CAMBRIDGE TEXTS IN THE
HISTORY OF POLITICAL THOUGHT

The Political Thought of the Irish Revolution

The Irish Revolution was a pivotal moment of transition for Ireland, the United Kingdom, and British Empire. A constitutional crisis that crystallised in 1912 electrified opinion in Ireland whilst dividing politics at Westminster. Instead of settling these differences, the advent of the First World War led to the emergence of new antagonisms. Republican insurrection was followed by a struggle for independence along with the partition of the island. This volume assembles some of the key contributions to the intellectual debates that took place in the midst of these changes and displays the vital ideas developed by the men and women who made the Irish Revolution, as well as those who opposed it. Through these fundamental texts, we see Irish experiences in comparative European and international contexts, and how the revolution challenged the durability of Britain as a global power.

Richard Bourke is Professor of the History of Political Thought and a Fellow of King's College at the University of Cambridge. His books include *Peace in Ireland: The War of Ideas* (2nd ed. 2012) and *Empire and Revolution: The Political Thought of Edmund Burke* (2016), which was joint winner of the István Hont Memorial Book Prize in Intellectual History in 2016. His work has been named a Book of the Year in *The Observer, The Irish Times*, *The Spectator, The Claremont Review of Books*, RTÉ, *The Indian Express*, and *The National Review*. He is co-editor of the *Princeton History of Modern Ireland* (2016) which was selected as a *Choice* Outstanding Academic Title.

Niamh Gallagher is Lecturer in Modern British and Irish History and a Fellow of St Catharine's College at the University of Cambridge. Her first book, *Ireland and the Great War: A Social and Political History* (2019), won the Royal Historical Society's Whitfield Prize in 2020, the first work of Irish history to win the prize since its establishment in 1976. She has since published on the cultural, political, and social history of the First World War and other aspects of Irish and British History, and appears regularly in the UK, Irish, and international media.

CAMBRIDGE TEXTS IN THE HISTORY OF POLITICAL THOUGHT

Cambridge Texts in the History of Political Thought is firmly established as the major student series of texts in political theory. It aims to make available all the most important texts in the history of political thought, from ancient Greece to the twentieth century, from throughout the world and from every political tradition. All the familiar classic texts are included, but the series seeks at the same time to enlarge the conventional canon through a global scope and by incorporating an extensive range of less well-known works, many of them never before available in a modern English edition, and to present the history of political thought in a comparative, international context. Where possible, the texts are published in complete and unabridged form, and translations are specially commissioned for the series. However, where appropriate, especially for non-western texts, abridged or tightly focused and thematic collections are offered instead. Each volume contains a critical introduction together with chronologies, biographical sketches, a guide to further reading and any necessary glossaries and textual apparatus. Overall, the series aims to provide the reader with an outline of the entire evolution of international political thought.

For a list of titles published in the series, please see end of book

The Political Thought of the Irish Revolution

EDITED BY

RICHARD BOURKE
King's College, University of Cambridge

NIAMH GALLAGHER
St Catharine's College, University of Cambridge

CAMBRIDGE
UNIVERSITY PRESS

University Printing House, Cambridge CB2 8BS, United Kingdom

One Liberty Plaza, 20th Floor, New York, NY 10006, USA

477 Williamstown Road, Port Melbourne, VIC 3207, Australia

314–321, 3rd Floor, Plot 3, Splendor Forum, Jasola District Centre, New Delhi – 110025, India

103 Penang Road, #05–06/07, Visioncrest Commercial, Singapore 238467

Cambridge University Press is part of the University of Cambridge.

It furthers the University's mission by disseminating knowledge in the pursuit of education, learning, and research at the highest international levels of excellence.

www.cambridge.org
Information on this title: www.cambridge.org/9781108836678
DOI: 10.1017/9781108874465

First published 2022

A catalogue record for this publication is available from the British Library.

ISBN 978-1-108-83667-8 Hardback
ISBN 978-1-108-79913-3 Paperback

Contents

Acknowledgements

The editors would like to express their gratitude to the following for providing comment or information in the process of producing this volume: Lauren Arrington, Duncan Bell, Richard Butterwick, Eugenio Biagini, Ultán Gillen, James McConnel, Margaret O'Callaghan, Tejas Parasher, Jonathan Parry, and Colin Reid. Thanks also to Quentin Skinner for seeing the potential in an edition such as this, to Liz Friend-Smith for including it in the series, to Anna Oxbury for meticulous copy-editing, and to Stephanie Taylor for overseeing the production process.

Introduction

The Character of the Conflict

During the seven-month long caretaker ministry headed by Lord Salisbury beginning in June 1885, William Ewart Gladstone converted to home rule. The measure was intended to pacify Ireland, which had been shaken by waves of agrarian unrest and a series of 'Fenian' outrages over recent decades. The first Home Rule Bill, introduced by Gladstone in the House of Commons on 8 April 1886, was supported with reservations by the leader of the Irish Parliamentary Party at Westminster, Charles Stewart Parnell, but vehemently opposed by the Conservatives and a section of Gladstone's Liberals. There were riots in Belfast in response to the proposals, though on 8 June the Bill was defeated by a margin of thirty votes. Over the next thirty-five years, the issue would prove divisive inside the United Kingdom parliament and polarise opinion out of doors. In Ireland itself, it added an extra dimension of strife to existing divisions.

Gladstone's new departure is often seen as inaugurating an era of rigid antagonism in Irish politics. An enduring cleavage is assumed to have emerged and to have lasted beyond partition and the War of Independence down to and including the Northern Ireland Troubles of 1968–98. This picture, however, has always involved considerable simplification. The idea of compact ideological structures spanning the twentieth century is far-fetched. Even the period of the Irish Revolution covered by this book cannot accurately be described as a monolithic struggle. Circumstances changed, the debate evolved, and commitments were gradually revised. This volume offers testimony to these dynamic shifts in allegiance and the unfolding conditions that shaped them. While it is obvious that animosity could run deep, it is also clear that hostilities were not uniform across time. The image of smouldering communal hatreds periodically reignited is an artful but distorting literary construction. Despite the distortion, the historiography of the period regularly depicts developments in terms of an abiding contest between nationalism and unionism.[1] Political scientists, and later journalists, have tended to follow suit, delineating a series of variable conflicts as a collision between fixed positions defined with reference to rival affiliations. This misrepresentation has been further contorted by the academic tendency to portray political loyalties by resort to the catch-all concept of identity.[2]

The attempt to schematise Irish history as a standoff between the discrete edifices of nationalism and unionism is reductive in two ways. First, unionism, like nationalism, denominates a form of allegiance. On that basis, both forms of attachment are 'nationalist' in character. Where they differ is in the object of their allegiance, and in each case the object was progressively redefined. Moreover, both are also best regarded as forms of democratic nationalism. Schisms over the future shape of a prospective Irish polity took place as the constitutional monarchies of Europe were challenged by democratic movements, and in due course undermined by recourse to democratic procedures. As these forces gained momentum over the course of the First World War, they exercised a steadily disaggregating effect on existing political structures. Empires fell, and governments were re-configured, as democratic norms secured an ascendancy over fading values.

A gradual transformation of the United Kingdom began earlier: franchise reform, extra-parliamentary party organisation and the rise of charismatic leadership were under way there before these processes proved decisive in central Europe.[3] Max Weber took Gladstone to have perfected

[1] Hugh Kearney, *The British Isles: A History of Four Nations* (Cambridge: Cambridge University Press, 1989); D. George Boyce, *Nationalism in Ireland* (London: Routledge, 1982, rev. 1995); Roy Foster, 'Something to Hate: Intimate Enmities in Irish History', *The Irish Review*, 30 (Spring-Summer 2003), pp. 1–12; Richard English, *Irish Freedom: The History of Nationalism in Ireland* (London: Macmillan, 2006).

[2] See for example Charles Townshend, 'Religion, War and Identity in Ireland', *The Journal of Modern History*, 76: 4 (December 2004), pp. 882–902.

[3] These processes are examined in Gary W. Cox, *The Cabinet and the Development of Political Parties in Victorian England* (Cambridge: Cambridge University Press, 1987); Eugenio F. Biagini, *British Democracy and Irish Nationalism, 1876–1906* (Cambridge: Cambridge University Press, 2007).

a new species of 'demagogy'; for A. V. Dicey he was a 'born enthusiast'.[4] At the same time, parliamentary representatives were increasingly drawn from the professional classes. Irish MPs were the first to be paid a stipend. The figure of the gentleman-politician was no longer fully dominant. Georges Sorel marvelled at Parnell's brand of agitational democracy, which piled on parliamentary pressure by a 'few acts of violence'.[5] Less insidiously, the abolition of the Lords veto in 1911 was yet another step in the disappearance of government by estates. With the passing of the Representation of the People Act in 1884, parliamentarism was challenged by an expanded electorate.[6] In Ireland, the number of men eligible to vote suddenly doubled to 500,000, many of whom were small farmers.[7] At the same time, the Irish Parliamentary Party was disciplined by an effective machine: the Irish National League expanded its network of branches throughout the country, candidates were vetted by the Party leadership, and MPs obliged to take a pledge. Although it is true that a far more extensive franchise was granted in 1918, the passage of the 1884 Act on the back of widening the suffrage in 1867 looked like a clear pattern, and commentators viewed the United Kingdom as approximating a democracy based on the existence of a mass voting public.[8] 'Up to 1895 English statesmen themselves did not, in general, fully appreciate the character of the revolution which they themselves had carried

[4] Max Weber, 'The Profession and Vocation of Politics' (1919) in *Weber: Political Writings*, ed. Peter Lassman and Ronald Spiers (Cambridge: Cambridge University Press, 1994), p. 242; A. V. Dicey, *A Fool's Paradise: Being a Constitutionalist's Criticism of the Home Rule Bill of 1912* (London: John Murray, 1913), p. xxi.

[5] Georges Sorel, *Reflections on Violence*, ed. Jeremy Jennings (Cambridge: Cambridge University Press, 1999), p. 67.

[6] On 'parliamentarism' as a distinct constitutional form that prevailed between the mid-eighteenth and mid-nineteenth centuries in Britain and France, see William Selinger, *Parliamentarism from Burke to Weber* (Cambridge: Cambridge University Press, 2019); on the challenges faced by parliamentary liberalism after 1884–6, see Jon Parry, *The Rise and Fall of Liberal Government in Victorian Britain* (New Haven: Yale University Press, 1993), ch. 12.

[7] On the impact of this see Margaret O'Callaghan, 'Franchise Reform, "First Past the Post" and the Strange Case of Unionist Ireland', *Parliamentary History*, 16: 1 (February 1997), pp. 85–106, p. 105: '1884 to 1885 made 1886 possible. Irish nationalist electoral power paved the way for Gladstonian action.'

[8] On these developments see Robert Saunders, *Democracy and the Vote in British Politics, 1848–1867: The Making of the Second Reform Act* (Farnham: Ashgate, 2011); Andrew Jones, *The Politics of Reform, 1884* (Cambridge: Cambridge University Press, 1972); Robert Blackburn, 'Laying the Foundations of the Modern Voting System: The Representation of the People Act 1918', *Parliamentary History*, 30: 1 (2011), pp. 33–52.

through by legislation extending from 1866 to 1884', observed Dicey.[9] Irish politics advanced in the shadow of these developments. Citizenship was democratised in the midst of social inequalities and the means of political struggle was opened to the nation. National rights, from this point on, were framed as democratic rights.

This brings us to the second interpretative framework that has encouraged a reductive approach to the period. While it is important, as already indicated, to appreciate what Irish nationalism and unionism had in common, it is also vital to appreciate the differences on either side. Animosity, in other words, was not binary. Opposing political persuasions were not formed into rival camps whose integrity persisted impervious to change. Nationalism, like unionism, did not comprise a single doctrine. While politics was polarising, opinion remained diverse. Antagonisms, therefore, were not static in content. The nature of the discord altered even as the fact of opposition endured. The terms of contention formed and reformed; fresh antipathies emerged inside rival positions. Given this underlying flux, it is at least understandable that the career of Irish unionism culminated in a form of home rule in the North; that large sections within nationalism converted to republicanism in the South; and that secession from the United Kingdom led to civil war.

Narrative of Events

In the face of these historical ironies, the train of events following on from the failure of Gladstone's Home Rule Bill of 1886 might usefully be recapitulated here. In 1891 the Irish Unionist Alliance was formed under Colonel Edward Saunderson. The organisation built upon the southern-based Irish Loyal and Patriotic Union, which had been formed in 1885 to promote collaboration between Liberals and Conservatives with a view to securing seats for pro-Union candidates at elections. The Alliance, which operated across all four provinces of Ireland, won considerable support in the House of Lords; it also attracted the future unionist leader Edward Carson into its ranks, along with the co-operative pioneer Horace Plunkett. On 17 June 1892, as opposition to home rule gained momentum, the Ulster Unionist Convention assembled 12,300 delegates in the Botanic Gardens in Belfast at the instigation of the Liberal unionist

[9] Dicey, *Fool's Paradise*, p. xxviii.

Thomas Sinclair to demonstrate their opposition to the creation of an Irish parliament. The Convention brought together an assortment of protestant creeds and classes reflecting the complexity of the coalition that would soon be marshalled in defence of the existing Union, particularly in the north-east of Ulster.[10] Devotees of the cause assembled to reject the devolution of legislative power to a band of representatives that included supporters of land agitation, many of them supposedly captivated by Roman Catholic clerical influence.

As Irish unionism grew more organised, the Irish Parliamentary Party fell into disarray. News of Parnell's adulterous relationship with Katherine O'Shea turned both Gladstone and the Catholic hierarchy against his leadership. The Party split in 1891, fomenting bitterness, and radically diminishing its influence as a force in Westminster politics until the general elections of 1910. Despite his faltering alliance with the Irish Party on account of the O'Shea scandal, Gladstone pursued a second Home Rule Bill, which passed in the Commons on 1 September 1893 by 30 votes, but was resoundingly defeated in the Lords by a margin of 378. The Irish Parliamentary Party would not recover its cohesion until John Redmond acceded to its leadership in 1900. In the interim, Irish policy at Westminster was channelled into 'constructive unionism', supported at the same time by coercive legislation.[11] The first sign of this change in direction came with the establishment by Arthur Balfour, then Chief Secretary for Ireland, of the Congested Districts Board in 1891 to alleviate poverty and halt emigration from the west of Ireland. This was followed by a series of measures introduced under a coalition government of Conservative and Liberal unionists that held office for a decade from 1895 to make the constitutional status quo appealing to Irish opinion. These measures included the extension of the tenant right to purchase property under the 1896 Land Act, although William O'Brien's United Irish League continued to agitate for land redistribution with a view to reallocating the uncultivated grasslands of the central plains to tenants and landless labourers based in Connaught. Two years later the introduction of a system of elected councils broke the stranglehold of the landlord class on local government.

[10] Alvin Jackson, *Home Rule: An Irish History, 1800–2000* (Oxford: Oxford University Press, 2003), ch. 6

[11] Andrew Gailey, *Ireland and the Death of Kindness: The Experience of Constructive Unionism 1890–1905* (Cork: Cork University Press, 1987).

The Conservative pursuit of political and social reform while sidelining the question of legislative devolution culminated in the 1903 Wyndham Land Act. The legislation extended opportunities for tenants to purchase farmland on a subsidised basis through a grant of government loans. The programme was expanded in 1909 with the result that by 1921 more than 310,000 former tenants had bought holdings from landlords amounting to nearly 12 million acres. The impact on the social structure of Ireland, with significant implications for its politics, was dramatic. Improvement became a watchword of policy, with 'conciliation' an expected consequence. The spirit of constructive amelioration proved controversial but still edged forward. A Department of Agriculture and Technical Instruction was established in 1900, drainage schemes as well as labour reforms were promoted, and there were plans for founding a Catholic university and overhauling public administration. All the while, the Liberal Party skirted the question of home rule as the Irish Party lost its momentum. But just when the great constitutional cause subsided, cultural innovation revived. From Horace Plunkett to James Joyce the prevailing mood was described in terms of spiritual 'paralysis', but in truth the enervation afflicted Members of Parliament while 'the rehabilitation of Ireland from within' – as Plunkett put it – began to blossom.[12]

For Plunkett rehabilitation was based on 'a new philosophy of Irish progress', which had come to express itself through a variety of projects.[13] The new strain of thought amounted to a programme of self-reliance: 'a profound revolution in the thoughts of Ireland about herself'.[14] This took multiple forms, from the co-operative movement championed by Plunkett to an array of schemes for cultural rejuvenation spanning language, sport, journalism, literature, and drama.[15] The Gaelic League, founded in 1893 with Douglas Hyde as its first president, was among the most consequential developments. Looking back in 1913, Patrick Pearse described the League as 'a prophet and more than a prophet'. It was, for him, 'the beginning of the Irish Revolution'.[16] In a lecture delivered on 25 November 1892 outlining the potential dividends to be derived from promoting the Irish language, Hyde also sought to advertise the virtues of Anglo-Irish literature: 'Every house should have a copy of

[12] James Joyce, *Letters*, ed. Stuart Gilbert (Faber and Faber: London, 1957), p. 55; Horace Plunkett, *Ireland in the New Century* (John Murray: London, 1904), pp. 148–9.

[13] Ibid., p. 6. [14] Ibid., p. 2.

[15] Erskine Childers, *The Framework of Home Rule*, below p. 66.

[16] Patrick Pearse, *The Coming Revolution* (1913), below p. 186.

Moore and Davis.'[17] Hyde further remarked that even though the Italian revolutionary Giuseppe Mazzini had detected the decline of Irish nationality, language revival and the reformation of taste would resuscitate a disappearing 'Celtic' culture that could appeal across religious and political divisions.[18] Only by means of a such a revival, Hyde thought, could the seemingly pathological impulse to disparage England, whilst at the same time neglecting domestic traditions, be made to cease. Native resources would become a national fund.

Competition to define the character of this new race ensued. W. B. Yeats contributed to the struggle with the establishment of the National Literary Society in 1892, before which Hyde had delivered his address on 'The Necessity for De-Anglicising Ireland'. In 1899, together with Augusta Gregory, George Moore, and Edward Martyn, Yeats also founded the Irish Literary Theatre as a vehicle for disseminating 'ancient idealism'.[19] Earlier, various endeavours to reappropriate past cultural treasures through folklore and history – or a mixture of both – had been pursued by figures like Standish O'Grady. For Yeats the strategy found echoes in Henrik Ibsen's *Peer Gynt* and Richard Wagner's *Parsifal*.[20] But as the National Literary Revival proceeded, the fashion for recovering superannuated customs in the hope of reshaping social attitudes drew criticism from numerous quarters. Yeats himself would progress through various stages in his renunciation of existing conditions by appeal to *faux*-patrician values, culminating in his rejection of 'this filthy modern tide'.[21] But, more immediately, strands of criticism began to assail the would-be guardians of an ancient Ireland. John Eglinton charged the revivalists' penchant for re-purposing archaic legends with evading modern life, while D. P. Moran accused them of ignorance and remoteness.[22]

[17] Douglas Hyde, 'The Necessity for De-Anglicising Ireland' (1892) in Charles Gavan Duffy, George Sigerson, and Douglas Hyde, *The Revival of Irish Literature and Other Addresses* (London: T. Fisher Unwin, 1904), p. 159.

[18] Ibid., p. 119. On membership of the League, see Timothy G. McMahon, *Grand Opportunity: The Gaelic Revival and Irish Society, 1893–1910* (New York: Syracuse University Press, 2008), ch. 3.

[19] Augusta Gregory, *Our Irish Theatre: A Chapter of Autobiography* (New York and London: G. P. Putnam's Sons, The Knickerbocker Press, 1913), p. 10.

[20] W. B. Yeats, 'A Note on National Drama' in John Eglinton, W. B. Yeats, and A. C. Larminie, *Literary Ideals in Ireland* (London: T. Fisher Unwin, 1899).

[21] W. B. Yeats, 'The Statues' (1938) in *The Collected Poems of W. B. Yeats* (London: Macmillan, 1950), p. 376.

[22] John Eglinton, 'What Should Be the Subjects of a National Drama' in John Eglinton et al., *Literary Ideals in Ireland*; D. P. Moran, *The Philosophy of Irish Ireland* (Dublin: James Duffy, 1905).

Alongside the National Literary Society in Dublin, there existed the Irish Literary Society in London. Several other associations prospered as well. William Rooney and Arthur Griffith's Leinster Literary Society formed the basis for the subsequent Celtic Literary Society which promoted the cause of independence together with Irish civilisation. Maud Gonne, a radical nationalist member of the Celtic Literary Society, founded Inghinidhe na hÉireann (Daughters of Ireland) in 1900 as a women's organisation devoted to advancing Irish separatism. Helena Molony, Mary MacSwiney, Constance Markiewicz, and Hanna Sheehy-Skeffington were all members.[23] Molony, a feminist and labour activist, edited the organisation's monthly newspaper, *Bean na hÉireann* (Woman of Ireland), while Rooney and Griffith edited the *United Irishman*. They also created Cumann na nGaedheal (Society of the Gaels) as an umbrella organisation under which assorted nationalist movements could be grouped. At the 1902 Cumann na nGaedheal convention, Griffith proposed the adoption of a policy of abstention for Irish MPs at Westminster. The approach was also adopted by the National Council, formed by Gonne and Griffith to protest against the royal visit of King Edward VII in 1903. When the National Council's first annual convention took place on 28 November 1905, it adopted what was now termed the Sinn Féin policy of abstentionism, which Griffith had elaborated in the pages of the *United Irishman*, into a theory of passive resistance that aimed at the establishment of a dual monarchy on the model of the 1867 Austro-Hungarian *Ausgleich*. In 1907 the National Council merged with Cumann na nGaedheal and the republican, paramilitary-backed Dungannon Clubs to form the Sinn Féin Party, committed to Griffith's 'Hungarian' policy.[24]

For many of these activists and commentators, an intellectual revolution had already occurred before the political upheavals that would erupt after 1912 – a general 'stir of thought' had surfaced, as Yeats famously put it, or a 'mouvement intellectuel' in the words of J. M. Synge.[25] The scene shifted from wrangling at Westminster to the cultivation of 'Irish Ideas', a clamour over 'ideals and principles', and hopes for a spiritual

[23] Senia Pašeta, *Irish Nationalist Women, 1900–1918* (Cambridge: Cambridge University Press, 2013), ch. 2.

[24] Michael Laffan, *The Resurrection of Ireland: The Sinn Féin Party, 1916–1923* (Cambridge: Cambridge University Press, 1999), ch. 1.

[25] W. B. Yeats, *Autobiographies* (London: Macmillan, 1955), p. 559; J. M. Synge, 'Le Mouvement intellectuel Irlandais', *L'Européen* , 31 May 1902, in *Collected Works II: Prose*, ed. Alan Price (Oxford: Oxford University Press, 1966).

'awakening'.[26] The revolution in thought is commonly described as a retreat from politics into art.[27] In truth the reorientation involved a rejection less of politics than of parliamentarism specifically. In his Introduction to the English translation of L. Paul Dubois' *L'Irlande contemporaine*, Thomas Kettle relayed the general 'outcry against parliamentarianism'.[28] That mood of scepticism was implicit in the founding of Sinn Féin and was still present in the late writings of James Connolly.[29] Michael Davitt regarded parliamentary procedures as under assault from the autocratic tendencies fostered by overseas expansion: 'In Great Britain, parliamentarism or imperialism must die.'[30] Electoral campaigning naturally persisted, but increasing resources of energy were focused on cultural revitalisation, much of this originally in a spirit of ecumenism. The ambition still remained one of political transformation – or, at least, of moral rebirth with vaguely projected political consequences. Perhaps inevitably, the spirit of inclusion steadily dwindled. Many, like Hyde, sustained the goal of transcending ecclesiastical and party-political sectionalism; however, intellectual experimentation bred its own differences and, before long, for every scheme encouraging national renewal there appeared a critique espousing an alternative vision.

George Bernard Shaw, for one, came to regard what he termed the 'neo-Gaelic' movement with a mixture of incredulity and disdain.[31] The aspiration to revive the Irish language, he thought, was quixotic and counter-productive, and the literary renaissance as conceived by Yeats seemed little more than 'a quaint little offshoot of English

26 William O'Brien, *Irish Ideas* (London: Longmans, Green, 1893; Æ (George Russell) to Yeats, 1 June 1896 in *The Field Day Anthology of Irish Writing*, ed. Seamus Deane (Derry: Field Day Publications, 1991), 3 vols., II, p. 341; Stephen Gwynn, *Today and Tomorrow in Ireland: Essays on Irish Subjects* (Dublin: Hodges, Figgis, 1903); Markievicz, *Women, Ideals and the Nation*, below p. 6.

27 Brian Ó Conchubhair, 'The Culture War: The Gaelic League and Irish Ireland' and Roy Foster, 'The Irish Literary Revival' in Thomas Bartlett ed., *The Cambridge History of Modern Ireland* (Cambridge: Cambridge University Press, 2018), IV.

28 Thomas M. Kettle, 'Introduction' to L. Paul Dubois, *Contemporary Ireland* (Dublin: Maunsel, 1908), p. ix.

29 Arthur Griffith, 'Preface to the Third Edition', *The Resurrection of Hungary: A Parallel for Ireland, with Appendices on Pitt's Policy and Sinn Fein* (Dublin: Whelan and Son, 1918), p. x; James Connolly, 'What Is a Free Nation?', below p. 229.

30 Michael Davitt, *The Fall of Feudalism in Ireland, or The Story of the Land League Revolution* (London and New York: Harper and Brothers, 1904), p. 723.

31 George Bernard Shaw, 'Preface for Politicians' in *John Bull's Other Island and Major Barbara* (New York: Brentano's, 1907), p. v.

pre-Raphaelitism' which appealed to national sentiment for leverage.[32] As with all instances of cultural and political idealism, the true character of such idealism was revealed in its secular ambition, yet for all that it remained ill-adapted to existing circumstances. Despite his own rejection of compulsive Irish nostalgia, Joyce was more sympathetic to the yearning for a new civilisation that would purge the country at once of Anglo-Saxon democracy and the Roman Catholic imperium.[33] An appeal to the past would not revive the old 'Hellas of the north', nor free it from the burdens of past failure and betrayal.[34] The hope of renovation could only be redeemed by bringing forth the 'uncreated conscience' of the 'race'.[35]

Although these calls for renewal were marked by their diversity, there were commonalities in the midst of this heterogeneity. Newfangled appeals to Celticism and cosmopolitanism alike spurned earlier characterisations of the Celtic mind. Theodor Mommsen had notoriously depicted the Celts as fundamentally incapable of political exertion.[36] Then, from Ernest Renan to Matthew Arnold, with assorted ends in view, a stream of portraits of the dreamy and ineffectual Celt poured forth.[37] Rebuffing this condescension, a procession of Irish publicists nonetheless urged opposition to 'Saxon' values. In this venture they had available to them a rich British tradition, epitomised by John Ruskin, of castigating the 'utilitarianism' of modern culture. Gandhi, likewise drawing on Ruskin, was still operating within this framework when in 1910 in *Hind Swaraj* he pleaded for the replacement of functional market relations by what he termed 'true' civilisation.[38] With a system of mass education in place in virtually every country in Europe by the start of the First World War, the creation and dissemination of cultural attitudes mattered. The

[32] Ibid., p. xxxvi.

[33] James Joyce, 'James Clarence Mangan' (1907), *The Critical Writings of James Joyce*, ed. E. Mason and R. Ellmann (New York: Viking Press, 1964).

[34] James Joyce, 'Ireland, Island of Saints and Sages' (1907) in ibid.

[35] James Joyce, *Portrait of the Artist as a Young Man* (1914–15), ed. Seamus Deane (Harmondsworth: Penguin: 1992) p. 276.

[36] Theodor Mommsen, *Römische Geschichte* (Leipzig: Weidmannsche Buchhandlung, 1854–6), 3 vols., III, p. 285.

[37] Seamus Deane, 'Arnold, Burke and the Celts' in *Celtic Revivals: Essays in Modern Irish Literature* (London: Faber and Faber, 1985); Seamus Deane, '"Masked with Matthew Arnold's Face": Joyce and Liberalism', *The Canadian Journal of Irish Studies*, 12: 1 (June 1986), pp. 11–22.

[38] M. K. Gandhi, *Hind Swaraj and Other Writings*, ed. A. J. Parel (Cambridge: Cambridge University Press, 1997, 2nd ed. 2009), ch. 13.

1870 Foster Act laid the foundations of elementary schooling in England and Wales. Compulsory enrolment then arrived in 1880 and was duly introduced in Ireland twelve years later. Through the nineteenth century, the Irish language declined and literacy in English spread.[39] The number of Catholics in secondary education more than doubled between the Disestablishment of the Church of Ireland in 1869 and the passage of the 1911 Parliament Act. The Royal University of Ireland was founded in 1880 and soon permitted students from the Catholic University, the forebear of University College Dublin, to take degrees. Thomas Kettle, Hanna Sheehy-Skeffington, Patrick Pearse, Éamon de Valera, Douglas Hyde, Eoin MacNeill, and James Joyce were among its earliest graduates. As education expanded, the reading public was enlarged, with audiences for literature, journalism, and more popular forms of entertainment increasing. In 1906 Stephen Gwynn, Joseph Hone, and George Roberts founded Maunsel and Company, a publishing house committed to the publication of Irish writers.

Given these developments, public opinion took on a vital significance, particularly as voting rights were extended. The North of Ireland Women's Suffrage Society was formed in 1872 and the Irish Women's Franchise League in 1912. The vote for women over the age of thirty with the requisite property qualifications did not arrive until 1918, with an equal franchise introduced by the new Irish parliament in 1922, although local suffrages at parish and district levels were granted to women at the end of the nineteenth century. The Local Government Act of 1898 extended the system of administration in operation in Britain to Ireland and in the process gave the vote to 100,000 women in council elections. A decade later they were made eligible to become candidates themselves.[40] The following year Markiewicz noted that women until recently stood 'far removed from all politics', comparing the situation in Ireland with the prominent role they played in radical movements in Russia and Poland.[41] Among men and women, enfranchised citizens were drawn into the battle of ideas. Where the public was invited to embrace new values in the

[39] The importance of literacy to the conceptualisation of citizenship is discussed in Ernest Gellner, 'Nationalism' in *Thought and Change* (London: Weidenfeld and Nicolson, 1964), p. 159; on assorted European campaigns for linguistic and cultural revival see Benedict Anderson, *Imagined Communities: Reflections on the Origin and Spread of Nationalism* (London and New York: Verso, 1983), ch. 5.

[40] Pašeta, *Irish Nationalist Women*, pp. 18–19.

[41] Constance Markievicz, *Women, Ideals and the Nation*, below p. 7.

guise of 'Irishness', these ideals were generally conceived in opposition to the spirit of selfishness, frequently connected to the commercial avarice of the seat of empire.

Egoism of the kind had of course also been subject to a series of indictments in Britain from Samuel Taylor Coleridge and Thomas Carlyle to Matthew Arnold and William Morris.[42] The grim forecasts that accompanied debate about the 'Condition of England' encouraged an appeal to restorative romanticism. In Ireland, as materialism similarly came to be denounced, it was often correlated with imperialism. Along with this, industrialism and individualism were castigated. So too was political trimming since it connoted the affairs of parliament. In place of all this, heroism was lauded; or, at least, passion and idealism were. These favoured mental dispositions implied at once authenticity and a degree of spiritualism. In Pearse, Yeats, and Connolly the resulting mindset involved extolling integrity and selflessness. The principle of nationality, according to Kettle, presupposed a capacity for 'sacrifice'.[43] For Markiewicz altruism depended in the end on a 'genius for sacrifice'.[44] A refurbished worldview awaited a new epoch. 'England has laboured to anglicize Ireland', observed the Earl of Dunraven in 1907.[45] The venture, he thought, had consistently failed. Native solutions, it was claimed all round, were required to tackle the problem of Ireland. There were echoes in this approach of Henry Sumner Maine's insistence after the Sepoy Rebellion in India on maintaining customary forms of life in traditional societies.[46] However, in the case of Ireland, reclaimed traditions were used as vehicles to disavow commercial civilisation even if the origins of the principles being promoted lay in a critique of metropolitan capitalism.

Clearly this project of ethical atonement was poorly designed to accommodate the qualities of 'thrift and industry' that Plunkett had observed admiringly in the north-east of Ulster.[47] There had been many visions of 'two nations' internally dividing both Britain and Ireland from the middle

[42] Donald Winch, *Wealth and Life: Essays on the Intellectual History of Political Economy in Britain, 1848–1914* (Cambridge: Cambridge University Press, 2009).

[43] Thomas M. Kettle, 'The Economics of Nationalism', below p. 148.

[44] Markievicz, *Women, Ideals and the Nation*, below p. 3.

[45] Earl of Dunraven, *The Outlook in Ireland: The Case for Devolution and Conciliation* (Dublin: Hodges, Figgis, 1907), p. 7.

[46] Karuna Mantena, *Alibis of Empire: Henry Maine and the Ends of Liberal Imperialism* (Princeton, NJ: Princeton University Press, 2010).

[47] Plunkett, *Ireland in the New Century*, p. 120.

of the nineteenth century. Benjamin Disraeli's 1845 *Sybil, or The Two Nations* was just one instance of a celebrated genre. The line of cleavage was variously drawn along the fault-lines of class and culture. For Paul Dubois there existed 'two Irelands' – 'two opposed nations' – defined in terms of settler and native and distributed across the island as a whole.[48] Six years later, W. F. Moneypenny declared in a pamphlet on home rule that, notwithstanding the existence of a large 'Protestant democracy' in Ulster, the partition of Ireland into 'two nations' corresponded to 'no real geographical line of division'. Instead, rival constituencies were parcelled into 'separate religions, separate ideals, separate traditions, and separate affinities' right across the territory.[49]

But the schism that would ultimately prove decisive was that between the 'north-east' and the 'south and west'. The topographical distinction was substantiated in terms of sundry contrasts – between Orange and Green, Presbyterian and Catholic, industry and indolence, or an amalgamation of each. For Thomas Macknight back in 1896 the main fissure in Ireland was captured by the contrasting reactions in Dublin and Belfast to the assassination of senior British political officials in the Phoenix Park in 1882.[50] The disparity suggested, he concluded, the existence of 'two antagonistic populations, two different nations on Irish soil'.[51] Plunkett, on the other hand, entertained the hope of harmony driven by the 'fruitful contact of North and South'. Toward this end, both extremes needed to modulate their characters. Protestant Ireland, the 'home of the strictly civic virtues and efficiencies', ought to purge accumulated bigotries while Catholic Ireland had to shake itself from lethargy. Both could equally embrace creativity and self-help.[52] This hybridisation would implicitly combine tradition and innovation, retrospect and modernity. The prospect put Plunkett in mind of Westernisation in Japan with the qualification that the Irish bid to forge 'a civilisation of their own' appeared at once more significant and interesting.[53]

As the British government pursued a policy of assuaging Ireland with constructive legislation, it faced what was often deemed 'another

48 Dubois, *Contemporary Ireland*, pp. 89 ff.

49 W. F. Moneypenny, *The Two Irish Nations: An Essay on Home Rule* (London: John Murray, 1913), p. 12.

50 Thomas Macknight, *Ulster as It Is, or Twenty-Eight Years' Experience as an Irish Editor* (London: Macmillan, 1896), 2 vols, II, pp. 27 ff.

51 Ibid., II, p. 380.

52 Plunkett, *Ireland in the New Century*, p. 121.

53 Ibid., pp. 165–6.

Ireland' in southern Africa. Between October 1899 and May 1902, the Empire struggled to contain a Boer insurrection in the Transvaal and the Orange Free State. Guerrilla tactics were met by the British with concentration camps and agrarian devastation leading to civilian deaths. Although, as D. P. Moran insisted, the analogy with Ireland was strained, it was nonetheless popular.[54] Volunteer recruits to the Boer cause and parliamentary agitation by members of the Irish Party at Westminster were an index of opposition to British jingoism. Notwithstanding this, some 47,000 Irishmen fought on the British side, while charity donations and public displays of support point toward widespread loyalty.[55] Even so, the character of Irish opposition to an assault on 'Boer freedom' reflects the development of resistance to the Empire and the Union – and thus the sense that Ireland, though a contributor to the Empire, was nonetheless subject to it. Yeats, Gregory, Redmond, Connolly, Griffith, Gonne, John MacBride, and Seán O'Casey were all active in protesting against British policy in the Transvaal. In 1904 Michael Davitt condemned the 'attack made upon the Transvaal by the forces of the British Empire, in furtherance of the purposes and plans of freebooters and financiers'.[56]

Davitt's rhetoric was derived from the burgeoning suspicion of sordid acquisitiveness hitched to the overseas exploitation of resources occasioned by the 'scramble' for Africa. Reacting against the war in South Africa, John Morley and J. A. Hobson had turned their fire against Joseph Chamberlain's brand of free trade expansionism. Hobson, who had reported on the Boer War for the *Manchester Guardian* in 1899, indicted the machinations of Jewish finance as a malevolent force.[57] But despite his adoption of Hobsonian idioms, Davitt's real concern was to wrest the control of the soil of Ireland from venal landlords while repudiating what he saw as the humiliation of Boer farmers at the hands of the British. He claimed that broad-based outrage at the abuse and denigration of South African insurgents had united Irish opinion behind Redmond.[58] Yet he also believed that British conduct was a product of sinister interests and

[54] Donal P. McCracken, *Forgotten Protest: Ireland and the Anglo-Boer War* (Belfast: Ulster Historical Foundation, 2003), pp. xv–xvi.

[55] Keith Jeffery, 'The Irish Soldier in the Boer War' in John Gooch ed., *The Boer War: Direction, Experience and Image* (London: Frank Cass, 2000), p. 142.

[56] Davitt, *Fall of Feudalism in Ireland*, p. 693.

[57] R. Koebner and H. D. Schmidt, *Imperialism: The Story and Significance of a Political Word, 1840–1960* (Cambridge: Cambridge University Press, 1964), p. 226.

[58] Davitt, *Fall of Feudalism in Ireland*, p. 694.

he was happy to align these with imperialism. The aggrandising ambition which drove imperial power had imposed a costly regime of taxation on the mother country, undermined the stability of parliamentary government, and contributed to progressive depopulation in Ireland. The Empire, he thought, would inevitably 'breed the diseases of its own decay and downfall'.[59] Despotism would lead to disaffection and kindle hopes of self-determination.

Davitt liked to cite J. A. Froude's assertion that the British could govern India but not Ireland. This confirmed, he thought, the right of nationality that the Irish enjoyed along with other small European states like 'Holland, Denmark, Belgium, Switzerland, Bulgaria, Servia, and Greece'.[60] Nonetheless, at the time Davitt wrote, Irish independence looked wholly improbable, relying on unlikely fantasies of the United States emancipating Ireland as she had liberated Cuba from Spain.[61] After an extended period of Conservative administration, it fell to the Liberal Party to manage Irish affairs from 1905, first under the leadership of Henry Campbell-Bannerman and then under Herbert Henry Asquith. While home rule remained a party aspiration, it had receded as a policy commitment. Instead, the Chancellor, David Lloyd George, supported by twenty-nine Labour Party MPs, concentrated on advancing a programme of social reform, culminating in the attempt to pass the People's Budget through parliament in 1909. The legislation proposed to tackle poverty through a welfare programme funded by tariffs and taxation, but it met with staunch opposition among Conservative MPs who looked to the House of Lords to strike the measure down. On 30 November, the Bill was vetoed, forcing a general election in January 1910 in which the Liberals threatened to neuter the upper chamber if the electorate returned them to power. The polls returned a hung parliament, with Asquith now dependent on Labour and the Irish Party. After a year of tensions, a second election followed in December 1910 with the result once more leaving the Liberals relying on John Redmond's support. The Parliament Act passed in August 1911, depriving the Lords of the right to block money bills and replacing its entitlement to stop other legislative provisions with the power to delay their passage for two years. Redmond had demanded a home rule bill as the price of his support for the

[59] Ibid., pp. 722–3. [60] Ibid., p. 717.

[61] A view expressed by the journalist Alfred Stead in 1901, cited in J. O. Baylen, '"What Mr Redmond Thought": An Unpublished Interview with John Redmond, December 1906', *Irish Historical Studies*, 19: 74 (September 1974), pp. 169–89, p. 172.

new government, and he could now look forward to assisting its advance without obstruction from the upper house. The Bill was duly introduced on 11 April 1912.

The third Home Rule Bill provided for a bicameral legislature in Dublin comprising a 40-member Senate and a 164-member Commons along with a reduction of the number of Irish MPs at Westminster from 103 to 42. Although the policy attracted broad Irish support, it was both federalist and devolutionary, and therefore hardly 'nationalist' in the technical sense: sovereignty would reside in the seat of empire. The execution of government business through the Dublin Castle administration would cease, although a Lord Lieutenant would be retained. Unionist opposition to the Bill was immediate and intense. Two days before its introduction, the leader of the Opposition, Andrew Bonar Law, together with Edward Carson, now leader of the Irish Unionist Alliance, reviewed 100,000 Ulster Volunteers in marching columns. The militia, led by Carson and James Craig, drew some of its strength from the lodges of the Orange Order and was tacitly supported by elements at the War Office in London. The Ulster Unionist Council, established in 1905, now became a central organ in the resistance to home rule as the centre of gravity within loyalism began to shift from the South. On 28 September 1912 the Ulster Covenant was signed at Belfast City Hall by a quarter of a million men while the accompanying Declaration was signed by a comparable number of women.[62] The feeling of peril and solidarity crystallised: 'We perish if we yield.'[63] There was a stay of execution in January 1913 when the Lords voted down the legislation, deferring the implementation of the Act by 24 months. At this point the Ulster Volunteers were reformed into the paramilitary Ulster Volunteer Force in an effort to block the creation of an all-Ireland parliament by the threat of arms. The following November the formation of the Irish Volunteers, a rival militia supported by the Irish Republican Brotherhood, was presented by Eoin MacNeill as a means of asserting that 'all Irish people, Unionist as well as Nationalist, are determined to have their own way'.[64] Cumann na mBan (The Women's Council), a paramilitary organisation formed by leading republican women and intended to reinforce the Volunteers, was formed in April 1914. A path to confrontation had been cleared.

[62] For the Covenant and the Declaration see below pp. 140–1

[63] Rudyard Kipling, 'Ulster 1912', *The Morning Post*, 9 April 1912.

[64] Eoin MacNeill, 'The North Began', 1 November 1913, below p. 183.

With a threat of resignation by senior Army officers stationed at the Curragh military camp in Co. Kildare announced in March 1914, the ability of the British government to control events appeared to diminish. An amending Bill providing for the temporary exclusion of Ulster from the jurisdiction of a home rule parliament was debated through the summer, although the number of counties subject to the exclusion had yet to be finalised. With the onset of the First World War at the end of July 1914, the amending Bill was abandoned due to a lack of consensus and home rule was suspended for the duration of the war. Consequently, the legislation was not revived until after 1918, although in the interim Lloyd George made covert concessions to unionism, alienating the Irish Party in the process. When an Irish Convention under Horace Plunkett was convened in 1917 to broker a deal, it ended in failure: agreement on Ulster remained intractable while devolution on Asquith's model was effectively dead. On the evidence at least of opinion in the Convention, a majority in the South favoured a dominion arrangement instead of a federal connection to the Westminster parliament – thereby seeking, in Plunkett's words, a 'government within the British Commonwealth of self-governing nations'.[65]

The impact of four years of a bloody conflagration in Europe on political attitudes in Ireland is not to be underestimated. Most immediately, it dissipated, or at least delayed, direct confrontation over the fate of Ulster as home rule loomed. Instead, senseless carnage on a far larger scale was pursued by the European powers. Although over 200,000 Irishmen fought on the Entente side and 40,000 lost their lives during the course of the war, the conflict had some potential to unify domestic dissensions. There was support for the British among the majority in the North, while a large preponderance in the South likewise pledged to join the effort. Members of the Ulster Volunteer Force streamed into the 36th (Ulster) Division to take up arms to defend the Empire, and the bulk of the Irish Volunteers formed the National Volunteers, who had a considerable presence in both the 10th and 16th (Irish) Divisions. In the House of Commons, after the opening of hostilities, Redmond declared that for the first time in over a century 'Ireland in this War feels her interests are precisely the same as yours.'[66] He expected that the shared experience of combat between nationalists and unionists would assuage bitterness

[65] Horace Plunkett, *A Defence of the Convention*, below p. 263.

[66] John Redmond, Speech on the Suspensory Bill, below p. 207.

leading to mutual accommodation of a kind that might form the basis of a post-war settlement. Soldiers of the 10th (Irish) Division fell in droves at Gallipoli in 1915 while the 16th and 36th Divisions were decimated at the Somme in 1916. Thomas Kettle died in action during the Somme offensive while Redmond's brother lost his life in the Battle of Messines the following year. Throughout the duration of the war – including the aftermath of the 1916 Rising and the conscription controversy – extensive evidence of quiet sympathy for the Allied effort points to significant areas of shared allegiance spread across religious denominations and rival political constituencies in Ireland.[67] However, when Armistice arrived on 11 November 1918, common sacrifice did not deliver unity of purpose.

Where there was opposition to the war, it was sometimes fierce. An experience that in many respects generated alliances could also be savagely divisive. Already at the start of the war, Connolly complained that the hard-won achievements of generations of toil were being 'blown into annihilation from a hundred cannon mouths' in the name of a sham 'civilisation'.[68] Accordingly, there was an absolute commitment inside Connolly's trade union militia, the Irish Citizen Army, to the wisdom and legitimacy of an armed insurrection against the Empire, which was launched on 24 April 1916. By comparison, councils within the Irish Volunteers, and even inside the Irish Republican Brotherhood, were divided. Confusion in the run-up to Easter week hamstrung the Rising from the start, largely confining its operations to the capital, where 1,000 rebels occupied key positions and held out against 20,000 British soldiers for six days, leaving 500 dead and the city centre in ruins.[69] It has been widely attested that the punitive military response in the aftermath of the Rising conferred retrospective credibility on the insurgency: the staggered execution of 16 rebel leaders along with the arrest and internment of thousands of suspects inspired sympathy for what was now seen as a dignified if desperate cause. Farce, it seemed, had been elevated inadvertently into tragedy.

For the main protagonists, the Rising had been principled rather than comical in the first place. The 'needless death' that Yeats invoked in

[67] Niamh Gallagher, *Ireland and the Great War: A Social and Political History* (London: Bloomsbury, 2019), p. 5.

[68] James Connolly, 'A Continental Revolution', below p. 200 and James Connolly, 'A War for Civilization', below p. 214.

[69] Fearghal McGarry, *The Rising: Ireland, Easter 1916* (Oxford: Oxford University Press, 2010), ch. 4.

connection with the event had for Connolly precisely captured the slaughter in the trenches.[70] 'Sacrifice' did not 'make a stone of the heart'.[71] It kindled passion. It meant devotion to a national ideal in place of futile butchery on the battlefields of foreign lands. As preparations for the Rising were in train, Connolly wrote that a 'destiny not of our fashioning has chosen this generation as the one called upon for the supreme act of self-sacrifice – to die if need be that our race might live in freedom'.[72] If the object of freedom proved immediately elusive, the ordeal would nonetheless set an example. It was, in the words of the Proclamation, a 'summons'. That task was carried out in the name of the 'common good'.[73] For Pearse, the spirit of nationality had become a 'forgotten truth', and the Rising was an invitation to revive – 'here in our day' – its persistent if sometimes hidden appeal, its 'august' dignity.[74] Should the action in the short term miscarry, it would still inspire and so be imitated, which of course it was. In its own terms, such a stand is hardly conceived as a purely symbolic gesture. As attempts to impose a military draft on Ireland in April 1918 met with opposition from trade unions, the Catholic Church, and mainstream opinion, attitudes hardened further against the administration in London. Redmondism, and the Irish Party, haemorrhaged support. In the general election of 14 December 1918, Sinn Féin swept to victory across the South. Exemplary sacrifice had indeed achieved some kind of awakening.

As the war brought devastation, so its aftermath triggered waves of upheaval across Europe and the world. Louie Bennett, reflecting on the general tumult in 1918, commented optimistically that 'Today a revolutionary ferment is stirring in the bewildered minds of the European nations, kindling a blaze of idealism in the hearts of the peoples before which the vices of Imperialism must presently shrink abashed.'[75] As she wrote, the dissolution of the Ottoman Empire proceeded apace. In the same year, the Romanovs were executed, King Ferdinand of Bulgaria abdicated, Ludwig of Bavaria fled the country, Wilhelm II abandoned the German throne, and Charles I of Austria ceded his powers. Assorted

[70] Yeats, 'Easter 1916', *Collected Poems*, pp. 202–5. [71] Ibid.
[72] Connolly, 'What Is a Free Nation?', below p. 232.
[73] *Proclamation of the Republic*, below p. 235.
[74] Patrick Pearse, *The Sovereign People*, below p. 254.
[75] Louie Bennett, *Ireland and a People's Peace*, below p. 272.

imperial maps were redrawn.[76] Woodrow Wilson revealed his commitment to the civil right of self-government, usually mistaken for an engagement to entrench the right of self-determination.[77] Months later, at Brest-Litovsk, the Bolshevik government sought to implement Lenin's advocacy of 'the right to free political secession' from oppressor nations.[78]

Finland declared its independence from Russia in January 1918, and a bloody civil war ensued. In the same month, the Ukrainian People's Republic was established, and Lithuania, Latvia, and Estonia soon withdrew from the Soviet federation. There was a Muslim revolt in Baku, and the Belarusian Republic was founded. On 22 April Armenia, Azerbaijan, and Georgia declared their independence. So too, on 28 October, did Czechoslovakia. Austria and Hungary established autonomous states, and Poland won its freedom. In Germany bands of soldiers and workers formed revolutionary councils and, on 9 November, a republic was declared. At the same time, Bavaria proclaimed its own socialist statelet, followed by the establishment of free states in Baden, Hesse, Coburg, and Mecklenburg-Schwerin. In the midst of the international turmoil, tens of thousands of war veterans returned to settle in Ireland, which by this point had its own self-declared parliament, Dáil Éireann, established in January 1919 without Westminster's consent. The Irish Parliament prepared to meet at the Mansion House in Dublin in its capacity as a sovereign authority in a nominally independent state. While Dáil representatives were assembling on 21 January 1919, the first shots of the War of Independence rang out in Co. Tipperary.

Violence escalated from the middle of 1919, involving guerrilla tactics supported by a campaign of assassination. Government property was vandalised, arms raids carried out, and prisoners freed from capture. At the same time, patrols were ambushed and barracks attacked,

[76] Maurice Walsh, *Bitter Freedom: Ireland in a Revolutionary World 1918–1923* (London: Faber and Faber, 2015), pp. 37–8.

[77] Trygve Throntveit, 'The Fable of the Fourteen Points: Woodrow Wilson and National Self-Determination', *Diplomatic History*, 35: 3 (June 2011), pp. 445–81. For the reconceptualisation of self-determination in the post-colonial context see Adom Getachew, *Worldmaking after Empire: The Rise and Fall of Self-Determination* (Princeton, NJ: Princeton University Press, 2019). For awareness in Ireland of Wilson's pronouncements see Alice Stopford Green, *Loyalty and Disloyalty: What it Means in Ireland*, below p. 280.

[78] V. I. Lenin, 'The Socialist Revolution and the Rights of Nations to Self-Determination' (1916), *Collected Works*, (Moscow: Progress Publishers 1964), 45 vols., XXII, p. 146. On the impact of Brest-Litovsk see Richard Bourke, 'Nationalism, Balkanization and Democracy' in *Schleifspuren: Lesarten des 18. Jahrhunderts*, ed. Anke Fischer-Kattner et al. (Munich: Dreesbach Verlag, 2011), pp. 77–89.

forcing the police force, the Royal Irish Constabulary, to withdraw from its rural bases. Westminster began to pay more attention to Irish affairs in 1920 and reinforcements – the so-called Black and Tans and Auxiliaries, drawn from the ranks of the British Army – were sent to assist the Royal Irish Constabulary. During this year, republican flying columns were used to assail British forces. Tax collection began to collapse while Sinn Féin-controlled councils appropriated rates and Westminster came to rely on emergency powers. Soon martial law was declared as the Dáil gradually built up a shadow government with its own judicial system across the south and west. During the conflict, the Irish Republican Army (IRA) was responsible for nearly half of all fatalities, the Crown forces for 42 per cent, and reprisals against civilians were common. One of the main resources on the Irish side was the effectiveness of its intelligence gathering under Michael Collins. A peak of violence was reached on 21 November 1920 when attacks by Collins's assassins were avenged by British forces shooting indiscriminately into the crowd at a football match in Dublin's Croke Park. Seven days later a west Cork IRA unit under Tom Barry ambushed a large patrol of Auxiliaries at Kilmichael. A spiral of violence endured until a truce was secured on 11 July 1921.[79]

Despite the truce, killing in the North saw little respite until after the summer of 1922. Under the 1920 Government of Ireland Act, the island had been partitioned, with the Belfast administration established on 3 May 1921. This meant that when preliminary talks were opened that summer between the President of Sinn Féin, Éamonn de Valera, and Lloyd George, the existence of Northern Ireland was a reality – albeit a contested one – and any negotiation regarding a future settlement would necessarily be conducted against that background. Five plenipotentiaries from the Irish side arrived for discussions in London with leading members of the British Cabinet in October and three months later a Treaty accord had been struck. But its adoption into Irish legislation would prove bitterly controversial. The Treaty provided for the establishment of Southern Ireland as a self-governing dominion within the British Commonwealth, including recognition of the King as the head of the Empire. Members of the Irish Parliament were required, in pledging their allegiance to the Dáil, to take a secondary oath to the British monarch. However, Crown forces were to withdraw from the jurisdiction of

[79] Michael Hopkinson, *The Irish War of Independence* (Dublin: Gill and Macmillan, 2000).

the new regime, although Britain would retain control of specified ports for naval purposes. Northern Ireland was awarded the option to opt out of the Treaty arrangements, while a Boundary Commission was set up to review the borders of the six counties in the expectation that the North might in due course come under the South.

The Treaty was debated in public sessions of the second Dáil between the middle of December 1921 and early January 1922, although disagreements deepened rather than being reconciled as the deliberations proceeded.[80] Ultimately these divisions led to civil war, shaping the character of the Free State, and subsequently the Republic. They also ensured that relations with Northern unionists would remain estranged and dogged by mutual recrimination. The opposing positions generated by the terms of the Treaty are commonly seen as distinguished in terms of attitudes rather than ideologies, whereas in fact the dissensions were manifestly driven by ideas.[81] The relationship between Ireland, the Crown, and the Empire was the central issue in contention. Dáil delegates shared a common objective: the establishment of an independent state. The question was how to achieve this, at what cost, and in what form. It was widely recognised on the pro-Treaty side, and by many of their opponents, that accepting the invitation to talks had inevitably meant compromise.[82] For Collins, Griffith, and their supporters, conceding ground meant accepting dominion status in the short term. In Collins's words, it awarded freedom – 'not the ultimate freedom that all nations desire and develop to, but the freedom to achieve it'.[83] There was much discussion about the meaning of honouring an 'ideal', and the difference between the 'substance' and the 'shadow' of liberty.[84] De Valera, with Childers's support, favoured a form of 'external' association between the Free State and the Empire, a specification that for Griffith amounted to a mere 'quibble of words'.[85] Markiewicz, against both these preferences, defended the right of republican sovereignty. Notwithstanding the existence of a shared political goal, there was thus endless scope for dissension.

[80] Jason Knirck, *Imagining Ireland's Independence: The Debates over the Anglo-Irish Treaty of 1921* (Lanham, MD: Rowman & Littlefield, 2006).

[81] *Pace* Fearghal McGarry, 'Revolution, 1916–1923' in Thomas Bartlett ed., *The Cambridge History of Modern Ireland* (Cambridge: Cambridge University Press, 2018), IV, p. 288.

[82] *Dáil Debates*, Vol. T, No. 6 (19 December 1921), Michael Collins's contribution.

[83] Ibid. [84] Ibid., contribution by Seán Mac Eoin.

[85] Arthur Griffith, 'Speech on the Treaty', below p. 343. For Childers's defence of de Valera's position see Erskine Childers, *Clause by Clause: A Comparison between 'The Treaty' and Document No. 2* (Dublin: Irish Nation Committee, 1922).

Contrary to expectations, secession had not unified viewpoints but rather proliferated disagreements. The very meaning of a republic was disputed on all sides. Instead of producing a common mind, the Revolution had generated multiple standpoints which only politics and arms could hope to reassemble, first into contending factions, and later into opposing parties within a constitutional regime.

Ideas in Contention

In his 1911 book, *The Framework of Home Rule*, Erskine Childers presented Ireland as 'the first and nearest of the British Colonies'.[86] What interested Childers was less the process of colonisation – conquest secured through plantation – than the resulting system of government under what used to be termed the 'old colonial system' whereby Ireland was tethered to Westminster on subordinate terms dictated by Poynings's Law and the Declaratory Act.[87] At that point Ireland was, in the words of George Cornewall Lewis, 'a dependent and subordinate kingdom'.[88] Childers recognised that this arrangement was succeeded in 1782 by legislative independence under Grattan's Parliament and the Renunciation Act of the following year. His point was that Grattan's Constitution was followed by the 1801 Act of Union – under which, ironically, Ireland approximated a dependency or Crown colony once more. In theory, under the Union, Ireland was an integral part of a unitary state, and thereby a participant in the management of its Empire. Yet in reality, Childers claimed, it was subject to unaccountable executive control. He thus wrote: 'Ireland is at the moment under a form of government unique, so far as I know, in the whole world, but resembling more closely than anything else that of a British Crown Colony'.[89] Childers's solution was to legislate for dominion home rule, precisely the arrangement he would reject in

[86] Erskine Childers, *The Framework of Home Rule* (London: Edward Arnold, 1911), p. 144.

[87] George L. Beer, *The Old Colonial System, 1660–1754* (New York: Macmillan, 1912), 2 vols. Although Ireland under the system was styled a kingdom and not a colony, its legislature and administration were subject to the British government, giving rise to the famous question in William Molyneux, *The Case of Ireland Being Bound by Acts of Parliament in England, Stated* (Dublin: Joseph Ray, 1698), p. 145: 'Do not the Kings of England bear the Stile of Ireland amongst the rest of their Kingdoms? Is this agreeable to the Nature of a Colony?'

[88] George Cornewall Lewis, *An Essay on the Government of Dependencies* (1841), with an Introduction by C. P. Lucas (Oxford: Clarendon, 1891), p. 152.

[89] Childers, *Framework of Home Rule*, p. 188.

1922.[90] In 1911 he asked what Ireland would have to gain by 'separation' and answered: 'Clearly nothing.'[91] At that stage, he believed, Fenianism was 'extinct', and quoted Redmond on the benefits of membership of the Empire.[92] On that basis, he sought for Ireland what Canada and other colonial dominions had secured – responsible government without a federal link to the Westminster parliament.

Self-government on this model, Childers noted, was distinct from the federated structures that characterised Switzerland, Germany, and the United States. However, in the British Empire – with New Zealand or South Africa, for example – dominions did not send representatives to the imperial parliament.[93] Still, there were debates about whether this degree of informality was sustainable.[94] By the start of the twentieth century there already existed a long-standing tradition of federalist argument in the United Kingdom, with proponents extending from Isaac Butt to Joseph Chamberlain, and including plans to federate the Empire pursued by the Round Table Movement.[95] On the other hand, at this point Childers advocated what he termed 'Colonial Home Rule' as the best means of correcting the negative consequences that followed from being a virtual crown colony, presenting his preferred system as 'an indispensable preliminary to the closer union of the various parts of the Empire'.[96] Under this version of home rule, Ireland would possess its own representative assembly with a responsible government whose link to Britain would be via the Crown and not the Westminster parliament. He cited W. E. H. Lecky as the author of the idea that Irish nationalism was a species of 'democratic revolt', although he discounted Lecky's fears about what this insurrection entailed.[97] It was simply intolerable, Childers believed, that 'one island democracy' should determine the destiny of 'another island democracy'.[98] Yet this was precisely what the

[90] He also, interestingly, defended federal home rule in Erskine Childers, 'The Home Rule Bill and the Unionist Alternative –A Contrast', *Contemporary Review*, June 1912.

[91] Childers, *Framework of Home Rule*, p. 147. [92] Ibid., p. 148.

[93] Ibid., p. 193.

[94] Lucas, Introduction in Lewis, *Essay on the Government of Dependencies*, pp. lxiv–lxviii.

[95] John Kendle, 'The Round Table Movement and "Home Rule All Round"', *The Historical Journal*, 11: 2 (1968), pp. 332–53; Colin Reid, '"An Experiment in Constructive Unionism": Isaac Butt, Home Rule and Federalist Political Thought during the 1870s', *The English Historical Review*, 129: 537 (April 2014), pp. 332–61; Duncan Bell, *Reordering the World: Essays on Liberalism and Empire* (Princeton, NJ: Princeton University Press, 2016), ch. 14.

[96] Childers, *Framework of Home Rule*, p. 148.

[97] Ibid., p. xi. [98] Ibid., p. xiii.

Union had meant for the smaller island. The United Kingdom executive as applied in Ireland, Childers complained, lacked all 'popular control'.[99] Although the Irish members at Westminster could obstruct business, they could not hold specific departments of government to account. The result was that the actual administration of Ireland was determined by British party-political interest. Although the country was adequately represented – and thus not strictly a Crown colony – its representation did not control how it was governed.

Childers's early advocacy of dominion home rule was singled out for discussion by both Dicey and Amery. It was the use of the dominion analogy that provoked Amery's criticism. Since Lord Durham's 1838 Report on the affairs of Canada, the extension of self-government to the colonies of white settlement was widely hailed as turning 'disaffection into loyalty'.[100] In proposing this arrangement for Ireland, Amery observed, advocates of Irish home rule conflated distinct aspects of the imperial set-up and sought to apply them to the incomparable case of a near-neighbour with a large constituency susceptible to secessionist hankering. Devolution to Ireland, he contended, would not result in a process of integration but in an increased incidence of friction between both countries, as happened with Newfoundland outside the Confederation of North American Colonies – except that Ireland was more commercially dependent on Britain than Newfoundland was on Canada.[101] The best indication of the likely future for relations between Britain and Ireland under home rule – dominion or otherwise – was the agitation that succeeded the grant of self-government to the Transvaal after the Battle of Majuba in 1881.[102] Irish alienation was a symptom of past policies that were no longer being pursued: 'Ireland suffers to-day economically and politically, from the legacy of political separation in the eighteenth century, and of economic disunion in the nineteenth.'[103] Now, however, the moral and material interests of both countries demanded an incorporating union.[104] Consolidation could further be secured by an appropriate regime of tariffs. In addition, Amery thought, while the two islands would thus be drawn together under the United Kingdom parliament, a separate imperial council could have oversight of the dominions.[105] In this way, the Union would be fused, and the Empire federated.

[99] Ibid., p. 188. [100] L. S. Amery, 'Home Rule and the Colonial Analogy', below p. 101.
[101] Ibid., p. 112. [102] Ibid., p. 115. [103] Ibid., p. 122. [104] Ibid. [105] Ibid., p. 103.

Dicey similarly regarded Childers's arguments as compelling but unpersuasive.[106] Dicey had been a stalwart campaigner against home rule since 1886. For him, the 1912 Bill reproduced all the failings of earlier renditions and added new deficiencies into the mix. Peculiarly destructive, he felt, was the federal component of the Bill, a feature it shared with the 1893 home rule scheme whose wisdom he had equally disputed.[107] For that reason, while the maintenance of a full incorporating or parliamentary union was the only credible arrangement for Ireland, dominion home rule, on Childers's model, along with full separation, were preferable to any proposal to retain Irish members at Westminster.[108] Each of the available models, however, suffered from a common misapprehension: they all presupposed the legitimacy of the principle of nationality – a vague notion, Dicey thought, whose appeal was rooted in the malleable concept of popular sovereignty. 'The theory of nationality', wrote Lord Acton in 1862, 'is involved in the democratic theory of the sovereignty of the general will.'[109] Dicey noted that the idea gained international prominence between 1848 and 1870, seducing Gladstone as it had done so many others who neglected to consider its application in practice. Lecky, an early advocate, came to rue his original commitment. Gladstone, on the other hand, never relented. Even the justification for Southern secession from the American Union, he believed, could be traced to the fact that 'they have made a nation'.[110] This simply pointed to a fact of modern politics: new nationalities would always lurk within an established nationality. The task for statecraft, Dicey suggested, was to compose a viable whole. Neither federal nor dominion home rule for Ireland could secure that objective. In the Irish case, both instruments were long-term recipes for separation, which in itself would not remove every cause of conflict. In the shorter term, he predicted, they guaranteed pernicious competition.

[106] Dicey, *Fool's Paradise*, p. 20.

[107] Successively in A. V. Dicey, *England's Case Against Home Rule* (London: John Murray, 1886); A. V. Dicey, *A Leap in the Dark: A Criticism of the Principles of Home Rule as Illustrated by the Bill of 1893* (London: John Murray, 1893). Dicey's arguments against federalism in 1913 were directed specifically against 'Pacificus' [F. S. Oliver], *Federalism and Home Rule* (London: John Murray, 1910).

[108] A. V. Dicey, *Fool's Paradise*, below p. 161.

[109] Lord Acton, 'Nationality' (1862) in *Selected Writings of Lord Acton: Essays in the History of Liberty*, ed. J. Rufus Fears (Indianapolis: Liberty Press, 1986), p. 423.

[110] John Morley, *The Life of William Ewart Gladstone* (London: Macmillan, 1903, 3rd ed. 1911), 3 vols., II, p. 61, cited by Dicey, *Fool's Paradise*, p. xix.

The vindication of the Union was, for Dicey, in part to be found in the prosperity and loyalty of Ulster. It was also to be found more generally in the success of Wyndham's land purchase scheme. As a result of it, small proprietors in Ireland no longer subscribed to constitutional innovation as a means of winning economic improvement.[111] Carson's arguments similarly relied on the tangible benefits of the Union: 'however Ireland might have suffered in the past, the day of her regeneration had already dawned'.[112] Although he counted himself at bottom a Liberal, he saluted the constructive measures pursued by successive Conservative governments. The opponents of unionism naturally countered these claims. For Markiewicz the Irish experience since 1801 had been one of over-taxation, underpopulation, and the decline of the Irish language.[113] Childers was happy to concede that advances in peasant ownership along with the impact of the 1898 Local Government Act had together 'destroyed the exceptional political privileges of the landlord class'. Yet still the overarching system of government deprived the country of 'national life' since the government at Westminster was never answerable to Irish interests.[114] Griffith likewise attributed Ireland's difficulties to constitutional causes, concentrating more specifically on their economic consequences.

Griffith's analysis appeared in a series of articles published in the pages of *Sinn Féin* in 1911. As indicated earlier, underlying his argument was a commitment to the Austro-Hungarian system of dual monarchy negotiated in 1867 by the imperial chancellor, Friedrich Ferdinand von Beust, and signed by Hungary's Ferenc Deák and Austria's Franz Joseph. Griffith had elaborated his 'parallel' for Ireland in *The Resurrection of Hungary* in 1904, and he now turned to reconstruct the manner in which the 1801 Union had been a betrayal of the principle of two realms under a single crown. In narrating this tale of treachery, Griffith claimed to have Irish unionists in sight as his target audience.[115] The aim was to show that a policy of British 'imperialism' subverted the interests of northern Protestants as much as it did those of southern Catholics by impoverishing the country under the zero-sum programme of securing English national greatness: 'English Imperialism decreed that Ireland must be struck down and kept down.'[116] This project, Griffith argued, had been

[111] Dicey, *Fool's Paradise*, below p. 164.
[112] Edward Carson, 'Settlement of an Old Controversy', below p. 128.
[113] Markievicz, *Women, Ideals and the Nation*, below p. 4.
[114] Childers, *The Framework of Home Rule*, below p. 81.
[115] Arthur Griffith, 'Pitt's Policy', below p. 60. [116] Ibid.

inaugurated by Pitt the Younger on the basis of ideas developed by Adam Smith. With Ireland tethered under the Union, free trade would be pursued to aggrandise England on the basis of the 'commercial conquest of the globe'.[117] Griffith's verdict on the outcome was vividly expressed in the words of an imagined British statesman: '"Behold. We graze the bullocks where the homesteads of four millions stood. We have made of Ireland the one country in Europe where the people yearly diminish. We have strengthened England. We have carried out Pitt's policy."'[118]

Griffith's thesis involved the rejection of a particular conception of imperialism – of which there were many incompatible theories in the period.[119] But it was not a rejection of empire as such. In fact, his purpose was to relaunch the goal of world hegemony on a more equitable basis: he wished to create, as he put it, 'an invincible naval and military Anglo-Hibernian Empire'.[120] Smith's critique of the mercantile system of political economy, Griffith thought, had in reality used the tool of free trade as a means of exclusive expansionism. According to Griffith, Friedrich List's scheme of 'national' economy had been the leading continental riposte, based on Henry Carey's plans for protectionism.[121] Kettle, unlike Amery, rejected the pursuit of protection while adhering to the conception of national interest promoted by the German historical school of economics.[122] However, Griffith defended a regime of tariffs to be jointly imposed under his Anglo-Hibernian condominium. Yet Britain would have to be brought to endorse the wisdom of this measure. The rise of Germany was the only inducement that might push statecraft in the right direction. Bismarck's victories over Austria and France and the subsequent increase in German naval power meant that sooner or later Britain would face its new rival in the theatre of war. In the absence of an equal partnership with Ireland, the Irish would 'hail her defeat as their

[117] Ibid., p. 41. [118] Ibid., p. 60.

[119] Among the most influential texts of the period was J. A. Hobson, *Imperialism: A Study* (New York: James Pott, 1902), which contributed to the transformation of the meaning of the term. Relevant also in associating overseas expansion with capitalist exploitation is Rudolf Hilferding, *Das Finanzkapital: Eine Studie über die jüngste Entwicklung des Kapitalismus* (Vienna: Wiener Volksbuchhandlung, 1910). See also V. I. Lenin, *Imperialism, the Highest Stage of Capitalism* (1917) in *Selected Works* (Moscow: Progress Publishers, 1963), 3 vols., I, pp. 667–766. However, for competing visions of imperialism as a constructive international policy, see Dicey, *Fool's Paradise*, pp. xxxi ff.

[120] Griffith, 'Pitt's Policy', below p. 38. [121] Ibid., p. 46.

[122] See Thomas M. Kettle, 'The Economics of Nationalism', below. For his response to the policy of dual monarchy and abstentionism see Thomas M. Kettle, 'Would the Hungarian Policy Work?', *New Ireland Review* (February 1905), pp. 321–8.

salvation'.[123] The military might of the Germans had created conditions resembling those faced by Britain in 1782. Pressed by foreign engagements again in the early twentieth century, Griffith concluded, Britain would be wise to renew the pact agreed with Ireland under Grattan.

For Griffith nationality could be reconciled with empire; but for Pearse they were intrinsically antipathetic. He believed that the nation was prior to politics – it was an expression of 'natural' human affection, animated by spiritual values. It was, in effect, an extension of family relations, imbued with divine purpose: 'The nation is of God, the empire is of man.'[124] While empire was founded on commercial utility, the nation was rooted in sentiments of mutual affiliation. Nonetheless, Pearse judged that in the Irish case this sensibility had been corrupted and would in practice have to be rekindled, not least by raising civic awareness through discipline and arms. Whether home rule was granted or not, Pearse reflected in 1913, 'the substantial task of achieving the Irish Nation' would remain.[125] Yet happily, since nationality was primordial, it was always available to be resurrected even when the memory of it had been virtually obliterated. The prospect of resuscitation held out the promise that 'the people itself will perhaps be its own Messiah, the people labouring, scourged, crowned with thorns, agonising and dying, to rise again immortal and impassible'.[126] Four years before Pearse's bid to appropriate the Christian ordeal in the service of national liberation, Markiewicz had declared that 'as the death of Christ brought a new hope and a new life to an old world, so the blood of each martyr shed in the cause of liberty will give a new impetus to the comrades who are left behind to continue the work'.[127] She too had recognised the decline of national feeling: modern transport, education, the postal service, the telegraph, and the press had shrunk distances and eroded customs. The shared project of national freedom would therefore have to be revived. Ireland, like Egypt and India, appeared to Markiewicz to be held in bondage and needed to be awoken by inspiring ideals. Empires, like the Macedonian, relied on force and could not survive; nationalities, like the Irish, relied on spiritual faith which could be replenished.[128]

This reinvigoration would not just be moral but also social in nature. The aim was 'to build up a great nation, noble and self-sacrificing,

[123] Griffith, 'Pitt's Policy', below p. 60.

[124] Pearse, *The Sovereign People*, below p. 240.

[125] Pearse, *The Coming Revolution*, below p. 187.

[126] Ibid., p. 185.

[127] Markievicz, *Women, Ideals and the Nation*, below p. 4.

[128] Ibid., p. 16.

industrious and free'.[129] For Pearse any programme of social reconstruction should be anchored in the 'democratic truths' underpinning the four 'gospels' of republican ideology developed by Wolfe Tone, Thomas Davis, Fintan Lalor, and John Mitchel.[130] But it was Connolly who developed this agenda into a programme of revolution. He envisaged transforming economic, social, and intellectual relations together. A 'reconquest' of Ireland implied, among other things, a species of ideological conversion. It was this aspect of Connolly's campaign that led him to present his *Labour in Irish History* 'as part of the literature of the Gaelic revival'.[131] He drew on Alice Stopford Green's historical study, *The Making of Ireland and Its Undoing*, to create a vision of primitive communism in pre-Norman Ireland. This followed a wider European trend of finding the antidote to exploitation in social systems that were unmolested by capitalist relations of production. The German *Mark*, the Russian *mir*, and the Indian village community epitomised primeval collectivism. Even Marx in his later writings came to value the ethos of archaic co-operation.[132] According to Connolly, the steady colonial reduction of Ireland had introduced a regime of private property and thus prepared the ground for modern commercial society. The last remnants of 'rude' social democracy expired in 1649. At the same time, ideological conquest followed material subjugation. With the education of the Irish clergy in 'the continental Schools of European despots' after Williamite Wars in Ireland, learning was steadily seduced by the corrupt principles of the *ancien régime*, completing the oblivion of Gaelic society. There followed the degradation of Irish manners in English literature and the self-abasement of Irish character in Anglo-Irish writing. Faced with the general decline in national self-respect, only the working classes offered the means of fundamental resistance. However, hitherto their attempts at insurrection had failed because the promise of political liberty since 1798 had not been systematically linked to the goal of economic freedom. Connolly reminded his readers that 'revolutions are not the product of our brains, but of ripe material conditions'.[133] But in fact he believed that

[129] Ibid. [130] Pearse, *The Sovereign People*, below pp. 241–50.

[131] James Connolly, *Labour in Irish History*, below p. 26.

[132] For Marx's shifting position on village communities and his absorption of arguments made fashionable by Maurer, Haxthausen, Stubbs, Freeman, and Maine see Gareth Stedman Jones, *Karl Marx: Greatness and Illusion* (London: Allen Lane, 2016), pp. 568 ff.

[133] Connolly, *Labour in Irish History*, below p. 32.

intellectual persuasion was also essential: labour had to be stirred by a vision of the future.

Carl Schmitt would argue in 1923 that successful mobilisation in the age of mass democracy required a principle (or 'myth') of cohesion. Since ideas of nationality or class might equally serve that purpose, it struck him as unsurprising that Connolly conspired with Pearse in prosecuting the Rising.[134] Yet collaboration does not entail concurrence. Having established the Irish Socialist Republican Party in 1896, Connolly was increasingly attracted by syndicalist methods after his experience of trade unionism during his period in the United States between 1903 and 1910. In *The Re-Conquest of Ireland* he would argue that the cause of social democracy was best advanced by a system of coordinated labour unions. While social power was being nurtured on the industrial 'battlefield', political agitation and revolutionary militancy would simultaneously promote the cause of public ownership.[135] This concerted programme required an alliance between day labourers and 'workers whose toil was upon the intellectual plane'.[136] The energies of literary and artistic life had been distracted, he thought, by the exclusive pursuit of national freedom. But now the aims of 'wage labourers and their intellectual comrades' would have to be harnessed to the cause of socialism.[137] Increasingly after the start of the First World War, Connolly meditated the possibilities of insurgency in the interest both of nationalism and socialism. The former, he thought, was a fitting instrument of the latter. He contemplated various methods for bringing about 'the final dethronement of the vulture classes that rule and rob the world'.[138] In the end he opted to throw in his lot with a republican rising against the Empire based on a revival of the 'tradition of nationhood' and aiming at 'the establishment of a permanent National Government'.[139] For him, a mixture of history and geography vindicated this national focus. In comparative terms, he thought, Belgium was but a creation of yesterday, while 'the frontiers of Ireland, the ineffaceable marks of the separate existence of Ireland, are as old as Europe itself, the handiwork of the Almighty, not of politicians'.[140]

[134] Carl Schmitt, *The Crisis of Parliamentary Democracy* (1923), trans. Ellen Kennedy (Cambridge, MA: MIT Press, 1985), p. 75.
[135] James Connolly, *The Re-Conquest of Ireland*, below p. 219.
[136] Ibid. [137] Ibid., p. 222. [138] James Connolly, 'Our Duty in the Present Crisis', below p. 196.
[139] *Proclamation of the Republic*, below p. 234.
[140] Connolly, 'Our Duty in the Present Crisis', below p. 231.

This conclusion could not accommodate Ulster's appeal to nationality. 'They have their own version of *Sinn Féin* – they, too, want to be left to themselves alone', declared Horace Plunkett in response to the southern Irish tendency to disregard the claims of the north-east to national legitimacy.[141] Carson maintained that reasoned apprehension among Protestants about impeding Catholic dominance was not based on expectations of open persecution. Instead, there was fear about the regular operation of democratic institutions as these were likely to impact upon the rights of minorities.[142] For Childers and Lynd, worries about intolerance were simply misplaced.[143] But this assessment was based on the evidence for Catholic prejudice, which was felt to be negligible, rather than on an appreciation of how Catholic democracy functioned. Espousing Irish republicanism in 1918, Stopford Green pronounced that 'the rule of one democracy by another is unthinkable'.[144] Yet for Ronald McNeill defending partition on the eve of the Irish civil war, this was exactly what the republican position entailed.[145] The division of the island into distinct jurisdictions was not, McNeill insisted, an act of dismemberment but merely the recognition of a *fait accompli*. This amounted to the contention that an Ulster democracy existed inside the population of the island as a whole demanding institutional recognition. This claim was the culmination of unionist polemic. However, technically, the proposition was not a defence of the 1801 Union but rather an assertion of its end.

Asquith had famously declared in the House of Commons in 1912 that Ireland must be regarded as a 'nation': 'What nation? The Irish nation – repeated and ratified time after time during the best part of the life of a generation.'[146] The statement was a perpetuation of Gladstonian faith. Yet the implications of the position pointed in numerous potentially contradictory directions. It meant that Ireland as a corporate entity should be taken as the democratic basis on which any rightful system of government ought to be constructed. Yet this left unresolved the form of administration that would best honour that foundation in popular legitimacy. Opinion

[141] Plunkett, *A Defence of the Convention*, below p. 267.
[142] Carson, 'Settlement of an Old Controversy', below p. 136.
[143] Childers, *The Framework of Home Rule*, below p. 77; Robert Lynd, 'Ulster the Facts of the Case', below p. 234.
[144] Stopford Green, *Loyalty and Disloyalty*, below p. 293.
[145] Ronald McNeill, *Ulster's Stand for Union*, below p. 364. For discussion see Colin Reid, 'Democracy, Sovereignty and Unionist Political Thought during the Revolutionary Period', *Transactions of the Royal Historical Society*, 27 (December 2017), pp. 211–32.
[146] Hansard, 11 April 1912, Vol. 36, cols. 1401–2.

in Ireland divided on this question, not simply between unionists and nationalists, as the ensuing conflict is usually portrayed, but within these respective bodies of thought as well. This left Ireland disjointed, but not along a single axis. Unionism splintered between maintaining the status quo and creating a home rule parliament in Belfast. At the same time, Protestant unionism fractured between North and South. The fissures within nationalism were more conspicuous still, rendering the very category an empty generalisation. Consequently, opponents of a parliamentary union argued on competing fronts: for the creation of a new imperial condominium; for self-government in various guises under the Westminster parliament; and for assorted forms of separatism leading to political outcomes ranging from capitalist democracy to socialist republicanism. Militant conflict streamlined this factionalism – on both sides of the border. Yet it was the original rupture stemming from 1886 that proved a decisive turning point for the history of these islands, and a defining moment for the Empire as a whole.

Bibliographical Essay

Accounts of the Period

There are numerous standard accounts covering the period in its various aspects. Among the most essential are: Joseph Lee, *The Modernisation of Irish Society, 1848–1918* (Dublin: Gill and Macmillan, 1973); D. G. Boyce ed., *The Revolution in Ireland, 1879–1923* (Basingstoke: Macmillan Education, 1988); David Fitzpatrick, *The Two Irelands, 1912–1939* (Oxford: Oxford University Press, 1998); and Eugenio Biagini, *British Democracy and Irish Nationalism, 1876–1906* (Cambridge: Cambridge University Press, 2007). For an overview of the Revolution, see John Crowley, John Borgonovo, Donal Ó Drisceoil, Mike Murphy, and Nick Hogan eds., *Atlas of the Irish Revolution* (Cork: Cork University Press, 2017). Home rule and the drama of high politics are captured in Alvin Jackson, *Home Rule: An Irish History, 1800–2000* (London: Weidenfeld & Nicolson, 2003) and Ronan Fanning, *Fatal Path: British Government and Irish Revolution, 1910–1922* (London: Faber and Faber, 2013). For a focus on the dynamics of the Revolution, see Fearghal McGarry, 'Revolution, 1916–1923' in Thomas Bartlett ed., *The Cambridge History of Ireland, 1880–Present*, IV (Cambridge: Cambridge University Press, 2018), pp. 258–95; see also Fearghal McGarry, *The Rising: Ireland, Easter 1916* (Oxford: Oxford University Press, 2010). Ireland in the War is covered by Niamh Gallagher, *Ireland and the Great War: A Social and Political History* (London: Bloomsbury, 2019). For the Anglo-Irish War and the Civil War, see Maurice Walsh, *Bitter Freedom: Ireland in a Revolutionary World, 1918–1923* (London: Faber and Faber, 2015). For the border, see Cormac Moore, *Birth of the Border: The Impact of Partition in Ireland* (Dublin: Merrion

Press, 2019). For the dynamics of Unionist politics, see Alvin Jackson, *The Ulster Party* (Oxford: Clarendon, 1989) and *Colonel Edward Saunderson: Land and Loyalty in Victorian Ireland* (Oxford, Clarendon, 1995). For the IRA in the context of the Revolution, see Peter Hart, *The IRA at War, 1916–1923* (Oxford: Oxford University Press, 2003). For the response in Ulster to home rule, see A. T. Q. Stewart, *The Ulster Crisis* (London: Faber, 1967). For the Irish Parliamentary Party, see Conor Mulvagh, *The Irish Parliamentary Party at Westminster, 1900–18* (Manchester: Manchester University Press, 2016); James McConnel, *The Irish Parliamentary Party and the Third Home Rule Crisis* (Dublin: Four Courts Press, 2013). For nationalism in the period, see Tom Garvin, *Nationalist Revolutionaries in Ireland, 1858–1928* (Oxford: Oxford University Press, 1987); Patrick Maume, *The Long Gestation: Irish Nationalist Life, 1891–1918* (Dublin: Gill and Macmillan, 1999); R. F. Foster, *Vivid Faces: The Revolutionary Generation in Ireland, 1890–1923* (London: Allen Lane, 2014); David Dwan, *The Great Community: Culture and Nationalism in Ireland* (Dublin: Field Day, 2008); and Paul Bew, 'Moderate Nationalism and the Irish Revolution, 1916–1923', *Historical Journal*, 42: 3 (1999), pp. 729–49. For women and nationalism, see Senia Pašeta, *Irish Nationalist Women, 1900-1918* (Cambridge: Cambridge University Press, 2013); for Ulster, see Diane Urquhart, *Women in Ulster Politics, 1890–1940* (Dublin: Irish Academic Press, 2000). For Northern Ireland, see Alan Parkinson, *A Difficult Birth: The Early Years of Northern Ireland, 1920-25* (Dublin: Eastwood Books, 2020). W. Alison Phillips, *The Revolution in Ireland, 1906–1923* (London and New York: Longmans, Green, 1923) offers a contemporary perspective on the politics of the period with a definite slant, and is itself for these reasons of historical interest.

Intellectual History and Political Thought

Nicholas Mansergh, *Ireland in the Age of Reform and Revolution* (London: Allen & Unwin, 1940), revised as *The Irish Question, 1840–1921: A Commentary on Anglo-Irish Relations and on Social and Political Forces in Ireland in the Age of Reform and Revolution* (London: Allen & Unwin, 1965) explores ideas of nationality. Paul Bew, *Ideology and the Irish Question: Ulster Unionism and Irish Nationalism, 1912–1916* (Oxford: Oxford University Press, 1994) tackles the principal ideological antagonisms around home rule. E. Rumpf and A. C. Hepburn, *Nationalism and Socialism in Twentieth-Century Ireland* (Liverpool: Liverpool University

Press, 1977) examines the relations between socialist ideas and nationalism. Oliver MacDonagh, *States of Mind: A Study of Anglo-Irish Conflict 1780–1980* (London: Allen & Unwin, 1983) covers aspects of intellectual and cultural developments in the period.

Twentieth-century Political thought in Ireland has received relatively little attention until recently, though for a pioneering collaborative effort see D. George Boyce, Robert Eccleshall, and Vincent Geoghegan eds., *Political Thought in Ireland Since the Seventeenth Century* (London: Routledge, 1994), particularly Margaret O'Callaghan, 'Denis Patrick Moran and "the Irish Colonial Condition", 1891–1921'. More recent research includes Richard Bourke, 'Reflections on the Political Thought of the Irish Revolution', *Transactions of the Royal Historical Society*, 27 (December 2017), pp. 175–91; 'Political and Religious Ideas of the Irish Revolution', *History of European Ideas*, 46: 7 (2020), pp. 997–1008; Colin Reid, 'Democracy, Sovereignty and Unionist Political Thought during the Revolutionary Period', *Transactions of the Royal Historical Society*, 27 (December 2017), pp. 211–32; and Senia Pašeta, 'Feminist Political Thought and Activism in Revolutionary Ireland, c. 1880–1918', *Transactions of the Royal Historical Society*, 27 (December 2017), pp. 193–209. Also important for grasping the political ideas of the period is Colin Reid, *The Lost Ireland of Stephen Gwynn: Irish Constitutional Nationalism and Cultural Politics, 1864–1950* (Manchester: Manchester University Press, 2011). A book which situates Ireland in the political thought of British and European thinkers is that of James Stafford, *The Case of Ireland: Commerce, Empire and the European Order, 1750–1848* (Cambridge: Cambridge University Press, 2022).

Individual Authors

Studies of individual authors are listed in the order of their appearance in this volume. The writings of several women activists are available in Angela Bourke et al. eds., *The Field Day Anthology of Irish Writing, vols. 4 & 5: Irish Women's Writings and Traditions* (Cork: Cork University Press, 2002). For Constance Markievicz, correspondence is available in Constance Markievicz, Eva Gore-Booth, and Esther Roper, *Prison Letters of Countess Markievicz* (London: Longmans, Green and Co., 1934). Important studies include Lauren Arrington, *Revolutionary Lives: Constance and Casimir Markievicz* (Princeton, NJ: 2016); Anne Haverty, *Constance*

Markievicz: Irish Revolutionary (Dublin: Lilliput Press, 2016); and Sonja Tiernan, *Eva Gore-Booth: An Image of Such Politics* (Manchester: Manchester University Press, 2010). For James Connolly, the most useful selection available is Conor McCarthy ed., *The Revolutionary and Anti-Imperialist Writings of James Connolly, 1893–1916* (Edinburgh: Edinburgh University Press, 2016); and the best biographical study is Donal Nevin, *James Connolly: 'A Full Life'* (Dublin: Gill & Macmillan, 2005). For Arthur Griffith, see Patrick Maume, 'The Ancient Constitution: Arthur Griffith and his Intellectual Legacy to Sinn Féin', *Irish Political Studies*, 10: 1 (1995), pp. 123–37; Patrick Maume, 'Young Ireland, Arthur Griffith, and Republican Ideology: The Question of Continuity', *Éire-Ireland*, 34: 2, (Summer 1999), pp. 155–74; and Richard Bourke, 'Perfidy: 1891–1923' in *Peace in Ireland: The War of Ideas* (London: Pimlico, 2003; rev. 2012). For Erskine Childers, see Jim Ring, *Erskine Childers* (London: John Murray, 1997); Andrew Boyle, *The Riddle of Erskine Childers* (London: Hutchinson, 1977); and the portrayal offered in Robert Brennan, *Allegiance* (Dublin: Browne and Nolan, 1950). The best source for L. S. Amery remains his autobiography, *My Political Life* (London: Hutchinson, 1953–55), 3 vols. A concise account of Edward Carson's career can be found in Alvin Jackson, *Sir Edward Carson* (Dundalk: Dundalgan Press, 1993). Also see Alvin Jackson, *Judging Redmond and Carson: Comparative Irish Lives* (Dublin: Royal Irish Academy, 2018). For Thomas Kettle, see Senia Pašeta, *Thomas Kettle* (Dublin: University College Dublin Press, 2008), and her chapter in Adrian Gregory and Senia Pašeta eds., *Ireland and the Great War: 'A War to Unite Us All'?* (Manchester: Manchester University Press, 2002); see also Margaret O'Callaghan, 'Political Formations in Pre-First World War Ireland: The Politics of the Lost Generation and the Cult of Tom Kettle' in Caoimhe Nic Dháibhéid and Colin Reid eds., *From Parnell to Paisley: Constitutional and Revolutionary Politics in Modern Ireland* (Dublin: Irish Academic Press, 2010). On A. V. Dicey, see Richard Cosgrove, *The Rule of Law: Albert Venn Dicey, Victorian Jurist* (London: Macmillan, 1980); in relation to Ireland, see Richard Bourke, 'Reversals: 1886–1920' in *Peace in Ireland: The War of Ideas* (London: Pimlico, 2003, rev. 2012). On Eoin MacNeill, see F. X. Martin and F. J. Byrne eds., *The Scholar Revolutionary: Eoin MacNeill, 1867–1945, and the Making of the New Ireland* (Shannon: Irish University Press, 1973) and Michael Tierney ed. *Eoin MacNeill: Scholar and Man of Action* (Oxford: Clarendon, 1980). For the writings of Patrick Pearse, see *The Collected Works of Patrick Pearse* (Dublin: Phoenix,1924), 5 vols.

For commentary, see Conor Cruise O'Brien, 'The Embers of Easter', *The Massachusetts Review*, 7: 4, (Autumn 1966), pp. 621–37; Conor Cruise O'Brien, *Ancestral Voices: Religion and Nationalism in Ireland* (Dublin: Poolbeg, 1994), pp. 159–60; and Joost Augsteijn, *Patrick Pearse: The Making of a Revolutionary* (Basingstoke: Palgrave Macmillan, 2010). On John Redmond there is Denis Gwynn, *The Life of John Redmond* (London: G. G. Harrap,1932); also relevant is Joseph P. Finnan, *John Redmond and Irish Unity, 1912–1918* (New York: Syracuse University Press, 2004); and Dermot Meleady, *John Redmond: The National Leader* (Newbridge: Merrion, 2013). On Hanna Sheehy Skeffington, see Margaret Ward, *Fearless Woman: Hanna Sheehy Skeffington, Feminism and the Irish Revolution* (Dublin: University College Dublin Press, 2019); and Maria Luddy, *Hanna Sheehy Skeffington* (Dundalk: Irish Historical Association, 1995). For Horace Plunkett, see Trevor West, *Horace Plunkett: Co-operation and Politics* (Gerrards Cross: Smythe, 1986). On Louie Bennett, see R. M. Fox, *Louie Bennett: Her Life and Times* (Dublin: Talbot Press, 1958). For both Sheehy Skeffington and Bennett, see Mary Cullen and Maria Luddy eds., *Female Activists: Irish Women and Social Change 1900–1960* (Dublin: The Woodfield Press, 2001); and the insights in Margaret Ward, *Maude Gonne: A Life* (London: Pandora, 1993). On Alice Stopford Green, see R. B. McDowell, *Alice Stopford Green: A Passionate Historian* (Dublin: A. Figgis, 1967). For Robert Lynd see D. MacCarthy, 'Introduction', in R. W. Lynd, *Essays on Life and Literature* (London: Dutton, 1951). For Ronald McNeill, see St. John Ervine, revised by Marc Brodie, 'McNeill, Ronald John, Baron Cushendun (1861–1934)' in the *Oxford Dictionary of National Biography* (online: https://doi.org/10.1093/ref:odnb/34816).

Chronology of Events

1886 *8 April:* First Home Rule Bill (i.e. Government of Ireland Bill) introduced in Commons by Liberal Prime Minister William Ewart Gladstone.

8 June: Home Rule defeated in Commons by 341 votes (including 93 Liberals) to 311.

1891 Irish Unionist Alliance formed, led by Colonel Edward Saunderson.

1893 *13 February:* Second Home Rule Bill introduced in Commons by Prime Minister Gladstone. Passed third reading on 1 Sept by 301 votes to 267.

31 July: The Gaelic League, an organisation to revive Irish language and culture, founded by Douglas Hyde, Eoin MacNeill, and Fr Eugene Downey.

9 September: Second Home Rule Bill rejected by Lords by 419 votes to 41.

1898 James Connolly launches *The Workers' Republic.*

1899 *4 March:* Arthur Griffith launches and becomes editor of *United Irishman.*

1900 Maud Gonne forms radical nationalist women's organisation, Inghinidhe na hÉireann (Daughters of Ireland). Constance Markievicz and Hanna Sheehy-Skeffington become members.

January–February: Irish Parliamentary Party (IPP) reunites after ten-year rift between factions under leadership of John Redmond.

1904 *2 January–July:* Griffith publishes *The Resurrection of Hungary* in weekly articles printed in *United Irishman.* Reprinted in book form at end of year.

1905 *3 March:* Ulster Unionist Council formed in Belfast.

28 November: First Annual Convention of Griffith's The National Council, at which he presents 'The Sinn Féin Policy'.

1907 *21 April:* Formation of Sinn Féin League.

1908 *21 February:* Sinn Féin stands for parliament for first time in North Leitrim by-election and is defeated by IPP.

11 November: Suffrage organisation Irish Women's Franchise League established by Hanna Sheehy-Skeffington and three others.

1909 *4 January:* James Larkin establishes trade union, the Irish Transport and General Workers' Union (ITGWU).

30 November: House of Lords rejects 'The People's Budget', precipitating constitutional crisis.

1910 *January:* UK general election. Hung parliament. Liberals retain power by forming government with IPP.

21 February: Edward Carson elected leader of Irish Unionist Alliance.

December: UK general election. Liberals retain power and form government with IPP. Last general election to be held until end of First World War.

1911 *18 August:* Parliament Act. Removes veto of House of Lords.

21 August: Louie Bennett and Helen Chenevix establish Irish Women's Suffrage Federation.

23 September: Ulster Unionist monster meeting at Craigavon, Belfast, to protest home rule. Organised by James Craig.

1912 *9 April:* Mass Unionist gathering at Balmoral Showground, Belfast. Conservative leader Andrew Bonar Law pledges unconditional support for Ulster Unionist resistance to home rule.

11 April: Third Home Rule Bill presented to Commons by Liberal Prime Minister Herbert H. Asquith.

9 May: Home Rule Bill passes second reading in Commons by 370 votes to 270.

11 June: Liberal MP Thomas Agar-Robartes proposes amendment to exclude northern Protestant majority counties of Antrim, Armagh, Derry, and Down from Home Rule Bill, the first formal parliamentary proposal to exclude part of Ulster. Motion defeated.

28 June: James Connolly founds Irish Labour Party.

28 September: Unionists declare this day 'Ulster Day'. 237,368 men sign Ulster Solemn League and Covenant; 234,046 women sign corresponding Women's Declaration.

1913 *16 January:* Third reading of Home Rule Bill in Commons. Passed by 368 votes to 258.

30 January: House of Lords reject Home Rule Bill by 326 votes to 69, delaying progress of legislation but not vetoing it. Home rule set to come into operation.

31 January: Formation of Ulster Volunteer Force (UVF).

26 August: General strike in Dublin. Approximately 20,000 workers go on strike against 300 employers. The 'Lockout' lasts until early 1914.

23 September: Ulster Unionist Council endorses Proclamation of a Provisional Government for Ulster.

1 November: Eoin MacNeill publishes 'The North Began' in *An Claidheamh Soluis.*

11–25 November: Irish Volunteers launched with Irish Republican Brotherhood (IRB) backing. MacNeill becomes leader.

19 November: James Larkin, James Connolly, and Jack White form Irish Citizen Army.

1914 *9 March:* Carson rejects Asquith's proposal for Ulster counties to opt out of home rule for six years.

20 March: Curragh incident. Senior British military officers refuse to deploy British Army against Ulster loyalists.

6 April: New Cabinet proposal that six counties of Ulster would not be included in home rule legislation 'unless by their own consent', effectively making partition proposal permanent.

24–5 April: UVF gunrunning in Larne, Donaghadee, and Bangor. Approximately 20,000 rifles and 3 million rounds of ammunition smuggled from Germany.

25 May: Unamended Home Rule Bill passes third and final reading in House of Commons with no agreement over Ulster.

10–16 June: Redmond wrests control of Irish Volunteers from IRB.

28 June: Archduke Franz Ferdinand, heir to Austro-Hungarian Empire, and his wife Sophia are assassinated in Sarajevo, Bosnia.

21–4 July: At the King's request, a conference of all parties is held at Buckingham Palace to resolve the 'Irish Question'. Conference fails.

26 July: Irish Volunteers' failed gunrunning at Howth, Dublin. British Army opens fire on a crowd in Bachelors Walk, killing four civilians and wounding thirty.

3 August:

- Germany declares war on France.
- Redmond commits Irish Volunteers to defence of Ireland.

4 August: Germany invades neutral Belgium. UK declares war on Germany.

8 August: UK Parliament passes Defence of the Realm Act.

18 September: Government of Ireland Act receives Royal Assent but suspended for one year or until end of European hostilities, pending resolution of Ulster question.

20 September: Redmond makes famous speech at Woodenbridge, Co. Wicklow, committing Irish Volunteers to going 'wherever the firing line extends'.

24 September: Irish Volunteers split into two groups over Redmond's declaration: the majority National Volunteers, who follow Redmond, and the minority Irish Volunteers, who retain the name.

2–4 December: Government suppresses Griffith's *Sinn Féin,* the IRB's *Irish Freedom*, and Connolly's *The Irish Worker*. Griffith launches *Eire/Ireland*.

1915 *Early 1915: Eire/Ireland* suppressed by government. Griffith launches *Scissors and Paste*. Suppressed in March.

1 May: IRB establishes new Military Committee, which contains members who play key role in 1916 rebellion.

25 May: Asquith forms coalition government. Carson appointed Attorney General. Redmond refuses appointment in new administration.

29 May: Connolly publishes new series of *The Workers' Republic.*

19 June: Griffith publishes *Nationality*.

1 August: Jeremiah O'Donovan Rossa's funeral used as propaganda event by republicans. Pearse delivers famous graveside oration.

1916 *19–22 January*: IRB Military Council agreed to instigate rebellion no later than Easter. Connolly joins Council.

1 March: IRB decide on Easter Sunday for rebellion, unbeknownst to Eoin MacNeill.

22 April: MacNeill revokes orders for Easter manoeuvres.

23 April: MacNeill's orders published in the *Sunday Independent*. IRB Military Council decide to go ahead with rebellion regardless.

24 April: First day of Easter Rising. Key locations seized in Dublin by 1,250 members of the IRB, Irish Volunteers, Cumann na mBhan, and Irish Citizen Army. Irish tricolour hoisted for first time outside captured General Post Office (GPO) and Pearse reads Proclamation. Smaller actions take place in Galway, Meath, and Wexford.

25 April: Francis Sheehy-Skeffington, husband of Hanna, shot dead by Captain J. C. Bowen-Colthurst. Martial law declared.

27 April: Connolly badly injured in GPO.

29–30 April: Unconditional surrender of rebels. 466 lives lost, including 254 civilians.

3–12 May: Fifteen rebel leaders executed including Pearse and Connolly. Roger Casement executed on 13 August.

May–July: David Lloyd George, Secretary of State for War, resumes negotiations with IPP and Ulster Unionists on basis of implementing home rule and excluding Ulster from settlement.

9 September: Thomas M. Kettle killed at Ginchy.

6 December: Lloyd George takes over prime ministership from Asquith and forms War Cabinet.

1917 *5 February*: Count Plunkett, father of executed rebel Joseph, wins Roscommon North by-election, the first of several by-election nationalist swings away from IPP.

9 May: Joseph McGuinness (Sinn Féin), imprisoned after the Rising, narrowly wins South Longford by-election.

16 May: Lloyd George proposes home rule for twenty-six counties (excluding Ulster) or convention of Irishmen to resolve impasse. Redmond declines home rule.

10 July: Eamon de Valera (Sinn Féin) wins East Clare by-election following death of Willie Redmond MP (brother of IPP leader) at Battle of Messines Ridge, Belgium.

25 July: First meeting of Irish Convention.

10 August: W. T. Cosgrave (Sinn Féin) wins by-election for Kilkenny City.

20 Sept: Thomas Ashe, the first of several republican hunger strikers, dies of force-feeding.

25–7 October: Eamon de Valera elected president of Sinn Féin at party's first ard-fheis (convention). Griffith does not contest election. De Valera also becomes president of Irish Volunteers.

1918 *2 February*: Patrick Donnelly (IPP) wins South Armagh by-election, defeating Sinn Féin.

6 February: Representation of the People Act receives Royal Assent. Enfranchises women aged thirty and above and all men aged twenty-one and above (with qualifications).

6 March: John Redmond dies.

12 March: John Dillon elected IPP leader.

21 March: German spring offensive begins.

5 April: Final meeting of Irish Convention.

9 April: Military Service Bill (including Ireland) introduced in Westminster and Irish Convention proposal rejected by government.

18 April:

- Military Service (No. 2) Act, 1918 receives Royal Assent, expanding age of compulsion to include all males aged eighteen to fifty-one (with qualifications).

- Representative gathering of nationalists (including Irish Labour, the Catholic Church, and all nationalist parties) at Mansion House, Dublin, to coordinate opposition to conscription.

21 April: Anti-conscription pledges signed across Ireland until late 1918.

17–18 May: Arrest of Sinn Féin leadership in intelligence fiasco known as 'German plot'.

20 June: Griffith (Sinn Féin) wins East Cavan by-election.

1 November: Irish Labour agrees to withdraw from contesting UK general election, positioning election as a referendum on the national question.

11 November: Armistice signed between the Allied and Associated Powers and Germany. Hostilities on Western Front cease at 11 a.m.

14–28 December: UK general election. Sinn Féin wins seventy-three seats on abstentionist platform. IPP win six. Unionists win twenty-six. Constance Markievicz (Sinn Féin) is first female MP to be elected in UK.

1919 *18 January:* Paris Peace Conference opens in Versailles, France.

21 January:

- First meeting of Dáil Éireann in Dublin. Sinn Féin declares Ireland independent
- Two Royal Irish Constabulary (RIC) men killed in Soloheadbeg Ambush in Tipperary by IRA volunteers. Initiates Irish War of Independence.

1 April: Second meeting of Dáil Éireann. De Valera elected President.

2 April: Markievicz appointed Minister for Labour: first Irish female Cabinet Minister (the only one for sixty years) and first in Western Europe.

18 April: De Valera elected president of Sinn Féin.

17 May: First Republican court established at Ballinrobe, Co. Mayo.

28 June: Treaty of Versailles signed, formally ending First World War.

12 September: Dáil Éireann proscribed by British authorities.

4 November: British Cabinet's Irish Committee led by southern Unionist Walter Long creates two home rule parliaments for Ireland (one in Dublin; one in Belfast) with a Council of Ireland to provide framework for unification.

1920 *25 February:* New Government of Ireland Bill introduced to Commons based on Long's proposal.

10 March: UUC accepts Long's proposal and parliament for Northern Ireland.

25 March: British servicemen ('Black and Tans' and Auxiliaries) arrive in Ireland to assist RIC.

31 March: Carson opposes partition of Ireland in second reading of Government of Ireland Bill, calling it a betrayal of unionists in the south and west.

23 July: 14 die and 100 injured in fierce rioting in Belfast.

13 August: Restoration of Order in Ireland Act receives Royal Assent. IRA activists to be tried by court martial rather than by jury in criminal courts.

19 August: Lord Mayor of Cork Terence MacSwiney embarks on hunger strike in Brixton Prison following conviction by court martial for sedition. Griffith delivers graveside oration in Cork on 31 October.

22 October: Ulster Special Constabulary formed: an armed (and predominantly northern Protestant) police reserve.

21 November: 'Bloody Sunday': IRA kill fourteen British undercover agents. Auxiliary Division of RIC retaliate, opening fire on spectators at football match in Croke Park, Dublin, killing thirteen.

28 November: 'Kilmichael ambush': two lorries carrying Auxiliaries ambushed by IRA at Kilmichael, killing seventeen. Three IRA men killed.

10 December: Martial law declared in counties Cork, Limerick, Kerry, and Tipperary.

11 December: Cork city centre burned in reprisal attacks by Crown forces.

23 December: Government of Ireland Act 1920 receives Royal Assent.

1921 *3:* Northern Ireland formally created under Government of Ireland Act 1920.

13 May: Irish elections in the South held under terms of the Government of Ireland Act 1920. All 128 candidates returned unopposed, including 124 Sinn Féin members who join Second Dáil.

24 May: Northern Irish elections held under terms of Government of Ireland Act 1920. Unionists win forty out of fifty-two seats.

7 June: James Craig elected first prime minister of Northern Ireland.

22 June: New Parliament of Northern Ireland meets at Belfast City Hall and is opened by King George V.

28 June: New Parliament of Southern Ireland meets at Royal College of Science, Dublin. Opened by the Lord Lieutenant of Ireland. Four unionist MPs representing University of Dublin attend. This is its only formal meeting.

8 July: De Valera accepts invitation to meet UK prime minister in London.

9 July: Truce signed between IRA and Crown Forces.

October–December: Negotiations begin between representatives of Dáil Éireann and British government in London for a bilateral agreement. De Valera does not attend.

6 December:

- Agreement reached between Irish and British representatives, creating Anglo-Irish Treaty. Key points include creation of an Irish Free State within the Commonwealth, an Oath of Allegiance to the Crown, and retention by the British naval services of certain ports.
- De Valera accuses Irish delegation of agreeing to demand which falls short of a Republic. Griffith, a signatory, refutes de Valera.

16 December: House of Commons accepts Treaty proposal.

1922 *7 January:* Dáil Éireann ratifies Treaty following Griffith's motion for approval. Sixty-four in favour; fifty-seven against. De Valera resigns as president of Dáil.

10 January: Griffith elected President of Provisional Government. Michael Collins, a signatory to the Treaty, becomes Minister for Finance. De Valera and fifty-six supporters walk out of Dáil Éireann.

14 January: Provisional Government of Ireland formed for administration of Southern Ireland.

31 January: First unit of new Irish National Army, a former IRA unit, takes possession of Beggars Bush Barracks: the first British military transfer to the new state (formal handover 1 February).

10 February: Irish Free State (Agreement) Act 1922 introduced in British House of Commons by Winston Churchill. Provides for dissolution of Parliament of Southern Ireland and election of a parliament to which the Provisional Government will be responsible.

14 April: Anti-Treaty IRA occupy Four Courts in Dublin to defy Provisional Government.

16 June: Southern Irish general election. Pro-Treaty candidates win 75 per cent of votes.

28 June: National Army, using armaments borrowed from British, bombard anti-Treaty IRA occupying Four Courts, initiating civil war.

4 July: Anti-Treaty IRA capture Skibbereen (Cork) and Listowel (Kerry), establishing 'Munster Republic'.

12 August: Death of Griffith in Dublin.

17 August: Dublin Castle formally handed to National Army. British Army leaves.

22 August: Michael Collins killed in ambush at Béal na Bláth, Cork.

9 September: First meeting of Provisional Parliament (Third Dáil). W. T. Cosgrave elected President of Dáil Éireann and Chairman of the Provisional Government.

26 October: Last meeting of standing committee of Sinn Féin before party de facto dissolves.

24 November: Erskine Childers (Anti-Treaty IRA) executed by firing squad at Beggars Bush Barracks, Dublin.

	5 December: UK Parliament enacts Irish Free State Constitution Act, legally sanctioning Constitution of the Irish Free State.
	6 December: Irish Free State formally comes into existence.
	7 December: Parliament of Northern Ireland votes to remain part of the United Kingdom.
	8 December: Northern Ireland rejoins United Kingdom.
1923	*24 May*: End of Republican military campaign, marking end of civil war.
	27 August: Cumann na nGaedheal, the party formed from Sinn Féin's pro-Treaty wing, wins first general election of Irish Free State. Cosgrave's party wins sixty-three seats. De Valera's Sinn Féin claim forty-four. Sinn Féin's representatives abstain from taking their seats until 1927.
1924–5	The Irish Boundary Commission, formed as part of the Anglo-Irish Treaty, meets to review delineation of the border in Ireland. Minor changes are proposed and MacNeill resigns. Commission's report is suppressed, making partition permanent in the form provided for in the Government of Ireland Act 1920.

Biographies

Leopold S. **Amery** (1873–1955), academic, journalist, and politician, was born in the North-Western Provinces of India. He attended Harrow School with Winston Churchill, read Classics at Balliol College, Oxford, and later became a Fellow in History at All Souls College, where he worked on the Austro-Hungarian and Turkish Empires, and reputedly acquired competence in some fourteen languages. He covered the build-up to the South African War of 1899–1902 for the *Times* before being called to the bar at the Inner Temple in 1902. His life-long commitment was to the British Empire as an object of patriotic attachment, having been influenced by Alfred Milner and patronised by Joseph Chamberlain. Amery won a seat in the House of Commons in 1911, which he held until 1945. He occupied the colonial secretaryship from 1924 to 1929 and became Secretary of State for India and Burma in Churchill's war ministry. He was a dedicated Zionist and collaborated with the Round Table movement, drafting the agreed text of the Balfour Declaration. Amery was opposed to imperial federation, supporting a looser and evolving structure of association based on equal membership for the Commonwealth. He later sought to strike a balance between the Commonwealth and Europe. He was a prolific author, editing *The Times History of the War in South Africa*, and intervening in national and imperial affairs with polemical works, including *The Fundamental Fallacies of Free Trade* (1906), *The Forward View* (1935), and *Thoughts on the Constitution* (1945). His speeches delivered during his tour of the Empire from 1927 to 1928 were collected as *The Empire in the New Era* (1928). In retirement, Amery published a three-volume autobiography, *My Political Life*.

Louie **Bennett** (1870–1956) was a suffragist, trade unionist, pacifist, journalist, and author. She was raised in a wealthy south Co. Dublin family as a member of the Church of Ireland. She was educated at Alexandra College in Milltown as well as at boarding school in England. In 1911, she co-founded the Irish Women's Suffrage Federation and, later, the Irish Women's Reform League, which addressed wider social issues, including working conditions and education. During the 1913 strike and lockout in Dublin, she appealed for funds to help strikers' families via the Irish Women's Franchise League's paper the *Irish Citizen*, which she took control of in 1920. She also became prominently involved in the Irish Women Workers' Union, founded in 1911 because other unions would not accept female members. Bennett was an active peace campaigner during the First World War. She was both an Irish representative for the Women's International League for Peace and Freedom, and the League of Nations. She worked on educational policy for the Irish Trade Union Congress, becoming its first female president in 1932. In 1943, she was elected as a Labour Party member for Dun Laoghaire borough council, later representing Ireland at the International Labour Organisation in Europe. In addition to journalism, she published two novels, *The Proving of Priscilla* (1902) and *A Prisoner of His Word* (1908).

Edward **Carson** (1854–1935) was a barrister and leading Unionist politician. Born in Dublin to Anglican parents, he was educated at Wesley College and then at Trinity College, Dublin, where he read law. He entered parliament in 1892 as a Liberal Unionist member for the University of Dublin. He pursued his legal practice in tandem with parliamentary and ministerial careers. In the former capacity he famously defended the Marquess of Queensberry against Oscar Wilde in a criminal libel action. He was appointed Solicitor General for Ireland in 1892 and Solicitor General for England and Wales in 1900. As a parliamentarian, he was appointed to the Irish Privy Council in 1896 and became leader of the Irish Unionist Alliance in 1910, putting him at the head of the campaign against home rule for Ireland. He soon established himself as the leading advocate of the rights of Ulster. He abhorred the prospect of partition, though his tactics ensured its introduction. His was the first signature to appear on *Ulster's Solemn League and Covenant* in 1912. In 1913, he sanctioned the foundation of the Ulster Volunteers and the Ulster provisional government. He briefly served as Attorney General under Asquith in 1915 and, later, as First Lord of the Admiralty, becoming Minister without Portfolio under Lloyd George. In 1921 he refused to lead the new government of Northern Ireland and opposed the Anglo-Irish Treaty. He resigned his leadership of the Irish Unionist Party and was made a life peer.

Erskine **Childers** (1870–1922) was an author and political activist who started life as a committed British imperialist and ended it as a dedicated Irish republican. He attended school at Haileybury College in Hertfordshire before studying classics and then law at Trinity College, Cambridge. He qualified as a parliamentary official, and then joined the City Imperial Volunteers (CIV) to fight the Boers in South Africa, after which point his views began to change. By 1910, he had converted to the cause of home rule and resigned his membership of the Liberal Party, becoming involved in 1914 in smuggling armaments from Germany into Ireland with the assistance of his wife, Mary 'Molly' Osgood, the disabled daughter of a leading anti-imperialist Boston family. Upon the outbreak of the First World War, he was commissioned as lieutenant in the Royal Naval Volunteer Reserve, earning the Distinguished Service Cross. He was vexed by wartime developments in Ireland, dismayed by the execution of participants in the 1916 Rebellion, and staunchly opposed the introduction of conscription in Ireland in 1918. He acted as a propagandist for Sinn Féin from 1919 to 1921, was elected to the second Dáil as a Sinn Féin member for the constituency of Kildare-Wicklow, and stood as an anti-Treaty candidate in the 1922 general election. He was executed by Free State forces during the Irish Civil War. In addition to his successful spy novel, *The Riddle of the Sands* (1903), Childers published a memoir of his time in the CIV (1901), *The Framework of Home Rule* (1911), *German Influence on British Cavalry* (1911), and several pamphlets on British policy in Ireland.

James **Connolly** (1868–1916) was a socialist, trade unionist, and revolutionary leader. He was born in Edinburgh to Irish parents, where he worked as a labourer before joining the British Army in 1877. He became involved in the local Labour movement in the 1880s where he fell under the influence of John Leslie and Keir Hardie, and secured the position of secretary of the Scottish Socialist Federation in 1892. In 1896 he moved to Dublin as organiser for the Dublin Socialist Club, committing himself to Irish republicanism, and helped establish the Irish Socialist Republican Party. Connolly founded the weekly journal, *Workers' Republic*, in 1898, and twice sought election to Dublin city council. In 1903 he moved to the

United States for seven years, getting involved successively in the Socialist Labour Party, the Socialist Party of America, the Industrial Workers of the World, and the Irish Socialist Federation. Returning to Ireland in 1910, he became organiser for the Socialist Party of Ireland and active in the Irish Transport and General Workers' Union (ITGWU) under James Larkin, spending time in this official capacity in Belfast. After the 1913 Dublin lockout and general strike, Connolly succeeded Larkin as acting leader of the ITGWU and founded the Irish Citizen Army. By 1915, his opposition to the First World War, the postponement of home rule, and the prospect of partition began to drive him closer to the Irish Republican Brotherhood, with whom, in due course, he conspired to launch and take part in the 1916 Rising. He was executed for his leading role in the rebellion in May. Connolly's journalistic output was prolific. His articles appeared in *Workers' Republic*, *Shan Van Vocht*, *The Harp*, and *Forward*. He also published several books on socialism and Irish history, including *Socialism Made Easy* (1909), *Labour, Nationality and Religion* (1910), *Labour in Irish History* (1910), and *The Re-Conquest of Ireland* (1915).

Albert Venn **Dicey** (1835–1922), British jurist and publicist, studied classical moderations and then *literae humaniores* at Balliol College, Oxford, graduating in 1858. He was elected to a fellowship at Trinity College, Oxford, but moved to London in 1861 to study for the bar, and was called to Inner Temple in 1863. In 1882 he was elected to the Vinerian professorship of English law at Oxford, from which he retired in 1909. During the course of his tenure at Oxford, he published his widely influential *Introduction to the Study of the Law of the Constitution* (1885), *A Digest of the Law of England with Reference to the Conflict of Laws* (1896), and *Lectures on the Relation between Law and Public Opinion in England during the Nineteenth Century* (1905). The maintenance of the Union became a dominant commitment after Gladstone's conversion to home rule, leading him to launch a series of polemics against devolution for Ireland in any form. This resulted in the publication of several books on the subject: *England's Case Against Home Rule* (1886), *Letters on Unionist Delusions* (1887), *A Leap in the Dark* (1893), and *A Fool's Paradise* (1913). He also published on Wordsworth and on the Scottish Union.

Alice Stopford **Green** (1847–1922) was a historian and Irish nationalist. She was born into an Anglican family in Co. Meath and was largely educated by governesses at home. In 1874 her family moved to Chester, where she met the historian John Richard Green, whom she married three years later. He died in 1883. Thereafter, Stopford Green dedicated herself to historical writing. She became involved in agitating against the Boer War and colonial policy in Africa at the same time as she became interested in the history of Ireland. Her most important works include *Irish Nationality* (1911), *The Old Irish World* (1912), and *History of the Irish State to 1014* (1925). In 1914 she became involved in importing arms into Ireland on behalf of the Irish Volunteers, but was opposed to the 1916 Rebellion and remained uncomfortable with using violence to achieve independence. She supported the Anglo-Irish Treaty and became a member of the senate of the Irish Free State. Stopford Green published important pamphlets on Irish independence, including *Ourselves Alone in Ulster* (1918) and *The Government of Ireland* (1921).

Arthur **Griffith** (1871–1922) was a writer, journalist, and politician who founded Sinn Féin. The son of a printer, he was educated in north inner-city Dublin, but left school at thirteen to work as a compositor and copywriter. He spent a year as a journalist in South Africa supporting the Boers, but returned to Ireland in 1898 to co-edit the *United Irishman*. An admirer of Parnell in his youth, he became for a time a member of the Irish Republican Brotherhood, but was uncertain about its use of violence, and soon developed the policies of dual monarchism and abstentionism, which he promoted through propaganda and party organisation. In 1906 he launched the newspaper, *Sinn Féin*; in 1915, after its suppression, he edited *Nationality*, and published other short-lived papers. Although Griffith did not participate in the 1916 Rebellion, he was arrested in its aftermath and imprisoned in Reading jail. He ceded the leadership of Sinn Féin to Éamon de Valera in 1917, becoming vice-president of the party. He was nominated to chair the Irish delegation at the talks to end the Anglo-Irish conflict in 1921. After two months of negotiations, he emerged as a supporter of the offer of dominion status for Ireland and fought to defend the Treaty until his sudden death from a cerebral haemorrhage. He was a prolific commentator on Irish affairs and collected one suggestive group of articles into the controversial volume *The Resurrection of Hungary* (1904), whose argument proved subtly influential in shaping modern Irish politics.

Thomas M. **Kettle** (1880–1916), academic, writer, and politician, attended the Christian Brothers' O'Connell School on Richmond Street in Dublin, and then boarded at Clongowes Wood in Co. Kildare. He graduated from the Royal University of Ireland in Mental and Moral Science in 1902, read law at King's Inns, but opted for journalism instead of practising at the bar. He supported the Irish Parliamentary Party and edited *The Nationist*, a paper friendly to the party's cause. Kettle entered the House of Commons as MP for Tyrone East in 1906 and held his seat in 1910. He secured a professorship of national economics but continued to be active in politics and journalism. He campaigned for women's enfranchisement and became involved with the Irish Volunteers in 1914. He was in Belgium upon the outbreak of the First World War where he witnessed German atrocities, prompting him to join the British Forces. He was a committed home ruler and opposed the 1916 Rebellion, though he recognised its impact on national opinion, noting that the rebels would 'go down in history as heroes and martyrs' while he would be remembered as 'a bloody British officer'. He was killed five months later during the Irish assault on Ginchy. Apart from *Home Rule Finance: An Experiment in Justice* (1911), his published writings mostly appeared as collections of essays, including *The Day's Burden* (1910), *The Open Secret of Ireland* (1912), and, posthumously, *Ways of War* (1917).

Robert **Lynd** (1879–1949) was an essayist and journalist. Born in Belfast to Presbyterian parents, he was educated at the Royal Belfast Academical Institute before studying classics at Queen's University, Belfast, from which he graduated in 1899. He served on the staff of the *Northern Whig* before moving to London, where he wrote successively for *Today*, *Daily News*, *The Nation*, and the *New Statesman*. He also wrote biting pamphlets and a range of books on topical issues, not least about the two islands, including *Rambles in Ireland* (1912), *If the Germans Conquered England* (1917), *Ireland a Nation* (1919), *The Passion of Labour* (1920), *The Pleasure of Ignorance* (1921), *The Sporting Life* (1922), *The Money Box* (1925), *The Orange Tree* (1926), *Dr. Johnson and Company* (1927), and *Searchlights and Nightingales* (1939). Early on, he was influenced by socialist republicanism (he wrote for *The Republic* in 1906–7), becoming more actively engaged with Irish politics as Ulster threatened to capsize home rule. He inveighed against British hypocrisy and imperialism. From his base in Hampstead he emerged as a centrally connected figure in the literary worlds of London and Dublin.

Eoin **MacNeill** (1867–1945), politician, activist, and academic, was born in Antrim and attended St. Malachy's College in Belfast before studying constitutional history, jurisprudence, and political economy at the Royal University of Ireland. After graduation, he secured a junior clerkship in the accountant-general's office in the Dublin law courts. From 1887 he took up the study of Irish, contributing articles to the *Irish Ecclesiastical Record* and the *Gaelic Journal*. In 1893 he played a leading role in the establishment of the Gaelic League. MacNeill went on to edit the *Gaelic Journal*, *Fáinne an Lae*, and *An Claidheamh Soluis*. In November 1913 he published 'The North Began', which helped launch the Irish Volunteers. He opposed Redmond's proposal to send Irishmen to the front and joined a splinter group of Irish Volunteers, some of whom, with Irish Republican Brotherhood backing, fomented plans for a rebellion. MacNeill initially supported the proposal to rebel, but later countermanded the orders to mobilise on Easter Sunday. In 1918, he was elected to the first Dáil for Sinn Féin and was appointed Minister for Finance in 1919, before becoming Minister for Industries. He acted as speaker in the second Dáil, generally supported the Treaty, and was elected as pro-Treaty TD for Clare in 1922. He defended government reprisals during the civil war, although his son was killed fighting on the republican side. He was the Irish representative on the 1924–5 Boundary Commission, formed as part of the provisions of the Anglo-Irish Treaty and charged with reviewing the border between North and South. MacNeill resigned from the Commission in November 1925 over its failure to substantially change the delineation of the border and the Commission's report was suppressed. Four days later, he resigned his cabinet post. MacNeill lost his seat in 1927 and returned to academia, retiring from a professorship of early and medieval Irish at University College Dublin in 1941. His academic work focused on the origins of Irish history, the history of St. Patrick, and early Irish law. Among his more popular publications were *Phases of Irish History* (1919) and *Celtic Ireland* (1921).

Ronald **McNeill** (1861–1934), lawyer, politician, and editor, was born in Devon to parents from Antrim. He attended Harrow and then read Modern History at Christ Church, Oxford, graduating in 1884. Four years later, he was called to the bar at Lincoln's Inn, though he rejected the law in favour of journalism. He started as an assistant editor at the *St. James's Gazette* in 1889, and, from 1904 to 1911, for the *Encyclopaedia Britannica*. He was elected as a Conservative member for the East division of Kent in 1911, a seat he held until 1927. He strenuously opposed the Parliament Act of the same year, and campaigned against home rule, following Carson in his stalwart defence of the rights of Ulster under the Union. In 1927 he was raised to the Peerage as Baron Cushendun. He briefly secured the position of chief British representative to the League of Nations, and for five months in 1928 became acting secretary of state for foreign affairs. In addition to *Ulster's Stand for Union* (1922), he published *Home Rule: Its History and Danger* (1907).

Constance **Markievicz** (née Gore-Booth) (1868–1927) was a prominent nationalist, feminist, revolutionary, and socialist. She was born into an Anglo-Irish landed family based in Sligo. From 1893 she studied at the Slade School of Art in London. In 1900 she married Casimir Markievicz, an artist from a wealthy Polish family from Ukraine. She became politically active in the later 1890s, joining the National Union of Women's Suffrage Societies, and later got involved in nationalist politics through her membership of Sinn Féin and Inghinidhe na hÉireann (Daughters of Ireland). Her immediate political, literary, and artistic circle included W. B. Yeats, Maude Gonne, and John Butler Yeats. In addition to painting, Markievicz acted regularly at the Abbey Theatre in Dublin. She also produced journalism, wrote pamphlets, and delivered speeches. With Bulmer Hobson she founded Fianna Éireann, a paramilitary youth organisation, and later joined James Connolly's Irish Citizen Army, in whose ranks she was active during the 1916 Rising. Markievicz was the first woman to be elected to the Westminster parliament in 1918. She vehemently opposed the Anglo-Irish Treaty and acted as propagandist for the republican cause before becoming an Irish TD for Fianna Fáil. She held the cabinet position of Minister for Labour between 1919 and 1922. She died of complications from appendicitis.

Patrick **Pearse** (1879–1916) was an educationalist, writer, and insurrectionary. He was born in Dublin to James Pearse, a stone carver from London, and Margaret Pearse, a shop assistant from Dublin. He attended the Christian Brothers' School on Westland Row, and enrolled for a BA in Irish, English, and French at the Royal University of Ireland. He also attended law lectures at the King's Inns and qualified for the bar, though he practised little as a barrister. He joined the Gaelic League in 1896 and founded the New Ireland Literary Society in 1897. Passionate about education, he established St. Enda's school in Cullenswood House in south Dublin in 1908. From 1913, he moved closer to the Irish Republican Brotherhood, under whose auspices he would play a leading role in planning the 1916 Rebellion. He took a prominent organisational part in the Irish Volunteers, leading the ranks of the splinter group which opposed Redmond's support for the British war effort. The Curragh mutiny, the Ulster unionist gun-running incident at Larne, and the outbreak of the First World War had a radicalising impact on Pearse and galvanised his commitment to fomenting insurrection. He drafted the Proclamation of the Irish Republic and occupied the role of President throughout the rebellion, surrendering on 29 April. He was condemned to death by firing squad on 2 May and executed the following day. In addition to his educational tract, *The Murder Machine* (1912), and a range of literary and journalistic writings, Pearse published several political pamphlets dedicated, *inter alia*, to reinventing a national tradition. These included *The Coming Revolution* (1913), *The Spiritual Nation* (1916), and *The Sovereign People* (1916).

Horace **Plunkett** (1854–1932), activist, politician, and cooperative movement pioneer, was born into an Irish aristocratic family and educated at Eton and University College, Oxford, where he read History. He returned to Ireland in 1889 following the death of his father, Baron Dunsany, to help run the family estate. After a decade spent in Wyoming, USA, where his views on agricultural reform were formed, he returned to Ireland to establish a cooperative store in Cork and a creamery in Limerick. Having been elected a Unionist MP for Dublin South in 1892, two years later he became president of the Irish Agricultural Organisation Society. The cooperative movement expanded under its aegis and in 1899 Plunkett was made vice-president of the Department of Agriculture and Technical Instruction for Ireland, a movement which reached across the political divide in both the north and south. As his career progressed, Plunkett switched from constructive unionism to support dominion home rule for Ireland. In 1917 he was appointed to chair the Irish Convention, and in 1919 founded the Irish Dominion League. He accepted a seat in the Irish senate after the establishment of the Free State, but when his house in Foxrock was destroyed in the civil war he resigned his post and resettled in England in 1923. Plunkett was elected to the Royal Society in 1902 and to the Royal Irish Academy in 1929. He authored several pamphlets on agricultural reform and is the author of the pioneering and controversial *Ireland in the New Century* (1904). He also published speeches on major issues, such as conscription in 1918, the radicalisation of Ulster, and Irish affairs in North American contexts.

John **Redmond** (1856–1918), committed home ruler and political leader, was born into a Catholic gentry family in Co. Wexford. He studied at Clongowes Wood and later for two years at Trinity College, Dublin, without taking a degree. He became a Parnellite MP for New Ross in 1881 and steadily rose through the ranks of the Irish Parliamentary Party. Having studied law intermittently, he was called to the bar in 1887. On the back of his managerial and oratorical skills he became a leading figure in the pro-Parnell faction after the 1891 split. Within a decade he was elevated to the position of chairman of a reunited party. The elections of January and December 1910 transformed Redmond's fortunes, as the Liberals depended on Irish votes. Redmond abandoned conciliatory tactics to demand the removal of the Lords' veto and introduction of a third Home Rule Bill, which were effected in 1911 and 1912 respectively. He was uneasy in his management of the Third Home Rule crisis of 1912–14, but nonetheless managed to place the Home Rule Act on the statute book in September 1914, albeit with qualifications. Redmond leant his full support to the British war effort and hoped that common participation with Ulster would bring Unionists around to the notion of self-government in an unpartitioned Ireland. The 1916 Rising and its aftermath disappointed his expectations. Redmond's agreement to the temporary partition of Ulster during the talks with Lloyd George in June 1916 haunted the Irish Parliamentary Party (IPP), which was ill-equipped to deal with the rapid rise of the better organised and pro-suffrage Sinn Féin, which eclipsed the IPP in the 1918 UK general election. His health deteriorated, and in the midst of a final push for a compromise settlement with Ulster in the 1917–18 Irish Convention, Redmond died of heart failure after an operation in London.

Hanna **Sheehy-Skeffington** (1877–1946), feminist, suffragette, nationalist campaigner, and teacher, was born in Cork to a mill owner but moved to Dublin as a child in 1887. She was educated at the Dominican Convent on Eccles Street in Dublin and later studied Modern Languages at the Royal University of Ireland, graduating in 1899. She then took an MA in 1902, and in 1903 married the pacifist, socialist, and feminist, Francis Sheehy-Skeffington. She joined the Irishwomen's Suffrage and Local Government Association, but became more militant in her tactics and in 1908 co-founded the Irish Women's Franchise League, which paralleled the militant activities of the British Women's Social and Political Union. Later, she became a member of the pacifist Women's International League for Peace and Freedom, of which she ultimately became vice-president. From 1912 she co-managed and contributed to *The Irish Citizen*, with which she was intermittently involved until 1920. In 1916, her husband was shot on the orders of J. C. Bowen-Colthurst, a British captain, after his attempt to prevent looting during the 1916 Rebellion. Her response is recorded in her speech, *British Militarism As I Have Known It*, published as a pamphlet in 1917. In 1919, she was elected as a Sinn Féin candidate to Dublin corporation and took the republican side in the civil war, campaigning across the USA for funds to relieve families of republican soldiers. In 1926 she was appointed to the executive of the new Fianna Fáil party. She lectured widely and continued to publish journalism in the *Irish World*. She also wrote for *An Phoblacht* and its successor *Republican File*. She studied the Soviet system of government first-hand in 1930 and, in 1937, actively campaigned against the recently promulgated Irish Constitution. During the course of her life, Hanna Sheehy-Skeffington was imprisoned and went on hunger strike on numerous occasions in connection with her activism.

Note on the Texts

The texts collected in this volume are reproduced where possible from their original sources or first editions rather than from subsequent editions. These sources include pamphlets, newspapers, and monographs. Details of original publications are footnoted at the start of each text. Typographical errors in the originals have been corrected, though punctuation has been retained. Spelling has been made uniform within each chapter and the use of accents for Irish nouns, like Sinn Féin, has been made consistent throughout the volume. Footnotes in the original texts are distinguished from editorial notes: the editors' notes are marked sequentially with Arabic numerals while authors' are signalled by using asterisks and daggers. Comments on author footnotes are contained within the note and introduced by '*Editorial note:*'.

1909

1 Constance Markievicz, *Women, Ideals and the Nation*[1]

I take it as a great compliment that so many of you, the rising young women of Ireland, who are distinguishing yourselves every day and coming more and more to the front, should give me this opportunity. We older people look to you with great hopes and a great confidence that in your gradual emancipation you are bringing fresh ideas, fresh energies, and above all a great genius for sacrifice into the life of the nation.

In Ireland the women seem to have taken less part in public life, and to have had less share in the struggle for liberty, than in other nations. In Russia, among the people who are working to overthrow the tyrannical and unjust government of the Czar and his officials, and in Poland where, to be a nationalist, men and women must take their lives in their hands, women work as comrades, shoulder to shoulder, with their men.[2] No duty is too hard, no act too dangerous for them to undertake. Many a woman has been incarcerated in the dungeons under St. Peter and St. Paul – to sit in the damp and mouldy gloom and watch – perhaps for a week, perhaps for a year – the little gate high up on the wall, where one day or other, sure enough, she would see a little stream of dirty water

[1] Constance Markievicz, *Women, Ideals and the Nation: A Lecture Delivered to the Students' National Literary Society, Dublin, by Constance de Markievicz* (Dublin: Inginide na hÉireann, 1909).

[2] The 1905 Russian Revolution led to the establishment of the State Duma, a multi-party system, and a national constitution. The Polish Revolution of the same year was triggered by a series of struggles focused on independence from Russia as well as workers' and peasant rights.

begin to trickle through, which would tell her that soon that which once had been her would drift out into the world again.[3]

Many another woman has dropped exhausted on the long, weary march through the snow-covered steppes to the land of exile. Weighed down by her chains, unable to stir herself, scarcely a groan escapes her, even under the lash of the knout – freely applied by the soldier in charge – she has sunk down hopeless and helpless, alone on the dreary plain, to watch for a few short hours the big black birds circling nearer and nearer, borne up and sustained by the knowledge that 'no sacrifice is ever in vain', and that as the death of Christ brought a new hope and a new life to an old world, so the blood of each martyr shed in the cause of liberty will give a new impetus to the comrades who are left behind to continue the work.

Now, England in this twentieth century is much more civilised, and much more subtle than Russia in her methods for subjugating a nation; therefore, more difficult to fight; and much more difficult to realise as an enemy. She deals out pennies liberally and noisily with her right hand, shouting into our ears all the time how good and how liberal she is to the mere Irish, while her left hand is busily engaged in feeling in our pockets and abstracting as many as she can of the few gold pieces we have earned by the sweat of our brows.[4] She trumpets her own praise loudly through the world – John Bull's bluntness, honesty, truth and bravery, his nobleness in dealing with his enemies – all this has been sung, shouted and declaimed throughout civilisation, so that Irish people, being very simple and honest themselves, have often taken a very long time to realise that we are being governed – not as we are told for the ultimate good of the Irish nation, but as an alien province, that must be prevented from interfering with the commerce of, and whose interest must always be kept subservient to, England.[5] She has systematically overtaxed us – for our own good; she has depopulated our country – and it is for our own good; she has tried to kill our language – for our own good; she entices our young men into her armies, to fight her battles for her – and still it is for

[3] The reference is presumably to the Peter and Paul Fortress in St. Petersburg, which incarcerated numerous political prisoners, including Peter Kropotkin, Mikhail Bakunin, and Leon Trotsky. The Church of St. Peter and St. Paul is located in Vilnius, a baroque masterpiece of the Polish-Lithuanian Commonwealth.

[4] Originally 'mere' Irish meant pure (native) Irish, unmixed by Norman stock or on account of subsequent colonial settlement. Here the term denotes the Irish as being of lesser status in relation to Britain.

[5] John Bull, created by John Arbuthnot (1667–1735) as a satirical character in the early eighteenth century, was commonly used thereafter to personify England.

our own good. She began this policy in 1800 when – entirely for our own good – our Parliament was disbanded, and we were given instead the great privilege of sending to Westminster a small band of representatives to make the best fight they could for Irish rights against an overwhelming majority; which, of course, while causing but a small annoyance to England, brought there with the representatives of Ireland, their families and the whole of the society in which they moved.[6] In fact the wealthiest and most influential section of the Irish nation was, at one fell swoop, transferred to London, there to spend its money, and to learn to talk about the 'Empire'. The immense privilege of belonging to the 'greatest Empire in the world', of being one with 'the greatest people in the world', has since been shouted and preached and sung to us, till many of us have been beguiled into believing this story of fairy gold only to be lost – lost to our country in her direst need!

In this desertion our women participated quite as much as our men, they abandoned their Dublin mansions, to hire or buy houses in London, they followed the English Court about and joined the English ranks of toadies and placehunters, bringing up their daughters in English ways and teaching them to make English ideals their ideals, and when possible marrying them to Englishmen.

Of course this could not go on for ever, and the Irish nation, at last realising that they and their interests had been sold for years, refused to be represented by them any longer … but it was too late – the rich and the aristocratic section of the men and women of Ireland had been lost to their country for years, if not for all eternity.

Now, I am not going to discuss the subtle psychological question of why it was that so few women in Ireland have been prominent in the national struggle, or try to discover how they lost in the dark ages of persecution the magnificent legacy of Maeve, Fleas, Macha and their other great fighting ancestors.[7] True, several women distinguished themselves on the battlefields of '98, and we have the women of the *Nation* newspaper, of the Ladies' Land League, also in our own day the few women who have worked their hardest in the Sinn Féin movement and in the Gaelic League, and we have the woman who won a battle for Ireland,

6 The Acts of Union were passed in 1800 and came into force on 1 January 1801, creating the United Kingdom of Great Britain and Ireland. The Acts are frequently referred to as the 1801 Act of Union, which abolished the Irish parliament, with Irish representatives henceforth elected to the Westminster parliament.

7 Irish female mythical characters.

by preventing a wobbly Corporation from presenting King Edward of England with a loyal address.[8] But for the most part our women, though sincere, steadfast Nationalists at heart, have been content to remain quietly at home, and leave all the fighting and striving to the men.

Lately things seem to be changing. As in the last century, during the sixties, a strong tide of liberty swept over the world, so now again a strong tide of liberty seems to be coming towards us, swelling and growing and carrying before it all the outposts that hold women enslaved and bearing them triumphantly into the life of the nations to which they belong.

We are in a very difficult position here, as so many Unionist women would fain have us work together with them for the emancipation of their sex and votes – obviously to send a member to Westminster. But I would ask every Nationalist woman to pause before she joined a Suffrage Society or Franchise League that did not include in their Programme the Freedom of their Nation.[9] 'A Free Ireland with No Sex Disabilities in her Constitution' should be the motto of all Nationalist women. And a grand motto it is.

There are great possibilities, in the hands and the hearts of the young women of Ireland – great possibilities indeed, and great responsibilities. For as you are born a woman, so you are born an Irelander, with all the troubles and responsibilities of both. You may shirk or deny them, but they are there, and some day – as a woman and as an Irelander – you will have to face the question of how your life has been spent, and how have you served your sex and your nation?

The greatest gifts that the young women of Ireland can bring into public life with them, are ideals and principles. Ideals, that are but the Inward Vision, that will show them their nation glorious and free, no longer a reproach to her sons and daughters; and principles that will give them

[8] Referring respectively to the 1798 Rebellion in Ireland; the weekly newspaper, *The Nation*, published between 1844 and 1849 and edited by Young Irelanders Charles Gavan Duffy (1816–1903), Thomas Davis (1814–45), and John Blake Dillon (1814–66); the women's auxiliary wing of the Irish National Land League between 1881 and 1882; the Gaelic League, founded in 1893 by Douglas Hyde, who served as its first president, and who promoted the use of the Irish language in everyday life; and King Edward VII's 1903 visit to Ireland.

[9] The Irish Women's Suffrage Society (originally the North of Ireland Women's Suffrage Society) was founded in 1872 by the unionist politician and campaigner Isabella Maria Susan Tod (1836–96). The Irish Women's Franchise League was established in Dublin in 1908 by Hanna Sheehy-Skeffington (1877–1946), Francis Sheehy-Skeffington (1878–1916), and James H. Cousins (1873–1956).

courage and strength – the patient toil of the worker, the brilliant inspiration of the leader.

Women, from having till very recently stood so far removed from all politics, should be able to formulate a much clearer and more incisive view of the political situation than men. For a man from the time he is a mere lad is more or less in touch with politics, and has usually the label of some party attached to him, long before he properly understands what it really means.

We all know that when you get quite close to a rock or to a waterfall you lose the general effect of the mountain of which it is only a small part; and it is just the same with politics. Men all their lives are so occupied in examining closely, from a narrow party point of view all the little Bills 'relating to Ireland' – that all parties in the British Houses of Parliament are so constantly throwing them, to fight and squabble over – that they often quite lose sight of their 'mountain' and forget that – as the greater contains the less, as the mountain contains the rocks and the waterfalls, so does the lost nationhood of their country contain class legislation, sex legislation, trade legislation.

Now, here is a chance for our women. Let them remind their men, that their first duty is to examine any legislation proposed not from a party point of view, not from the point of view of a sex, a trade, or a class, but simply and only from the standpoint of their Nation. Let them learn to be statesmen and not merely politicians. Let them consider how their action with regard to it may help or hinder their national struggle for independence and nothing else, and then let them act accordingly.

Taking my simile from another point of view, as surely that a few stones, and a few pails of water, though improving our garden, are but a poor substitute for our great mysterious mountain, so these little Bills, though improving the conditions of our people, are at the best but a poor substitute for our Nation's freedom, which in the meantime has been shelved and almost forgotten. Now, let our women come forward with the determination that we must obtain possession of the mountain itself – not contenting ourselves with buying or stealing bits of rock and pails of water.

Fix your mind on the ideal of Ireland free, with her women enjoying the full rights of citizenship in their own nation, and no one will be able to side-track you, and so make use of you to use up the energies of the nation in obtaining all sorts of concessions – concessions, too, that for the most part were coming in the natural course of evolution, and were perhaps just hastened a few years by the fierce agitations to obtain them.

Catholic emancipation must have come; it has come even in Russian Poland, where the whole nation was in arms against Russia as late as '63, and where it stands for a much greater thing than it does here.[10]

Catholicism is an integral part of a Pole's Nationality, the Orthodox religion an integral part of a Russian's, for all Poles are Catholic, all Russians Orthodox – and a Pole of the Orthodox religion would even now be regarded with suspicion in Poland and could not possibly enter any Polish National Movement; while a Russian who was a Catholic would find it difficult even to live in his country.

Tenant right and peasant proprietorship, extension of the franchise and universal suffrage, are all but steps in the evolution of the world; for, as education and with it the knowledge of the rights of a man or a woman to live, is gained by the masses of mankind, so gradually they push their way – individually and collectively – into the life of their nation, and being in the majority, the moment they realise their power, the world may be theirs for the taking.

But our national freedom cannot, and must not, be left to evolution. If we look around us, we will find that evolution – as far as Ireland is concerned – is tending rather to annihilate us as a nation altogether. We seem day by day to be brought more and more in touch with England, and little by little to be losing all that distinctiveness which pertains to a nation, and which may be called nationality. London seems to be coming nearer and nearer to us till quite imperceptibly it has become the centre of the universe to even many good Irishmen.

Of course all modern inventions have helped England in the task of submerging our interests in hers – trains, the penny post, the telegraph system, have all brought her nearer, and given her more power over us. More especially the daily papers, forcing England upon us as the headquarters of our politics, our society, our stock exchange, our sport, teaching us to regard her foreign policy and her wars from the point of view of one or other of her political parties – all this, I say, wears away the rock of our national pride, and little by little we drift nearer to the conventional English views on life.

[10] The 1863 'January Uprising' was an insurrection within the Russian portion of Poland that sought the restoration of the Polish-Lithuanian Commonwealth. Catholic Emancipation in Ireland culminated in the 1829 Roman Catholic Relief Act.

The educational systems through the country have also been used to work for the destruction of our nationality, from the smart English governess who despised the mere Irish, to the village schoolmaster forced to train up his scholars in ignorance of Ireland's wrongs, in ignorance of Ireland's language and history.

The schools, too, were usually under the patronage of the priest or parson of the district, and therefore very naturally concentrated on developing strong sectarian feelings in the children, instead of the broader creed of nationalism.

Every right granted to us by England has been done in such a way that it helped to split us up into divisions and sub-divisions. That policy is being continued now. We have had landlords and tenants, Catholics and Protestants, North and South, besides the sub-divisions into the different sections of the English political parties. We are rapidly adding graziers and peasants, farmers and labourers, to the list of Irishmen who are all losing sight of their ideal, and sordidly scrambling for what they hope to get.[11] They are curiously blind and inconsistent, too, for no great and real prosperity can be ours, while our interests are always the very last to be considered in an Empire.

To prove this, take a glance at two of the Bills that are being very much discussed at this moment.

The Liberals are talking of Land Tax.[12] This may suit the needs of England very well, with her big, rich proprietors, who can well afford to pay it; but over here, where the land is at this moment gradually becoming the property of the farmer, big and small, through a system of paying a certain rent to the Government, it will mean that this rent has been raised, and nothing more, and that, in spite of England's promises. The rent goes into England's pockets, so also does the Land Tax. Therefore, except in the terms, where is the difference? And who cares whether the extra charge is called rent or 'Land Tax'? It will have to be paid, and that is the only point of any importance to the farmer.

[11] Markiewicz is referring to the series of land acts passed by both Liberal and Conservative governments since 1870, the most significant of which was in 1903 under George Wyndham. The Act bought out absentee landlords and facilitated the transfer of huge tracts of land to Irish tenants. She is also referring to the Labourers (Ireland) Act 1906, which granted state-funded rural social housing.

[12] Land taxes were included in a package of reforms introduced by the Liberal government in Britain between 1906 and 1914.

Then take the great Conservative cry of Tariff Reform.[13] We are all told that Cobden ruined Ireland's milling industry with Free Trade, and we are all familiar with the pitiful ruins of mills, great and small, through the country.[14] Round Dublin, along the Dodder banks, one ruin after another, tells its sad tale of unemployment and emigration to the holiday wanderer. In Sligo – my own county – every little stream has the same tale to tell; and where, even the bleak walls have vanished, you often find a record of bygone prosperity in names such as Milltown or Millbrook.

But conditions, have changed all over the world since Cobden's day, and tax on flour now would only mean that the wheat-growing industry of Canada would benefit largely. 'Colonial Preference' would mean that Canada would get every advantage over Russia and other wheat-growing countries in our markets, while Ireland would possibly have to pay more for bread.

In the ready-made clothing trades, England with her Black Country, with her great manufacturing towns, has always been our worst enemy, and a tax on foreign ready-made clothes would tend to close the markets to all but English goods – the very ones (that once grant we require Protection at all) we require to be protected the most against. England's greatest rival in ready-mades is Germany. We, at present, count for nothing, and, of course, German goods excluded by a prohibitory tariff, England would do practically what she liked with the markets over here. Her firms would be in the position of a certain English boot factory which established a shop in Limerick in competition to a Limerick boot factory. Being a rich firm, they were able to sell their wares under cost price to the unsuspicious people of Limerick, till the day when the Limerick factory closed its doors, unable to stand up against the competition, and from that day the people of Limerick have had to pay through the boots they wear – the expenses of the fight, and a huge dividend to the English company, as well as having the unemployed from the ruined industry to support, unless they emigrate.

All this points to the one way in which the women of Ireland can help their country; and, indeed, many of them are already doing so; and it is a movement too that all creeds, all classes, and all politics can join in. We

13 Tariff Reform, associated with the national campaign by Liberal Unionist MP Joseph Chamberlain (1836–1914) for an imperial preference on imports, became popular among Conservative grassroots from 1903.

14 Richard Cobden (1804–65) was an English manufacturer and statesman who supported the repeal of the Corn Laws and the introduction of free trade.

have the Irish Industrial Development Associations, and the Sinn Féin organisations both working very hard for this object, but still there is much to be done.[15]

It is not enough just vaguely to buy Irish goods where you can do so without trouble, just in a sort of sentimental way. No; you must make Irish goods as necessary to your daily life, as your bath or your breakfast. Say to you yourselves, 'We must establish here a Voluntary Protection against foreign goods.' By this I mean that we must not resent sometimes having to pay an extra penny for an Irish-made article – which is practically protection – as the result of protection is that native manufacturers are enabled to charge the extra penny that will enable their infant factory to live and grow strong, and finally to compete on absolutely equal terms with the foreign-made article.

Every Irish industry that we manage even to keep in existence is an added wealth to our nation, and therefore indirectly to ourselves. It employs labour which serves to keep down the poor rates, and to check emigration. The large sums of money it turns over benefits every other trade in the country. So you also will benefit, for the richer the country, the better price you will be able to command for your services in the professions and trades, and the more positions will be created to which you may aspire.

Besides, as in the case of the boot factory in Limerick, so in the other industries. If we allow England to ruin them, it is we that will have to pay up in the end.

An Irishman is but a poor match for an Englishman in trade, because he is such an extraordinary good hand in driving a bargain.

This may sound paradoxical, but you will find that nevertheless it is true. Who can sell a horse better at a fair than an Irishman? – abstracting the uttermost farthing from his English customer. But in his heated arguments, and in his gentle persuasiveness, he entirely omits to mention that his animal has staggers, is a crib-biter, or some other such trifle.[16] The Irishman will tell you with pride for years after of the wonderful bargain

[15] The Irish Industrial Development Associations were an informal federation of organisations, the first established in Cork in 1903, to promote Irish manufactures. Sinn Féin, founded by Arthur Griffith in 1905, was, in addition to its policy of parliamentary abstentionism, also dedicated to the protection of Irish industries.

[16] Crib-biting (or cribbing) involves horses chewing or gnawing on a fence or a rail giving rise to a characteristic grunt.

he struck, but he will draw a veil over the fact that he has lost his best customer, and a good market for many horses in the succeeding years.

Now, it is the same spirit that prompts us to glory in bargains we make when we are buying, and boast when we return home one shilling the richer than we expected from buying foreign-made articles, forgetting that the shillings spent on foreign goods and the shillings saved are both robbed from our Nation – our Nation is the poorer for them, and we as parts of our nation are the poorer for them too.

If the women of Ireland would organise the movement for buying Irish goods more, they might do a great deal to help their country. If they would make it the fashion to dress in Irish clothes, feed on Irish food – in fact, in this as in everything, LIVE REALLY IRISH LIVES, they would be doing something great, and don't let our clever Irish colleens rest content with doing this individually, but let them go out and speak publicly about it, form leagues, of which 'No English Goods' is the war-cry.[17] Let them talk, and talk, publicly and privately, never minding how they bore people – till not one even of the peasants in the wilds of Galway but has heard and approved of the movement.

I daresay you will think this all very obvious and very dull, but Patriotism and Nationalism and all great things are made up of much that is obvious and dull, and much that in the beginning is small, but that will be found to lead out into fields that are broader and full of interest. You will go out into the world and get elected on to as many public bodies as possible, and by degrees through your exertions no public institution – whether hospital, workhouse, asylum or any other, and no private house – but will be supporting the industries of your country.

Ireland wants her girls to help her to build up her national life. Their fresh, clean views of life, their young energies, have been long too hidden away and kept separate in their different homes. Bring them out and organise them, and lo! you will find a great new army ready to help the national cause. The old idea that a woman can only serve her nation through her home is gone, so now is the time; on you the responsibility rests. No one can help you but yourselves alone; you must make the world look upon you as citizens first, as women after.[18] For each one of you there is a niche waiting – your place in the nation. Try and find it. It may be

[17] Colleens from the Irish *cailín* meaning girl or young woman.

[18] The reference to 'yourselves alone' is likely a riff on 'ourselves alone', the meaning of the Irish phrase Sinn Féin. Markiewicz joined the Sinn Féin party in 1908.

as a leader, it may be as a humble follower – perhaps in a political party, perhaps in a party of your own – but it is there, and if you cannot find it for yourself, no one can find it for you.

If you are fitted for public work take up any that is within your reach, so long as you feel that you can do it. Ireland wants reforming, sweeping clean from ocean to ocean; and it is only the young people can do it.

Since the Union we have been steadily deteriorating; all our ideals have been gradually slipping from us. Let us look all these facts bravely in the face, and make up our minds to change them.

We know that the Government of England is responsible for all this. First, for the famine with its deaths and desolations, by which our people were taught to beg and to appeal and look to England, and our fine national spirit was taught to be submissive.[19]

Emigration – another policy sent to us from England – has helped to build up another great nation at Ireland's expense.[20] The men and women whom she could least afford to lose were the ones who so often had to go, leaving the weak and the feeble to continue their own race.

But what has done us most harm of all is a system of Government calculated to foster all that was low or mean in our nature – treachery, place-hunting, besides all the petty, mean vices that follow on the idea that commercial prosperity and nothing else is the highest ideal of life. These ideas, and many more, we have been allowing a subtle foe to graft on our national character at her will.

But we have seen it in time; and a nation of idealists and soldiers has only to see it, and she will prune off the bad growths, as a strong nature will throw off an unclean sickness.

Drunkenness is one of the great national evils for us to fight. It has caused more harm to our nation than at first seems possible. Many and many a defeat and massacre in '98 were facilitated by the drunkenness of the patriot army.[21] To quote 'The Boys of Wexford':

> We bravely fought and conquered
> At Ross and Wexford town;

[19] The reference is to the Great Irish Famine of 1845–52. During this period about 1 million people died from starvation and disease, and a further 1.25 million emigrated.

[20] The 'other great nation' is the United States. Approximately 4.5 million Irish arrived in the US between 1820 and 1930, with the rate of emigration increasing during and in the aftermath of the Famine. There was also extensive Irish immigration into Britain, Australia, and Canada.

[21] A reference to the Irish Rebellion of 1798.

And if we failed to keep them,
'Twas drink that brought us down.
We had no drink beside us
On Tubberneering's day,
Depending on the long bright pike,
And well it won its way.[22]

Again, another way of helping Ireland – make this country untenable for the British Army – let them be taught to paraphrase the Cromwellian cry and say when ordered to Ireland, 'To Hell or Ireland.'[23] Take a leaf from the book of the Italian ladies in their treatment of the armies of the Austrian usurper. Boycott them, men and officers, let them realise what the sight of a red or khaki coat means to a right-thinking Irishman or woman; let them feel that you would force them to leave, that you would fain see in their place the gorgeous uniforms of an Irish army, the brilliant ranks of regiments like the Volunteers of '82.[24] Make public opinion so strong that no Irish lad will ever again join the army of his country's enemies, to be at any moment called upon to 'quell sedition' in his own country or to fight against other noble nations in the same plight as themselves.

If Irish boys could realise the contempt the British army is held in abroad, if they heard it talked of as the last relic of barbarism, a 'mercenary army', and, as the most immoral army in the world, they would indeed hesitate before they entered it.

Then, again, you can educate your universities, colleges and schools. Don't permit pro-English propaganda, vice-regal patronage. I saw the other day a lecture advertised to be given by Father Maturin, Dr. Delany, S. J., in the chair, under the patronage of *Her Excellency, the Countess of Aberdeen*.[25] How long are the students of Ireland going silently to acquiesce in insults such as these? Many of us had great hopes of a new

[22] The ballad commemorates the 1798 Rebellion, specifically the Wexford Rebellion of May 1798.

[23] Oliver Cromwell (1599–1658) brought Ireland into an 'incorporating' union with Britain in the aftermath of the military conquest of the island, which took place between 1649 and 1653. In popular memory the putatively Cromwellian injunction 'to Hell or Connaught' connoted the expropriation and expulsion of Catholics to the barren territories of the western province during the conquests of the 1640s.

[24] The Irish Volunteers, established in 1778, supported the demand for legislative independence that resulted in Grattan's Parliament of 1782.

[25] Lady Aberdeen (Ishbel Hamilton-Gordon, 1857–1939), philanthropist and advocate of women's interests, was wife of the Viceroy of Ireland from 1906 to 1915.

order of things when 'God Save the King' was rioted down by some brave young men, but that protest does not seem to have led to anything more.[26]

The '63 revolution in Poland was chiefly organised by students. Cannot the young men and women realise their strength? It is they who are the universities and colleges of the country; without them the schools would cease to be. Let them force their senates or governing bodies into line and not allow them to tolerate, or worse still, to solicit any English patronage however they may be tempted. Let the maiden of Ireland, fleet as Atalanta, never pause in the race for freedom; let her shut her eyes to the golden apples that England will strew on her path, wisely understanding the bitter disappointment that must have been the lot of the other Atalanta, when she had realised that she had lost her race, her great prestige, her sex's prowess.[27] And all for what? For some fruit to eat.

As I write this a couple of lines from a Scotch poet are running in my head, which apply very aptly to us and to Ireland –

> Breathes there a man with soul so dead,
> Who never to himself has said,
> This is my own my Native Land?[28]

I think that there are very few Irishwomen whose souls are so dead that they would answer that question in the negative, but how many of them have realised the responsibility they have admitted when they say, 'My own, my native land'? Those words applied to our nation exclude all other nations from your possession. No man can apply the words, 'My native land' to two countries – to Ireland and England, or to Ireland and any other country. That we still can use those words proves that our souls incorporate in the soul of our nation are free still. The great soul of Ireland is still unconquered, and it is to the free souls of her sons and her daughters that she looks to free her body.

Each one of us has a soul, an Irish soul, a tiny atom of the great national soul of Ireland. Let us give that soul her chance; let us listen to her lofty aspirations, to the truth and justice of her claims. Ireland's soul was born free; it is we must free her body too.

[26] Referring to the visit of King Edward VII to Ireland in 1903.

[27] Atalanta, a character in Greek mythology, sought to avoid marriage by challenging suitors to a foot race, though she was ultimately beaten by Hipponemes who tempted her with apples.

[28] Walter Scott, *Lay of the Last Minstrel*, canto VI, 'My Native Land'.

In every action we do in life, the idea behind it is the thing that counts – if you go deep enough – the soul as it were. And so it is only by realising that unless the ideal, the spirit of self-sacrifice and love of country, is at the back of our work for commercial prosperity, sex emancipation, and other practical reforms, that we can hope to help our land. Every little act 'for Ireland's sake' will help to build up a great nation, noble and self-sacrificing, industrious and free.

Do you think that Christ would have conquered so much of the world, and held it for nearly 2,000 years, with a selfish practical policy and nothing more? No; Christianity, and other religions which have prevailed, have done so through their ideals, for which men and women were not afraid to die. Why did the Macedonian Empire break up? Why have we nothing left of the glories of the great Kingdom of Spain? What was the cause of the fall of Napoleon, and why did the French Empire crumble away? Because they were founded upon usurpation and sustained by physical force, that most unstable of human powers, and no physical force can hold forever a free-souled and steadfast people.

England is now holding by force three civilised nations – nations whose ideals are Freedom, Justice and Nationhood – Ireland, India and Egypt, not to consider her savage territories and South Africa. Her colonies have to be coaxed into loyalty, and her House of Commons goes into hysterics over the news that Germany is building ships.[29] Does that look like an Empire that is replete with a great National confidence, that is going to last for all eternity?

Wherever Ireland is known in the world, she is known by the great legacy her martyrs have left her, tales of noble deeds, of fearless deaths, of lives of self-denial and renunciation. Her name stands for the emblem of all that is brave and true, while England, her conqueror, has but gained for herself universally among the nations, the sobriquet of 'La Perfide Albion'.[30]

To sum up in a few words what I want the Young Ireland women to remember from me. Regard yourselves as Irish, believe in yourselves as Irish, as units of a nation distinct from England, your conqueror, and as determined to maintain your distinctiveness and gain your deliverance.

[29] The Anglo-German naval race became more intense from 1906 when both countries sought to build a new class of battleship, the dreadnought.

[30] The slogan 'Perfidious Albion' gained traction in Germany before the First World War but had its origins in French diplomatic history, rising to prominence during the French Revolutionary wars.

Arm yourselves with weapons to fight your nation's cause. Arm your souls with noble and free ideas. Arm your minds with the histories and memories of your country and her martyrs, her language, and a knowledge of her arts, and her industries. And if in your day the call should come for your body to arm, do not shirk that either.

May this aspiration towards life and freedom among the women of Ireland bring forth a Joan of Arc to free our nation!

1910

2 James Connolly, *Labour in Irish History*[1]

Foreword

In her great work, *The Making of Ireland and its Undoing*, the only contribution to Irish history we know of which conforms to the methods of modern historical science, the authoress, Mrs. Stopford Green, dealing with the effect upon Ireland of the dispersion of the Irish race in the time of Henry VIII and Elizabeth, and the consequent destruction of Gaelic culture, and rupture with Gaelic tradition and law, says that the Irishmen educated in schools abroad abandoned or knew nothing of the lore of ancient Erin, and had no sympathy with the spirit of the Brehon Code, nor with the social order of which it was the juridical expression.[2] She says they 'urged the theory, *so antagonistic to the immemorial law of Ireland*, that only from polluted sinks of heretics could come the idea that the people might elect a ruler, and confer supreme authority on whomsoever pleased them'.[3] In other words the new Irish, educated in foreign standards, had adopted as their own the feudal-capitalist system, of which England was the exponent in Ireland, and urged it upon the Gaelic Irish. As the dispersion of the clans, consummated by Cromwell, finally completed the ruin of Gaelic Ireland, all the higher education of

1 James Connolly, *Labour in Irish History* (Dublin: Maunsel, 1910), was originally published in monthly instalments in the *Irish Workers' Republic*. The Forward and Chapter 1 of the monograph version are included here.

2 Alice Stopford Green, *The Making of Ireland and Its Undoing, 1200–1600* (London: Macmillan, 1908). The Brehon code comprised laws regulating life in early medieval Ireland, many of whose provisions survived the Norman conquest, reviving in particular between the thirteenth and seventeenth centuries.

3 Ibid., p. 448. Italics added by Connolly.

Irishmen thenceforward ran in this foreign groove, and was coloured with this foreign colouring.[4]

In other words, the Gaelic culture of the Irish chieftainry was rudely broken off in the seventeenth century, and the continental Schools of European despots implanted in its place in the minds of the Irish students, and sent them back to Ireland to preach a fanatical belief in royal and feudal prerogatives, as foreign to the genius of the Gael as was the English ruler to Irish soil. What a light this sheds upon Irish history of the seventeenth, eighteenth, and nineteenth centuries! And what a commentary it is upon the real origin of that so-called 'Irish veneration for the aristocracy', of which the bourgeois charlatans of Irish literature write so eloquently! That veneration is seen to be as much of an exotic, as much of an importation, as the aristocratic caste it venerated. Both were

> ... foul foreign blossoms
> Blown hither to poison our plains.[5]

But so deeply has this insidious lie about the aristocratic tendencies of the Irish taken root in Irish thought that it will take a long time to eradicate it from the minds of the people, or to make the Irish realise that the whole concept of orthodox Irish history for the last 200 years was a betrayal and abandonment of the best traditions of the Irish race. Yet such is undoubtedly the case. Let us examine this a little more closely!

Just as it is true that a stream cannot rise above its source, so it is true that a national literature cannot rise above the moral level of the social conditions of the people from whom it derives its inspiration. If we would understand the national literature of a people we must study their social and political status, keeping in mind the fact that their writers were a product thereof, and that the children of their brains were conceived and brought forth in certain historical conditions. Ireland at the same time as she lost her ancient social system, also lost her language as the vehicle of thought of those who acted as her leaders.[6] As a result of this two-fold loss the nation suffered socially, nationally and intellectually from a

[4] Oliver Cromwell (1599–1658) brought Ireland into an 'incorporating' union with Britain in the aftermath of the military conquest of the island, which took place between 1649 and 1653.

[5] The lines come from John Banim's (1798–1842) attack on Sir Arthur Wellesley, 1st Duke of Wellington (1769–1852). 'He Said that He was not Our Brother' was intended as an indictment of the plantation or colonial class.

[6] Irish remained the language of the majority of the population until the eighteenth century. In the first half of the nineteenth century, Irish was still the primary language of three

prolonged arrested development. During the closing years of the seventeenth century, all the eighteenth, and the greater part of the nineteenth, the Irish people were the lowest helots in Europe, socially and politically. The Irish peasant, reduced from the position of a free clansman owning his tribeland and controlling its administration in common with his fellows, was a mere tenant-at-will subject to eviction, dishonour and outrage at the hands of an irresponsible private proprietor.[7] Politically he was non-existent, legally he held no rights, intellectually he sank under the weight of his social abasement, and surrendered to the downward drag of his poverty. He had been conquered, and he suffered all the terrible consequences of defeat at the hands of a ruling class and nation who have always acted upon the old Roman maxim of 'Woe to the vanquished.'[8]

To add to his humiliation, those of his name and race who had contrived to escape the general ruin, and sent their children to be educated in foreign schools, discovered with the return of those 'wild geese' to their native habitat that they who had sailed for France, Italy or Spain, filled with hatred of the English Crown and of the English landlord garrison in Ireland, returned as mere Catholic adherents of a pretender to the English throne, using all the prestige of their foreign schooling to discredit the Gaelic ideas of equality and democracy, and instead instilling into the minds of the growing generation feudal ideas of the divine right of kings to rule, and of subjects to unquestioningly obey.[9] The Irish students in the universities of the Continent were the first products of a scheme which the Papacy still pursues with its accustomed skill and persistence – a persistence which recks little of the passing of centuries – a scheme which looks upon Catholic Ireland simply as a tool to be used for the spiritual re-conquest of England to Catholicity. In the eighteenth century this scheme did its deadliest work in Ireland. It failed ridiculously to cause a single Irish worker in town or country to strike a blow for the

million members of a population of around eight million, but dramatically declined after the Great Irish Famine.

7 Connolly is referring to the customs of tanistry and gavelkind under the Brehon law which determined succession to high office and property.

8 The phrase *vae victis* – woe to the conquered – derives from the Gauls' treatment of the Romans after the Battle of Allia in 390 BC as reported in Livy, Book 5, 34–49.

9 The 'Flight of the Wild Geese' refers to the departure of an Irish Jacobite army under Patrick Sarsfield to France as agreed under the terms of the 1691 Treaty of Limerick. In general terms, the phrase designates those Irish soldiers who left to fight in continental armies between the sixteenth and eighteenth centuries or, as here, the departure and return of the Catholic aristocracy in the penal era.

Stuart cause in the years of the Scottish Rebellions in 1715 and 1745, but it prevented them from striking any blows for their own cause, or from taking advantage of the civil feuds of their enemies.[10] It did more. It killed Gaelic Ireland; an Irish-speaking Catholic was of no value as a missionary of Catholicism in England, and an Irish peasant who treasured the tongue of his fathers might also have some reverence for the principles of the social polity and civilisation under which his forefathers had lived and prospered for unnumbered years. And such principles were even more distasteful to French, Spanish or Papal patrons of Irish schools of learning on the Continent than they were to English monarchs. Thus the poor Irish were not only pariahs in the social system of their day, but they were also precluded from hoping for a revival of intellectual life through the achievements of their children. Their children were taught to despise the language and traditions of their fathers.

It was at or during this period, when the Irish peasant had been crushed to the very lowest point, when the most he could hope for was to be pitied as animals are pitied; it was during this period Irish literature in English was born.[11] Such Irish literature was not written for Irishmen as a real Irish literature would be, it was written by Irishmen, about Irishmen, but for English or Anglo-Irish consumption.

Hence the Irishman in English literature may be said to have been born with an apology in his mouth. His creators knew nothing of the free and independent Irishman of Gaelic Ireland, but they did know the conquered, robbed, slave-driven, brutalised, demoralised Irishman, the product of generations of landlord and capitalist rule, and him they seized upon, held up to the gaze of the world, and asked the nations to accept as the true Irish type.

If he crouched before a representative of royalty with an abject submission born of a hundred years of political outlawry and training in foreign ideas, his abasement was pointed to proudly as an instance of the 'ancient Celtic fidelity to hereditary monarchs'; if with the memory of perennial famines, evictions, jails, hangings, and tenancy-at-will beclouding his brain he humbled himself before the upper class, or attached himself like

[10] The 1715 and 1745 Jacobite rebellions were attempts by the Stuarts to regain the thrones of England, Scotland, and Ireland.

[11] The era of Jonathan Swift (1667–1745), Edmund Burke (1730–97), Oliver Goldsmith (1728–74), Richard Brinsley Sheridan (1751–1816), and Maria Edgeworth (1768–1849). In Sheridan's *The Rivals*, the typically 'stage Irish' character of Lucius O'Trigger is presented as an impoverished and hot-headed baronet.

a dog to their personal fortunes, his sycophancy was cited as a manifestation of 'ancient Irish veneration for the aristocracy', and if long-continued insecurity of life begat in him a fierce desire for the ownership of a piece of land to safeguard his loved ones in a system where land was life, this new-born land-hunger was triumphantly trumpeted forth as a proof of the 'Irish attachment to the principle of private property'. Be it understood we are not talking now of the English slanderers of the Irishman, but of his Irish apologists. The English slanderer never did as much harm as did these self-constituted delineators of Irish characteristics. The English slanderer lowered Irishmen in the eyes of the world, but his Irish middle-class teachers and writers lowered him in his own eyes by extolling as an Irish virtue every sycophantic vice begotten of generations of slavery. Accordingly, as an Irishman, peasant, labourer, or artisan, banded himself with his fellows to strike back at their oppressors in defence of their right to live in the land of their fathers, the 'respectable' classes who had imbibed the foreign ideas publicly deplored his act, and unctuously ascribed it to the 'evil effects of English misgovernment upon the Irish character'; but when an occasional Irishman, abandoning all the traditions of his race, climbed up upon the backs of his fellows to wealth or position, his career was held up as a sample of what Irishmen could do under congenial or favourable circumstances. The seventeenth, eighteenth and nineteenth centuries were, indeed, the Via Dolorosa of the Irish race. In them the Irish Gael sank out of sight, and in his place the middle-class politicians, capitalists and ecclesiastics laboured to produce a hybrid Irishman, assimilating a foreign social system, a foreign speech, and a foreign character. In the effort to assimilate the first two the Irish were unhappily too successful, so successful that to-day the majority of the Irish do not know that their fathers ever knew another system of ownership, and the Irish Irelanders are painfully grappling with their mother tongue with the hesitating accent of a foreigner.[12] Fortunately the Irish character has proven too difficult to press into respectable foreign moulds, and the recoil of that character from the deadly embrace of capitalist English conventionalism, as it has already led to a revaluation of the speech of the Gael, will in all probability also lead to a re-study and appreciation of the social system under which the Gael reached the highest point of civilisation and culture in Europe.

[12] A reference to D. P. Moran, *The Philosophy of Irish Ireland* (Dublin: James Duffy, 1905), a celebration of 'Gaelic', spiritual, Catholic Ireland in the face of perceived anglicisation.

In the re-conversion of Ireland to the Gaelic principle of common ownership by a people of their sources of food and maintenance, the worst obstacle to overcome will be the opposition of the men and women who have imbibed their ideas of Irish character and history from Anglo-Irish literature. That literature, as we have explained, was born in the worst agonies of the slavery of our race; it bears all the birth-marks of such origin upon it, but irony of ironies, these birth-marks of slavery are hailed by our teachers as 'the native characteristics of the Celt'.

One of these slave birth-marks is a belief in the capitalist system of society; the Irishman frees himself from such a mark of slavery when he realises the truth that the capitalist system is the more foreign thing in Ireland.

Hence we have had in Ireland for over 250 years the remarkable phenomenon of Irishmen of the upper and middle classes urging upon the Irish toilers as a sacred national and religious duty the necessity of maintaining a social order against which their Gaelic forefathers had struggled, despite prison cells, famine, and the sword, for over 400 years. Reversing the procedure of the Normans settled in Ireland, who were said to have become 'more Irish than the Irish', the Irish propertied classes became more English than the English, and so have continued to our day.[13]

Hence we believe that this book, attempting to depict the attitude of the dispossessed masses of the Irish people in the great crisis of modern Irish history, may justly be looked upon as part of the literature of the Gaelic revival. As the Gaelic language, scorned by the possessing classes, sought and found its last fortress in the hearts and homes of the 'lower orders', to re-issue from thence in our own time to what the writer believes to be a greater and more enduring place in civilisation than of old, so in the words of Thomas Francis Meagher, the same 'wretched cabins have been the holy shrines in which the traditions and the hopes of Ireland have been treasured and transmitted'.[14]

The apostate patriotism of the Irish capitalist class, arising as it does upon the rupture with Gaelic tradition, will, of course, reject this conception, and saturated with foreignism themselves, they will continue to hurl the epithet of 'foreign ideas' against the militant Irish democracy. But the present Celtic revival in Ireland, leading as it must to a reconsideration

[13] The phrase 'more Irish than the Irish themselves' (Hiberniores Hibernis ipsis or, in Irish, Níos Gaelaí ná na Gaeil féin) was originally used by the scholar and priest, John Lynch (c. 1599–c. 1677) to refer to the Gaelicisation of the Normans in Ireland.

[14] Thomas Francis Meagher (1823–67) was a prominent Young Irelander in the 1840s.

and more analytical study of the laws and social structure of Ireland before the English Invasion, amongst its other good results, will have this one also, that it will confirm and establish the truth of this conception. Hitherto the study of the social structure of Ireland in the past has been marred by one great fault. For a description and interpretation of Irish social life and customs the student depended entirely upon the description and interpretation of men who were entirely lacking in knowledge of, and insight into, the facts and spirit of the things they attempted to describe. Imbued with the conception of feudalistic or capitalistic social order, the writers perpetually strove to explain Irish institutions in terms of an order of things to which those institutions were entirely alien. Irish titles, indicative of the function in society performed by their bearers, the writers explained by what they supposed were analogous titles in the feudal order of England, forgetful of the fact that as the one form of society was the antithesis of the other, and not its counterpart, the one set of titles could not possibly convey the same meaning as the other, much less be a translation.

Much the same mistake was made in America by the early Spanish conquistadores in attempting to describe the social and political systems of Mexico and Peru, with much the same results of introducing almost endless confusion into every attempt to comprehend life as it actually existed in those countries before the conquest. The Spanish writers could not mentally raise themselves out of the social structure of continental Europe, and hence their weird and wonderful tales of despotic Peruvian and Mexican 'Emperors' and 'Nobles' where really existed the elaborately organised family system of a people not yet fully evolved into the political state. Not until the publication of Morgan's monumental work on 'Ancient Society' was the key to the study of American native civilisation really found and placed in the hands of the student.[15] The same key will yet unlock the doors which guard the secrets of our native Celtic civilisation, and make them possible of fuller comprehension for the multitude.

Meanwhile we desire to place before our readers the two propositions upon which this book is founded – propositions which we believe embody alike the fruits of the experience of the past and the matured thought of the present upon the points under consideration.

[15] Lewis H. Morgan, *Ancient Society or Researches in the Lines of Human Progress from Savagery through Barbarism to Civilization* (Chicago: Charles H. Kerr, 1877).

First, that in the evolution of civilisation the progress of the fight for national liberty of any subject nation must, perforce, keep pace with the progress of the struggle for liberty of the most subject class in that nation, and that the shifting of economic and political forces which accompanies the development of the system of capitalist society leads inevitably to the increasing conservatism of the non-working-class element, and to the revolutionary vigour and power of the working class.

Second, that the result of the long drawn out struggle of Ireland has been, so far, that the old chieftainry has disappeared, or through its degenerate descendants has made terms with iniquity, and become part and parcel of the supporters of the established order; the middle class, growing up in the midst of the national struggle, and at one time, as in 1798, through the stress of the economic rivalry of England almost forced into the position of revolutionary leaders against the political despotism of their industrial competitors, have now also bowed the knee to Baal, and have a thousand economic strings in the shape of investments binding them to English capitalism as against every sentimental or historic attachment drawing them toward Irish patriotism; only the Irish working class remain as the incorruptible inheritors of the fight for freedom in Ireland.

To that unconquered Irish working class this book is dedicated by one of their number.

Chapter I: The Lessons of Irish History

'What is History but a fable agreed upon.'

– *Napoleon I*

It is in itself a significant commentary upon the subordinate place allotted to labour in Irish politics that a writer should think it necessary to explain his purpose before setting out to detail for the benefit of his readers the position of the Irish workers in the past, and the lessons to be derived from a study of that position in guiding the movement of the working class to-day. Were history what it ought to be, an accurate literary reflex of the times with which it professes to deal, the pages of history would be almost entirely engrossed with a recital of the wrongs and struggles of the labouring people, constituting, as they have ever done, the vast mass of mankind. But history, in general, treats the working class as the manipulator of politics – treats the working man, that is to say, with contempt when he remains passive, and with derision, hatred and misrepresentation whenever he dares evince a desire to throw off the yoke of political or social servitude. Ireland is no exception to the rule. Irish history has ever been written by the master class – in the interests of the master class.

Whenever the social question cropped up in modern Irish history, whenever the question of labour and its wrongs figured in the writings or speeches of our modern Irish politicians, it was simply that they might be used as weapons in the warfare against a political adversary, and not at all because the person so using them was personally convinced that the subjection of labour was in itself a wrong.

The present series of articles are intended primarily to prove that contention. To prove it by a reference to the evidence – documentary and otherwise – adduced illustrating the state of the Irish working class in the past, the almost total indifference of our Irish politicians to the sufferings of the mass of the people, and the true inwardness of many of the political agitations which have occupied the field in the eighteenth and nineteenth centuries. Special attention is given to the period preceding the Union and evidence brought forward relative to the state of Ireland before and during the continuance of Grattan's Parliament; to the condition of the working people in town and country, and the attitude towards labour taken up by politicians of all sides, whether patriot or ministerialist. In other words, we propose to do what in us lies to repair the deliberate neglect of the social question by our historians, and to prepare the way in order that other and abler pens than our own may demonstrate to the reading public the manner in which economic conditions have controlled and dominated our Irish history.

But as a preliminary to this essay on our part it becomes necessary to recapitulate here some of the salient facts of history we have elsewhere insisted upon as essential to a thorough grasp of the 'Irish Question'.

Politically, Ireland has been under the control of England for the past 700 years, during the greater part of which time the country has been the scene of constant wars against her rule upon the part of the native Irish. Until the year 1649, these wars were complicated by the fact that they were directed against both the political and *social* order recognised by the English invader. It may surprise many readers to learn that up to the date above-mentioned the basis of society in Ireland, except within the Pale (a small strip of territory around the Capital city, Dublin), rested upon communal or tribal ownership of land.[16] The Irish chief, although recognised in the courts of France, Spain, and Rome, as the peer of the reigning princes of Europe, in reality held his position upon the sufferance of his people, and as an administrator of the tribal affairs of his people, while the land or territory of the clan was entirely removed from his private jurisdiction. In the parts of Ireland where for 400 years after the first conquest (so-called) the English governors could not penetrate except at the head of a powerful army, the social order which prevailed in England – feudalism – was unknown, and as this comprised the greater portion of the country, it gradually came to be understood that the war against the foreign oppressor was also a war against private property in land. But with the forcible break up of the clan system in 1649, the social aspect of the Irish struggle sank out of sight, its place being usurped by the mere political expressions of the fight for freedom. Such an event was, of course, inevitable in any case. Communal ownership of land would, undoubtedly, have given way to the privately owned system of capitalist-landlordism, even if Ireland had remained an independent country, but coming as it did in obedience to the pressure of armed force from without, instead of by the operation of economic forces within, the change has been bitterly and justly resented by the vast mass of the Irish people, many of whom still mix with their dreams of liberty longings for a return to the ancient system of land tenure – now organically impossible. The dispersion of the clans, of course, put an end to the leadership of the chiefs, and in consequence, the Irish aristocracy *being all of foreign or traitor origin*, Irish patriotic movements fell entirely into the hands of the middle class, and became, for the most part, simply idealised expressions of middle-class interest.

Hence the spokesmen of the middle class, in the Press and on the platform, have consistently sought the emasculation of the Irish National movement, the distortion of Irish history, and, above all, the denial of all relation between the social rights of the Irish toilers and the political rights of the Irish nation. It was hoped and intended by this means to create what is termed 'a real National movement' – *i.e.*, a movement in which each class would recognise the rights of the other classes and

[16] The suggestion is that the final remnants of the Brehon laws were extinguished by Oliver Cromwell. On common ownership see Green, *Making of Ireland and Its Undoing*, p. 107: 'The propertied classes evidently feared the Irish land system as expressing what might be called the Socialism of the time.'

laying aside their contentions would unite in a national struggle against the common enemy – England. Needless to say, the only class deceived by such phrases was the working class. When questions of 'class' interests are eliminated from public controversy a victory is thereby gained for the possessing, conservative class, whose only hope of security lies in such elimination. Like a fraudulent trustee, the bourgeois dreads nothing so much as an impartial and rigid inquiry into the validity of his title deeds. Hence the bourgeois press and politicians incessantly strive to inflame the working-class mind to fever heat upon questions outside the range of their own class interests. War, religion, race, language, political reform, patriotism – apart from whatever intrinsic merits they may possess – all serve in the hands of the possessing class as counter-irritants, whose function it is to avert the catastrophe of social revolution by engendering heat in such parts of the body politic as are farthest removed from the seat of economic enquiry, and consequently of class consciousness on the part of the proletariat. The bourgeois Irishman has long been an adept at such manoeuvring, and has, it must be confessed, found in his working-class countrymen exceedingly pliable material. During the last hundred years every generation in Ireland has witnessed an attempted rebellion against English rule.[17] Every such conspiracy or rebellion has drawn the majority of its adherents from the lower orders in town and country, yet under the inspiration of a few middle-class doctrinaires the social question has been rigorously excluded from the field of action to be covered by the rebellion if successful; in hopes that by such exclusion it would be possible to conciliate the upper classes and enlist them in the struggle for freedom. The result has in nearly every case been the same. The workers, though furnishing the greatest proportion of recruits to the ranks of the revolutionists, and consequently of victims to the prison and the scaffold, could not be imbued *en masse* with the revolutionary fire necessary to seriously imperil a dominion rooted for 700 years in the heart of their country. They were all anxious enough for freedom, but realising the enormous odds against them, and being explicitly told by their leaders that they *must not expect any change in their condition of social subjection, even if successful*, they as a body shrank from the contest, and left only the purest minded and most chivalrous of their class to face the odds and glut the vengeance of the tyrant – a warning to those in all countries who

[17] For example, in 1798, 1803, 1848 and 1867.

neglect the vital truth that successful revolutions are not the product of our brains, but of ripe material conditions.[18]

The upper class also turned a contemptuously deaf ear to the charming of the bourgeois patriot. They (the upper class) naturally clung to their property, landed and otherwise; under the protecting power of England they felt themselves secure in the possession thereof, but were by no means assured as to the fate which might befall it in a successful revolutionary uprising. The landlord class, therefore, remained resolutely loyal to England, and while the middle-class poets and romanticists were enthusing on the hope of a 'union of class and creeds', the aristocracy were pursuing their private interest against their tenants with a relentlessness which threatened to depopulate the country, and led even an English Conservative newspaper, the London *Times*, to declare that 'the name of an Irish landlord stinks in the nostrils of Christendom'.[19]

It is well to remember, as a warning against similar foolishness in future, that the generation of Irish landlords which had listened to the eloquent pleadings of Thomas Davis was the same as that which in the Famine years 'exercised its rights with a rod of iron and renounced its duties with a front of brass'.[20]

The lower middle class gave to the National cause in the past many unselfish patriots, but, on the whole, while willing and ready enough to please their humble fellow-countrymen, and to compound with their own conscience by shouting louder than all others their untiring devotion to the cause of freedom, they, as a class, unceasingly strove to divert the public mind upon the lines of constitutional agitation for such reforms as might remove irritating and unnecessary officialism, while leaving untouched the basis of national and economic subjection. This policy enables them to masquerade as patriots before the unthinking multitude, and at the same time lends greater force to their words when as 'patriot leaders' they cry down any serious revolutionary movement that might demand from them greater proofs of sincerity than can be furnished by the strength of their lungs, or greater sacrifices than would be suitable to their exchequer. '48 and '67 , the Young Ireland and the Fenian

[18] A reference to the 'materialist' conception of history, associated with Karl Marx (1818–83).

[19] The statement was originally made in 1852, and thereafter widely quoted, for example by Wilfrid Lawson during debate on the Land Purchase Bill of 1890. See Hansard, House of Commons Debates 27 November 1890, vol. 349, col. 153.

[20] Thomas Davis (1814–45) was a leading member of the Young Ireland movement.

Movements, furnish the classic illustrations of this policy on the part of the Irish middle class.[21]

Such, then, is our view of Irish politics and Irish history. Subsequent chapters will place before our readers the facts upon which such a view is based.

[21] A Young Ireland uprising was staged in Tipperary in 1848; the Irish Republican Brotherhood launched a Fenian rebellion in 1867.

1911

3 Arthur Griffith, from 'Pitt's Policy'[1]

IX. The Fundamentals of English Statecraft

When the Norman conquerors of England were definitely defeated in their attempt to seize the crown of France they were compelled to build a strong navy to secure themselves independence in the island to which they were then restricted.

As the commercial era followed the military era and England aimed at becoming a great trading nation it became vital to her that the countries facing her on the south-east should not be occupied by a strong naval or military power. The wars of England with Spain and of England with France in centuries past were waged to prevent Holland and Belgium becoming appanages of Spain or France. By the end of the seventeenth century Spain's strength was broken. The eighteenth century witnessed England concentrating her power to break France.[2] It was at the moment when this traditional policy of England seemed to be defeated that William Pitt became Minister.[3] The revolt of the American colonies gave France and Spain the opportunity of humbling England for ever.[4] The combined Spanish and French fleets exceeded the strength of the English

[1] The material that follows was for the most part originally published as a series of articles in the newspaper *Sinn Féin* in 1911. The articles were then collected and reproduced as an appendix to Arthur Griffith, *The Resurrection of Hungary: A Parallel for Ireland, with Appendices on Pitt's Policy and Sinn Féin*, 3rd ed. (Dublin: Whelan, 1918). The sections included here can be found in ibid., pp. 119–38.

[2] Referring to the wars of 1778–83.

[3] William Pitt the Younger (1759–1806) became Prime Minister in 1783 with the fall of the Fox–North Coalition.

[4] The 1779–83 wars are also known as the American Revolutionary Wars and involved Spain, France, the American Continental Congress, and the Netherlands against Britain.

fleet. The English fleet was defeated, but owing to the gross mis-management of the war by the Allies it was not conquered. England escaped destruction as a great naval Power in 1778–82 by the blunders of her foemen. She had invited it by permitting her fleet, for motives of economy, to fall below the standard of her traditional policy, i.e., equality with that of the combined fleets of the Bourbon Powers – then the only Powers in Europe strong enough to thwart her.[5]

Pitt was called to the helm at the time when as the first men in England despairingly proclaimed 'the sun of England's glory had set'. He must either give England a new policy or show her how to reassert the old.

He resolved to reassert the old. Ireland was on his flank. Ireland had profited by the collapse of English sea-power to reassert its independence. It remained, however, voluntarily associated with the Crown of England.[6] The new policy was obvious. England had shown herself unequal to defending her Empire. Ireland had shown itself equal to defending itself.[7] Ireland was filled with vigour, hope and enthusiasm, and produced in abundance the raw material of conquest. The new policy was, therefore, to accept the end of the English Empire as a fact and to reconstruct on its ruins an invincible naval and military Anglo-Hibernian Empire. This policy, which in similar circumstances eighty years later Austria accepted, Pitt rejected. He stood for England Absolute as those in Austria who opposed Beust's solution of the Hungarian problem stood for Austria absolute.[8] There was no Beust in the England of Pitt. Pitt's policy was the policy of a daring gambler. He set the fate of his country on the chance of destroying the power of victorious France. Twice under his guidance England trembled on the brink of annihilation. He even died believing he had ruined his country, and his death alone saved him from denunciation in the English Parliament as the destroyer of the Empire. Yet in the

[5] In the eighteenth century, the House of Bourbon held thrones in Italy, Spain, Luxembourg, and France.

[6] In 1782 the Irish parliament in Dublin was freed from restrictions that had been successively imposed on it since Poynings's Law in 1494, thereby bringing 'Grattan's Parliament' into existence. This was followed in 1783 by the Renunciation Act, under which the British parliament renounced the right to legislate for Ireland.

[7] Ireland raised its own Protestant militias known as the Irish Volunteers in 1778 to secure the defence of the island while British troops were withdrawn to fight in the American War of Independence.

[8] Count Friedrich Ferdinand von Beust (1809–86) negotiated the Austro-Hungarian Compromise (*Ausgleich*) establishing the dual monarchy, an event that formed the exemplary basis for Griffith's original 1904 *The Resurrection of Hungary*.

end his policy won in so far as it involved the pulling down of France, and the restoration of English control of the seas. And for eighty years no man has been honoured and worshipped by England as William Pitt has been. Every English politician realises that Pitt performed an almost impossible feat when he preserved the Empire without admitting Ireland to be a co-partner.

To understand the last hundred years of history it is necessary to realise that the English foreign policy which went down in 1782 and was successfully revived by Pitt postulates four things, which are these:–

(1) In the control and direction of Empire England must be absolute.
(2) The maintenance of Empire depends upon the maintenance of an English fleet more powerful than the combined fleets of rival Powers.
(3) The Low Countries – Belgium and Holland – must not be permitted to become in themselves great naval Powers or to fall under the control of a great naval or military Power.
(4) No one Continental Power must be permitted to dominate the Continent. Against any Power seeking the hegemony of the Continent combinations of other Continental Powers supported by the English fleet must be formed.

This was England's policy for two centuries before Pitt. It was the policy that had failed when Pitt was called to power. Pitt restored it, and made it run for a century. It necessitated the Union. It necessitated the English policy that prevailed in Ireland for the whole of the nineteenth century. What we shall consider later on is whether it has failed – and why.

Since the two steps necessary to Pitt in the policy were the overthrow of France and the subjection of Ireland, Pitt's action in Ireland is explicable. His support of the French Revolution for four years is also explicable.[9] The French Monarchy was the ancient enemy of England. Pitt backed the Revolution in order to overthrow the Monarchy. He did not believe that under a Republic France could remain a formidable Power. The invasion of the Low Countries by the French in 1793 awakened him to the fact that French Republicanism was not less imperialistic than French Monarchism. He therefore declared war against his former friends. The

[9] Britain was at war with France from 1 February 1793 until the end of the French Revolutionary Wars. Pitt initially adopted a policy of neutrality towards the Revolution.

rise of Napoleon deranged his calculations, and he was forced in 1802 to face the fact that France was now in possession of the strongholds of the Low Countries, and that England's power of opposition was exhausted. To avoid the necessity of concluding peace on terms which admitted the failure of his policy, he resigned office, alleging that he did so on the Catholic question – and Addington concluded the Treaty of Amiens.[10] Since this Treaty kept the Low Countries as a pistol at England's head, it was clear that England must by war or diplomacy secure the evacuation of these countries by France or England must go under. Diplomacy failed, although it offered Malta to France in exchange for the neutralisation of Holland. England then had no choice left. The war which followed the Peace of Amiens was England's fight for life.[11]

If the impartial reader will keep before his mind the four fundamentals of Pitt's policy we shall conduct him to the conviction hereafter that that policy, which necessitated the Act of Union, has to-day failed, because of that Act of Union.

X. The Origin of Free Trade

The battle of Austerlitz killed Pitt, and Fox, the man who might have reversed his policy, joined him in his grave.[12] The disciples of Pitt regained power, and among them there was none so strong as Lord Castlereagh.[13] Since the choice of Ministers lay between working Pitt's ideas to the full or abandoning them in favour of an agreement with France, the Pittite Ministry fell under the sway of Castlereagh. He guided its policy, although never nominally its head. The one man to challenge his authority was a brother Irishman – George Canning.[14] A duel between Castlereagh and Canning settled the question. Canning lost power in his party, and did not recover it whilst Castlereagh lived.

The history of England, then, from the death of Pitt until 1823 is little more than the history of an apostate Irishman carrying out resolutely the policy he had been taught by Pitt.

[10] Signed on 27 March 1802.

[11] The Napoleonic Wars following the Treaty of Amiens (1802) lasted from 1803 to 1815.

[12] The Battle of Austerlitz took place on 2 December 1805. Pitt died in the same year as Charles James Fox (1749–1806), a prominent Whig statesman and Pitt's rival.

[13] Robert Stewart (1769–1822), 2nd Marquess of Londonderry, also styled Lord Castlereagh, was a British statesman born in Ireland – hence Griffith's charge of apostasy.

[14] George Canning (1770–1827) was appointed foreign secretary under the Duke of Portland in 1807.

When in 1815 France fell before an embattled Europe, the Kingdom of the Netherlands was established with the Prince of Orange as Monarch.[15] The Kingdom was given sixty million francs to construct a line of fortresses to keep France in check. Thus Pitt's policy seemed to have absolutely triumphed. England was not merely the chief naval Power in the world, but the only naval Power. France, her one serious rival in a hundred years, was dethroned and the Low Countries converted into sentinels on French ambition. To overthrow France, resume the Empire of the sea, establish suzerainty over the Low Countries, and kick Ireland into a cellar was not the end of a policy, but means to an end. The end was the commercial conquest of the world. In the early eighteenth century this aim was freely avowed. The subsequent misfortunes of England compelled her to wear a mask. Adam Smith, Mr. Pitt's mentor, supplied the mask. His *Wealth of Nations* was, is, and will remain the best example of a subtle scheme for English world-conquest put forward under the guise of an essay on political economy flavoured with that love of man which hooks in the sentimentalists of all countries.[16] The fall of Napoleon left the way clear for England to monopolise the manufacturing power of the world. If she had thrown her ports open in 1815 instead of thirty years later there is no doubt all Europe would have gone down before her – rushing to exchange its raw materials for English manufactured goods. But, as Frederick List afterwards said, Providence has taken care that trees shall not grow quite up to the sky.[17] Castlereagh gave over the commercial policy of England into the hands of the landed aristocracy, and it killed the goose which had laid the golden eggs. The Pittites preached open markets to the world, but kept their own closed. France, observing this, shut her ports against England, and to all remonstrances from the Friends of Man and Pioneers of Progress pointed to the closed ports of England. The Secret Service of England was able to incline Germany, Russia, and North America to the policy of opening their markets free to English manufactured goods. But France's resolute refusal blocked the way to the conquest of the Continent. The landed magnates who had

[15] Referring to William VI of Orange, also known as William I of the Netherlands (1772–1843), who was declared sovereign prince of the Netherlands in 1813 and king in 1815.

[16] Adam Smith (1723–90) published *An Inquiry into the Nature and Causes of the Wealth of Nations* in two volumes in 1776.

[17] Friedrich List (1789–1846), a German-American economist, subjected Adam Smith and the doctrine of free trade to extensive criticism in *Das nationale System der politischen Oekonomie* in 1841.

backed Pitt refused assent to a policy of Free Trade which promised to decrease their importance whilst it increased that of the mercantile element. After the suicide of Castlereagh the dispute came to a head. All England – Whig and Tory – agreed that the glory of God and the interests of civilisation required that the Continent should buy its manufactures from England, whilst England in return would take raw material from the Continent – 'and agricultural produce', added others. 'No, no,' shouted the landowners. Canning tried to avert a conflict between the English commercial and the English landed interests. He went to France himself and tried his power of cajolery on the Ministers, pointing out to them how much they had to gain by opening their ports. They told him they had resolved not to worry on the right or wrong of Free Trade until England herself opened her ports. He returned to England in a fury and threatened he would hang a mill-stone around France's neck. But France, unmoved, kept her ports fast locked. Thus England was forced to go to war within herself as a preliminary to the commercial conquest of Europe: The merchants and capitalists who believed that by opening the English ports France would be forced to open her own versus the landholders who didn't believe anything of the kind.

What Pitt would have done had he been alive in 1815 is uncertain. It is clear that with England's supremacy in Europe re-established and the commercial conquest of the Continent as the objective that the ports of England ought to have been thrown open in 1815. But there were powerful interests in England opposed to such a course, interests powerful enough to drag Pitt down. Castlereagh must have seen clearly enough that Pitt's policy pointed to Free Trade, and that Free Trade was the natural and immediate sequel of the overthrow of Napoleon by England, but the disciple shrank from the fate that awaited him if he attempted to carry to the end his master's policy.

France was the key of the position. To force France to open her ports the Free Trade movement was begun by the British industrialists and opposed by the British landholders. The year 1824 marks the definitive quarrel of Pitt's disciples as to the means of carrying out his policy and the birth of the parties we know to-day as Liberals and Conservatives as distinguished from the old hereditary parties of Whig and Tory.[18]

[18] William Huskisson (1770–1830), president of the board of trade from 1824 to 1827, permitted foreign countries to trade with the colonies and lowered duties on imports.

XI. List and Carey

Up to the year 1824, when the commercial and the landed classes of England divided into hostile camps, England's economic policy had been the most rigidly protective in the world. Prohibitive duties were levied on the importation of the manufactures of the Continent, and the foodstuffs of these countries were all but interdicted. The navigation laws of England until the end of the Napoleonic wars provided that foreign commodities could only be imported in British ships or in ships of the country from which the goods were exported or of which they were the produce, and the trade of the British Colonies was restricted to British vessels. Goods exported could only be exported in British ships. The latter law was modified after the fall of Napoleon, but otherwise the navigation laws were kept intact. In 1824, when modern English history starts, the policy of England was to ensure that the foreigner bought from England and to prevent England buying from the foreigner. The doctrines of Adam Smith were sedulously promoted on the Continent by England while she kept her own ports closed. The Secret Service money of England was lavished with no niggard hand on Continental journalists and Continental theorists to influence them to advocate opening the Continental ports to English products. Whilst the French Government stood firm against such a policy the French public was profoundly agitated in its favour by professors and progressive writers. Germany, enamoured of the beautiful theories spun for it inclined its eager ear. It was at this time a man appeared in Germany whose keen mind, intense patriotism, and fearless character laid the foundation for the German power of to-day.

The man was Frederich List, the son of a Württemberg tanner. Beginning life as an enthusiastic Free Trader, he was led to investigate more deeply, and arrived at the conclusion that what Germany stood in need of was a rigid Protection. In 1822 he appeared as the head of a German Commercial Union whose doctrines were a direct challenge to England. Fearing his propaganda would displease England, he was expelled from his native Württemberg by its servile Government. Seeking refuge in other States of Germany, he was in turn by the same influence expelled from them. Fleeing to France, he was welcomed, but later returning to his own country he was cast into prison. On his release he retired to America. Here he fell under the influence of the two Irishmen, Carey, whose ideas, incorporating with his own, formed the foundation of his doctrine of National Economy, on which modern Germany is built.[19]

Carey the elder was an Irishman forced to flee his country by Mr. Pitt. Settling in America, he married, and his famous son, Henry Carey, elaborated the doctrine of Protection which the United States adopted in opposition to the doctrine of Smith. Henry Carey is the author of the United States as England's commercial rival. List, his colleague, is the author of Germany as England's competitor in sea power.

If at the end of the Napoleonic wars England, then standing supreme in manufacturing power, had itself adopted Free Trade, it is humanly probable that all Europe would have succumbed. The Ministers of England, however, considered they could force the opening of foreign ports without opening their own. For ten years they strove to attain this end, and failed. Instead opposition grew in strength on the Continent, and in 1824 England was faced with the certainty that she could not force the Continental ports to open to her Sesame without first modifying her own prohibitive policy. The landed interest, which regarded the free import of produce as certain to reduce its strength and importance, stood rigidly opposed to any relaxation in the English system. The manufacturing interest saw in the open ports of Europe the road to a wealth and importance unequalled in the history of the world. It had nothing to fear from opening the ports to manufactured goods – the Continent, it knew, was not able to compete with the home manufacturer in the English market. If the landed interest suffered some loss, the loss would be as nothing in comparison with the prosperity England could acquire by such a policy. The landed interest could not see this. It opposed doggedly. Under the influence of the commercial interest the British Government in 1824 began cautiously to move towards the abrogation of its prohibitive policy. The opposition of the landed interest proving too strong, the commercial interest threw in its power on the side of 'Reform', and the Reform Act of the Thirties, breaking down the strength of the territorialists, opened the way for the reversal of England's ancient trade policy.[20]

[19] Matthew Carey (1760–1839) was an Irish-born economist and publicist whose son, Henry Carey (1793–1879), singled out the 'British system' of free trade for criticism in his *The Harmony of Interests: Agricultural, Manufacturing, and Commercial* (Philadelphia: J. S. Skinner, 1851).

[20] The Representation of the People Act (1832), also known as the First Reform Act, introduced significant changes to the electoral system.

The history of British Parliamentary politics from 1824 to 1846 is the history of a struggle between the British shipowners and manufacturers, in which they used the multitude as their tool, and the British landed proprietors. The 'Reform and Anti-Corn Law' agitations were different phases of the fight between the two monied classes.[21] The commercials won in 1845, and Free Trade became the declared policy of England.[22] The English ports were thrown open, and the English manufacturer, cheered on by Cobden, who assured him that soon all the countries of Europe must open their ports, went forth to the conquest of the world. Incidentally some millions of Irish were famished or expatriated, and the price of food increased to their posterity. The delusion that Free Trade has cheapened food in Ireland is sedulously inculcated on a people ignorant of their history. The following prices of food in Ireland outside Dublin in the decade 1830–40, when Protection was in force, will dispel the delusion: – Beef, 4d. per lb.; mutton, 5d. to 6d.; bacon, 2d. to 4d.; pork, 2d. to 5d.; butter, 9d. per lb.; fowls, 1s. the couple. In Dublin 10 to 20 per cent. might be added to these prices. But this is of interest to none save the Irish themselves.

France, refusing to fall in with Cobden's idea, was discovered to be living in an intolerable state of tyranny, and the supersession of Louis Philippe by a Government of Liberal ideas became an object of English policy. Of that hereafter. The position of Germany requires a few words. Frederich List, returning thither years after he had been expelled, impressed its thoughtful people by his work on 'The National System of Political Economy'. He promised his countrymen a glorious future if they would act on his propositions, which were: –

'All nations have a common interest in protecting themselves against the destructive competition of England.'

'All nations have a common interest in preventing England holding the absolute mastery of the seas.'

'Germany's interest demanded that reciprocity treaties should be entered into by her with the United States and countries of the Continent, **but not with England.**'

[21] A nationwide Anti-Corn Law League was founded in 1838, with Richard Cobden (1804–65) and John Bright (1811–89) among its most prominent leaders. The aim of the League was to liberalise the international trade in wheat.

[22] John Russell (1792–1878), 1st Earl Russell, came out in favour of the repeal of the Corn Laws in 1845, forcing Robert Peel (1788–1850), then prime minister, to follow suit.

'An association of the States of Germany in a common flag, a common fleet and a mercantile marine is politically essential, and cannot be attained if the first three propositions are not accepted and acted on.'

List was bitterly opposed in his own country, where Dr. Bowring, paid by the British Government, lectured to discredit him.[23] In the reptile Press of List's native land he was held up in turn as an ignoramus, an adventurer, as a man who by bringing down England's displeasure on Germany endangered his country's safety, as at best a dreamer of dreams. Uncowed by attack and unmoved by ingratitude, List fought on against English policy, gaining recruits day by day. But the opening of her own ports by England dealt him a fatal blow. In holding the common mind of Germany against open ports, he had always pointed to England's keeping her own closed. When England flung them free, boasting as she did so that within a few years all Europe would be forced to follow her example, List, despairing of his countrymen's virtue to resist, killed himself. Belittled in his life, the dead man appeared to Germany in all his greatness and patriotism. His tragic death achieved what his continued life might have failed in. It impelled Germany to keep her sentinels on her ports and raise the call for a German flag and a German fleet.

Modern Germany and modern America – England's political rivals and commercial competitors – are the creation of List and Carey. We have turned somewhat aside to trace the origin of Free Trade with which the children of Pitt went forth to conquer the world. We shall now see how Pitt's policy was faithfully carried on against France, while despised Germany, silently working on the propositions of List, gathered strength to set it at defiance.

XII. Palmerston

From the day of Canning's death until the end of his own days Palmerston dominated English foreign policy, and with small interruption it was confided to his direction.[24] He slaughtered brown and yellow men for the benefit of British speculators and the opium trade, but these things were by the way, mere trade-wars. He bullied little Kingdoms such as Portugal and Greece and supplied munitions of war from his Government

[23] John Bowring (1792–1872) was a political economist who promoted the cause of free trade in the *Westminster Review*.

[24] Henry John Temple (1784–1865), 3rd Viscount Palmerston, served twice as British prime minister (1858–9; 1859–65).

Ordnance factories to insurgents in countries whose rulers were too weak to make England respect international law. But such things the commonplace English Foreign Minister can always do. The enthusiasm that his name aroused in England – which sustained him for forty years against all combinations in that country – was due to his vigour in carrying out Pitt's propositions of English foreign policy, viz.:–

(1) In the control and direction of Empire England must be absolute.
(2) The maintenance of Empire depends upon the maintenance of an English fleet more powerful than the combined fleets of rival powers.
3) The Low Countries – Belgium and Holland – must not be permitted to become in themselves great naval Powers or to fall under the control of a great naval or military Power.
(4) No one Continental Power must be permitted to dominate the Continent. Against any Power seeking the hegemony of the Continent combinations of other Continental Powers supported by the English fleet must be formed.

Palmerston added nothing to English foreign policy. But he enforced it as he had learned it from Pitt with the strength of Pitt.

When Belgium revolted against the role of Britain's policeman over French ambition, and France came to her aid, Palmerston effectively showed France that Pitt's policy had a strong man behind it.[25] The French armies which marched to the assistance of Belgium marched out again when Palmerston pointed the guns of the British fleet towards the coast of France. The French dream of Belgium as a sword brandished against England vanished. 'We have you down, gentlemen', said Palmerston to the French, 'and down you stay.'

France, baffled but unconquered, attempted to build up her power in the Mediterranean.[26] She played for an independent Egypt, which as her ally would aid her to successfully dispute England's mastery of the centre sea. Palmerston let her play a while. Then he slipped in and knocked Egypt down with a club. 'Gentlemen', said the English Foreign Minister to the French, 'the Mediterranean is an English lake, and an English lake it is going to remain.'

[25] The Belgian Revolution of 1830–1 led to the secession of the southern provinces from the Netherlands and establishment of an independent Kingdom of Belgium.

[26] In 1830, the French captured Algiers, which remained a colony until 1962.

France, held up in the Channel and held up in the Mediterranean, looked to alliance with Russia. Palmerston locked up Russia in the Black Sea, and retorted on France's attempt to find a Mediterranean ally by planning Italy a Mediterranean Netherlands. Liberty-loving England became aflame with enthusiasm for Italian freedom, and Austria, much annoyed, could only growl and swear.[27]

The year 1848 brought matters in France to a head. The continued defeat of French foreign policy by Palmerston had aroused discontent against the Monarchy amongst Monarchists and Imperialists, who remembered in bitterness the days when France gave the law to Europe. The internal policy of the Government of Louis Philippe increased the discontent by striving to drive it beneath the surface.[28] Republicans, Liberals and Bonapartists, mutually detesting each other, united in detesting Louis Philippe more. The unlucky Citizen-King resolved on a bold policy. France was to assert itself once again – by arms if necessary – against England. It asserted itself in connection with an affair of Spain, and Palmerston replied by a French Revolution. The British Embassy in Paris, with admirable skill, utilised French discontent to the end of firing Louis Philippe off the Throne. The French Republic of 1848 was inaugurated with great éclat and received with great enthusiasm.[29] All that appeared to the public eye was that a somewhat mean and despotic monarch had been overthrown, and all that resounded in the public ear was 'Tremble, Tyrants'. Young Ireland, with a dream that this regenerate France would unsheathe its sword for Ireland, hastened to Paris to congratulate M. Lamartine, apostle of liberty and high priest of the Republic, and M. Lamartine bowed Young Ireland out, informing it, much to its astonishment, that the French Republic was on excellent terms with England, and could not dream of interfering with the right of that country to dispose as it pleased of its subjects – willing or unwilling.[30] Thus did Lamartine pay some of the debt he owed England's Foreign Minister.

[27] The 1848 Revolutions sparked the Italian Wars of Independence.

[28] Louis Philippe I (1772–1850) reigned from 1830 to 1848. He earned the title of 'Citizen King' by disdaining outward shows of regal pomp.

[29] The second French Republic lasted from February 1848 until the coup d'état by Charles-Louis Napoléon Bonaparte (1808–73), Napoleon III, of 2 December 1851.

[30] Alphonse de Lamartine (1790–1869) played a prominent role in the establishment of the second French Republic. Young Ireland was a movement of the 1840s committed to the revival of Irish culture and the pursuit of political ideals of national freedom. William Smith O'Brien (1803–64) and Thomas Francis Meagher (1823–67) made up the delegation that appealed to the French Republic in April 1848.

The French Revolution of 1848 saved England from the danger of a war with France at a time when England was not on good terms with Russia and Austria. Its echoes resounded through Europe, and inimical Austria found her hands so full with her own Republicans and with the insurgent Italians and Hungarians that her unfriendliness to England counted for nothing. Palmerston, having thus settled France and the Mediterranean, turned his attention to clipping the wings of Russia. Glancing at the States of Germany, in his wisdom he remarked that it would not be a bad thing if Prussia grew stronger and assumed their leadership – thus serving England as a guarantee against France and Austria – and then he passed on. Like his master Pitt, Lord Palmerston did not foresee the possibility of Germany playing a hand for itself, and discreet Prussia, silently plodding on its way as an humble second-rate Power void of ambition, gave him no hint that with France out of the way there could ever arise a Power in Europe to challenge British supremacy.

XIII. The Crimean War

The Crimean War was the work of Lord Palmerston.[31] He believed some heavy blow should be struck at the naval and territorial power of Russia, and, in defiance of treaty and obligation, he made war on Russia; for the war with Russia was a shameless violation of the secret arrangement of 1844 by which England had acknowledged the right of Russia on every point on which England afterwards declared war. Palmerston, who believed that with Louis Napoleon at the helm France was in his grasp – later on he revised his opinion of Louis Napoleon – induced France to make common cause with England. Napoleon was not loth to do so, for in the tangled state of affairs in France a foreign war was good policy. When England, France and Turkey went to war with Russia they were joined by Sardinia – a little Kingdom dominated by a great man. The adhesion of Sardinia was regarded by the combatants in the light of a joke. But Sardinia was the one country in the war which gained out of the war. The Crimean War ended in a nominal victory for England and France. In reality it left matters where they were. For Sardinia it ended most satisfactorily. As Cavour, who planned a Kingdom of Italy with Sardinia at the

[31] The Crimean War lasted from October 1853 to February 1856, during which time Russia lost out to an alliance between the Ottoman Empire, the United Kingdom, Sardinia, and France.

head, foresaw when he sent his little forces to the front, in the settlement of affairs after peace, Sardinia necessarily secured representation, and stood on an equal footing for the time with the Great Powers.[32] Her representative was Cavour himself – the ablest man in the conference. He thus secured the foothold he wished in European affairs for his country and out of the blundering Crimean War built up the modern Kingdom of Italy.

The end of the Crimean War found Palmerston with his views of Louis Napoleon completely altered. He had regarded the Frenchman as his dupe – he found him cunning and dangerous. The Anglo-French Alliance went smash, and Palmerston roused England to the cry 'Delenda est Carthago.'[33] This Heaven-sent Foreign Minister, as he was termed, carrying blindly on the anti-French policy of Pitt, openly advocated a 'strong Germany with Prussia at the head'. The strong Germany was to be England's catspaw in keeping France down. English policy set itself to back Prussia against Austria, which was precisely what Prussia wanted.

Palmerston in his day was acclaimed the greatest of European Ministers. Compared with Cavour and Bismarck he was a child.[34] They used him to forward their own schemes – the one to make a united Italy, the other a German Empire. The united Italy did not matter to English policy, the German Empire mattered much.

Not until 1864 did any suspicion arise in England of Prussia – not for twenty years afterwards did she begin to take Prussia seriously. Her Heaven-sent statesman had learned from Pitt that France must be kept down. The possibility that another European Power could grow strong enough to challenge England as France had done never entered their minds. Palmerston for thirty years was the ruler of English foreign policy. He kept France in the place Pitt had designed for her and he let Germany get out of her bonds.

XIV. The Danish War

In 1850 Menzel wound up his history of Germany in a wail of despair.[35] The idea of Germany one and strong was all but dead. Her nobles were

[32] Camillo Paolo Filippo Giulio Benso, Count of Cavour, Isolabella and Leri (1810–61).

[33] 'Carthage must be destroyed.' The phrase is attributed to Cato the Censor during the debates in the Roman Senate over the Second Punic War.

[34] Otto Eduard Leopold (1815–98), Prince of Bismarck, Duke of Lauenburg, masterminded the unification of Germany and served as its first chancellor.

[35] Wolfgang Menzel (1798–1873), poet, critic, and historian, author of *The History of Germany from the Earliest Period to 1842* (London: G. Bell, 1871), 3 vols.

indifferent, her people deserters. Emigrants, they sought abroad comfort for themselves and forgot their Fatherland. Germany was a dead lion.

How oddly this sounds sixty years later – yet there was much truth in it in the day of its writing. A few years before Menzel shed his tears List had died likewise despairing of the country in whose service he had spent his life and which repaid him with imprisonment, poverty and exile. Germany in 1850 counted for little or nothing. Twenty years later she was a Great Power. The man who worked the miracle was a private gentleman named Bismarck.

Bismarck had read his List and his Menzel. He went into politics to carry out their ideas – to re-make Germany a Great Power. In the making he became the best hated man in Germany and the best abused man in Europe. He fought his own King, his own Parliament, his own people, and the jealousy of Europe, and overcame all. German Nationalism had got itself mixed up with ideas of democracy and universal brotherhood. Bismarck candidly and brutally told Germany that democracy and universal brotherhood were not in his line. He had no use for them. All he cared about was making Germany Germany. He was a German, nothing more. He laughed at the doctrinaires and university professors who dominated German politics, and who sought to re-make Germany by drafting paper Constitutions. Germany, he told them, could be re-made only by blood and iron. When the German Parliament denounced him he crushed the German Parliament beneath his heel and went on to make Germany with his specific. He had no notion of letting the babblers drive him to death as they had driven List.

Bismarck did not come into leadership until the period of the Franco-Prussian War.[36] He was, as the head of Prussian politics before that time remarked, too much of an idealist for the positive art of politics. During the Franco-Austrian War the subordinate idealist influenced his leaders sufficiently to keep Prussia well out of the conflict. Later on his lot was cast in Paris and London, where the great politicians were highly amused at him. 'You are not a serious man,' said Napoleon III. to Bismarck in Paris. Disraeli in London was highly diverted by the Prussian Baron who talked so frankly about a regenerated Germany.[37] He caricatured him in

[36] The Franco-Prussian War lasted from 19 July 1870 to 28 January 1871. The German states were victorious and subsequently established the German Empire under Bismarck.

[37] Benjamin Disraeli (1804–81), 1st Earl of Beaconsfield and British prime minister from 1874 to 1880. In his 1880 novel *Endymion*, the character of Count Ferrol is generally thought to represent Bismarck.

the name of Count Ferroll, and gave him a place in one of his novels, where he made him say, 'I will never have anything to do with new Constitutions. Instead of making a new Constitution I shall make a nation – by blood and iron.' When Bismarck returned to Prussia the King made him his right-hand man. The Press of Europe was very much amused. The Press of Germany was savage. The Press of Europe spoke of Bismarck as a demented Minister. The Press of Germany represented him as a tyrant – which he was for Germany's sake. When the Parliament refused to vote him supplies to govern, he most unconstitutionally ignored the Parliament and took the supplies. When it frantically denounced him, he laughed in its face. He was there to make Germany, he told his enemies defiantly, and he would make it in spite of Parliaments and people who had no sense whatever. Probably no man ever exasperated his countrymen more than Bismarck did – they assailed his life, and he smiled back at them – loving them all the time. Nothing they could say, no blow they could strike [against] him, made him swerve from his object. The Germans are children – they must be made into men – blood and iron is the medicine. That was Bismarck's creed.

In 1863 his first collision with England came. The Russian Poles had risen in revolt. Prussia had her own Poles to fear.[38] England expressed great indignation at the action of Prussia. The Prussian Liberals and Democrats did the same. Bismarck remained unmoved. Napoleon III. suggested to England that France and England should jointly Intervene. But this was not in the English programme. Her sympathy was not intended to be active. Instead she suggested to Russia that the Russians should permit the Poles to look after their own affairs. The Russian Press advised England to apply her own advice to Ireland first. England retired, and the Poles were speedily subdued. Bismarck became equally unpopular with the English and the majority of the Germans. To English criticism he made no reply – to his own countrymen he bluntly said his role was not the friend of man, but the friend of Germany.

The next year increased his unpopularity. The King of Denmark, who was also Duke of Schleswig-Holstein, as the Kings of England had at one time been also Kings of Hanover, died.[39] Schleswig-Holstein was three-fourths German, and Denmark, holding that Schleswig-Holstein should

[38] After the January Uprising in the Russian Kingdom of Poland, Prussia signed the Alvensleben Convention on 8 February with the Russians to secure its own Polish territories.

[39] King Frederick VII of Denmark (1808–63).

be a part of Denmark, had been long engaged in its Danification. Bismarck desired the provinces principally because the possession of Kiel was essential to Germany becoming a naval Power. Denmark incorporated the provinces by Act of Parliament. Bismarck urged strong action. He found the King, the Parliament, and the people against him and England threatening. 'If', said Lord Palmerston in the English House of Commons, 'any attempt be made to violate the rights of Denmark, those who make the attempt will find that it is not with Denmark only they have to count'. The *Times* newspaper announced that if war were made on Denmark, Denmark could rely on England. War was made on Denmark.[40] Denmark, relying on England, refused Bismarck's offer of compromise, and dared him to come on. Bismarck, by a dexterous move, induced Austria to join with him, and the two Powers fell upon the Danes, who fought bravely, waiting for England to come to their help. But England stayed at home and sent her sympathy instead. Lord Palmerston informed them that they had English public opinion with them, and 'opinion was stronger than arms'.

In the result Schleswig-Holstein was taken from Denmark and divided between Austria and Prussia. Bismarck had now the foundation on which to make Germany a sea Power. He applied to Parliament for money to start his navy with, and his Parliament, hating him, refused it - what did Germany want with warships? Bismarck then went ahead to make his navy without Parliament.

Why did England not go to the assistance of Denmark in 1864? Why did she permit Bismarck to get possession of Kiel? There were several reasons.

War with Prussia in 1864 meant war with Austria and all the States of Germany. This would have been a costly and expensive affair.

Bismarck's idea of a regenerated and powerful Germany was laughed at by all English statesmen, and formed food for jokes in *Punch* and satire in Disraeli's novels.[41]

The possibility of a permanently united Germany with a powerful German fleet was never once contemplated.

[40] The Second Schleswig War lasted from 1 February until 30 October 1864.

[41] *Punch* was a weekly, satirical magazine that circulated in the United Kingdom (predominantly within Britain) from the 1840s and commented on political affairs, mainly through humorous illustration with captions.

France, in the tradition of Pitt, was regarded by all English statesmen as the enemy, and it was held that a weakened Germany would strengthen France.

The Fenian movement in Ireland was at its zenith, and a war between England and Prussia and Austria would have precipitated insurrection in Ireland, and necessitated a large part of the British army being kept in Ireland.[42]

These were the considerations that induced England to break her pledges to the Danes in 1864, and let Prussia, by seizing Kiel, get her foot in the stirrup. Having got it there, Bismarck proceeded with the second part of his policy. His whole policy may be stated in four lines.

(1) To secure Kiel as a base for a German navy.
(2) To dethrone Austria from the hegemony of Germany and to weld the States of Germany together under the leadership of Prussia.
(3) Having thus secured German military unity, to attack and defeat France and make the German Empire the first land Power.
(4) Thereafter to build up German naval power to the end of challenging English dominance on the ocean.

Not a single statesman in Europe saw where Bismarck was going. Had they done so, Prussia would have been cut in pieces by England, France and Austria. The annexation of Kiel and the hegemony of Germany won at Sadowa meant little to English statesmanship. It was engaged in dragooning Ireland when Bismarck was engaged in clearing the way for Germany to seize England's place in the world. If there had been no Mr. Pitt to pass the Act of Union there would have been no Ireland whose necessary repression occupied English statesmen and blinded them to what the seizure of Kiel and the submission of the German States to the King of Prussia spelled.

XV. The Franco-Prussian War

The Austro-Prussian war that followed on the defeat of Denmark was inevitable, yet Bismarck found difficulty in persuading Prussia to undertake it.[43] Saxony, Bavaria, and some of the smaller States joined Austria against Prussia. Prussia secured Italy as an ally, and flung herself like a tornado

[42] The Fenian Brotherhood was founded in Dublin in 1858. Often associated with the Irish Republican Brotherhood, it was a transatlantic fraternal radical nationalist association that staged rebellions against Britain in Ireland in 1867 and Canada from 1866 to 1871.

[43] The Austro-Prussian War took place in 1866.

on her foes. The Austrians went down before her like chaff before the wind. Austria had no friendly Hungary to help her this time. Six weeks after the declaration of war Prussia dictated the terms of peace in Prague. By the peace of Prague Austria lost her headship of the German Empire, Prussia became head of the North German States, but South Germany remained outside. Italy secured repossession of Venice. Hungary received back the Free Constitution which in 1848 Austria had suppressed.[44]

Bismarck could not stop here. It was necessary to the unification of Germany that France should be met and beaten. So long as France remained the power she was, the South German States could not be combined in the grand Germany he had planned. The Franco-Prussian War was a sequel inevitable to the Austro-Prussian War. France recognised this, but despised her enemy. She counted on South Germany either actively supporting her or maintaining a benevolent neutrality. When war broke out, France found that the dislike of Prussia cherished by the South German States was not strong enough to make German war on German or even stand aside. The Southern States of Germany made common cause with Prussia, and France fell even more completely before the Prussian arms than Austria had done. On the 18th of January, 1871, the King of Prussia was crowned German Emperor in Versailles by the unanimous vote of all the German States.[45]

The sympathy of England was with Germany in the Franco-Prussian War. Faithfully following out Pitt's idea that France was the one enemy to fear, England regarded France's annihilation as a gain to herself. She failed to realise at the time that the Germany which rose upon France's ruin would become a more serious menace than France had been since Napoleon's day. It was good policy from the English standpoint to let France be defeated. It was the worst of policy to let her be annihilated. A bold English statesman, not obsessed by the Pitt policy, would have followed one of two courses. He would either have joined the strength of England with that of Germany in attacking France and taken the lion's share of the fruits of victory, or he would have intervened on the French side when it was evident that France was bound to fail, and dictated the terms of peace. To let France be so utterly crushed that she no longer formed even

[44] The Austrian monarch, Franz Joseph I (1830–1916), arbitrarily revoked what were known as the Twelve Points, sometimes called the March Laws or April Laws, which had been passed by the Batthyány government and effectively made Hungary an independent state.

[45] Wilhelm I (1797–1888), of the House of Hohenzollern, was King of Prussia from January 1861 until he became German Emperor in January 1871.

a menace to Germany was the acme of stupidity when England gained nothing by the crushing. The intervention of England in the war in its middle stage would have forced Prussia to be content with much less than she obtained and secured that neither France nor Germany could hope for generations to effectively challenge English supremacy. France would have been stronger to-day than she is – Germany weaker, and the two Powers would have fairly balanced power on the Continent, leaving England to play the part Lord Palmerston described as the 'Judicious Bottle-holder'. The Franco-Prussian War made Germany a unit, as the Danish War made her a sea-power, and there was no statesman in England to understand the meaning in 1865 of the seizure of Kiel, or in 1871 of the Coronation of a German Emperor in Versailles. All that England saw, in the light of the policy Pitt left her, was the annihilation of her old enemy, France. That Germany could ever menace her as France had done was unthinkable.

Bismarck, who understood the English politicians better than any man in Europe, foresaw this. He knew England would not intervene, for, as he implies in his memoirs, he knew England had no statesmen.[46] He realised that if England joined with Germany in attacking France, Germany would not reap the reward he wished. He therefore refrained from anything that might induce her to do so, and he felt that English policy, obsessed by the vision of France as the enemy to fear, would keep England from coming to France's aid. His conclusions were fully justified.

English mobs in English towns cheered the news of Prussia's victories in 1870. In 1911 England is forced to arrange an entente cordiale with France, a treaty with Japan, and make overtures to the United States, to ensure her against the ultimate results of the victories she hailed with enthusiasm, believing with the man who garrotted the Irish Parliament and made the Empire wholly an English possession, that with France humbled England must rule the world.[47]

XVI. Mr. Gladstone

The Franco-German War relieved England from serious fear of France, but it did not warn her of the obvious – the emergence of Germany as a rival. From 1870 to 1890 England entertained nothing stronger than dislike

[46] O. E. L. Bismarck, *Bismarck, the Man and the Statesman; Being the Reflections and Reminiscences of Otto, Prince von Bismarck*, 2 vols. (London: Smith, Elder, 1898).

[47] The 1904 Entente Cordiale marked the end of almost one thousand years of intermittent conflict. The Anglo-Japanese Alliance (1902) was an attempt to contain Russia.

of Germany. Her active hostility was transferred to Russia. Disraeli was chiefly responsible for this policy. A brilliant and audacious man without depth, he inaugurated that era of dramatic statesmanship in English politics which has produced Mr. Balfour, Mr. Lloyd George, Mr. Churchill and Mr. Austen Chamberlain.[48] Gladstone, a profounder type, who saw clearly that an anti-Russian policy could not serve England, saved English interests for the time by adopting Disraelian tactics, and raising a melodramatic agitation over 'Bulgarian atrocities' which were chiefly manufactured at the English Liberal headquarters.[49] Gladstone thus averted war with Russia, which, although England might have been nominally victorious, would have permanently injured her. In two years he beat Disraeli and assumed office. The policy he inaugurated was extension of the Empire without conflict with European Powers. By improving his friendship with Russia he got guarantees for his Indian frontier which the Disraelian wars in Afghanistan had endangered, and by his seizure of Egypt in 1882 he secured the only other real road to India against all rivals.

In South Africa his policy was marked by the same caution. The revolt of the Transvaal Boers, to whom after he had returned to office he broke his word, threatened at one time to interfere with the plans he had made for the subjugation of Egypt. After Majuba, when the Orange Free State Boers notified him privately that if he persisted they would go to the help of their Transvaal brethren, Gladstone had the courage to haul down his flag in Africa – a courage none of the limelight statesmen who succeeded him in office could ever display.[50] Gladstone had to choose between South Africa and Egypt, and he chose Egypt.[51] South Africa it was possible to get back later on, but Egypt not seized on at once was lost for ever.

Yet Gladstone, although infinitely superior to his rivals, the Disraelis and the Salisburys, as a statesman, was equally blind as them to the menace of

[48] Arthur James Balfour (1848–1930), 1st Earl of Balfour; David Lloyd George (1863–1945), 1st Earl Lloyd-George of Dwyfor; Winston Leonard Spencer Churchill (1874–1965); Joseph Austen Chamberlain (1863–1937).

[49] William Ewart Gladstone (1809–98) served as Liberal prime minister for twelve years spread over four terms beginning in 1868 and ending in 1894. In 1876 he published a pamphlet titled *Bulgarian Horrors and the Question of the East*, seeking to expose Ottoman brutality while also attacking the Disraelian policy of 'indifference' in his celebrated Midlothian campaign.

[50] The First Boer war, ending with the Battle of Majuba, lasted from 16 December 1880 until 23 March 1881.

[51] The Anglo-Egyptian War of July–September 1882 ended in British victory.

Germany.[52] Day by day that nation grew in strength – slowly but certainly its toy navy grew into the fifth class, then the fourth, then the third, and England did not read the meaning. In Africa and in Asia England extended her Empire, and did not understand the significance of Bismarck's pronouncement that Europe had become an armed camp because England was eating up the earth and leaving no outlet for other nations to expand. England seemed to grow in wealth and power each day, until when the Triple Alliance and the Dual Alliance were formed, and both sought England's partnership, she replied that she stood alone, supreme, in 'Splendid Isolation'.

It is little more than twenty years since that boast was made by the British Government and echoed by the British Press – England's haughty defiance of the whole world in arms. It is within the memory of every man of forty years of age that England with contempt refused alliance with every other Power, and asserted in her Press that she was in herself more than a match for Germany, Austria and Italy combined on the one hand, or France and Russia combined on the other. And not only did she believe her own boast, but the other nations believed it also. From that time until 1899 England was mistress of the world. She slighted Austria, snubbed Italy, insulted France, and ignored Russia and Germany. But all the time Germany continued building up her fleet.

In 1899, Gladstone being dead, she embarked on the South African War.[53] While Gladstone lived it was impossible for any English Government to make such a war, for he had threatened to return to public life and oppose the Government that did so with the same methods, if necessary, with which he dished Disraeli. Gladstone's plan for the absorption of the Boer Republics did not include war. His plan was to hem the Boers in a ring-fence of British Colonies and permit them no outlet to the sea. In time he calculated that as they could make no progress they would yield peacefully and take the status of British Colonies. This policy had been tacitly agreed to by both Parties in England after 1881, but the discovery of gold in the Transvaal and the impatience of Cecil Rhodes to become head of an United States of South Africa, determined the South African War once Gladstone was dead.[54] So when Gladstone – her last semi-statesman – had been a little

52 Robert Arthur Talbot Gascoyne-Cecil (1830–1903), 3rd Marquess of Salisbury, served as Conservative prime minister three times for a total of over thirteen years, acting as his own foreign minister but avoiding alliances, thereby maintaining a policy of splendid isolation.

53 The Second Boer War lasted from October 1899 until May 1902.

54 Cecil John Rhodes (1853–1902) was an arch-imperialist mining magnate in southern Africa, prime minister of the Cape Colony from 1890 to 1896, and founder of the territory Rhodesia (now Zambia and Zimbabwe).

over a year in his grave England embarked on the crowning blunder of her adherence to the Pitt policy – the war against the Boer Republics.

XVII. Conclusion

England came back from the Boer War – which she entered with the usual declaration from her Premier (Mr. Balfour) that she was fighting for 'Liberty and Righteousness' – with her prestige lower than it had been for a hundred years. 'Splendid Isolation' was no longer possible, and she was compelled to seek Alliances. She found Allies in her old enemies France and Russia, and since she found them her statesmen have been busy in encircling Germany in a ring of steel.

This is Pitt – the A B C of Pitt's Continental policy – 'No one Continental Power must be permitted to dominate the Continent. Against any Power seeking the hegemony of the Continent combinations of other Continental Powers, supported by the English fleet, must be formed.' Germany in the twentieth century is to England as France in the eighteenth and nineteenth, and Spain in the sixteenth. It is the fortune, or misfortune, of the German Kaiser to stand in the same relation to English policy as did Philip of Spain, Louis XIV., and Napoleon Bonaparte. One day that ring of steel will be drawn tight, and then war will happen. One day England will again stand at the head of a strong European Coalition; and Germany, in its turn, like France, must face a world in arms.

It needs no gift of prophecy to foresee so much. It is plain to the student of English policy. It may be in a few years, or it may not be for twenty, but the world will assuredly rock with a war waged to secure the hegemony of Europe – a war that Pitt's policy has made inevitable. If England win that war, then for another century Pitt's name will be glorified and Pitt's policy will continue to rule and ruin our country. If England lose that war, then the doctrine of England Over-All, which Pitt labelled 'Imperialism', will go out of fashion. England will realise that the man who substituted Patriotism by Imperialism was not a real statesman, but a very daring gambler.

In the day when England is again fighting for her absolutism her leaders will look for Ireland's aid, and they will shriek 'Loyalty to the Empire' in Ireland's ear. Thus Austria shrieked in Hungary's ear when Austria was grappling with Prussia. But Ireland, if she be in sanity, will not be deluded. The fruits of Pitt's policy to her have been the extermination of half her people, the paralysis of her commerce and industry, the devastation of her soil, and the loss of her place in Europe.

And now to the Irish Unionists – those so-called Imperialists – to whom I have really written these articles, I say: William Pitt, whose Act of Union you laud, was not only the destroyer of Ireland's organised nationhood. He will prove in time the destroyer of England's Empire. In his time there was an organised Irish nation co-equal with England. He struck it down. He served out to Ireland degradation and misery to the end that his England might be the more prosperous and exalted. He taught by example that the weakness of Ireland was the strength of England, and the statesmen of England have consistently followed his implicit teaching. A hundred years after his death they can look upon Ireland and say, 'Behold. We graze the bullocks where the homesteads of four millions stood. We have made of Ireland the one country in Europe where the people yearly diminish. We have strengthened England. We have carried out Pitt's policy.'

It is true. They have made England tenfold richer and Ireland tenfold poorer than when William Pitt walked the earth. But, while they were busy so doing, there grew up unnoticed in their preoccupation a challenge to their life stronger than the challenge of Spain or France. The spectre of Germany to-day hagrides English statesmanship.

When William Pitt struck down Ireland by the Act of Union he made modern Germany possible. When William Pitt made it certain that, instead of an independent and prosperous Ireland in the year A.D. 1911, with 20,000,000 of people in friendly relations with the neighbouring islanders, there should be an enslaved and impoverished Ireland with 4,000,000 of people hating most justifiably their neighbouring oppressors, he made the European situation of 1911. English Imperialism decreed that Ireland must be struck down and kept down. English Imperialism succeeded so well that England's rival will have no Irish enemy to face. England produced a Pitt – Austria produced a Beust. When England fights for its life there will be no Ireland to support her – when Austria fights for its life Hungary will stand with Austria. England has taught Ireland to abandon hope of freedom except through England's destruction. This teaching she has styled Imperialism. In the day of her stress she will find that Irishmen have learned the true lesson of her Imperialism, and that they will hail her defeat as their salvation.

4 Erskine Childers, from *The Framework of Home Rule*

'Ireland To-day'[1]

Why does present-day Ireland need Home Rule? I put the question in that way because I am not going to question the fact that she wants Home Rule. She has always said she wanted it: she says so still, and that is enough. There is a powerful minority in Ireland against Home Rule.[2] There always have been minorities more or less powerful against Home Rule in all ages and places. That does not alter the national character of the claim. If once we go behind the voice of a people, constitutionally expressed, we court endless risks. National leaders have always been called 'agitators', which, of course, they are, and non-representative agitators, which they are not. To deny the genuineness of a claim which is feared is an invariable feature of oppositions to measures of Home Rule. The denial is generally irreconcilable with the case made for the dangers of Home Rule, and that contradiction in its most glaring shape characterizes the present opposition to the Irish claims. But Unionists should elect to stand on one ground or the other, and for my part I shall assume that the large majority of Irishmen, as shown by successive electoral votes, want Home Rule. Precisely what form of Home Rule they want is another and by no means so clear a matter, on which I shall presently have a word to

1 This document forms chapter 9 of Erskine Childers, *The Framework of Home Rule* (London: Edward Arnold, 1911), pp. 150–87.

2 Childers has Irish unionists in mind, many of whom, particularly in parts of Ulster, opposed home rule.

say. But they want, in the general sense, to manage their own local affairs. Her best friends would despair of Ireland if that was not her desire.

What, in the Colonies, Ireland, and everywhere else, is the deep spiritual impulse behind the desire for Home Rule? A craving for self-expression, self-reliance. Home Rule is synonymous with the growth of independent character. That is why Ireland instinctively and passionately wants it, that is why she needs it, and that is why Great Britain, for her own sake, and Ireland's, should give it. If that is not the reason, it is idle to talk about Home Rule; but it is the reason.

Character is the very foundation of national prosperity and happiness, and we are blind to the facts of history if we cannot discern the profound effect of political institutions upon human character. Self-government in the community corresponds to free will in the individual. I am far from saying that self-government is everything. But I do say that it is the master-key. It is fundamental. Give responsibility and you will create responsibility. Through political responsibility only can a society brace itself to organized effort, find out its own opinions on its own needs, test its own capabilities, and elicit the will, the brains, and the hands to solve its own problems.

These are such commonplaces in every other part of the Empire, which has an individual life of its own, that men smile if you suggest the contrary. But ordinary reasoning is rarely applied to Ireland. There 'good government' has been held to be 'a substitute for self-government' and a regime of benevolent paternalism to be a full and sufficient compensation for cruel coercion and crueller neglect. In this paternal *régime* it is impossible to include those great measures of land reform passed in 1870, 1881, and 1887,[3] which revolutionized the agrarian system, and converted the cottier tenant into a judicial tenant.[*] Although these measures, which fall into an altogether different category from the subsequent policy of State-aided Land Purchase,[†] were inspired by an earnest desire to mitigate frightful social evils, they cannot be regarded as voluntary. They

[3] Childers is referring to a series of Land Acts dealing with tenancy contracts and peasant proprietorship. Taken together, the Acts radically reduced the concentration of ownership of Irish land, gradually creating a class of small independent farmers.

[*] See pp. 13–17 and 66–71. *Editorial note:* Childers is referring respectively to sections of chapters on 'The Colonization of Ireland and America' and 'The Union'.

[†] Dealt with fully in Chapter XIV. *Editorial note:* this refers to Childers's chapter on 'Land Purchase Finance'.

were extorted, shocking as the reflection is, by crime and violence, by the spectacle of a whole social order visibly collapsing, and by the desperate efforts of a handful of Irishmen, determined at any cost, by whatever means, to save the bodies and souls of their countrymen.[4] The methods of these men were destructive. They were constructive only in this, the highest sense of all, that while battling against concrete economic evils, they sought to obtain for Ireland the right to control her own affairs and cure her own economic evils. It is often said that Parnell gave a tremendous impetus to the Home Rule movement by harnessing it to the land question. True; but what a strange way of expressing a truth! Anywhere outside Ireland men would say that self-government was the best road to the reform of a bad land system.

With the tranquillity which was slowly restored by the alterations in agrarian tenure and the immense economic relief derived from the lowering of rents, a change came over the spirit of British statesmanship. With the exception of the short Liberal Government of 1892–1895, which failed for the second time to carry Home Rule, Conservatives were responsible for Ireland from 1886 to 1905. They felt that opposition to Home Rule could be justified only by a strenuous policy of amelioration in Ireland, and the efforts of three Chief Secretaries, Mr. Arthur Balfour, Mr. Gerald Balfour, and Mr. George Wyndham – efforts often made in the teeth of bitter opposition from Irish Unionists – to carry out this policy, were sincere and earnest.[5] The Act of 1891, with its grants for light railways, its additional facilities for Land Purchase, and its establishment of the Congested Districts Board to deal with the terrible poverty of certain districts in the west, may be said to mark the beginning of the new era.[6] The Land Act of 1896 was another step, and the establishment of a complete system of Irish Local

[4] Childers is in effect criticising the methods pursued by the Land League and then the Plan of Campaign led by, among others, Michael Davitt (1844–1906) and Charles Stewart Parnell (1846–91) to secure tenant rights against landlordism.

[5] Arthur James Balfour (1848–1930) was prime minister from 1902 to 1905; Gerald Balfour (1853–1954) served as Chief Secretary for Ireland from 1895 to 1900; George Wyndham (1863–1913), having been private secretary to Gerald Balfour, succeeded him as chief secretary in 1900, and gave his name to the 1903 Wyndham Land Act.

[6] The Purchase of Land (Ireland) Act 1891.The Congested Districts Board for Ireland was designed to alleviate poverty and congested living conditions mainly in the west of Ireland.

Government in 1898 another.[7] In the following year came the Act setting up the Department of Agriculture, and in 1903 Mr. Wyndham's great Land Purchase Act.[8] Then came the strange 'devolutionist' episode, arising from the appointment of Sir Antony (now Lord) MacDonnell to the post of Under-Secretary at Dublin Castle, the Government who selected him being fully aware that he was in favour of some change in the government of Ireland.[9] He entered into relations with a group of prominent Irishmen, headed by Lord Dunraven, who were thinking out a scheme for a mild measure of devolution.[10] When the fact became known, there was an explosion of anger among Irish Unionists. Mr. Wyndham, who had been a popular Chief Secretary, resigned office, and was succeeded by Mr. Walter Long;[11] perhaps the most dramatic and significant example in modern times of the policy of governing Ireland in deliberate and direct defiance of the wishes and sentiments of the vast majority of Irishmen.

The Liberal Government of 1906, coming into office under a pledge to refrain from a full Home Rule measure, confined itself to the introduction of the Irish Council Bill of 1907, which, rightly, in my opinion, was repudiated by the Irish people, and accordingly dropped. But the Government was in general sympathy with Nationalist Ireland, so that a number of useful measures were added to the statute books; for example, the Labourers (Ireland) Act of 1906, empowering Rural Councils, with the aid of State credit, to acquire land for labourers' plots and cottages; the Town Tenants Act, extending the principle of compensation for improvements at the termination of a lease to the urban tenant;[12] the very important Irish Universities Act of 1908, which gave to Roman

[7] The Land Law (Ireland) Act 1896; the Local Government (Ireland) Act 1898 was implemented ten years after a similar Act was passed for England, Scotland, and Wales in 1888.

[8] The Agriculture and Technical Instruction (Ireland) Act 1899 was the inspiration behind the Department of Agriculture and Technical Instruction, inaugurated in 1900 by Horace Plunkett, which designed to improve Irish agriculture and industry through practical education and local co-operation.

[9] Sir Antony Patrick MacDonnell (1844–1925), 1st Baron MacDonnell, an Irish civil servant also extensively involved in the administration of India.

[10] Windham Thomas Wyndham-Quin (1841–1926), 4th Earl of Dunraven and Mount-Earl, Under-Secretary of State for the Colonies and chairman of the 1902 Land Conference Ireland.

[11] Walter Hume Long (1854–1924), 1st Viscount Long, an Irish Unionist politician, held the position of Chief Secretary for Ireland, March–December 1905. He later led the Irish Unionist Party in the House of Commons from 1906 to 1910.

[12] Town Tenants (Ireland) Act 1906.

Catholics facilities for higher education which they had lacked for centuries, and, lastly, Mr. Birrell's Land Act of 1909, which was designed partly to meet the imminent collapse of Land Purchase, owing to the failure of the financial arrangements made under the Wyndham Act of 1903, and partly to extend the powers of the Congested Districts Board.

To these measures must be added another which was not confined to Ireland, but which has exercised a most potent influence, and by no means a wholly beneficial influence, on Irish life and Irish finance, the Old Age Pensions Act of 1908, under which the enormous sum of two and three-quarter millions is now allocated to Ireland.*

The best that can be said of the legislation since 1881 is that it has laid the foundations of a new social order. Agrarian crime has disappeared and material prosperity has greatly increased. Government in the interests of a small favoured class has almost vanished. It survives to this extent, that civil administration and patronage, which are still, be it remembered, removed from popular control, remain, in fact, in Protestant and Unionist hands to an extent altogether disproportionate to the distribution of creeds, classes, and opinions. And, of course, in the major matter of Home Rule, the power of the Unionist minority, as represented in the Commons by seventeen out of the thirty-three Ulster representatives, and in the House of Lords by an overwhelming preponderance of Unionist peers, is still enormous. But within Ireland itself, central administration apart, the exceptional privileges and exceptional political power of Protestants and landlords, which lasted almost intact until forty years ago, is now non-existent. The Disestablishment Act of 1869, while immensely enhancing the moral power and religious zeal of the Church of Ireland, and even strengthening its financial position, took away its political monopoly, and through the final abolition of tithes, its baneful and irritating interference with economic life.[13] The successive measures of land legislation, culminating in the transfer of half the land of Ireland from landlord to peasant proprietorship, and the Local Government Act of 1898, surrendering at a stroke the whole local administration of the

[13] The Irish Church Act 1869 separated the Church of Ireland from the Church of England and disestablished the former in the process. Full relief from tithes came with the Act.

* In 1910–11, £2,408,000 (Treasury Return No. 220, 1911); plus £225,000 estimated increase owing to removal of Poor Law disqualification (Answer to Question in House of Commons, February 15, 1911).

country into popular control, destroyed the exceptional political privileges of the landlord class.

Ascendancy, then, in the old sense, is a thing of the past. What has taken its place? What is the ruling power within Ireland? Is it a public opinion derived from the vital contact of ideas and interests, and taking shape in a healthy and normal distribution of parties? Is thought free? Has merit its reward? Is there any unity of national purpose, transcending party divisions? If it were necessary to give a categorical 'Yes' or 'No' to these questions, the answer would be 'No'. Sane energizing politics, and the sovereign ascendancy of a sane public opinion, are absolutely unattainable in Ireland or anywhere else without Home Rule. It is all the more to the credit of Irishmen that, in the face of stupendous difficulties, and in a marvellously short space of time since the attainment, barely twenty years ago, of the elementary conditions of social peace, they have gone so far as they have gone towards the creation of a self-reliant, independently thinking, united Ireland. The whole weight of Imperial authority has been thrown into the scale against them. Whatever the mood and policy of British upholders of the Union, whether sympathetic or hostile, wise or foolish, their constant message to both parties in Ireland has been, 'Look to us. Trust in us. You are divided. We are umpires', and the reader will no doubt remember that the theory of 'umpirage' was used in exactly the same way in the Colonies, notably in Upper Canada,[*] to thwart the tendency towards a reconciliation of creeds, races, and classes. Fortunately, there have been Irishmen who have laboured to counteract the effects of this enervating policy, and to reconstruct, by native effort from within, a new Ireland on the ruins of the old. Whether or not they have consciously aimed at Home Rule matters not a particle. Some have, some have not; but the result of these efforts has been the same, to pull Irishmen together and to begin the creation of a genuinely national atmosphere.

It is not part of my scheme to describe in detail the various movements, agricultural, industrial, economic, literary, political, which in the last twenty years have contributed to this national revival. Some have a world-wide fame, all have been excellently described at one time or another by writers of talent and insight.[†] My purpose is to note their

[*] See p. 101. *Editorial note:* in the chapter on 'Canada and Ireland'.

[†] See particularly 'Ireland in the New Century', Sir Horace Plunkett; 'Contemporary Ireland', E. Paul-Dubois; 'The New Ireland', Sydney Brooks. *Editorial note:* Sydney Brooks (1872–1937) published *The New Ireland* in 1907.

characteristics and progress, and to estimate their political significance. In the first place it must be remembered that some of the most important of the modern legislative measures have been initiated and promoted by Home Rulers and Unionists, Roman Catholics and Protestants, acting in friendly co-operation and throwing aside their political and religious antagonisms. Such was the origin of the great Land Purchase Act of 1903, which Mr. Wyndham drafted on the basis of an agreement reached at a friendly conference of landlords and representatives of tenants. But a far more interesting and hopeful instance of co-operation had taken place seven years earlier. One of the very few really constructive measures of the last twenty years, the Act of 1899 for setting up the Department of Agriculture and Technical Instruction, was the direct outcome of the recommendations of the Recess Committee brought together in 1895 and 1896 by Sir Horace Plunkett;[14] a Committee containing Nationalist and Unionist Members of the House of Commons, Tory and Liberal Unionist peers, Ulster captains of industry, the Grand Master of the Belfast Orangemen, and an eminent Jesuit.[*] In its reunion of men divided by bitter feuds, it was just the kind of Conference that assembled in Durban in 1908, six years after a devastating war, to discuss and to create the framework of South African Union.[15] That Conference was the natural outcome of the grant of Home Rule to the defeated Boer States. The Irish Conference, succeeding a land-war far more destructive and demoralizing, was brought together in spite of the absence of Home Rule, and the prejudice it had to overcome,[†] is a measure of the fantastically abnormal conditions produced by the

[14] Sir Horace Curzon Plunkett (1854–1932), cooperative pioneer, agricultural reformer and Irish Unionist MP from 1892 to 1900.

[15] The National Convention, also known as the Convention on the Closer Union of South Africa, was a constitutional convention held between 1908 and 1909 in Durban, Cape Town, and Bloemfontein.

[*] 'Report of the Recess Committee', New Edition (Fisher Unwin). *Editorial note:* the original report was composed by Horace Plunkett and published as *Report of the Recess Committee on the Establishment of a Department of Agriculture and Industries for Ireland* (Dublin: Browne & Nolan, 1896).

[†] Colonel Saunderson, for example, the leader of the Irish Unionists in the Commons, refused publicly to be a member of a committee on which Mr. Redmond sat. Mr. John Redmond himself wrote that he could not take a very sanguine view of the Conference, but that he was 'unwilling to take the responsibility of declining to aid in any effort to promote useful legislation in Ireland'. *Editorial note:* Colonel Edward James Saunderson (1837–1906) led the Unionist Alliance from 1891 to 1906, while John Redmond (1856–1918) led the Irish Parliamentary Party from 1891 to 1918.

denial of self-government. There lay Ireland, an island with a rich soil and a clever population, yet terribly backward, far behind England, far behind all the progressive nations of Europe in agriculture and industry, her population declining, her land passing out of cultivation,* her strongest sons and daughters hurrying away to enrich with their wits and sinews distant lands. There, in short, lay a country groaning for intelligent development by the concentrated energies of her own people.

'We have in Ireland', runs the first paragraph of the Report of the Committee, 'a poor country practically without manufactures – except for the linen and shipbuilding of the north, and the brewing and distilling of Dublin – dependent upon agriculture, with its soil imperfectly tilled, its area under cultivation decreasing, and a diminishing population without industrial habits or technical skill.'

The leeway to make up was enormous. To go no farther back than the institution of the Penal Code and the deliberate destruction of the woollen industry, two centuries of callous repression at the hands of an external authority had maimed and exhausted the country whose condition the Committee had met to consider.[16] These facts the members of the Committee frankly recognized in that part of the Report which is entitled with gentle irony 'Past Action of the State'. Here, then, was a purely Irish problem, intimately concerning every Irishman, poor or rich, Roman Catholic or Protestant, a problem of which Great Britain, though responsible both for its existence and its solution, knew and cared little. The really strange thing is, not that representative Irishmen should have met together to consider and prescribe for the deplorable economic condition of their country, but that they should not also, like the South African Conference, have drafted a Constitution for Ireland, on the sound ground that a system of government which had promoted and sustained the evils they described could never, with the best will in the world, become a good government for Ireland. Yet for a brief space of

[16] A series of Penal Laws against Roman Catholics were introduced by the Irish parliament, beginning in 1695. The Irish Wool Act of 1699 sought to constrain the manufacture and export of Irish wool products in order to benefit the English trade.

* Area under cultivation in 1875, 5,332,813 acres; in 1894, 4,931,011 acres (in 1899, 4,627,545 acres; in 1900, on a system of classification dividing arable land more accurately from pasture, there were only 3,100,397 acres arable, and in 1905 the figures were 2,999,082 acres) (Official Returns). Population in 1841, 8,175,124; in 1851, 6,552,385; in 1861, 5,798,976; in 1871, 5,412,377; in 1881, 5,174,836; in 1891, 4,704,750; in 1892, 4,633,808; in 1893, 4,607,462; in 1894, 4,589,260; in 1895, 4,559,936 (in 1901, 4,458,775; in 1905, 4,891,543) – Census Returns and *Thoms' Directory*.

time these men actually had Home Rule, and by virtue of that privilege they did better work for Ireland in six months than had been done in two centuries.

What is more, they used the Home Rule principle in their recommendations for the establishment of a Department of Agriculture and Technical Instruction. 'We think it essential', they reported on p. 101, 'that the new Department should be in touch with the public opinion of the classes whom its work concerns, and should rely largely for its success upon their active assistance and co-operation.' Its chief, they added, should be a Minister directly responsible to Parliament, and on p. 103 they advocated a Consultative Council, whose functions should be – (1) To keep the Department in direct touch with the public opinion of those classes whom the work of the Ministry concerns; and (2) to distribute some of the responsibility for administration amongst those classes. Now these, in Ireland, were revolutionary proposals. The idea of any part of the Government 'being in touch with public opinion' was wholly new. The idea of 'distributing responsibility for administration' amongst the subjects of administration was startlingly novel. Ireland, both before and after the Union, had always been governed on a diametrically opposite principle. Since the Union, when Irish departmental Ministers, never responsible to the people, disappeared, not one of the host of nominated Irish Boards was legally amenable to Irish public opinion. Not one had a separate Minister responsible even to the Parliament at Westminster, which was not an Irish Parliament. *A fortiori*, not one relied on the co-operation and advice of the classes for whose benefit it was supposed to exist.

Proposed, nevertheless, by a group of representative Irishmen, the scheme for a democratically constituted Department of Agriculture passed smoothly into law as soon as the machinery for ascertaining public opinion on the matters at issue had been brought into existence. Mr. Gerald Balfour, the Chief Secretary, was engaged at the time upon his measure for the extension of Local Government to Ireland. This measure became law in 1898, and the Department Act in 1899.[17] Under that Act, the duty was laid upon each of the new County Councils of electing two members to serve upon a Consultative Council of Agriculture, to which a minority of nominated members was added, and this Council in its turn elects two-thirds of the members of an Agricultural Board, and supplies

[17] Agriculture and Technical Instruction Act (Ireland) 1899.

four representatives to a Board of Technical Instruction, which, like the Council and the Agricultural Board, has a predominantly popular character.*

At the summit stands the Minister, or Vice-President, as he is called (for in accordance with ancient custom, the Chief Secretary is nominally in supreme control of this as of all other Irish Departments), and a large and efficient staff of permanent officials. He and his staff have a large centralized authority, but this authority is subject to a constitutional check in the shape of a veto wielded by the Boards over the expenditure of the Endowment Fund. What is more important, policy tends to be shaped in accordance with popular views by the existence of the Council and the Boards.

Here, then, is the germ of responsible government. At first sight a critic might exclaim: 'Why, here is democracy pushed to a point unknown even in Great Britain, where Government Departments are wholly independent of Local Councils.' That is in a limited sense true, and it is quite arguable that British Departments would be the better for an infusion of local control. But we must not be misled by a false analogy. Great Britain reaches the Irish ideal by other means. Her departmental Ministers are directly responsible to a predominantly British House of Commons where a hostile vote can at any moment eject them from office.† There is no Irish Parliament, nor any kind of predominantly Irish body which is vested with the same power. The Vice-President of the Irish Department of Agriculture, an institution concerned exclusively with Irish affairs, whether he sits in the House of Commons or not (and for two years Mr. T. W. Russell had not a seat at Westminster),[18] could not be ejected from office even by a unanimous vote of Irish Members of the House,

[18] Thomas Wallace Russell (1841–1920) was a Liberal MP for Tyrone who stood as a Liberal Unionist after 1886. Between 1895 and 1900 he was Parliamentary Secretary to the Local Government Board under the Conservatives.

* *Council of Agriculture:* 68 members elected by County Councils; 34 appointed by the Department from the various provinces. Total 102. *Board of Agriculture:* 8 members elected by Council of Agriculture; 4 appointed by the Department. Total 12. *Board of Technical Instruction:* 10 members appointed by County Boroughs; 4 elected by Council of Agriculture; 6 appointed by the various Government Departments; 1 by a joint Committee of Dublin District Councils. Total 21.

† I am not forgetting Scotland. Her few local departments are theoretically, but not practically, at the mercy of English votes and influence. Scotch opinion, broadly speaking, governs Scotch affairs. Precisely to the extent to which it does not so govern them, is a demand for Home Rule likely to grow.

with the moral backing of a unanimous Irish people.* That is one of the anomalous results of the Union, and it was a recognition, though rather a confused one, of this anomaly, that inspired the ingenious compromise invented by the Recess Committee for introducing an element of popular control. But what a light the compromise throws on the anomaly which evoked it! Is it common sense to make these elaborate arrangements for promoting an Irish Department on an Irish popular basis while recoiling in terror from the prospect of crowning them with a Minister responsible to an Irish Parliament? The consequence is that even in this solitary example of an Irish Department under semi-popular control we see the subtle taint of Crown Colony Government. Popular opinion, acting indirectly, first through the Council and then through the Boards, can legally paralyze the Department by declining to appropriate money in the way it prescribes, while possessing no legal power to enforce a different policy or change the personnel of administration. This is only an object-lesson. I hasten to add that such a paralysis has never taken place, though some acrimonious controversy, natural enough under the anomalous state of things, has arisen over the office of Vice-President. There is now only one means by which Irish opinion can, if it be so disposed, displace the holder of the office, and that is a thoroughly unreliable and unhealthy means, namely, through pressure brought to bear by one or other of the Irish Parliamentary parties upon a newly elected British Ministry.† But why in the world should the British party pendulum determine an important Irish matter like this? Why, *a fortiori*, should it determine the appointment to the office of Chief Secretary, the irresponsible Prime Minister,

* Even the Recess Committee (and we cannot wonder) but dimly grasped the constitutional position when they laid stress on the necessity for an Agricultural Minister 'directly responsible to Parliament'. Logically, they should have first recommended the establishment of an Irish Parliament to which the Minister should be responsible. To make him responsible to the House of Commons was absurd; and a Departmental Committee of 1907 has, in fact, recommended that the Vice-President should not have a seat in Parliament, but should remain in his proper place, Ireland. Meanwhile, the original mistake has caused friction and controversy. Soon after the Liberal Ministry took office in 1906, Sir Horace Plunkett, the first Vice-President, as a Unionist, was replaced by Mr. T. W. Russell, a Home Ruler. [*Editorial note:* Russell was in fact against home rule.] On the assumption that such an Office was Parliamentary, its holder standing or falling with the British Ministry of the day, the step was quite justifiable, and even necessary. On the opposite assumption, confirmed by the Departmental Committee, the step was unjustifiable, that is, on the theory of the Union. An Irish Parliament alone should have the power of displacing Irish Ministers.

† See footnote, p. 159. *Editorial note:* this refers to the immediately preceding footnote.

or, rather the autocrat of Ireland? It is the *reductio ad absurdum* of the Union.

The Department commands a large measure of confidence. It would command far greater confidence if it were responsible to an Irish Parliament; but Irishmen are sensible enough to perceive that as long as the Union lasts, everyone is interested in making the existing system work smoothly and well. The general policy as laid down in the first instance, by the first Vice-President, Sir Horace Plunkett, has been sound and wise;* to proceed slowly, while building up a staff of trained instructors, inspectors, organizers; to devote money and labour mainly to education, both industrial and agricultural, and to evoke self-reliance and initiative in the people by, so far as possible, spending money locally only where a local contribution is raised and a local scheme prepared. The last aim met with a fine response. Every County Council in Ireland raises a rate, and has a scheme for agricultural and technical instruction. I can only enumerate some of the multifarious functions which the Department evolved for itself or took over from various other unrelated Boards and concentrated under single control. It gives instruction in agriculture and rural domestic economy (horticulture, butter-making, bee-keeping, poultry-keeping, etc.) through schools, colleges, or agricultural stations under its own direction, through private schools for both sexes, and through an extensive system of itinerant courses conducted (in 1909) by 128 trained instructors. It gives premiums for the breeding of horses, cattle, asses, poultry, swine. It conducts original research, it experiments in crops, and, among other things, is slowly resuscitating the depressed industry of flax-growing, and starting a wholly new industry in the southern counties, that of early potatoes. It sprays potatoes, prescribes for the diseases of trees, crops, and stock, advises on manures and feeding-stuffs, teaches forestry, and gives scholarships at various colleges for proficiency in agricultural science. On the side of Technical Instruction it teaches and encourages all manner of small industries, such as lace-making. It superintends all technical instruction in secondary schools, and organizes and subsidizes similar instruction in a multitude of different subjects under schemes prepared by local authorities, while at the same time carrying on an important and extensive system of training teachers. It also superintends sea-fisheries and improves harbours.

* 'Organization and Policy of the Department', Official Pamphlet.

The material results have been great; the moral results perhaps even greater. Just as we should expect, wherever education goes, and wherever men work together for economic improvement, unnatural antagonisms of race and religion tend to disappear. This is not the result of any direct influence wielded by the Department, which never finds it necessary to lecture people on the duty of mutual tolerance; it is the result of common sense and a small experience in Home Rule. High officials of the Department have informed me that their work, for all intents and purposes, is unhampered by local religious prejudices. A spirit of keen and wholesome rivalry permeates the people. County and Borough Committees in districts almost wholly Roman Catholic, with large powers of patronage, almost invariably appoint the best men, regardless of creed and local influence. Anyone who wishes to gain a glimpse of the real Belfast of the present and the future, as distinguished from the ugly, bigoted caricature of a great city which some even of its own citizens perversely insist on displaying to their English friends, a Belfast as tolerant and generous as it is energetic and progressive, should visit the magnificent Municipal Technical Institute, where 6,000 boys and girls, Roman Catholic and Protestant, mix together on equal terms, and derive the same benefit from an extraordinary variety of educational courses in a building furnished with lecture-rooms, laboratories, experimental plant, and gymnasia, of a perfection hardly to be surpassed in any city of the United Kingdom.

Here is something grand and fruitful accomplished in eleven years, and it is the outcome, be it remembered, of original, constructive thought devoted by Irishmen to the needs of their own country.

Let us also remember that it represents the application of State-aid to economic development. But with the utmost caution, and the utmost efforts to elicit self-help, one may go too far in the direction of State-aid, and even in this sphere it is by no means certain that Ireland is free from danger. Let us pass to another movement whose essence is self-help: I mean the movement for Agricultural Co-operation. Here again Sir Horace Plunkett was the originator. Indeed, with him and his able associates and advisers, of whom Lord Monteagle and Mr. R. A. Anderson, the Secretary of the I.A.O.S., were the first, the twin aims of self-help and State-aid were combined as they should be, in one big, harmonious policy.[19] Self-help must, indeed, they held, be antecedent to, and

[19] The acronym refers to the Irish Agricultural Organisation Society, which organised a system of agricultural cooperativism including shared credit facilities.

preparatory for, State-aid. The position confronting them was that half a million unorganized tenant farmers, for the most part cultivating excessively small holdings, and just beginning to emerge after generations of agrarian war from an economic serfdom, were face to face with the competition of highly organized European countries, and of vast and rapidly developing territories of North and South America. It was as far back as 1889 that the first propaganda was begun, and in 1894, a year before the Recess Committee met, the Irish Agricultural Organization Society was formed. By unwearied pains and patience, seemingly hopeless obstacles had been overcome, apathy, ignorance, and often contemptuous opposition from men of both political parties. For, with that ruinous pessimism always endemic in countries not politically free, and exactly paralleled in the Canada described by the Durham Report of 1839, extremists were inclined to suspect any movement which drew recruits from both political camps.[20] Nevertheless, the island is now covered with a network of 886 co-operative societies, creameries, agricultural societies (for selling implements, foodstuffs, etc.), credit banks, poultry societies, and other miscellaneous organizations. The total membership is nearly 100,000, the total turnover nearly two and a half millions.* Nearly half the butter exported from Ireland is made in the 392 co-operative creameries, and at the other end of the scale extraordinarily valuable work is done by the

[20] Lord Durham's Report on the Affairs of North America recommended the introduction of responsible government into Upper and Lower Canada and the fusion of both territories into a single province.

* Statistics of the Irish Agricultural Organization Movement to December 31, 1909, with Number of Societies in Existence on December 31, 1910 (supplied by the I.A.O.S.):

Description.	Number of Societies. 1910.	Number of Societies. 1909.	Membership.	Paid-up Shares.	Loan Capital.	Turnover.
Creameries	392	380	44,213	138,354	111,365	1,841,400
Agricultural	169	155	16,050	6,253	40,326	112,222
Credit	237	234	18,422	–	56,469	57,641
Poultry	18	18	6,152	2,292	4,026	64,342
Industries	21	21	1,375	1,267	1,450	7,666
Miscellaneous	37	15	4,633	15,015	2,864	48,987
Flax	9	9	589	482	5,796	2,286
Federations	3	3	227	6,753	6,360	259,925
	886	835	91,661	170,416	228,656	2,394,469

237 agricultural credit banks, which supply small loans, averaging only £4 apiece, for strictly productive purposes on a system of mutual credit.

Moral and material regeneration go together. The aim is to build up a new rural civilization, to put life, heart, and hope into the monotony of country life and unite all classes in the strong bonds of sympathy and interest: a splendid ideal, applicable not to Ireland alone, but to all countries, and Ireland may truly be said to be pointing the way to many another country, Great Britain included.

The Co-operative movement attracts the most intelligent and progressive elements of the rural population. Strictly non-political itself, it unites creeds and parties. It is as strong in predominantly Roman Catholic districts as in predominantly Protestant districts, strongest of all in Catholic Wexford. Probably two-thirds or more of the co-operators are Home Rulers, but that only accidentally reflects the distribution of Irish parties. On the local committees political animus is unknown. The governing body contains members, lay and clerical, of all shades of opinion. Step into Plunkett House, that hospitable headquarters of the Organization Society, and if you have been nurtured in legends about inextinguishable class and creed antipathies, which are supposed to render Home Rule impossible and the eternal 'umpirage' of Great Britain inevitable, you will soon learn to marvel that anyone can be found to propagate them. Here, just because men are working together in a practical, self-contained, home-ruled organization for the good of the whole country, you will find liberality, open-mindedness, brotherhood, and keen, intelligent patriotism from Ulsterman and Southerners alike. The atmosphere is not political. But you will come away with a sense of the absurdity, of the insolence, of saying that a country which can produce and conduct fine movements like this is *unfit* for self-government. I should add a word about a new organization which only came into being this year, and which also has its home at Plunkett House, the United Irishwomen, whose aim, in their own words, is to 'unite Irishwomen for the social and economic advantage of Ireland'.[21] 'They intend to organize the women of all classes in every rural district in Ireland for social service. These bodies will discuss, and, if need be, take action upon any and every matter which concerns the welfare of society in their several localities. So far as women's knowledge

[21] The movement was formed by Anita Lett and Ellice Pilkington. It promoted teaching, home-care, arts and crafts and even sports to rural housewives, and encouraged women to take a greater role in public and intellectual life.

and influence will avail, they will strive for a higher standard of material comfort and physical well-being in the country home, a more advanced agricultural economy, and a social existence a little more in harmony with the intellect and temperament of our people.' Anyone who wants to understand something of the spirit of the new self-reliant Ireland which is springing up to-day should read the thrilling little pamphlet (I cannot describe it otherwise) from which I quote these words, and which introduced the United Irishwomen to the world, with its preface by Father T. A. Finlay, and its essays by Mrs. Ellice Pilkington, Sir Horace Plunkett, and Mr. George W. Russell, better known as 'Æ', poet, painter, and Editor of the Co-operative weekly, the *Irish Homestead*.[22] Nor can I leave this part of my subject without referring to that amazing little journal.[23] No other newspaper in the world that I know of bears upon it so deep an impress of genius. There are no 'politics', in the Irish sense, in it. It would be impossible to infer from its pages how the Editor voted. What fascinates the reader is the shrewd and witty analysis of Irish problems, the high range of vision which exposes the shortcomings and reveals the illimitable possibilities of a regenerated Ireland and the ceaseless and implacable war waged by the Editor upon all pettiness, melancholy, and pessimism.

What the Agricultural Organization Society is doing for agriculture the Industrial Development Associations, formed only in quite recent years, are doing, in a different way, for the encouragement of Irish industries. The Associations of Belfast, Cork, and other cities work in harmony, and meet in an annual All-Ireland Industrial Conference. Their effort is to secure the concentration of Irish brains and capital on Irish industrial questions, to promote the sale of Irish goods, both in Ireland, Great Britain, and foreign countries, and to protect these goods against piracy and illicit competition.* Here again co-operation for Irish welfare brings together the creeds and races, and tends to extinguish old bigotries and antipathies. Here again the truth is recognized that Ireland is a dis-

[22] The pamphlet, *The United Irishwomen: Their Work, Place and Ideals*, jointly authored by Pilkington, Plunkett, and Russell, appeared in 1911.

[23] *The Irish Homestead* was a weekly publication founded by Horace Plunkett in 1895. The paper's first editor was Thomas A. Finlay (1848–1940). George Russell (1867–1935) became editor in 1905.

* An Irish Trademark has been secured, and has proved of great value. 'Irish Weeks', for the furtherance of the sale of Irish products, are held. The organ of the Association is the *Irish Industrial Journal*, published weekly in Dublin.

tinct economic entity whose conditions and needs demand special study from her citizens. In a country of which that basal truth is recognized it would seem inexplicable that Protestants and Catholics who meet in committee-rooms and on platforms to promote, outside Parliament, the common interests of Ireland, should not unite as one man to demand an Irish Legislature in which to focus those interests and make them the subjects of direct legislative enactment, free both from the paternal and the coercive interference of a country differently situated, and absorbed in its own affairs.

I pass from the agricultural and industrial movements to another powerful factor in the reconstruction of Ireland, namely, the Gaelic League, founded in 1893, whose success under the Presidency of Dr. Douglas Hyde in reviving the old national language, culture, and amusements, is attracting the attention of the world.[24] Fortunately the League encountered some ridicule at the outset and prospered proportionately. Some of its work is not above criticism, but few persons – and none who have the least knowledge of such intellectual revivals elsewhere – now care to laugh at it. The League is non-political and non-sectarian. Strange, is it not, that such a movement should have to emphasize the fact? Strange paradox that in a country which is being re-born into a consciousness of its own individuality, which is regaining its own pride and self-respect, recovering its lost literature and culture, and vibrating to that 'iron string, Trust thyself', the conflict for self-government, that elementary symbol of self-trust, should still retain enough intestinal bitterness to compel men to label national movements as non-political and non-sectarian! It would be idle, of course, to pretend that this national movement, like all others in Ireland, does not strengthen, especially among the younger generation, which grows increasingly Nationalist, the sentiment for Home Rule. If it did not, we should indeed be in the presence of something miraculously abnormal.

Meanwhile the Celtic revival does visible good. The language is no longer a fad; it is an envied accomplishment, a mark of distinction and education. Wherever it goes, North and South, it obliterates race and creed distinctions, and all the terrible memories associated with them. There are Ulstermen of Saxon or Scottish stock in whom the fascination of Irish art and literature has extirpated every trace of Orangeism and all

[24] The Gaelic League was founded by Douglas Hyde, who served as its first president, and promoted the use of the Irish language in everyday life.

implied in it. The language revivifies traditions, as beautiful as they are glorious, of an Ireland full of high passions and stormy domestic feuds, but united in sentiment, breeding warriors, poets, lawgivers, saints, and fertilizing Europe with her missionary genius. However far those times are, however grim and pitiful the havoc wrought by the race war, it is nevertheless a fact for thinkers and statesmen to ponder over, not a phantasy to sneer at, that Celtic Ireland lives. Anglicization has failed, not because Celts cannot appreciate the noblest manifestations of English genius in art, letters, science, war, colonization, but because to repress their own culture and nationality is at the same time to repress their power of appreciation and assimilation.[25] Until comparatively recent times, it was only the worst of English literature and music, the cheapest newspaper twaddle, the inanest music-hall songs, which penetrated beyond a limited circle of culture into the life of the country. The revolt against this sterilizing and belittling side of anglicization is strong and healthy. It affects all classes. Farmers, labourers, small tradesmen, who had never conceived the idea of learning for learning's sake, and who had grown up, thanks to the national system of education, in all but complete ignorance of their own country's history and literature, spend time on reading and study and in the practice of the old indigenous dances and music, which was formerly wasted in idleness or dissipation. Temperance and social harmony are irresistibly forwarded. Nor is it a question of a few able men imposing their will on the many, or of an artificial, State-aided process. Though the language has obtained a footing in more than a third of the State schools and in the National University,[*] the motive force behind it comes from the people themselves. In the country district, with which I am best acquainted, boys and girls from very poor families are clubbing together to pay instructors in the Irish language and dances, and the same thing is going on all over Ireland.

The brilliant modern school of poets and playwrights who, steeped in the old Celtic thought and culture, have found for it such an exquisite vehicle in the English tongue, speak for themselves and are winning their

[25] Douglas Hyde delivered a lecture in 1892 on 'The Necessity for De-Anglicising Ireland' to the Irish National Literary Society.

[*] On December 31, 1909, Irish was taught as an 'extra subject' in 3,006 primary schools out of 8,401, and in 161 schools in Irish-speaking districts in the West a bi-lingual programme of instruction was in force (Report of Committee of National Education, 1910). Forty-six thousand pupils passed the test of the inspectors. Irish in 1910 was made a compulsory subject for matriculation at the National University.

own way to renown.[26] The only criticism I venture to make is that some of them are too much inclined to look backward instead of forward, to idealize the far past rather than to illuminate the future, and to delineate the deformities of national character produced by ages of repression, rather than to aid in conjuring into being a virile, normal nation.

The name of the last movement to be referred to sums up all the others, Sinn Féin.[27] Unlike the others, it had a purely political origin, and for that reason, probably, never made the same progress. Yet the explanation is simple. In pursuance of the general purpose of inspiring Irishmen to rely on themselves for their own salvation, economic and spiritual, Sinn Féiners, like John Mitchel and others in the past,[28] and like the Hungarian patriots,[29] attacked, with much point and satire, the whole policy of constitutional and Parliamentary agitation for Home Rule. The policy, they said, had failed for half a century; it was not only negative and barren, but positively harmful. Nationalists should refuse to send Members to Westminster and abide by the consequences. Sensibly enough, most Irishmen, while recognizing that there was an element of indisputable and valuable truth in this bold diagnosis, decided that it was premature to adopt the prescription. Public opinion in Britain was slowly changing, and confidence existed that this opinion would be finally converted. If the Sinn Féin alternative meant anything at all, it meant complete separation, which Ireland does not want, and a final abandonment of constitutional methods. If another Home Rule Bill were to fail, Sinn Féin would undoubtedly redouble its strength. Its ideas are sane and sound. They are at bottom exactly the ideas which actuate every progressive and spirited community, and which in Ireland animate the Industrial Development Associations, the Co-operative movement, the thirst for technical instruction, the Gaelic League, the literary revival, and the work of the

[26] The Irish Literary Revival, sometimes dubbed the Celtic Twilight, is associated with the establishment in 1892 of the Irish Literary Society in London and the National Literary Society in Dublin. W. B. Yeats played a prominent role in both organisations. Along with Lady Gregory and Edward Martyn, he also founded the Irish Literary Theatre in 1897.

[27] Founded in 1905 by Arthur Griffith, it became a political party in 1907 under the name, the Sinn Féin League.

[28] John Mitchel (1815–75) was an Irish nationalist author and MP who wrote for radical nationalist papers and spent time in Tasmania (as a prisoner) and America (as a pro-slavery Confederate and Irish activist). In *The Last Conquest of Ireland (Perhaps)*, published in 1866, he wrote a popular and influential scathing attack on British governance in Ireland during the 1840s famine.

[29] A reference to the followers of Lajos Batthyány (1807–49), who insisted on Hungary's independence from Austria. He was subsequently executed.

only truly Irish organ of government, the Department of Agriculture and Technical Instruction.

Now, where do we stand? Are the phenomena I have reviewed arguments for Home Rule or against Home Rule? Do they tend to show that Ireland is 'fitter' now for Home Rule, or that she manages very well without Home Rule? These are superfluous questions. They are never asked save of countries obviously designed to govern themselves and obstinately denied the right. Who would say now of Canada or Australia that they ought to have solved their economic, agrarian, and religious problems and have evolved an indigenous literature before they were declared fit for Home Rule, or – still more unreasonable proposition – that their strenuous efforts after self-help and internal harmony in the teeth of political disabilities proved, in so far as they were successful, that external government was a success?

Yet these questions were, as a fact, asked of the Colonies, as they are asked of Ireland. And misgovernment increased, and passions rose, and blood flowed, while, in the guise of dispassionate psychologists, a great many narrow, egotistical, and bullying people at home propounded these arid conundrums. Where is our common sense? The Irish phenomena I have described arise in spite of the absence of Home Rule, and the denial of Home Rule sets an absolute and final bar to progress beyond a certain point.

That is certain; one cannot live in Ireland with one's eyes and ears open without realizing it. All social and economic effort, successful as it is up to a certain point, and strong as its tendency is to promote nationalist feeling of the noblest kind, has to struggle desperately against the benumbing influence of abstract 'politics'. Suspicion comes from both sides. Both Unionists and Nationalists, for example, at one time or another have looked askance on the Co-operative movement and on the Department of Agriculture as being too Nationalist or too Unionist in tendency. Unionists caused Sir Horace Plunkett to lose his seat in Parliament in 1905; and Nationalists, though with some constitutional justification, secured his removal from office in 1907. At this moment there is friction and suspicion in this particular matter which seems to the impartial observer to be artificial, and which would not exist, or would be transmuted into something perfectly harmless, and probably highly beneficial, were there any normal political life in Ireland and a central organ of public opinion. As long as Great Britain insists, to her own infinite inconvenience, upon deciding Irish questions by party majorities fluctuating from Toryism to Radicalism, and thereby compels Ireland to send parties to Westminster whose *raison d'être* is, not to represent crystallized Irish opinion on Irish domestic questions – that is at present wholly impossible – but to assert or deny the fundamental right for Ireland to settle her own domestic questions, so long will these dislocations continue, to the grave prejudice of Ireland and the deep discredit of Great Britain.

Ireland, like Canada in 1838, has no organic national life.[30] Apart from the abstract but paramount question of Home Rule, there are no formed political principles or parties. Such parties as there are have no relation to the economic life of the country, and all interests suffer daily in consequence. In a normal country you would find urban and agricultural interests distinctly represented, but not in Ireland. We should expect to find clear-cut opinions on Tariff Reform and Free Trade. No such opinions exist. On the other hand, agreement on important industrial and agricultural questions finds not the smallest reflection in Parliamentary representation. Education, and other latent issues of burning importance, are not political issues. A Budget may cause almost universal dissatisfaction, but it goes through, and the amazing thing is that Unionists complain of its going through! Most of the Parliamentary elections are uncontested, though everybody knows that a dozen questions would set up a salutary ferment of opinion if they were not stifled by the refusal of Home Rule. The Protestant tenant-farmers of Ulster have identical interests with those of other Provinces, and have profited largely by the legislation extorted by Nationalists; but for the most part, though by no means wholly, they vote Unionist. The two great towns, Dublin and Belfast, are divided by the most irrational antagonism. Labourers, both rural and urban, have distinct and important interests; the rural labourers have no spokesman, the town-labourers only one. It was admitted to me by a Unionist organizer in Belfast that that city, but for the Home Rule issue, would probably return four labour members. Nor have parties any close relation to the distribution of wealth. In the matter of incomes the prosperous traders of Cork, Limerick, and Waterford are in the same case as regards taxation with those of Londonderry and Belfast. Publicans are Unionists in England, Nationalists in Ireland, both in

30 Two insurrections took place in Canada during 1837–8 due to political frustrations with governance.

Ulster and elsewhere. Before the Home Rule issue was raised, Ulster was largely Liberal. Ulster Liberalism is almost dead.[31] Extreme Socialism may almost be said to be non-existent in Ireland, yet Ireland is not only administered on semi-collectivist principles, but continually runs the risk of being involved in legislation of a Socialistic kind, which, rightly or wrongly, she heartily dislikes.

As for the landed aristocracy all over Ireland, their historic alliance with the intensely democratic tenant-farmers of one small corner of Ireland, North-East Ulster, against those of all the rest, presented strange enough features in the past, and is now becoming artificial in the highest degree. Thanks to Land Purchase, no landed aristocracy in the world now has a better chance of throwing its wealth and intelligence into public life for the good of the whole country, of thinking out problems, of conciliating factions, and of ennobling public life. The landlord who has sold his land is a free man, far freer than the English landlord from misgivings caused by divergency of interest. The opportunity is still there. Will they profit by it? One thing is essential: they must become Nationalists, and in breathing that phrase, one is conscious of all the misleading implications and the bitter historical feuds it suggests. Yet a small but powerful group of landlords is already leading the way. And the way, even before Home Rule, in reality is so simple. I speak from close observation. If a man is a good man, and worthy to represent a constituency, he has only to declare his belief that he thinks that he and his own fellow-citizens are fit to govern themselves. Irishmen, especially in Roman Catholic districts, and, indeed, as an indirect result of Catholicism, have never lost their belief in aristocracy. When a landlord, or any other Protestant, comes forward as a Nationalist, he is welcomed. His religion, whatever it may be, does not count. Parnell and Smith O'Brien were Protestant landlords.[32] Many of the most trusted popular leaders, Tone, Robert Emmet, John Mitchel, Isaac Butt, and others in the past have been Protestants.[33] Ten Members of the present Nationalist party are Protestants. The Home Rule issue would have lost some of its bitterness if a Unionist electorate had ever elected a Catholic to Parliament.

[31] In the 1880 UK general election, the Liberal Party won fifteen seats across Ireland, the Conservatives won twenty-three, while the Home Rule Party won sixty-three.

[32] William Smith O'Brien (1803–64).

[33] Wolfe Tone (1763–98), Robert Emmet (1778–1803), John Mitchel (1815–75), Isaac Butt (1813–79).

Still, it is unfortunately true that the great bulk of the landlords and ex-landlords stand aloof from the Home Rule movement. The collateral result is that far too many of them instinctively stand aloof even from those purely economic and intellectual movements which tend to make a living united Ireland out of chaos. The national loss is heavy; the waste of talent and of driving-power, for Ireland needs driving-power from her leisured and cultured classes, is melancholy to contemplate.

Everywhere one sees waste of talent in Ireland. The land abounds in men with ideas and potentialities waiting for those normal chances of development which self-governed countries provide. Much of this good material is crushed under unnatural political tyrannies caused by ceaseless agitation for and against an abstract aim which should have been satisfied long ago, so that the energies it absorbed might have been diverted into practical channels. There is too much moral cowardice, too little bold, independent thought and action. Nobody knows what Ireland really is, and of what she is capable. Nobody can know until she has responsibility for her own fate.

Local government, where popular opinion is nominally free, suffers from the absence of free central government. Is it not on the face of it preposterous to give complete powers of local taxation and administration to a country while withholding from it, as unsafe and improper, central co-ordinating control? For any country but Ireland – at any rate, in the British self-governing Colonies and the United States – such a policy would be regarded as crazy. Still more unreasonable is it to complain that local authorities under such a system spend part of the energy which should be devoted wholly to local affairs in abstract politics. I forbear from engaging in the statistical war over the numbers of Catholics and Protestants employed and elected by local bodies. One must remember, what Unionists sometimes forget, that Ireland is, broadly speaking, a Roman Catholic country, and that until thirteen years ago local administration and patronage were almost exclusively in Protestant hands. We should naturally expect a marked change; but, with that reminder, I prefer to appeal to the reader's common sense. Deny national Home Rule, and give local Home Rule. What would one expect to happen? What would have happened in any Colony? What would Mr. Arthur Balfour himself have prophesied with certainty in the case of any other country but Ireland? Why, this, that each little local body would become an outlet for suppressed agitation, and that national or anti-national politics, not urgent local necessities, would enter into local elections and influence the composition of local bodies. And what would be the further consequence? That numbers of the best local men would stand aloof or be rejected, and that favouritism would find a congenial soil.

In point of fact, Irish local authorities, under the circumstances, are wonderfully free from these evils, only another proof of the resilience and vitality of the country under persistent mismanagement. On the whole they bear comparison with British local authorities in thrift, purity, and efficiency. None of them has ever yet had a scandal like that of Poplar. All of them have shown sense and spirit in forwarding sanitation and technical education. They vary widely, of course, the lowest units in the scale being the least efficient, as in England. County Councils, for example, are better than Rural District Councils. On the other hand, Dublin Corporation, though not so bad as it is sometimes painted, occasionally sets a very bad example. The standard of efficiency is higher in the Protestant north than in the Catholic south, the standard of religious toleration lower. But at bottom it is not a question of theology, as every well-informed person knows, but a question of politics. The same causes that keep the landed gentry out of Parliament keep them, although not to the same degree, out of local politics. Sometimes this is their own fault, for declining to take part in them; for many of the Protestant upper class in Nationalist districts obtain election in spite of being Unionists. Tolerance is slowly growing in Nationalist, though not, it is to be feared, in Unionist, districts; again a quite intelligible fact.* But when all is said and done, it is an undeniable fact that Irish local authorities, especially those in the poverty-stricken west, where all social activities are more retrograde than elsewhere, are capable of great improvement, and that improvement can come only by allowing them to concentrate on local affairs, and obtain the co-operation of all classes and religions. The very existence of a central Government of which Irishmen were proud would influence the tone and standard of all minor authorities to the bottom of the scale.

Meanwhile, obvious and urgent problems, which no Parliament but an Irish Parliament can deal with, cry aloud for settlement. The Poor Law, railways, arterial drainage, afforestation, are questions which I need only refer to by name, confining myself to the greater issues. Education, primary and intermediate, is perhaps the greatest. The present system

* The election by Nationalist votes of Lord Ashtown, a militant Unionist peer of the most uncompromising type, in the spring of 1911 to one of the Galway District Councils is a good recent example of this tendency.

is almost universally condemned, and its bad results are recognized. It has got to be reformed. By no possibility can it be reformed so long as the Union lasts, not only because the Boards, National and Intermediate, which control education, are composed of un-elected amateurs, but because there is no means of finding out what the national opinion is as to the course reform is to take. Meanwhile the children and the country suffer. The Intermediate Board is a purely examining and prize-giving body, and its system by general agreement is imperfect. In the National or Primary schools the percentage of average daily attendance (71.1 per cent.), though slowly improving, is still very bad.* Many of the schoolhouses are, in the words of the Commissioners, 'mere hovels', unsanitary, leaky, ill-ventilated. The distribution of schools and funds is chaotic and wasteful. Out of 8,401 schools (in 1909–10)† nearly two hundred have an average daily attendance of less than fifteen pupils. In 1730 the number is less than thirty, and it is not only in sparsely inhabited country districts, but in big towns, that the distribution is bad. The power of the Commissioners to stop the creation of unduly small schools, and even semi-bogus establishments which come into being in the great cities, is imperfect. Another example of the curious mixture of anarchy and despotism that the system of Irish government presents may be seen in the Annual Report of the Commissioners. With a mutinous audacity which would be laughable, if the case were one for laughing, the Commissioners openly rail at the Treasury for the parsimony of its grants, and, in order to stir its compassion, paint the condition of Irish education in black colours. Imagine the various Departmental Ministers in Great Britain publicly attacking in their Annual Reports the Cabinet of which they were members! The Treasury, needless to say, is not to blame. It pays out of the common Imperial purse all but a negligible fraction of the cost of primary education in Ireland. Nothing is raised by rates, and only £141,096 (in 1909–10) from voluntary and local sources, as compared with £1,688,547 from State grants. The Treasury has no guarantee that this money is well spent; on the contrary, it knows from the Reports of the Commissioners themselves that a great deal of it is very badly spent. The business is a comic opera, but it has a tragic significance for Ireland. Primary education is so bad that a great number of the pupils are absolutely unfit to receive the expensive and excellent technical instruction organized by the

* Permissive powers exist for County Councils to enforce compulsory attendance.

† Including 342 convent, 54 monastery, 125 workhouse, and 71 model schools.

Department of Agriculture and Technical Instruction, and contributed to by the ratepayers. The Belfast Technical Institute, for example, has to go outside its proper functions, and spend from its too small stock in providing introductory courses in elementary subjects, so as to equip children for the reception of higher knowledge.* All over the country the complaint is the same. No machinery whatever exists for co-ordinating primary, secondary, technical, and University education, and apportioning funds in an economical and profitable manner.

Religion is the immediate cause of the trouble; absence of popular control the fundamental cause. The national system of primary education, designed originally in 1831 to be undenominational, has become rigidly denominational. Out of 8,401 primary schools, 2,461 only are attended by both Protestants and Roman Catholics. The rest are of an exclusively sectarian character. Even the Protestants do not combine. The Church of Ireland, the Presbyterians, the Methodists, and other smaller denominations, frequently have small separate schools in the same parish. The management (save in the model schools, which are attended only by Protestants) is exclusively sectarian, the local clergyman, Roman Catholic, Church of Ireland, or Nonconformist having almost autocratic control over the school.

This education question has got to be thrashed out by a Home Ruled Ireland, and the sooner the better. After Home Rule the Treasury grant will stop, and Ireland will have to raise and apportion the funds herself, and set her house in order. At whatever sacrifice of religious scruples, and, it is needless to add that to the Roman Catholic hierarchy the sacrifice will be the greatest, the Irish people must control and finance its schools, whether through a central department alone, or through local authorities as well. There is no reason in the world why a compromise should not be arrived at which would secure vastly increased efficiency and leave the teaching of denominational religion uninjured. Other countries, where the same religions exist side by side, have attained that compromise. Ireland will be judged by her success in attaining it.

Another important question is the treatment of the Congested Districts. More than a third of Ireland is now under the benevolent jurisdiction of a despotic Board.† So long as its funds are raised from general Imperial taxation, the inevitable tendency is to shirk the thorough dis-

* See 'Prospectus of the Municipal Technical Institute, Belfast', 1910–11, pp. 55 and 57–58. Reading, Grammar, and Simple Arithmetic are taught.

† See Report of the Congested Districts Board, 1909–11.

cussion of this grave subject, to lay the responsibility on Great Britain, to acquiesce in a policy of extreme paternalism, and to appeal for higher and higher doles from the Treasury. This cannot go on. Whoever, in the eyes of Divine Justice, was originally responsible for the condition of the submerged west, and for the ruin of the evicted tenants, Ireland, if she wants Home Rule, must shoulder the responsibility herself, and think out the whole question independently. The Congested Districts Board has done, and continues to do, good work in the purchase and resettlement of estates; but even in this sphere there are wide differences of opinion as to the proper methods and policy to be employed, especially with regard to the division of grasslands and the migration of landless men. Its other remedial work (part of which is now taken over by the Department of Agriculture under the Land Act of 1909), in encouraging fisheries, industries, and farm improvements out of State money, is open to criticism on the ground of its tendency to pauperize and weaken character. I do not care to pronounce on the controversy, though I think that there is much to be said for the view that money is best spent by encouraging agricultural co-operation. Many able and distinguished men have devoted their minds to the subject, but it is plain that Ireland as a whole has not thought, and cannot think, the matter out in a responsible spirit, and that the only way of reaching a truly Irish decision is through an Irish Parliament, which both raises and votes money for the purpose.* The reinstatement of evicted tenants teems with practical difficulties which can only be solved in the same way.[34] As long as Great Britain remains responsible, errors are liable to be made which one day may be deeply regretted.

The same observation applies to all future land legislation, not excepting Land Purchase, which I deal with fully in a later chapter.† That great department of administration must, for financial reasons, be worked in harmonious consultation with the British Government; but it ought to be controlled by Ireland, and a free and normal outlet given to criticisms like those emanating from Mr. William O'Brien, whatever the intrinsic value of these criticisms. Purchase itself settles nothing beyond the bare ownership of the land. It leaves the distribution and use of the land, except in

[34] The Evicted Tenants (Ireland) Act 1907 aimed to give purchasing rights to certain tenants who had been evicted from their holdings.

* See Report of Royal Commission on Congestion in Ireland (Cd. 4097); especially a Memorandum by Sir Horace Plunkett, published as a separate pamphlet by the Department of Agriculture and Technical Instruction.

† See Chapter XIV. *Editorial note:* the chapter is on 'Land Purchase Finance'.

the 'resettled' districts, where it was, with a third or a quarter of the holdings so small as to be classed as 'uneconomic'. Ireland is not as yet awake to the possibilities of the silent revolution proceeding from the erection of a small peasant proprietorship. The sense of responsibility in these new proprietors will be quickened and the interests of the whole country forwarded by a National Parliament.

Temperance will never be tackled thoroughly but by an Irish Parliament. All Irishmen are ashamed in their hearts of the encouragement given to drunkenness by the still grossly excessive number of licensed houses, which in 1909 was 22,591, and of the National Drink Bill, which in the same year was £13,310,469,[*] or £3 11d. per head of a population not rich in this world's goods. Temperance is not really a party or a sectarian question. All the Churches make noble efforts to forward reform, and in a rationally governed Ireland reform would be considered on its merits. At present it is inextricably mixed up with Nationalist and anti-Nationalist politics, and with irrelevant questions of Imperial taxation.

The latest examples of the embarrassment into which Ireland without Home Rule is liable to drift from the absence of a formed public opinion and the means to give it effect, are the labour troubles and the National Insurance scheme.[35] There are signs that English labour is thrusting forward Irish labour in advance of its own will and in advance of general Irish opinion. In all labour questions Ireland's position as an agricultural country is totally different from that of Great Britain. The same legislation cannot be applicable to both. Ireland should frame her own. Under present conditions it is impossible to know the considered judgment of Ireland. There is certainly much opposition to Insurance, and if all Irishmen thoroughly realized that the scheme might complicate the finance of Home Rule and involve a greater financial dependence on Great Britain than exists even at present, they would study it with still more critical eyes,[†] as they would certainly have studied the Old Age Pensions scheme with more critical eyes.

[35] The scheme became the National Insurance Act (1911) whereby employers, the government, and workers made compulsory payments into health and unemployment insurance.

[*] Annual Report (1910) of the 'Irish Association for the Prevention of Intemperance'. The estimate is that of Dr. Dawson Burns. By the Licensing (Ireland) Act of 1902, the issue of any new licenses was prohibited.

[†] I write before the scheme has been fully discussed in Parliament.

Here I am led naturally to the great and all-embracing questions of Irish finance and expenditure, which lie behind all the topics already discussed and many others. The subject is far too important and interwoven with history to be dealt with otherwise than as an historical whole, and that course I propose to take in a later part of the book. It is enough to say that all the arguments for Home Rule are summed up in the fiscal argument. Every Irishman worth his salt ought to be ashamed and indignant at the present position.

The whole machinery of Irish Government, and the whole fiscal system under which Ireland lives, need to be thoroughly overhauled by Irishmen in their own interests, and in the interests of Great Britain. Among many other writers, Mr. Barry O'Brien, in his 'Dublin Castle and the Irish People', Lord Dunraven in 'The Outlook in Ireland', and Mr. G. F.-H. Berkeley in a paper contributed to 'Home Rule Problems', have lucidly and wittily described the wonderful collection of sixty-seven irresponsible and unrelated Boards nominated by the Chief Secretary, or Lord-Lieutenant, which, with the official services beneath them, constitute the colonial bureaucracy of Ireland; the extravagance of the judicial and other salaries, and the total lack of any central control worthy of the name.[36] By omitting a number of insignificant little bureaux, the figure 67, according to Mr. Berkeley's classification, may be reduced to 42, of which 26 are directly under Castle influence, and the rest either branches of British Departments or directly under the Treasury. In 1906, out of 1,611 principal official posts, 626 were obtained purely by nomination, and 766 by a qualifying examination only. In an able-bodied male population, which we may estimate at a million, there are reckoned to be about 60,000 persons employed by the State, or 1 in 18. If we add 180,000 Old Age Pensioners, we reach the figure of nearly a quarter of a million persons, out of a total population of under four and a half millions, dependent wholly or partially for their living on the State, exclusive of Army and Navy pensioners; again about 1 in 18. Four millions of money are paid in salaries or pensions to State employees, and two and three-quarter millions to Old Age Pensioners.

36 Richard Barry O'Brien (1847–1918) published *Dublin Castle and the Irish People* (London: K. Paul, Trench, Trübner, 1909); Lord Dunraven published *The Outlook for Ireland: The Case for Devolution and Conciliation* in 1897 (Dublin and London: Hodges, Figgis, & Co., John Murray, reissued in 1907); George Fitz-Hardinge Berkeley (1870–1955) contributed an essay on 'The Present System of Government in Ireland' to Basil Williams ed., *Home Rule Problems* (London: P. S. King & Son, 1911).

It is so easy to make fun about Irish administration that one has to be cautious not to mistake the nature or exaggerate the dimensions of the evil. The great defect is that the expenditure is not controlled by Ireland and has no relation to the revenue derived from Ireland. The Castle is not the odious institution that it was in the dark days of the land war;[37] but it is still a foreign, not an Irish institution, working, like the Government of the most dependent of Crown Colonies, in a world of its own, with autocratic powers, and immunity from all popular influence. Beyond the criticism that one religious denomination, the Church of Ireland, is rather unduly favoured in patronage, there is no personal complaint against the officials. They are as able, kindly, hard-working, and courteous as any other officials. Some of the principal posts are held by men of the highest distinction, who will be as necessary to the new Government as to the old. It is absolutely essential, but it will not be easy, to make substantial administrative economies at the outset, not only from the additional stress of novel work which will be thrown upon a Home Rule Government, but from the widespread claims of vested interests. It will require courageous statesmanship, backed by courageous public opinion, to overhaul a bureaucracy so old and extensive. Take the police, for example, the first and most urgent subject for reduction. Adding the Royal Irish Constabulary and the Dublin Metropolitan Police together,[38] we have a force of no less than 12,000 officers and men, a force twice as numerous in proportion to population as those of England and Wales, and costing the huge sum of a million and a half; and this in a country which now is unusually free from crime, and which at all times has been naturally less disposed to crime than any part of Great Britain. It is the forcible maintenance of bad economic conditions that has produced Irish crime in the past. Irishmen hotly resent that symbol of coercion, the swollen police force, which is as far removed from their own control as a foreign army of occupation. On the other hand, the force itself is composed of Irishmen, and is a considerable, though an unhealthy, economic factor in the life of the country. It performs some minor official duties outside the domain of justice; it is efficient, and its individual members are not unpopular. Reduction will be difficult. But drastic reduction, at least by a half, must

[37] Dublin Castle was the seat of British administration in Ireland from 1800 to 1922. The Land Wars (1879–82) were a period of rural agitation in mainly the west of Ireland.

[38] The Royal Irish Constabulary was Ireland's police force from 1822 to 1922. The Dublin Metropolitan Police was the police force for Dublin from 1836 to 1925.

eventually be brought about if Ireland is to hold up her head in the face of the world.

The difficulty will extend through all the ramifications of public expenditure. Ireland, through no fault of her own, against her persistent protests, has been retained in a position which is destructive to thrifty instincts. A rain of officials has produced an unhealthy thirst for the profits of officialdom. No one feels responsibility for the money spent for national purposes, because no one in Ireland is, in any real sense, responsible. There is no Irish Budget or Irish Exchequer to make a separate Irish Government logically defensible. The people are heavily taxed, but, rightly, they do not connect their taxes with the expenditure going on around them. On the contrary, their mental habit is to look to Great Britain as the source of grants, salaries, pensions.

And the worst of it is that they are now at the point of being financially dependent on Great Britain. After more than a century of Union finance, after contributing, all told, over three hundred and twenty millions of money to the Imperial purse over and above expenditure in Ireland, they have now ceased to contribute a penny, and are a little in debt. As we shall see, when I come to a closer examination of finance, the main factor in producing this result has been the Old Age Pensions. The application of the British scale, unmodified, to Ireland is the kind of blunder which the Union encourages. Ireland, where wages and the standard of living are far lower than in England, does not need pensions on so high a scale, and already suffers too much from benevolent paternalism. It was an unavoidable blunder, given a joint financial system, but it has gravely compromised Home Rule finance.

For acquiescing in this and similar grants, beyond the ascertained taxable resources of the country; for the general deficiency of public spirit and matured public opinion in Ireland; for the backwardness of education, temperance legislation, and other important reforms, the Irish Parliamentary parties cannot be held responsible. They are abnormal in their composition and aims, and, beyond a certain limited point, they are powerless, even if they had the will, to promote Irish policies. That is the pernicious result of an unsatisfied claim for self-government. It is the same everywhere else. While an agitation for self-government lasts, a country is stagnant, retrograde, or, like Ireland, progressive only by dint of extraordinary native exertions. Read the Durham report on the condition of the Canadas during the long agitation for Home Rule, and you will recognize the same state of things. The leaders of the agitation have to concentrate on the abstract and primary claim for Home Rule, and are reluctant to dissipate their energies on minor ends. Yet they, too, are liable to irrational and painful divisions, like that which divides Mr. O'Brien from Mr. Redmond; symptoms of irritation in the body politic, not of political sanity. They cannot prove their powers of constructive statesmanship, because they are not given the power to construct or the responsibility which evokes statesmanship. The anti-Home Rule partisans degenerate into violent but equally sincere upholders of a pure negation.

Many of the able men who belong to both the Irish parties will, it is to be hoped, soon be finding a far more fruitful and practical field for their abilities in a free Ireland. But the parties, as such, will disappear, on condition that the measure of Home Rule given to Ireland is adequate. On that point I shall have more to say later. If it is adequate, and Irish politicians are absorbed in vital Irish politics, the structure of the existing parties falls to pieces, to the immense advantage both of Ireland – including the Protestant sections of Ulster – and of Great Britain. At present both parties, divided normally by a gulf of sentiment, do combine for certain limited purposes of Irish legislation, but both are, in different degrees and ways, sterile. The policy of the Nationalist party has been positive in the past, because it wrung from Parliament the land legislation which saved a perishing society. It is essentially positive still in that it seeks Home Rule, which is the condition precedent to practical politics in Ireland. More, the party is independent, in a sense which can be applied to no other party in the United Kingdom. Its Members accept no offices or titles, the ordinary prizes of political life. But they themselves could not contend that they are truly representative of three-quarters of Ireland in any other sense than that they are Home Rulers. Half of the wit, brains, and eloquence of their best men runs to waste. Some of them are merely nominated by the party machine, to represent, not local needs, but a paramount principle which the electors insist rightly on setting above immediate local needs.

The purpose of the Irish Unionist party in the Commons is purely negative, to defeat Home Rule. It does not represent North-East Ulster, or any other fragment of Ireland, in any sense but that. It is passionately sentimental and absolutely unrepresentative of the practical, virile genius of Ulster industry. The Irish Unionist peers, in addition to voicing the same negative, are for the most part the spokesmen of a small minority of Irishmen in whom the long habit of upholding landlord interests has begun to outlive the need.

I have said little directly about the problem of modern Ulster, not because I underrate its importance, which is very great, but because I have some hope that my arguments up to this point may be perceived to have a strong, though indirect, bearing upon it.[*] The religious question I leave to others, with only these few observations. It is impossible to make out a historical case for the religious intolerance of Roman Catholics in Ireland, or a practical case for the likelihood of a Roman Catholic tyranny in the future. No attempt which can be described as even plausible has ever been made in either direction. The late Mr. Lecky, a Unionist historian, and one of the most eminent thinkers and writers of our time, has nobly vindicated Catholic Ireland, banishing both the theory and the fear into the domain of myth.[†]

He has shown, what, indeed, nobody denies, that, from the measures which provoked the Rebellion of 1641, through the Penal Code, to the middle of the nineteenth century, intolerance, inspired by supposed political necessities, and of a ferocity almost unequalled in history, came from the Protestant colonists.[39] In that brilliant little essay of his Nationalist youth, 'Clerical Influences' (1861), he described the sectarian animosity which was raging at that period as 'the direct and inevitable consequence of the Union', and wrote as follows: 'Much has been said of the terrific force with which it would rage were the Irish Parliament restored. We maintain, on the other hand, that no truth is more clearly stamped upon the page of history, and more distinctly deducible from the constitution of the human mind, than that a national feeling is the only check to sectarian passions.' He was himself an anti-Catholic extremist in the sense of holding (with many others) that 'the logical consequences of the doctrines of the Church of Rome would be fatal to an independent

[39] The Irish Rebellion of 1641 was an Irish Catholic uprising against the Protestant settlers of Ireland and anti-Catholic discrimination.

[*] It is scarcely necessary for me to remind the reader that the word 'Ulster', as used in current political dialectics, is misleading. Part of Ulster is overwhelmingly Catholic; in part the population is divided between the two creeds, and in two counties it is overwhelmingly Protestant. In the whole province the Protestants are in a majority of 150,000, but since a number of Protestants vote Nationalist, the representation of the province is almost equal, the Unionists holding seventeen seats out of thirty-three.

[†] 'Ireland in the Eighteenth Century', 'Leaders of Public Opinion in Ireland', 'Clerical Influences'. *Editorial note:* These works by W. E. H. Lecky were originally published, respectively, in 1878, 1861, and 1911. *Clerical Influences*, published as a pamphlet, was excerpted from *Leaders of Public Opinion in Ireland* (London: Saunders, Otley, and Co., 1861).

and patriotic policy in any land'. But he insists in the same passage 'that nothing is more clear than that in every land where a healthy national feeling exists, Roman Catholic politicians are both independent and patriotic'.

He never recanted these opinions (which are confirmed by the subsequent course of events) even after his conversion to Unionism, but derived his opposition to Home Rule from a dread of all democratic tendencies,* the only ground on which, if men would be willing to confess the naked truth, it can be opposed. There the matter ought to rest. If the doctrines of the Church of Rome are, in fact, inconsistent with political freedom – I myself pronounce no opinion on that point – it is plain to the most superficial observer that the Church, as a factor in politics, stands to lose rather than to gain by Home Rule. British statesmen have often accepted that view, and have endeavoured to use the Roman Catholic hierarchy against popular movements, just as they enlisted its influence to secure the Union. The Roman Catholic laity have often subsequently rejected what they have considered to be undue political dictation from the seat of authority in Rome.

If I may venture an opinion, I believe that both of these mutually irreconcilable propositions – that Home Rule means Rome Rule, and that Rome is the enemy to Home Rule – are wrong.† Such ludicrous contradictions only help to destroy the case against trusting a free Ireland to give religion its legitimate, and no more than legitimate, position in the State. Ireland is intensely religious, and it would be a disaster of the first magnitude if the Roman Catholic masses were to lose faith in their Church. The preservation of that faith depends on the political Liberalism of the Church.

Corresponding tolerance will be demanded of Ulster Protestants. At present passion, not reason, governs the religious side of their opposition to Home Rule. It is futile to criticize Ulster Unionists for making the religious argument the spear-head of their attack on Home Rule. The argument is one which especially appeals to portions of the British electorate, and the rules of political warfare permit free use of it. It was

* See 'Democracy and Liberty'. *Editorial note:* This refers to W. E. H. Lecky, *Democracy and Liberty* (London: Longmans, Green and Co., 1896).

† Many Unionists are to be found in the same breath prophesying Catholic tyranny under Home Rule and averring without any evidence that clerical influence caused the repudiation in 1907 of the Council Bill, because it placed education under a semi-popular body.

pushed beyond the legitimate point, to actual violence, in the Orange opposition to responsible government in Canada in 1849.[40] And it has more than once inflamed and embittered Australian politics, as it inflames the politics of certain English constituencies. But it is hardly to be conceived that Ulster Unionists really fear Roman Catholic tyranny. The fear is unmanly and unworthy of them. To anyone who has lived in an overwhelmingly Catholic district, and seen the complete tranquillity and safety in which Protestants exercise their religion, it seems painfully abnormal that a great city like Belfast, with a population more than two-thirds Protestant, should become hysterical over Catholic tyranny. It would be physically impossible to enforce any tyrannical law in Ulster or anywhere else, even if such a law were proposed, and many leading Protestants from all parts of Ireland have stated publicly that they have no fear of any such result from Home Rule.[*]

'Loyalty' to the Crown is a false issue. Disloyalty to the Crown is a negligible factor in all parts of Ireland. Loyalty or disloyalty to a certain political system is the real matter at issue. At the present day the really serious objections to Home Rule on the part of the leading Ulster Unionists seem to be economic. They have built up thriving trades under the Union. They have the closest business connections with Great Britain, and a mutual fabric of credit. They cherish sincere and profound apprehensions that their business prosperity will suffer by any change in the form of government. To scoff at these apprehensions is absurd and impolitic in the last degree. But to reason against them is also an almost fruitless labour. Those who feel them vaguely picture an Irish Parliament composed of Home Rulers and Unionists, in the same proportion to population as at present, and divided by the same bitter and demoralizing feuds. But there will be no Home Rulers after Home Rule, that is to say, if the Home Rule conceded is sufficient. I believe that Ulster Unionists do not realize either the beneficent transformation which will follow a change from sentimental to practical politics in Ireland, as it has followed a similar change in every other country in the Empire, or the enormous

[40] The 1848 riots were caused by the Orange Order in Saint John, New Brunswick, due in part to increased Irish Catholic immigration, and to support Newfoundland's continued confederation with Canada, thus opposing the Catholic bishops' support for a measure of independence.

[*] 'Religious Intolerance under Home Rule: Some Opinions of Leading Irish Protestants', pamphlet (1911) compiled by J. McVeagh, M.P.

weight which their own fine qualities and strong economic position will give them in the settlement of Irish questions.

Nor do they realize, I venture to think, that any Irish Government, however composed, will be a patriotic Government pledged and compelled for its own credit and safety to do its best for the interests of Ireland. I have never met an Irishman who was not proud of the northern industries, and it is obvious that the industrial prosperity of the north is vital to the fiscal and general interests of Ireland, just as the far more wealthy mining interests of the Rand are vital to the stability and prosperity of the Transvaal, and were regarded as such and treated as such by the farmer majority of the Transvaal after the grant of Home Rule. Those interests have prospered amazingly since, and in that country, be it remembered, volunteer British corps raised on the Rand had been the toughest of all the British foes which the peasant commandos had to meet in a war ended only four years before.

If the fears of Ulster took any concrete form, it would be easier to combat them; but they are unformulated, nebulous. Meanwhile, it is hard to imagine what measure of oppression could possibly be invented by the most malignant Irish Government which would not recoil like a boomerang upon those in whose supposed interests it was framed. I shall have to deal with this point again in discussing taxation, and need here only remind the reader that Ulster is not a Province, any part of which could possibly be injured by any form of taxation which did not hit other Provinces equally.

It is the belief of Ulster Unionists that their prosperity depends on the maintenance of the Union, but the belief rests on no sound foundation. Rural emigration from Ulster, even from the Protestant parts, has been as great as from the rest of Ireland.* It is easy to point to a fall in stocks when the Home Rule issue is uppermost, but such phenomena occur in the case of big changes of government in any country. They merely reflect the fact that certain moneyed interests do, in fact, fear a change of government, and whether those fears are irrational or not, the effect is the same. It is an historical fact, on the other hand, that political freedom in a white country, in the long run invariably promotes industrial expansion and financial confidence. Canada is one remarkable example, Australia is

* The Census of 1911 shows that the population of Ireland is still falling. The province of Leinster, mainly Catholic, alone shows a small increase, derived from the counties of Dublin (including Dublin City) and Kildare. In Ulster, Down and Antrim, which include the city of Belfast, alone show an increase, but not so great as that of County Dublin.

another. The Balkan States are others. Not that I wish to push the colonial example to extremes. Vast undeveloped territories impair the analogy to Ireland; but it is none the less true that when a country with a separate economic life of its own obtains rulers of its own choice, and gains a national pride and responsibility, it goes ahead, not backward.

Intense, indeed, must be the racial prejudice which can cause Ulstermen to forget the only really glorious memories of their past. Orange memories are stirring, but they are not glorious beside the traditions of the Volunteers. The Orange flag is the symbol of conquest, confiscation, racial and religious ascendancy. It is not noble for Irishmen to celebrate annually a battle in which Ireland was defeated, or to taunt their Catholic compatriots with agrarian lawlessness to which their own forefathers were forced to resort, in order to obtain a privileged immunity from the same scandalous land laws. Ulstermen reached spiritual greatness when, like true patriots, they stood for tolerance, Parliamentary reform, and the unity of Ireland. They fell, surely, when they consented to style themselves a 'garrison' under the shelter of an absentee Parliament, which, through the enslavement and degradation of the old Irish Parliament, had driven tens of thousands of their own race into exile and rebellion.

They cherish the Imperial tradition, but let them love its sublime and reject its ignoble side. It is sublime where it stands for liberty; ignoble – and none knew this better than the Ulster-American rebels – where it stands for government based on the dissensions of the governed.

The verdict of history is that for men in the position of the Ulster Unionists, the path of honour and patriotism, and the path of true self-interest, lies in co-operation with their fellow-citizens for the attainment of political freedom under the Crown. It is not as if they had to create a tradition. The tradition lives.

1912

5 L. S. Amery, 'Home Rule and the Colonial Analogy'[1]

There is no argument in favour of Home Rule for Ireland which is more frequently used to-day than that which is based on the analogy of our Colonial experience. In the history of every one of our Colonies – so runs one variant of the argument – from Lord Durham's report on Canada down to the grant of responsible government to the Transvaal, 'Home Rule' has turned disaffection into loyalty, and has inaugurated a career of prosperity.[2] Why should we then hesitate to apply to Irish discontent the 'freedom' which has proved so sovereign a remedy elsewhere? Again, if our Dominions have been able to combine local Home Rule with national unity – so runs another variant – why should a policy which works successfully in Canada or Australia not work in the United Kingdom? Another suggestion freely thrown out is that Home Rule is only the beginning of a process of federalisation which is to bring us to the goal of Imperial Federation. In one form or another the Colonial Analogy occupies the foreground of almost every speech or article in favour of Irish Home Rule. The ablest, as well as the most courageous, piece of Home Rule advocacy which has so far appeared, Mr. Erskine Childers's *Framework of Home Rule*, is based from first to last on this analogy and on little else.

1 This essay appeared as chapter 5 in S. Rosenbaum ed., *Against Home Rule: The Case for the Union* (London: Frederick Warne, 1912), pp. 128–52.

2 John Lambton (1792–1840), 1st Earl of Durham and a Whig, wrote a *Report on the Affairs of British North America* (1839) which proposed, amongst other things, responsible government in Canada in light of the 1837–8 Rebellions. The Transvaal was granted responsible government on 6 December 1906.

That the argument is effective cannot be gainsaid. It is the argument which appeals most strongly to the great body of thoughtful Liberals who from every other point of view look upon the project with unconcealed misgiving. It is the argument which has appealed to public opinion in the Dominions, and has there secured public resolutions and private subscriptions for the Nationalist cause. In one of its forms it appealed to the imagination of an Imperialist like Cecil Rhodes.[3] In another it has, undoubtedly, in recent years attracted not a few Unionists who have been prepared to approach with, at any rate, an open mind the consideration of a federal constitution for the United Kingdom. And, indeed, if the analogy really applied, it would be difficult to resist the conclusion. If Ireland has really been denied something which has proved the secret of Colonial loyalty and prosperity, what Englishman would be so short-sighted as to wish to deprive her of it for the mere sake of domination? If Home Rule were really a stepping-stone towards Imperial Federation, how insincere our professions of 'thinking Imperially', if we are not prepared to sacrifice a merely local sentiment of union for a great all-embracing ideal!

But, as a matter of fact, there is no such analogy bearing on the question which, here and now, is at issue. On the contrary the whole trend of Colonial experience confirms, in the most striking fashion, the essential soundness of the position which Unionists have maintained throughout, that the material, social and moral interests, alike of Ireland and of Great Britain, demand that they should remain members of one effective, undivided legislative and administrative organisation.

The whole argument, indeed, plausible as it is, is based on a series of confusions, due, in part, to deliberate obscuring of the issue, in part to the vagueness of the phrase 'Home Rule', and to the general ignorance of the origin and real nature of the British Colonial system. There are, indeed, three main confusions of thought. There is, first of all, the confusion between 'free' or 'self-governing' institutions, as contrasted with unrepresentative or autocratic rule, and separate government, whether for all or for specified purposes, as contrasted with a common government. In the next place there is the confusion between the status of a self-governing Dominion, in its relations to the Imperial Government, and the status of a Coloni-

[3] Cecil John Rhodes (1853–1902), a self-avowed devotee of British imperialism, was a mining magnate and politician in southern Africa. He served as Prime Minister of the Cape Colony from 1890 to 1896.

al state or provincial government towards the Dominion of which it forms a part. A truly inimitable instance of this confusion has been provided by Mr. Redmond in a declaration made on more than one occasion that all that Ireland asks for, is, 'What has already been given to twenty-eight different portions of the Empire.'* Considering that the 'portions' thus enumerated include practically sovereign nation states like Canada, provinces like those of the South African Union, with little more than county council powers, and stray survivals, like the Isle of Man, of an earlier system of government, based on the same principle of ascendency and interference as the government of Ireland under Poynings's Act, it is difficult to know which to admire most, Mr. Redmond's assurance, or his cynical appreciation of the ignorance or capacity for deliberate self-deception of those with whom he has to deal.[4] The third confusion is that between Imperial functions and national or Dominion functions, due to the fact that the two are combined in the United Kingdom Parliament, which is also, under present conditions, the Imperial Parliament, and to the consequent habitual use of the word 'Imperial' in two quite different senses. It is this last confusion which makes such a declaration as Mr. Asquith's about safeguarding 'the indefeasible authority of the Imperial Parliament' a mere equivocation, for it affords no indication as to whether the supremacy retained is the effective and direct control maintained by Canada over Ontario, or the much slighter and vaguer supremacy exercised by the United Kingdom over the Dominions. It is this same confusion, too, which is responsible for the notion that the problem of creating a true Imperial Parliament or Council by a federation of the Dominions would be assisted, either by creating an additional Dominion in the shape of Ireland, or by arranging the internal constitution of the United Kingdom, as one of the federating Dominions, on a federal rather than on a unitary basis.

The confusion of ideas between self-government and separate government pervades the whole argument that the granting of 'Home Rule' to Ireland would be analogous to the grant of responsible institutions to

[4] Poynings's Law (1494), also known as the Statute of Drogheda, was an archaic piece of legislation which proclaimed that legislation for Ireland could not be passed until it had been approved by Ireland's Privy Council and Lord Deputy in addition to the English monarch and Privy Council.

* Speech at Whitechapel, Oct. 10, 1911. There is an almost identical passage in Mr. Redmond's article in *McClure's Magazine* for October, 1910. Sir J. Simon, the Solicitor-General, has since perpetrated the same absurdity (Dewsbury, Feb. 6, 1912). *Editorial note:* John Edward Redmond (1856–1918), leader of the nationalist Irish Parliamentary Party.

the Colonies. The essence of Home Rule is the creation of a separate government for Ireland. The essence of our Colonial policy has been the establishment of popular self-government in the Colonies. That this self-government has been effected through local parliaments and local executives, and not by representation in a common parliament, is a consequence of the immense distances and the profound differences in local conditions separating the Dominions from the Mother Country. It is an adaptation of the policy to peculiar conditions, and not an essential principle of the policy itself.

This is obvious from any consideration of the circumstances under which the policy of Colonial self-government originated. Under the old Colonial system which preceded it, the Governor not only controlled the executive government, whose members were simply his official subordinates, but also controlled legislation through a nominated Upper Chamber or Legislative Council. The object of this restrictive policy was not interference with local affairs, but the supposed necessity of safeguarding general Imperial interests. Local affairs were, in the main, left to the local government. But the peculiar constitution of that government rendered it almost inevitable that the practical control of those affairs should fall into the hands of a narrowly limited class, clustering round the Governor and his circle, and by its privileges and prejudices creating in those excluded from that class a spirit of opposition, which extended from its members to the whole Imperial system which they were supposed to personify. In each of the North American Colonies a small oligarchy, generally known as the 'Family Compact', was able to 'monopolise the Executive Council, the Legislative Council, the Bench, the Bar, and all offices of profit'.[5] It was against this system, and not against the Imperial connection or even against undue interference from England, that the Canadian rebellion of 1837 was directed. In 1838 Lord Durham made his famous report in which he attributed the troubles to their true cause, the disregard of public opinion, and proposed that the Governor should in future govern, in local affairs, in accordance with the advice given by Colonial Ministers enjoying the confidence of the popular Assembly. A few years later his policy was put into execution by Lord Elgin in Canada, and rapidly

[5] The phrase 'family compact' was used as a derisory description of the political establishment in the 1810s and 1820s which monopolised office in Upper Canada, becoming a target for the Rebellions of 1837–8, prompting the Durham Report leading to the creation of responsible government.

extended to other Colonies.[6] Five years ago the same system of government was applied to the Transvaal and to the Orange River Colony.*

From the foregoing brief summary, it is sufficiently clear that the really vital feature of the policy inaugurated by Lord Durham was the acceptance of responsible popular government in local affairs, and not the separation of Colonial government from Imperial control. The policy did not involve the setting up of new legislative machinery or a new definition of Imperial relations. For an existing system of separate government in local affairs, which created friction and discontent, it simply substituted a new system which has, in the main, worked smoothly up to the present. From the success of this policy, what possible direct inference can be drawn as to the effect of setting up in Ireland, not a similar system of government, for Ireland already enjoys political institutions as fully representative as those of any Colony, or of any other portion of the United Kingdom, but a separate centre of government?

At the same time the success of responsible government in the Colonies is, on closer examination, by no means without bearing on the problem of Ireland. That system of Colonial responsible government which seems to us so simple and obvious is, on the contrary, one of the most artificial systems the world has ever known, based as it is upon conditions which have never been present before in the world's history, and which are now rapidly disappearing, never, perhaps, to recur. That a popular assembly in complete control of the executive, should respect an unwritten convention limiting its powers and rights to purely local affairs, and submit to a purely external control of its wider interests and destinies, seemed to most of Lord Durham's contemporaries almost unthinkable. Not only those who opposed the policy, but many of those who advocated it, were convinced that it would lead to complete separation. Nor were

[6] James Bruce (1811–63), 8th Earl of Elgin and 12th Earl of Kincardine, served as Governor of Jamaica (1842–6), Governor General of the Province of Canada (1847–54), and Viceroy of India (1862–3).

* The usual rhetorical appeal to 'What Home Rule has done in South Africa' presents, indeed, a most perfect specimen of the confusion of thought which it is here attempted to analyse. For no sooner had the Transvaal received 'Home Rule' (*i.e.* responsible government) than it surrendered the 'Home Rule' (*i.e.* separate government) which it had previously enjoyed in order to enter the South African Union. Stripped of mere verbal confusion the argument from the Transvaal analogy then runs somewhat as follows: 'The Transvaal is now contented because it enjoys free representative institutions as an integral portion of a United South Africa; therefore, Ireland cannot be contented until she ceases to be a freely represented integral portion of the United Kingdom!'

their fears or hopes by any means ill-grounded. That they were not justified by the event was due to an altogether exceptional combination of factors. The first of these was the overwhelming supremacy of the United Kingdom in commerce and naval power, and its practical monopoly of political influence in the outer world. Sheltered by an invincible navy, far removed from the sound of international conflict, the Colonies had no practical motive for concerning themselves with foreign affairs, or with any but purely local measures of defence. Even when, as in 1854, they were technically involved by the United Kingdom in war with a great Power, they were not so much as inconvenienced.[7] The United Kingdom, on the other hand, incurred no serious expenditure for their defence beyond what was in any case required for the defence of its sea-borne commerce, nor was its foreign policy at any time seriously deflected by regard for Colonial considerations. Even when the Colonies encroached on the original limits set them, and began to establish protectionist tariffs against the Mother Country, British manufacturers could afford to disregard a handicap of which they were at first scarcely sensible, while British statesmen smiled condescendingly at the harmless aberrations of Colonial inexperience. Another factor was the very fact that it was Colonies that the United Kingdom was dealing with, new countries where every other interest was secondary to that of opening up and developing the untamed wilderness, to creating the material framework which, in fulness of time, might support a complete national life. There was consequently little real interest in external policy in the Colonial assemblies, little leisure for criticism of the Imperial authorities, little desire to assert any particular point of view. Last, but not least, was the factor of distance, interposing a veil of obscurity between the different communities in the Empire, mitigating minor causes of friction, keeping Colonial politics free from being entangled in the British Party system.

The British system of Colonial self-government has so far proved workable because of the exceptional circumstances in which it originated. But its success cannot be regarded as wholly unqualified. The failure to provide any direct representation of Colonial interests and aspirations in the Imperial Parliament may not have mattered as far as foreign policy and defence were concerned. But it did affect the colonies most seriously from the economic point of view, for it precluded them from pressing with any effect for the development of inter-Imperial communications, or from resisting the

[7] During, that is, the Crimean War (1853–6).

abolition of the system of preferential trade which meant so much to their prosperity. Under the influence of a narrowly selfish and short-sighted policy, inspired by English manufacturing interests, Canada saw the stream of commerce and population pass by her shores on its way to the United States. The relative progress of the British Colonies and of the United States since the abolition of preference is some measure of the economic weakness of a political system which has no common trade policy. In any case the British Colonial system, as we have known it, is inevitably moving towards its crisis. The conditions under which it originated are fast disappearing. The commercial and political expansion of Europe, of America, of Asia, are bringing the Dominions more and more into the arena of international conflict. The growth of foreign navies is forcing them to realise the necessity of taking a larger part in their own defence. Their growing national self-consciousness demands not only that they should cease to be dependent on the Mother Country for their safety, but also that they should exercise control over the foreign policy of which defence is merely the instrument. There are only two possible solutions to the problem which is now developing: the one is complete separation, the other is partnership in an Imperial Union in which British subjects in the Dominions shall stand on exactly the same footing, and enjoy the same powers and privileges in Imperial affairs, as British subjects in the United Kingdom.

The conditions – geographical, economic, political – which, in the Colonies, made the grant of free institutions, unaccompanied by some form of political federation or union, even a temporary success, were, indeed, exceptional. None of them were present in the circumstances of Ireland before the Union. They are not present to-day. Geographically the United Kingdom is a single compact island group, of which Ireland is by no means the most outlying portion. No part of Ireland is to-day, or ever was, as inaccessible from the political centre of British power as the remoter parts of the Highlands, not to speak of the Shetlands or Hebrides. Racially, no less than physically, Ireland is an integral part of the United Kingdom, peopled as it is with the same mixture of racial elements as the main island of the group. The blend of Celt with Dane, with Normans and English of the Pale, with English citizens of the seaports and Cromwellian settlers, which constitutes Celtic Ireland, so-called, is less Celtic both in speech and in blood than either Wales or the Highlands. Religion alone has maintained a difference between a predominantly Celtic and a predominantly Teutonic Ireland which would otherwise have disappeared far more completely than the difference between Celtic and

Teutonic Scotland. Economically, the connection between Ireland and Great Britain, always close, has become such that to-day Ireland subsists almost wholly upon the English market. In these respects, at least, there is no resemblance between the conditions of Ireland and that of any of the Colonies.

On the other hand, politically, Ireland was for centuries treated as a colony – 'the first and nearest of the Colonies', as Mr. Childers puts it.[8] The difficulties and defects of early Colonial government were intensified by the great conflict of the Reformation, which made Ireland a centre of foreign intrigue, and by the long religious and constitutional struggle of the seventeenth century, which fell with terrible severity upon a population which had throughout espoused the losing cause. Cromwell, realising that 'if there is to be a prosperous, strong and United Kingdom there must be one Parliament and one Parliament only', freed Ireland from the Colonial status.[9] Unfortunately, his policy was reversed in 1660, and for over a century Ireland endured the position of 'least favoured Colony' – least favoured, partly because, with the possible exception of linen, all her industries were competitive with, and not complementary to English industries, and so were deliberately crushed in accordance with the common economic policy of the time, partly because the memories of past struggles kept England suspicious and jealous of Irish prosperity. Every evil under which the old colonial system laboured in Canada before the rebellion was intensified in Ireland by the religious and racial feud between the mass of the people and the ascendant caste. The same solvent of free government that Durham recommended was needed by Ireland. In view of the geographical and economic position of Ireland, and in the political circumstances of the time, it could only be applied through union with Great Britain. Union had been vainly prayed for by the Irish Parliament at the time of the Scottish Union. Most thoughtful students, not least among them Adam Smith,[*] had seen in it the only cure for the evils which afflicted the hapless island.

[8] Erskine Childers, *The Framework of Home Rule* (London: Edward Arnold, 1911), p. 144.

[9] Oliver Cromwell (1599–1658) brought Ireland into an 'incorporating' union with Britain in the aftermath of the military conquest of the island. Lasting from 1653 until 1660, parliamentary union did not bring a customs union.

[*] Quoted on p. 54. *Editorial note:* J. R. Fischer's contribution of a 'Historical Retrospect' to *Against Home Rule* cites Adam Smith, *An Inquiry into the Nature and Causes of the Wealth of Nations* (London: W. Strahan and T. Cadell, 1776), 2 vols., II, book 5, ch. 3 on the merits of a British union with Ireland.

Meanwhile, in 1782, the dominant caste utilised the Ulster volunteer movement to wrest from Great Britain, then in the last throes of the war against France, Spain, and America, the independence of the Irish Parliament.[10] Theoretically co-equal with the British Parliament, Grattan's Parliament was, in practice, kept by bribery in a position differing very little from that of Canada before the rebellion.[11] Still the new system in Ireland might, under conditions resembling those of Canada in 1840, have gradually evolved into a workable scheme of self-government. But the conditions were too different. A temporary economic revival, indeed, followed the removal of the crippling restrictions upon Irish trade. But, politically, the new system began to break down almost from the start. Its entanglement in English party politics, which geography made inevitable, lead to deadlocks over trade and over the regency question, the latter practically involving the right to choose a separate sovereign. The same geographical conditions made it impossible for Ireland to escape the influence of the French Revolution.[12] The factious spirit and the oppression of the ruling caste did the rest. There is no need to dwell here on the horrors of the rising of 1798, and of its repression, or on the political and financial chaos that marked the collapse of an ill-starred experiment.[13] England, struggling for her existence, had had enough of French invasion, civil war, and general anarchy on her flank. The Irish Parliament died, as it had lived, by corruption, and Castlereagh and Pitt conferred upon Ireland the too long delayed boon of equal partnership in the United Kingdom.[14]

The mistakes which, for a century, deprived the Union of much of its effect – the delay in granting Catholic emancipation, the folly of Free Trade, acquiesced in by Irish members, by which agrarian strife was intensified, and through which Ireland again lost the increase of

[10] In fact, legislative independence was secured under the influence of the Irish Volunteers, a Protestant militia stationed across the island.

[11] Grattan's Parliament (1782–1801), named after Henry Grattan (1746–1820), refers to the parliament of Ireland, which replaced many of the legislative restrictions under Poynings's Law and was subordinate to the Crown of England.

[12] The French Revolution (1789–99) abolished the Ancien Régime and replaced it with a constitutional monarchy.

[13] The 1798 Rebellion in Ireland was a concerted uprising against British authority, organised under the banner of the United Irishmen.

[14] Amery is referring to the 1801 Act of Union. Robert Stewart (1769–1822), 2nd Marquess of Londonderry, also styled Lord Castlereagh, was a British statesman born in Ireland. William Pitt the Younger (1759–1806) became prime minister in 1783 with the fall of the Fox–North Coalition.

population which she had gained in the first half century of Union – need not be discussed here.[15] The fact remains that to-day Ireland is prosperous, and on the eve of far greater prosperity under a sane system of national economic policy. What is more, Ireland is in the enjoyment of practically every liberty and every privilege that is enjoyed by any other part of the United Kingdom, of greater liberty and privilege than is enjoyed by Dominions which have no control of Imperial affairs. The principle which in the case of the Colonies was applied through separate governments has, in her case, been applied through Union. It could only have been applied through Union in 1800. It can only be applied through Union to-day. Railways and steamships have strengthened the geographical and economic reasons for union; train-ferries and aircraft will intensify them still further. Meanwhile the political and strategical conditions of these islands in the near future are far more likely to resemble those of the great Napoleonic struggle than those of the Colonial Empire in its halcyon period.

In one aspect, then, the Union was the only feasible way of carrying out the principle which underlay the successful establishment of Colonial self-government. In another aspect it was the last step of a natural and, indeed, inevitable process for which the history of the British Colonies since the grant of self-government has furnished analogies in abundance. It has furnished none for the reversal of that process. It is only necessary to consider the reasons which, in various degrees, influenced the several groups of independent Colonies in North America, Australia, and South Africa to unite under a single government, whether federal or unitary, thus wholly or partially surrendering the 'Home Rule' previously enjoyed by them, in order to see how close is the parallel. The weak and scattered North American Colonies were at a serious disadvantage in all political and commercial negotiations with their powerful neighbour, the United States, a fact very clearly emphasised by the termination of Lord Elgin's reciprocity treaty in 1864.[16] None of them was in a position to deal with the vast territories of the North-West, undeveloped by the Hudson's Bay Company, and in imminent danger of American occupation. A common trade policy, a common railway policy, and a common banking system were essential to a rapid development of their great resources, and only

[15] Catholic Emancipation culminated in the 1829 Roman Catholic Relief Act.

[16] The Reciprocity Treaty between Canada and the US was a free trade deal agreed by Britain. It was in fact signed in 1854.

a common government could provide them. In Australia the chief factor in bringing about federation was the weakness and want of influence of the separate Colonies in dealing with problems of defence and external policy, impressed upon them by German and French colonial expansion in the Pacific, and by the growth of Japan. In South Africa, on the other hand, the factors were mainly internal. The constant friction over railway and customs agreements, continually on the verge of breaking down, embittered the relations of the different Colonies and maintained an atmosphere of uncertainty discouraging to commercial enterprise. Four different governments dealt with a labour supply mainly required in one colony. Four agricultural departments dealt with locusts and cattle plagues, which knew no political boundaries, and which could only be stamped out by the most prompt and determined action. Four systems of law and four organisations for defence secured, as Lord Selborne pointed out in a striking Memorandum (Blue Book Cd. 3564) a minimum of return for a maximum of expense.[17] A native rising in Natal warned South Africans that the mistake of a single Colony might at any moment set the whole of South Africa ablaze with rebellion.[18] In the absence of larger issues local politics in each Colony turned almost exclusively on the racial feud. A comprehensive union alone could bring commercial stability and progressive development, mitigate race hatred, and pave the way to a true South African nationality.

All the weakness in external relations, all the internal friction and impediment to progress, all the bitterness and pettiness of local politics, which marked the absence of union among neighbouring colonies, also characterised the relations of Great Britain and Ireland in the eighteenth century. But there was this difference: the immense disproportion in wealth and power, and the political control exercised by the greater state, caused all the evils of disunion to concentrate with intensified force upon the smaller state. To undo the mischief of eighteenth-century disunion required at least a generation. A series of political mistakes and mischances, and a disastrous economic policy, have left the healing task of union incomplete after a century. But renewed disunion to-day would only mean a renewal of old local feuds to the point of civil war, a renewal of old economic friction, in which most of the injury would be suffered by the

[17] William Waldegrave Palmer (1859–1942), 2nd Earl of Selborne, served as high commissioner for Southern Africa from 1905 until 1910.

[18] The Zulu or Bambatha Rebellion of 1906 was directed against British rule and taxation in the colony of Natal, South Africa.

weaker combatant, the indefinite postponing for Ireland of the prospect, now so hopeful, of national development and social amelioration, a weakening of the whole United Kingdom for diplomacy or for defence. It is a policy which no Dominion in the Empire would dream of adopting – a policy which every Dominion would most certainly resist by force, just as the United States resisted it when attempted, with more than a mere pretext of constitutional justification, by the Southern States.

Now for the 'exception which proves the rule': there is one Colonial analogy for what would be the position of Ireland under Home Rule, namely, the position of Newfoundland outside the confederation of the other North American Colonies.* The analogy is only partial, for this reason, that whereas Ireland is almost wholly dependent economically on Great Britain, Newfoundland has little direct trade with Canada, and moreover enjoys a virtual monopoly of one particular commodity, namely codfish, by which it manages to support its small population. Nevertheless, no one can doubt that with its favoured geographical position, and with its great natural resources, Newfoundland would have been developed in a very different fashion if for the last forty years it had been an integral part of the Dominion.[19] Nor is the loss all on the side of Newfoundland, as the history of even the last few years has shown. In 1902, Newfoundland negotiated a commercial Convention with the United States which, in return for a free entry for Newfoundland fish into the United States, practically gave the Newfoundland market to American manufacturers, and explicitly forbade the granting of any trade preference to the United Kingdom or to Canada. When, fortunately, the American Senate rejected the Convention, Newfoundland embarked on a course of legislative reprisal against American fishing. But this involved the Imperial Government in a diplomatic conflict which, but for the excellent relations subsisting with the United States, might easily have led to a grave crisis. The inconveniences and dangers which Irish trade policy might lead to under Home Rule can easily be inferred from this single example, all the more if Irish policy should be influenced, as Newfoundland's policy certainly was not, by a bias of hostility to the Empire.

[19] Newfoundland rejected Confederation with Canada in 1869.

* The position of New Zealand, outside the Australian Commonwealth, is no parallel. New Zealand is almost as far from Australia as Newfoundland is from the British Isles; it differs from Australia in every climatic and physical feature; there is comparatively little trade between them.

So much for the first confusion, that which would base the case for a *separate government* in Ireland on the success of *free institutions* in the Colonies, entirely ignoring the whole movement for union, which has made every geographical group of Colonies follow the example of the Mother Country. We must now deal with the second confusion, that which is based on a hazy notion that Home Rule is only a preliminary step to endowing the United Kingdom as a whole with a working federal constitution like that of Canada or Australia. Ireland, in fact, so runs the pleasing delusion, is to be set up as an experimental Quebec, and the other provinces will follow suit shortly. Not all Home Rulers, indeed, are obsessed by this confusion. Mr. Childers, for instance, makes short work of what he calls the 'federal chimera', dismissing the idea as 'wholly impracticable', and pointing out that Home Rule must be 'not merely non-federal, but anti-federal'.[20] But the great majority of Liberals to-day are busy deluding themselves or each other, and the Nationalists are, naturally, not unwilling to help them in that task, with the idea of Home Rule for Ireland followed by 'Home Rule all round'.[21]

The new Home Rule Bill has not yet appeared, but certain main features of it can be taken for granted.[22] It will be a Bill which, save possibly for a pious expression of hope in the preamble, will deal with Ireland only. It will set up in Ireland an Irish legislature and executive responsible for the 'peace, order, and good government' of Ireland, subject to certain restrictions and limitations. It will assign to Ireland the whole of the Irish revenues, though probably retaining the control of customs and excise, and in that case retaining some Irish representatives at Westminster. So far from fixing any contribution to Imperial expenditure from Ireland, it will, apparently, include the provision of an Imperial grant in aid towards Land Purchase and Old Age Pensions. Any such measure is wholly incompatible with even the loosest federal system. A federal scheme postulates the existence over the whole confederation of two concurrent systems of government, each exercising direct control over the citizens within its own sphere, each having its legislative and executive functions, and its sources of revenue, clearly defined. The Home Rule Bill will certainly not set up any such division of government and its

20 Childers, *Framework*, p. 200.

21 The idea of 'Home Rule All Round' had been canvassed since the late nineteenth century and aimed at achieving a federal structure for the United Kingdom.

22 The third Home Rule Bill was introduced by H. H. Asquith (1852–1928) on 11 April 1912.

functions in Great Britain. Nor will it, in reality, set up any such effective double system of government in Ireland. What it will set up will be a national or Dominion government in Ireland, separate and exclusive, but subject to certain restrictions and interferences which it will be the first business of the Irish representatives, in Dublin or Westminster, to get rid of. Long before Scotland or Wales, let alone England, get any consideration of their demand for Home Rule, if demand there be, the last traces of any quasi-federal element the Bill may contain will have been got rid of.

In a federation every citizen, in whatever state or province he resides, is as fully a citizen of the federation as every other citizen. He not only has the same federal vote, and pays the same federal taxes, but he has the same access to the federal courts, and the same right to the direct protection of the federal executive. In what sense are any of these conditions likely to be true of, let us say, an Irish landlord under this Home Rule Bill? Again, federalism implies that all the subordinate units are in an equal position relatively to the federal authority. Is this Bill likely to be so framed that its provisions can be adapted unchanged to Scotland, Wales, or England? And if they could, what sort of a residuum of a United Kingdom government would be left over? Take finance alone: if every unit under 'Home Rule all round' is to receive the whole product of its taxation, what becomes of the revenue on which the general government of the United Kingdom will have to subsist? The fact is that the creation of a federal state, whether by confederation or by devolution of powers, must be, in the main, a simultaneous act. Additional subordinate units may subsequently join the confederation under the conditions of the federal constitution. Backward areas which are unable to provide for an efficient provincial expenditure, over and above their contribution to federal expenditure, may be held back as territories directly controlled by the federal authorities till they are financially and in other respects ripe for the grant of provincial powers. If a federal scheme were really seriously contemplated by the present Government they would have to adopt one of two courses. They would either have to establish it simultaneously for the whole United Kingdom, and in that case limit the powers and functions of the provinces so narrowly as to make it possible for Ireland to raise its provincial revenue without undue difficulty, the rest of Ireland's needs being met by a substantial federal expenditure carried out by federal officials. Or else they might begin by the creation of a federal constitution with considerable provincial powers for England, Scotland, and Wales, keeping back Ireland as a federal territory till its economic and social conditions justified the establishment of provincial institutions. The converse policy of treating the case of Ireland as 'prior in point of time and urgency',* of giving the poorest and most backward portion of the United Kingdom the whole of its revenue and a practically unfettered control of its territory, is, indeed, 'not merely non-federal, but anti-federal'.

The truth is that the federal element in this Home Rule Bill, as in that of 1893, will be merely a pretence, designed to keep timid and hesitating Home Rulers in line – a tactical manoeuvre of much the same character as the talk about a reformed Second Chamber which preceded the Parliament Act, and found due burial in the preamble to that Act.[23] In essence the Bill will set up Ireland as an entirely separate state subject to certain restrictions which the Government have no serious intention of enforcing, and the Irish every intention of disregarding, or abolishing as the outcome of further agitation. For this policy of pretence there is one admirable parallel in our Colonial history – the policy by which 'Home Rule' was 'given' to the Transvaal after Majuba.[24] It was the same policy of avoiding expense and trouble, political or military – the policy, in fact, of 'cutting the loss' – tricked out with the same humbug about 'magnanimity' and 'conciliation', about trust in Boer (or Nationalist) moderation when in power, the same contemptuous passing over of the loyalists as persons of 'too pronounced' views, or as 'interested contractors and stock-jobbers'.† It was embodied in a Convention by which the 'inhabitants of the Transvaal territory' were 'accorded complete self-government, subject to the suzerainty of Her Majesty' under a series of limitations which, if enforced, would have implied a measure of British control in many respects greater than that exercised over a self-governing Colony, and with a number of guarantees to protect the loyalists. The Government was able to 'save its face', while its hesitating followers were able to quiet their consciences, by the reassuring phrases

[23] Referring to the second Home Rule Bill of 1893.

[24] The Transvaal Boers secured a decisive victory against the British at the Battle of Majuba Hill on 27 April 1881, leading to the signing of the Pretoria Convention, which bestowed self-government to the South African Republic under nominal suzerainty of the Crown.

* Mr. Asquith at St. Andrews, Dec. 7, 1910. *Editorial note:* Asquith's speech, touching on the federal concept, was reported in *The Times* on 8 December 1910.

† See 'The *Times*' History of the South African War', vol. 1 pp. 67 *et seq. Editorial note:* this refers to L. S. Amery, Erskine Childers, G. P. Tallboy, and Basil Williams, *The 'Times' History of the War in South Africa, 1899–1902* (London: S. Low, Marston and Co., 1900–9), 7 vols. The quotations that follow are, as indicated, from this work.

of the Convention. The Boer Volksraad frankly declared itself still dissatisfied, but ratified the Convention, 'maintaining all objections to the Convention ... and for the purpose of showing to everybody that the love of peace and unity inspires it, for the time being, and provisionally submitting the articles of the Convention to a practical test'. If any Nationalist Convention in Dublin should accept the new Home Rule Bill, we can take it for granted that it will be in exactly the same spirit, and possibly in almost the same phraseology.*

From the first the limitations of the Convention were disregarded. Short of armed intervention there was no machinery for enforcing them, and the Boers knew perfectly well that there was no real desire on the part of an embarrassed Government to raise a hornet's nest by making the attempt. The British resident, with his nominally autocratic powers, was a mere impotent laughing stock. The ruined loyalists left the country, or remained to become the most embittered enemies of the British Government. In three years a new Convention was drafted – an even greater masterpiece of make-believe than the first – which could be expounded to Parliament as a mere modification of certain unworkable provisions, but which the Boers took as a definite surrender of all claims to suzerainty, and as a definite recognition of their position as an 'independent sovereign state', bound temporarily by the provisions of a treaty, which could have no permanent force in 'fixing the boundary to the march of a nation'.[25] So far from being reconciled they were only emboldened to embark on a policy of aggression, which in 1885 involved the British Government in military measures costing nearly as much as would have been required to suppress the whole rising in 1881. For the time being the stagnation and chronic bankruptcy which followed the removal of British rule and the exodus of the loyalists limited Transvaal ambitions. The gold discoveries both increased that ambition by furnishing it with revenue, and at the same time brought about a close economic intercourse with the neighbouring colonies which, under the political conditions of disunion,

[25] The London Convention succeeded the Pretoria Convention in 1884.

* *Cf.* Mr. J. Redmond on the third reading of the Home Rule Bill of 1893. 'The word 'provisional', so to speak, has been stamped in red ink across every page of the Bill. I recognise that the Bill is offered as a compromise and accepted as such. ... England has no right to ask from Irish members any guarantee of finality in its acceptance.' *Editorial note:* Redmond's statement appears in Hansard, House of Commons Debates, 30 August 1893, vol. 16 cols. 1504–5. The statement was frequently quoted back at Redmond, e.g. by Edward Carson (1854–1935) in the House of Commons on 11 April 1912.

was bound to create friction. In the end the policy of make-believe and 'cutting the loss' had to be redeemed at the cost of 20,000 lives and of £200,000,000. Reconciliation, in large measure, has come since. But it has only come because British statesmen showed, firstly, in the war, their inflexible resolution to stamp out the policy of separation, and secondly, after the war, their devotion to the real welfare of South Africa in a policy of economic reconstruction, and in the establishment of those free and equal British institutions under which – by the final dying out of a spurious nationalism based on racial prejudice and garbled history – South Africa may become a real, living nation.

The reservations and guarantees which this Home Rule Bill may contain cannot possibly constitute the framework of a federal constitution. All they can guarantee is a period of friction and agitation which will continue till Ireland has secured a position of complete separation from the United Kingdom. At the best the Home Rule experiment would then reduce Ireland to the position of another Newfoundland; at the worst it might repeat all the most disastrous features of the history of 'Home Rule' in the Transvaal. At the same time it may be worth inquiring how far there would really be any valid Colonial analogy for the introduction of a federal system of 'Home Rule all round' if such a scheme had been honestly contemplated. The first thing to keep in mind is that the internal constitution of the Dominions presents a whole gradation of constitutional types. There is the loose federal system of Australia, in which the Commonwealth powers are strictly limited and defined, and all residuary powers left to the States. There is the close confederation of Canada in which all residuary powers are vested in the Dominion. There is the non-federal unitary government of South Africa with a system of provincial local governments with somewhat wide county council powers. There is, lastly, the purely unitary government of the two islands of New Zealand. Each of these types is the outcome of peculiar geographical, economic, and historical conditions. To understand the federal system of Australia it is essential to remember that till comparatively recent times Australia consisted, to all intents, of four or five seaport towns, each with its own tributary agricultural and mining area, strung out, at distances varying from 500 to 1300 miles, along the southern and eastern third of a coast line of nearly 9000 miles looped round an unexplored and reputedly uninhabitable interior. Each of these seaports traded directly with the United Kingdom and Europe in competition with the others. With economic motives for union practically non-existent, with external factors awakening a general apprehension rather than confronting Australia with any immediate danger, it was impossible to find the driving power to overcome local jealousies sufficiently to secure more than a minimum of union. The Commonwealth Constitution is a makeshift which, as the internal trade of Australia grows and as railway communications are developed, will inevitably be amended in the direction of increasing the power of the Commonwealth and diminishing that of the States. In Canada the economic link between Canada proper and the Maritime Provinces was, before Confederation, almost as weak as that of Australia. British Columbia, which it was hoped to include in the Confederation, was then separated by a journey of months from Eastern Canada, and was, indeed, much nearer to Australia or New Zealand. Quebec, with its racial and religious peculiarities, added another problem. That the Confederation was nevertheless such a close and strong one was due both to the menace of American power in the south, and to the terrible example of the weakness of the American constitution as made manifest by the Civil War. Yet even so, Sir John Macdonald, the father of Confederation, frankly declared the federal constitution a necessary evil –

> As regards the comparative advantages of a Legislative and a Federal Union I have never hesitated to state my own opinions. … I have always contended that if we could agree to have one government and one Parliament … it would be the best, the cheapest, the most vigorous, the strongest system of government we could adopt.[26]

This also was the view of the framers of the South African Union. The circumstances of South Africa enabled them to carry it into effect. For all its extent, South Africa is geographically a single, homogeneous country with no marked internal boundaries. It is peopled by two white races everywhere intermixed in varying proportions and nowhere separated into large compact blocks. The immense preponderance and central position of the Rand mining industry makes South Africa practically a single economic system. The very bitterness of the long political and racial struggle which had preceded intensified the argument for really effective union.

If we compare the conditions in the United Kingdom with those of the Dominions it is obvious at once that there is no possible analogy with the conditions of Canada or Australia, but a considerable analogy with South Africa and New Zealand. The British Isles are but little larger than the

[26] John Alexander Macdonald (1815–91), the first Canadian prime minister, made this statement before the legislative assembly on 6 February 1865.

New Zealand group, and much more compact and homogeneous. Their close economic intercourse, the presence of two races with a history of strife behind them, but compelled by their inextricable geographical blending to confront the necessity of union, are reproduced in the conditions of South Africa. In so far then as the Colonial analogy bears upon the question at all, it cannot be said to be in favour of Federal Home Rule any more than of Separatist Home Rule. The most it can fairly be said to warrant is the establishment of provincial councils with powers akin to those of the South African Councils. For such councils, built up by the federation of adjoining counties and county boroughs, carrying out more effectively some of the existing powers of those bodies, and adding to them such other powers, legislative or administrative, as it may be convenient to bestow on them, a very strong case may be made on the grounds of the congestion of Parliamentary business. But that has nothing to do with Home Rule, either Separatist or Federal.

But if the congestion of Parliamentary business might be appreciably relieved by some such provincial bodies – larger 'national' bodies would only duplicate work, not relieve it – the true remedy for the confusion of principles and objectives which, rather than the mere waste of time, is the chief defect of our Parliamentary system, lies in a proper separation of the local affairs of the United Kingdom from the general work of the Empire, in other words, in some form of Imperial federation. What is needed is not the creation of separate parliaments *within* the United Kingdom, but the creation of a separate Parliament *for* the United Kingdom, a Parliament which should deal with the affairs of the United Kingdom considered as one of the Dominions, leaving the general problems of Imperial policy to a common Imperial Parliament or Council equally representative of the citizens of every Dominion. No form of Home Rule can in any sense advance that desirable solution of our Imperial problems. The creation of an additional Dominion in the shape of Ireland would merely add one to the number of units to be considered, and would be contrary to the spirit of the resolution passed at the 1897 Conference, that it was desirable 'wherever and whenever practicable, to group together under a federal union those Colonies which are geographically united'.[27] The problem would be no more affected by the setting up of a federal constitution for the United Kingdom, than it

[27] The Colonial Conference of 1897 brought together the secretary of state for the colonies and eleven representatives of the self-governing colonies of the British Empire.

would be if South Africa decided, after all, to give her provinces federal powers, or Australia carried unification by a referendum. The notion that the Dominions could simply come inside the United Kingdom federation, though it sometimes figures in Home Rule speeches, is merely a product of the third form of confusion of ideas previously referred to, and is a sheer absurdity. The terms and conditions of a United Kingdom federation would necessarily differ in almost every respect from those of an Imperial Federation, and a constitution framed for the one object would be unworkable for the other. Nor would it ever be acceptable to the Dominions, which regard themselves as potentially, if not actually, the equals of the United Kingdom as a whole. From their point of view the United Kingdom might almost as well be asked to step inside the Australian Commonwealth on the footing of Tasmania, as that they should be asked to join in, in the capacity of an additional Ireland, Scotland, or Wales, under any scheme of 'Home Rule all round'.

It should be sufficiently clear from the foregoing analysis that the vague and confused claim that the success of British Colonial policy is an argument for the Home Rule Bill has no shadow of justification. It has been shown, first of all, that the factor of success in our Colonial policy was not the factor of separatism implied in Home Rule, but the factor of responsible government already secured for Ireland by the Union. It has been shown, secondly, that the experience of the Colonies since the establishment of responsible government has in every case forced union upon them, and union in the closest form which the facts of trade and geography permitted of. Colonial experience is thus no argument even for a federal scheme of 'Home Rule all round', if such a scheme could possibly result from an Irish Home Rule Bill, which it cannot. The disadvantages and dangers of the contrary policy of disunion have been shown, in their least noxious form in the case of Newfoundland, which has simply remained outside the adjoining Dominion, and in their deadliest form in the case of the Transvaal, where 'Home Rule' was given in 1881, as it would be given to Ireland to-day, if the Government succeeded, not from conviction and wholeheartedly, but as a mean-spirited concession, made to save trouble, and under the most disingenuous and least workable provisions. Lastly, it has been made clear that Home Rule cannot possibly assist, but can only obscure and confuse, the movement for the establishment of a true Imperial Union. Unionists and Imperialists can choose no better ground for their resistance to Home Rule than the wide and varied field of Colonial experience.

But Colonial experience can give us more than that. It can provide us not only with an immense mass of arguments and instances against disruption, but with invaluable instances of what can be done to strengthen and build up the Union against all possible future danger of disruptive tendencies. The confederation of Canada was accomplished in the teeth of all the geographical and economic conditions of the time. Canadian statesmanship thereupon set itself to transform geography, and to divert the course of trade in order to make the Union a reality. The Intercolonial Railway, the Canadian Pacific, the Grand Trunk Pacific, the proposed Hudson Bay Railway, and the Georgian Bay Canal schemes, all these have been deliberate instruments of policy, aiming, first of all, at bridging the wilderness between practically isolated settlements scattered across a continent, and creating a continuous Canada, east and west; and, secondly, at giving that continuous strip depth as well as extension. Hand in hand with the policy of constructing the internal framework of transportation, which is the skeleton of the economic and social life of a nation, went the policy of maintaining a national tariff to clothe that skeleton with the flesh and blood of production and exchange, and, as far as possible, to clothe it evenly. Australia, too, is waking, though somewhat hesitatingly, to the need of transcontinental railways, for the protection of new industries and for the even development and filling up of all her territories. In South Africa the economic process preceded the political. It was the dread of the breakdown of a temporary customs union already in existence that precipitated the discussion of union. And it was the development of the Rand as the great internal market of South Africa, and the competitive construction of railway lines from the coast, that really decided the question of legislative union against federation. All three instances lead to the same conclusion that union to be really effective and stable needs three things: firstly, a developed system of internal communications reducing all natural barriers to social, political, and commercial intercourse to the very minimum; secondly, a national tariff, protective or otherwise, sufficient at least to encourage the fullest flow of trade along those communications rather than outside of them; thirdly, a deliberate use of the tariff and of the national expenditure to secure, as far as possible, the even development of every portion of the national territory.

In the United Kingdom all these instruments for making the Union real are still unutilised. The system of *laissez-faire* in the matter of internal communications has allowed St. George's Channel still to remain a real barrier. A dozen train-ferries, carrying not only the railway traffic between Great Britain and Ireland, but enabling the true west coast of the United Kingdom to be used for transatlantic traffic, would obliterate that strip of sea which a British minister recently urged as an insuperable objection to a democratic union.* To construct them would not be doing as much, relatively, as little Denmark has long since done, by the same means, to unite her sea-divided territory. The creation of a tariff which shall assist not only manufactures, but agriculture and rural industries, is another essential step. In view of Ireland's undeveloped industrial condition the giving of bounties to the establishment in Ireland of new industries, such as the silk industry, would be a thoroughly justifiable extension of the Unionist policy carried out through the Congested Districts Board and the Department of Agriculture.[28] The diversion to Ireland of a larger part of the general national and Imperial expenditure, whether by the establishment of a naval base, or the giving out of battleship contracts, or even only of contracts for Army uniforms, would also be of appreciable assistance to Ireland and to the Union. Ireland suffers to-day economically and politically, from the legacy of political separation in the eighteenth century, and of economic disunion in the nineteenth. It is the business of Unionists not only to maintain the legal framework of the Union, but to give it a vitality and fulness of content which it has never possessed.

[28] The Congested Districts Board for Ireland was designed to alleviate poverty and congested living conditions in mainly the west of Ireland. The Department of Agriculture and Technical Instruction was inaugurated in 1900 by Horace Plunkett and aimed to improve Irish agriculture and industry through practical education and local co-operation.

* Colonel Seely at Newry, December 9, 1911. *Editorial note:* John Edward Bernard Seely (1868–1947), 1st Baron Mottistone, sat as a Liberal MP from 1904 to 1922 and then from 1923 to 1924.

6 Edward Carson, 'Settlement of an Old Controversy'[1]

I do not mind in the least if I am accused of adopting what the Prime Minister calls the 'new style' if I say that, in my opinion, and I think there will be many both in the House and outside who will agree with me, more ridiculous or fantastic proposals than those which have been so clearly outlined by the Prime Minister have never been put before this or any other Parliament. I am one of the survivors of the old fight in 1893.[2] I am sorry I have not got the energy I had then, but while the proposals of Mr. Gladstone were difficult and complex, the proposals that we have heard made here to-day are, as I believe will be shown in the course of the Debate we will have, absolutely unworkable and ridiculous. The new Senate, the great safeguard of that contemptible minority which I attempt to represent in this House, is to be a nominated body.[3] That is a Radical proposition.[4] Any such proposal as that is a deliberate insult to this House of Commons. What is the use of it? Nominated by whom? Nominated, I suppose, by the Imperial Government. Will it be nominated, or could it be nominated, against the wish of the hon. Members who

1 Speech in the House of Commons, Hansard, 11 April 1912, vol. 36, cols. 1427–514, responding to Prime Minister Herbert Henry Asquith's introduction of the third Home Rule Bill.

2 Referring to the battle over the second Home Rule Bill introduced by Prime Minister William Ewart Gladstone (1806–98) in that year.

3 The 1912 Bill proposed to introduce a nominated senate with forty members in addition to an elected lower chamber as a protection for the Protestant minority on the island of Ireland. By 'contemptible' Carson means that Unionists, a largely Protestant minority in Ireland, were being held in contempt.

4 A nominated upper house would be 'Radical' since assorted radicals historically opposed a hereditary chamber.

will be retained in this House, and supported by a Parliament in Dublin which you yourselves created?[5] The thing is fantastic. It is worth nothing, like all the other safeguards that you have put forward. Take the safeguard of the supremacy of the Imperial Parliament. Does the right hon. Gentleman really think that he is adding anything by putting that into the Bill? He knows well it adds nothing.[6] It is put there merely as a picture, merely as something of a palliative for those who have some conscience left. I do not think there are any such words in the British North American Act.[7] [HON. MEMBERS: 'There are.'] They add nothing there to the Act.

This Parliament which passes an Act has an inherent right necessarily to alter or change or repeal any Act that is passed. Therefore these and the other great safeguards put there, and announced by the Prime Minister, are simply delusions. At all events, they are nothing to us. We care nothing about them. I rise at the earliest moment to say that, so far as I am concerned, I oppose even the introduction of this Bill, and I do so for this reason, that I gather – and with me, at all events, this is the main principle that I have to consider – I gather that we will no longer have in Ireland the protection of an Executive which is responsible to this Parliament. That is what we have now. That is what this country invited us to have.[8] That is what we loyally accepted, that is what, with those matchless phrases but I do not think always with great sincerity, the Prime Minister now asks us to abandon. The Prime Minister waxed very warm and eloquent over the charges made by the Leader of the Opposition at Belfast the other day.[9] I shall put a question in a moment to the Prime Minister. We are now here opposing a policy which has been twice rejected by the electorate. [HON. MEMBERS: 'NO, no,' and HON. MEMBERS: 'Only once,' and HON. MEMBERS: 'Twice.'] It has been twice rejected by the electorate.

5 The House of Commons was to retain 42 Irish members, reduced from 103.

6 Asquith had declared at the start of his speech (Hansard, 11 April 1912, vol. 36, col. 1424) that 'We maintain in this Bill unimpaired, and beyond the reach of challenge or of question, the supremacy, absolute and sovereign, of the Imperial Parliament.'

7 Carson presumably meant the Declaratory Act of 1766 under which British sovereignty over the North American colonies was asserted in the context of the repeal of the Stamp Act.

8 Carson is referring to the 1801 Act of Union between Great Britain and Ireland, based on what Carson calls an 'invitation' by Britain to Ireland to establish a united parliamentary polity.

9 The Conservative, Andrew Bonar Law (1858–1923), leader of the Opposition (1911–15) and later prime minister (1922–3). Asquith quotes a speech from him earlier in the same week alleging that 'In order to remain for a few months longer in office, His Majesty's Government have sold the Constitution.'

More than that, it is a policy which has been rejected upon the only occasions upon which it was ever put into concrete form. The late Duke of Devonshire said, and I think said very truly, speaking on the Home Rule Bill in 1893: – 'Before this measure is passed into law we have a right to demand that the judgment of the country shall be given not upon a cry, not upon an aspiration, not upon an impatient impulse, but upon a completed work, and that this measure, the result of the collective wisdom of the Government and Parliament, shall be submitted for the approval of the country aye or no.'[10] The Prime Minister is angry at being charged with selling us to the Irish party.[11] I ask him this question: Is he going to allow this Bill to be submitted to the electorate? [HON. MEMBERS: 'Answer.'] Will he assert in this House that that Bill which he outlined to-day before this House has even been approved of by the electorate? It was the details of the other Bills that were rejected. [An HON. MEMBER: 'Not the principle.'] I am on the question of submitting the Bill to the country at the present time. It was the details of the Bill that were rejected. The details of this Bill are far worse for England, and, in my opinion, are far worse for Ireland, but that is not all. What is the moment at which you are bringing in this Bill? You are bringing it in while the Constitution of the country is in suspense.[12] You are bringing it in while the lying Preamble remains unrepealed. We believe that you passed that Bill, and certainly that you got the Irish assistance – the Irish Nationalist assistance – to pass it for the purpose of passing Home Rule while the Constitution was suspended. [HON. MEMBERS: 'Hear, hear.'] Hon. Members opposite cheer that. If that is true, every word that was said by my right hon. Friend as to the disreputable bargain is true also. You cannot plead now that you have no time to carry out the Preamble of the Parliament Bill. [Several HON. MEMBERS: 'Parliament Act.'] Parliament Act – if hon. Members opposite get a little comfort from the fact that it is an Act. You cannot plead that you have no time, because you are

[10] Spencer Compton Cavendish (1833–1908), 8th Duke of Devonshire, formally moved for the rejection of the second Home Rule Bill of 1893.

[11] The Irish Parliamentary Party held the balance of power between the Conservatives and the Liberals after the general elections of January and December 1910.

[12] The Parliament Act was passed in 1911 in response to the rejection by the House of Lords of the 1909 'People's Budget'. It had the effect of cancelling the upper chamber's veto over legislation, thereby blocking its power to stymie legislation in favour of home rule. The Preamble to the Parliament Act referred to the creation of a second chamber on the basis of popular mandate rather than the hereditary principle, though this provision was not brought forward, leaving the constitution, as Carson saw it, 'in suspension'.

at the present moment entering upon this controversy, which not only sets up two new Houses in Ireland, but smashes this House in this country and for the United Kingdom. The truth of the matter is that, so far as this Home Rule Bill is concerned, you are compelled to do what you are doing by the necessity of retaining the Irish votes in this House. That is a matter that is demonstrable. As long as you had a majority independent of them we heard nothing of Home Rule. It was then, as I think the Prime Minister called it, an abstract or academic question.

THE PRIME MINISTER

On the contrary. In the Parliament to which the right hon. Gentleman referred, a Resolution in favour of Home Rule was moved by the hon. and learned Member for Waterford (Mr. J. Redmond) and supported by me on behalf of His Majesty's Government.

SIR E. CARSON

That is what I call an academic question. They did not bring in a Bill. No; on the contrary, they said that the proper policy and the one they believed in was a Council Bill.[13] Why did they bring in a Council Bill if they believed in a Home Rule Bill? Are they ever genuine? They brought in a Council Bill; the Council Bill was submitted to an Irish Convention; and the Irish Convention rejected it. Then, of course, they toed the line, and we heard no more of the Irish Council Bill. It was not the House of Lords who threw it out; it was something far more important to the right hon. and hon. Gentlemen opposite; it was the Irish Convention. The great Government of England, with the largest majority that any Government has ever had, bowed the knee to the Irish Convention. Then they say, forsooth, that they have always acted upon the highest motives and with the greatest independence, and they repudiate even any kind of transaction or bargain for the sake of votes.

Since these proposals were last before the House, as the right hon. Gentleman has said, a great deal has happened in Ireland. Nearly twenty years have passed.[14] Yes, but all that has passed has gone to show how right we were and how wrong the Government of the day was. The right

[13] Under the 1907 Irish Council Bill, the Campbell-Bannerman ministry proposed to devolve administrative powers to Ireland without conceding home rule. In the absence of support from a convention of the United Irish League and the Irish Parliamentary Party, the Bill was dropped.

[14] Nineteen years had passed since the second Home Rule Bill.

hon. Gentleman has asked what is our alternative. Our alternative then was to maintain the union and to do justice to Ireland. That has been done with results which, I venture to think, so great have they been in the direction of the prosperity of Ireland, could not have been contemplated by even the most optimistic Member of this House of either party. On the other hand, what about the finance of both those Home Rule Bills? Is there any man who, having gone into the subject, will deny what was stated the other day at a meeting of the General County Councils Assembly in Ireland by Mr. Ellis, one of the witnesses before the expert Committee, namely, that if the finance of 1893 had become law in Ireland, Ireland would long since have been in a state of bankruptcy? Surely after twenty years it is something for us to start with this, that you were demonstrably wrong and we were demonstrably right. What has been done since then? County councils have been set up in Ireland. I am not prepared to join in the panegyric which the right hon. Gentleman has pronounced about them. I think that if he knew a little more about them he would not have been so lavish with his praises of them. The University question has been settled.[15] Primary education has been enormously improved. Above all, land purchase has been brought not to completion – because you for your political purposes have checked it – but a sum of some £115,000,000 raised upon British credit has been either paid over or agreed to be paid over under the land purchase system.[16] Where would all that have come from if Home Rule had been granted in 1893?

I go further. What are now the outstanding grievances in Ireland? I know of none. I do not say that there are not many things to be remedied there as there are here. Primary education is one of them. But it will want money, and the way we are going to get money – I hope Irish Members will go down and candidly say so in Ireland – is by taxing land subject to instalments, and, I suppose, by taxing the industries in the North of

[15] The Irish Universities Act (1908) established a National University of Ireland, the seat of which was in Dublin, and three constituent colleges across Ireland were established by charter (University College, Dublin; University College, Cork; and University College, Galway). It dissolved the Royal University and created Queen's University, Belfast. Here, Carson is referring to the fact that the Act gave Roman Catholics facilities for higher education, which resolved an age-old dispute.

[16] Carson is referring to the series of land acts passed by the government, which had allowed Irish peasants to buy land from landlords by borrowing money at generous interest rates. Landlords in turn received generous payments for their holdings financed by the government. Together, the acts radically reduced the concentration of ownership of Irish land and gradually created a class of small independent farmers.

Ireland. I noticed an emphatic phrase of the Prime Minister that the Irish Parliament will have the power of taxing everything. That is a pleasant outlook. I shall deal in a few moments with the argument about Ireland not paying its way, but before I do that I should like, because I do not think its importance can be exaggerated, to say a few words more about what has happened under Unionist policy in Ireland since the last Home Rule Bill was rejected. Take a speech made by Lord MacDonnell on 29th November.[17] He said: – Within the last eight years he had seen marvellous improvements in the state of Ireland. He had seen confidence growing up. Men looked them in the face. Men were no longer afraid of the future. He put that down not to taxation of this or that; he put it down to land purchase, the first great remedial measure that had been introduced. He himself was a Liberal; but counting the measures that had been introduced into Ireland in the last twenty years, the great majority had been introduced by the Conservative party. They would give them credit for that. From Mr. Balfour's time in 1891 up to the present day there had been a succession of great things. Consequently they must admit that however Ireland might have suffered in the past, the day of her regeneration had already dawned. The Vice-President of the Board of Agriculture a short time ago said: – 'People talk about poor Ireland, but I have the opinion that relatively Ireland is doing quite as well as any part of the Empire.' I will not trouble the House by going into figures to show that prosperity. The right hon. Gentleman has admitted it. But if anybody likes to go into the matter they will find that, whereas we were always being taunted in the old Home Rule discussions about the illiberality of this country towards Ireland, about the want of development in Ireland and the poverty of her citizens, the one boast of every Irishman now, whatever his political creed may be, is the advancing prosperity of his country and the progress that her citizens have made. It is that moment, when Ireland was progressing – to use the words of the Vice-President of the Board of Agriculture[18] – as fast and as greatly as any other portion of the Empire, when confidence was largely restored, when great differences were dying down, when men of all creeds were meeting each other in a spirit that, I think, has never existed there before – it is that moment that you select, before even these measures of which I have been speaking have reached

[17] For Lord MacDonnell see p. 64 n. 9.

[18] Thomas Wallace Russell (1841–1920), 1st Baronet, succeeded Horace Plunkett as vice-president of the Irish Department of Agriculture and Technical Instruction in 1907.

their full fruition, to pack Ireland into the melting pot of discussion and the melting pot of all those political and religious passions which have in the past so distracted her from true economic progress and co-operation. I was surprised at the Prime Minister's claim to-day about the cost of Ireland to the Exchequer of the United Kingdom. I think his argument was a false one, and, if I may say so without wishing in the least to say offensive things – [Several HON. MEMBERS: 'Hear, hear.'] – If you like, I will say them – I think the argument was a foolish one. What was his argument? Of course, I know what he was leading up to. He was leading up to this: Taking the finance of Ireland, he had to announce to this House that in getting rid of Ireland, or, rather, in putting Ireland 'on its own', so to speak, in the new Parliament, this country would have to give her a free Grant of £2,000,000 a year. That is what it comes to; also that for ever this country would give up the power under any circumstances, or under any difficulties, of ever again taxing Ireland for any contribution. I do not envy the Prime Minister who ever tries to do it. When you start with this state of finance, when you advance £2,000,000 a year over which you are to have no control, and you are to ask for no contribution, either towards Imperial purposes or the National Debt – not forgetting always that you took over the National Debt of Ireland in 1817 – or towards the upkeep of the Empire![19] The Prime Minister affects to think – of course he does not really do so – that it is the same thing to give away £2,000,000 a year to Ireland over which you have no control, as Ireland being deficient £2,000,000, when Ireland forms a part of the United Kingdom, and you have control of everything. I venture to think that argument will not stand a moment's examination.

What is the object of the United Kingdom? As I understand it, it is that all parts of that Kingdom should be worked together as one whole; under one system, and with the object that the poorer may be helped by the richer, and the richer may be the stronger by the co-operation of the poorer. If you were to take certain counties in England at the present moment – I shall not name any, as it might seem invidious – and work out what their contribution to the United Kingdom is, you will find that many of them do not pay for their upkeep. Is that a reason that they should be deprived of that upkeep? No; and I say this further, that a worse, a more foolish, and a more impossible policy it would be impossible

[19] Referring to the Consolidated Fund Act (1816), which united the public revenues of Great Britain and Ireland into one fund.

to inaugurate than to suggest that either Ireland, or any other part of the United Kingdom, whether large or small, should be allowed to go back in the race of progress, and civilisation, and not to be kept up to the same standard as you yourselves, or as near thereto as possible. The whole of this argument is based upon a fallacy, because the moment you make a common Exchequer you have no right to segregate any unit paying into that Exchequer towards local or Imperial upkeep. As Ireland pays exactly the same taxes as Great Britain pays, you have no right whatsoever to segregate her. It is not true in argument to say that Ireland contributes nothing at the present time to the Imperial upkeep.

There was one observation made by the right hon. Gentleman to which I must reply somewhat. He says, as I understand, that this Bill is to be the precursor of similar devolution to the other countries of the United Kingdom. [HON. MEMBERS: 'Hear, hear.'] That is cheered. We also know that a Resolution was passed by this House – a pious Resolution supported by Members of the Government – calling upon the Government, in the same Parliament, to pass a scheme of Home Rule for Scotland.[20] I am not sure whether poor England was mentioned at all! Just let us look at this for a moment. We are told there was a mandate for this Home Rule Bill at the last Election.[21] I believe that to be false myself; but take it so for the moment. Was there a mandate for Home Rule for England? Was there a mandate for Home Rule for Scotland? I believe the whole of this question as regards the giving of 'Home Rule All Round' – as you call it – or Federal Government, to be absolutely hypocritical as regards this argument.[22] It is put forward simply for the purpose of pretending that you are only giving to Ireland something that you would also give to England and Scotland. You have not the least intention of doing any such thing. You may as well put it in your Preamble; we will then know it is false. I remember all this same pretence years ago. Why, twenty years ago, there was even a Scottish Home Rule Association got

[20] The Resolution was moved by William Chapple (1864–1936) on 28 February 1912.

[21] Asquith followed Gladstone in arguing that the Reform Act of 1884 made it possible to ascertain the levels of support in Ireland for policy developed at Westminster through the outcomes of general elections, not least the election of 1886, which implicitly approved home rule. Asquith went on: 'Eighty per cent at the last Election of the Nationalist Members were returned without opposition.'

[22] 'The Home Rule All Round' proposal, also known as federalism, recommended the creation of four provincial parliaments across the United Kingdom in England, Ireland, Scotland, and Wales, with each also represented in the imperial parliament at Westminster.

up.[23] What has it done for the last twenty years? Has it ever produced a scheme?

Sir HENRY DALZIEL[24]
There is one before the House.

SIR E. CARSON
Has it taken twenty years to grow?

Sir H. DALZIEL
It is produced every year.

SIR E. CARSON
What about Home Rule for England? You will see in a moment how important it is to take the thing together. If you are going to have a federal system, if that is really your view, you are now laying the foundations of these Bills – if you are doing anything at all! Was there a mandate for this at the last Election? Was there a mandate for Home Rule for England? Where are the offices of the English Home Rule Association? Let me in this context try to deal with the argument of the right hon. Gentleman. He says this is to be the foundation of Home Rule all round, including Home Rule for England.[25] The only reason he gives as to why it should be granted is because there is a majority of Irish Members in favour of it, and the congestion of business in this House. Very well. But mainly, he says – and this is the unanswerable argument – it is because a majority of Irish Members are in favour of it. Will the right hon. Gentleman refuse it to England if a majority of the English Members are against it, or, as at the present moment, even against this beginning? How do you know you are ever going to have a majority of English Members in favour of English Home Rule? If you do not get it, are you going to force it upon them? Are you going to do exactly the opposite to what you say you are going to do as regards Ireland? If you are going to act upon the principle that you have laid down, this separatist doctrine, with regard to the majority, and taking each of the three Kingdoms in this way, is the only country that is never going to get Home Rule to be England? And what becomes of your pretence that this is the basis of a great system of devolution all

[23] The Scottish Home Rule Association was set up in 1886.

[24] Henry Dalziel (1868–1935), MP for Kirkaldy Burghs.

[25] Asquith had claimed: 'this Imperial Parliament will have begun to break its own bonds and will be set free by the process, of which this is the first stage, for a fuller and more adequate discharge of its Imperial duties'.

round, for which you have never had even a majority of the constituencies of the country, which you say is necessary before you enter upon it? There is even more than that. If you are going to rely on giving federal government, you must give it in one measure, or you must have it at one and the same time. For this reason: what is the first thing you will have to do? The first thing you will have to do is to lay down what is to be the Imperial system of taxation, not as regards any one of the Kingdoms, but as regards all; secondly, you will have to lay down not the relations of one of them, but the relations of all of them to this House, or rather to the Imperial Houses; thirdly, you will have to lay down the relations of each of them to the other. Have you done that? Why have you not? Because you are only pretending. I go further.

Does the right hon. Gentleman really tell this House that he is going to have Home Rule all round? Does he say that until the other Constitutions are completed the Irish Members are to be here dealing with the local affairs of England and Scotland, and England and Scotland are to have nothing to say about the local affairs of Ireland? No. If you were in earnest you would have these schemes, whether brought in in one Bill or three all operating together. I will put it to the test. I will ask the right hon. Gentleman a question which will test his sincerity upon the subject. Will he agree to hang up this Bill until he has framed the others? Of course he will not. Do hon. Members think he would be allowed? The truth of the matter is that all this is simple hypocrisy. When you are granting to Ireland this system, which is said to be part of the federal system, there is really behind it a much deeper matter than the right hon. Gentleman has dealt with. Before you can grant a federal system at all you must make up your mind as to what is the demand, the real demand, of Ireland. Does Ireland demand national independence – 'Ireland a nation'.[26] Is that her demand? If it is, what has a federal system to do with it? It is inconsistent. You say: 'We cannot grant you national independence. It would not be safe for this country' – though I do not know how that operates upon the argument as to yielding to the majority of Members – 'we cannot have a second independent nation, such as Canada is, practically at our doors'. How much of the feeling I have mentioned do you satisfy by the federal system? Nothing. All you do by your federal system – and indeed there

[26] Asquith had argued that the refusal to meet Irish demands amounted to a failure to recognise 'the deliberate constitutional demands of the vast majority of the nation, repeated and ratified... What nation? The Irish nation – repeated and ratified time after time during the best part of the life of a generation.'

is a great deal of confusion of thought upon this matter – is to give a larger and a greater power to the new Parliament – that is to Ireland, than ever it had before; a power which I believe – and which I think time will show – is irresistible if those concerned persist in their demands in the direction in which they are going – that is of national independence, of 'Ireland a nation'!

Just picture what you are setting up. Do picture it in relation to the complicated system of taxation you are setting up, and which I venture to think will not last six months, and try to realise what it is that will then happen. Just think of the Irish Chancellor of the Exchequer bringing in his Budget and explaining to an Irish House of Commons mainly composed of agricultural Members that it is necessary to raise more money, and that it must come from the land, or if he had the power, which he never will have, from the industries of Ulster. What will be his argument? He would tell the Irish House of Commons, 'This is a very bad system; you have got your instalments to pay to that brutal English Government; they have reserved that to themselves. You have got a great many other taxes to pay, but the one thing we are not allowed to set up is a system of taxation which we know and believe would be best for our own country. We cannot help it. It is the brutal English Government that has done this.' You will not find everybody at that time with all sorts of pleasant death-bed repentances like the hon. and learned Member for Waterford, and then in addition to that you will have your forty Irish Members over here.[27] I doubt if you will have one who will be on the side of England. I do not know why you should. You will have your forty Irish Members over here probably holding the balance between both parties in this House, and they will be asking you not paltry questions about a post office at Ballaghaderreen or some other place,[28] but they will be directing your serious attention probably to an outbreak against taxation in Ireland which has all been caused by the artificial system of taxation you have set up, and by your partial gift which only gives power to ask for more. That is all you are doing by setting up a federal system. Lord Derby in 1887 wrote this,[29] which is mentioned in the Life of the Duke of Devonshire: – 'I hold, and have held full along, that there is no middle course possible,

[27] John Redmond (1856–1918), leader of the Irish Parliamentary Party, was the MP for Waterford City.

[28] A town between Roscommon and Mayo in the west of Ireland.

[29] Frederick Arthur Stanley (1841–1908), 16th Earl of Derby.

if Ireland and England are not to be one.[30] Ireland must be treated like Canada or Australia. All between is delusion and fraud.' Yes, Sir, and delusion and fraud is what you are adopting. But whatever limitations you put into your Bill, and whatever reservation and whatever limitation of taxation you make in your Bill, believe me once your Bill passes you will have no power on earth to resist. Will the Irish Members tell us that this is going to be accepted as a final settlement? I venture to think that not one of them will. The hon. and learned Member for Waterford himself was the Member who got up when Mr. Gladstone's 'final settlement' was passing its Third Reading, and told us this: – 'As the Bill now stands no man in his senses can regard it as a full, final, and satisfactory settlement of the Irish question.'[31] Sir, the word 'provisional', so to speak, has been stamped in red ink across every page of this Bill. I venture to say in addition to the word 'provisional' the word 'fantastic' will be found on every Section of this Bill. Anybody who has watched the movement in Ireland will see that at the present moment, even before your Bill is brought in, there is an outcry against the very limitations you are attempting to impose by it. The hon. Member for East Mayo said in 1904: – 'I say deliberately that I should never have dedicated my life as I have done to this great struggle if I did not see at the end of this great struggle the crowning and consummation of our work in a free and independent nation.'[32] What has that got to do with Federalism? We have had very little discussion of the Bill by English Ministers during the autumn or up to the present. I imagined the reason was they did not know what they would be allowed to put into the Bill. The right hon. Gentleman the First Lord of the Admiralty made a speech at Belfast,[33] and that speech was adopted, as I understand it, by the hon. and learned Member for Waterford. Two or three days afterwards one of his followers, the Member for North Meath,[34] said this: – On the question of legislative freedom he noticed that Mr. Churchill was silent, but that was no reason why they should be silent. Wherever Irishmen met they must declare they would not be satisfied with anything short of a free and unfettered Parliament. Irishmen

[30] Bernard Holland, *The Life of Spencer Compton, Eighth Duke of Devonshire* (London: Longmans, 1911), 2 vols., II, ch. 21.

[31] Referring to John Redmond MP.

[32] John Dillon (1851–1927), Irish Parliamentary Party MP.

[33] Winston Churchill (1874–1965) visited Belfast in February 1912 where he made a pro-home rule speech alongside John Redmond in front of a large crowd of nationalists.

[34] Patrick White (1860–1935), Irish Parliamentary Party MP.

had always maintained that Ireland was a nation, but Mr. Churchill was somewhat inconsistent, for subsequently he said the Imperial Parliament could repeal a Bill passed by the Irish Parliament. Was there any free Parliament in the world that would allow an outside Parliament to repeal its laws? If the Irish Parliament is to be dominated by the English Parliament, and if the English Parliament has power to repeal a law which is passed then that Irish Parliament would only be a sham, and in less than twenty years the people of this country will find themselves worse off than they are now. The extraordinary part of it all is that we are always being told we ought to trust the Irish Nationalist Member. I believe myself it is only in trust, if you can trust them, that any guarantee counts at all. But on what ground are we asked to trust them? Upon the ground that we ought not to believe a single word they have ever said. Now the right hon. Gentleman took some time in developing the guarantees that we are to have. There is not one of them worth the paper it is written on. There can be no guarantees of an administration unless you have confidence in the Parliament to which that administration is to be responsible. The Executive is everything. It is idle to tell us that the Lord Lieutenant is to exercise his veto. Is it upon the advice of his Executive in Ireland or is it upon the advice of the Cabinet in England? Is it upon both, or is it sometimes upon the one and sometimes upon the other? What a farce it is to tell us you are going to establish a Parliament, and all the paraphernalia of an independent Executive, answerable alone to that Parliament, and the moment anything arises you are to send over here to Downing Street and say, 'Stop the Parliament you set up! Stop the nominated Chamber you yourselves have nominated! Override the Lord Lieutenant, and tell him to set at nought your Parliament and your nominative Chamber!'

What a position for any country to be in. No, Sir, the veto of the Lord Lieutenant is worth nothing. Instructions from His Majesty are worth nothing in this Bill 'to bring about better relations; and for the better government of the two-countries'. And just think, the Lord Lieutenant is to hold office for six years; he cannot be changed when there is a change of Ministers in this House, and he is to receive his directions from the Government of the day in power. The next Government, coming in a few days afterwards, can upset every one of them. What other guarantees are there? If anything is done *ultra vires* [35] you can go before the Privy Council in England. That is a good thing to tell a man who feels that he has

[35] That is, beyond one's legal power or authority.

been unfairly dealt with: 'What grievance have you – you man in a dockyard or in a factory? Go before the Privy Council of England?' No, Sir, the guarantees are valueless. I do not often agree with the hon. Member for East Mayo, but he said this, speaking in November last at Salford: – Then there was the question of guarantees. The Irish party were asked if they were willing that guarantees should be inserted in the Home Rule measure to protect the Protestant minority. He attached no importance to those guarantees at all. He did not believe that artificial guarantees in an Act of Parliament were any real protection. That is why they have allowed the Government so profusely to put them in. Let me take one example of what I mean by administration throwing over any guarantees even under our present system. You passed the University Bill. It was a Bill which Nonconformists opposite were very careful to see had safeguards against it being turned into a denominational Bill. I was under no such delusion. I remember seeing posted up somewhere on one of your organisations, or some place that was in sympathy with you, a document giving a list of your great aims, and bearing the statement that this was the greatest Protestant Parliament that ever existed since the time of Cromwell.[36] That was a great boast, and it did them great credit to pass that Bill; they took great care that there should be safeguards in it to prevent its being turned to denominational purposes. And to follow this you must remember that the Bill provided that county councils were allowed to give scholarships to the University, and what is the first thing they did? Did they care about your safeguards? Here is what Cardinal Logue said:[37] – 'No matter what obstacles the Nonconformists of England may have inserted in the constitution of the University to keep it from being made Catholic we will make it Catholic in spite of them.'

I am not blaming him. I am only calling attention to the fact. Then what becomes of your scholarships? When you have made the University Catholic the county councils give the scholarships, but they tell you they will not allow them to be held unless you go to that University because it has been made Catholic. What becomes of your elaborate provision that they are not to be allowed to endow any religion? They will tell you that there will be no open persecution. Of course not. Nobody suggests that anybody will go and shoot a man because he is a Protestant

[36] Oliver Cromwell (1599–1658) brought Ireland into an 'incorporating' union with Britain in the aftermath of the military conquest of the island, which took place between 1649 and 1653.

[37] Michael Logue (1840–1924), a prominent Irish Catholic prelate.

or a Catholic or vice versa. That is not the way it is done, and nobody is afraid of that. That is the kind of thing they represent us as being afraid of. No, Sir, it is the working of the institution for political or for religious purposes and objects, and that no guarantee set up by any Parliament can prevent. What we may look for, too, can be seen by the threats that have already been made. The hon. Member for East Mayo (Mr. Dillon), speaking last October when he wanted to put pressure on certain landlords to compel them to sell their land, said: – 'I tell these men that the sands in the hour-glass are running out fast. Home Rule is coming and we will get it whether they like it or not, and when Home Rule has come and there is an Irish Parliament sitting in Dublin I do not think they will get English Ministers to trouble themselves much about their woes in future. They will make their bed with the people of Ireland and, be it short or long, they will have to be on that bed. It is better for them to make friends with their own people while there is yet time.' Yes, we know what 'making friends' means. No wonder that the hon. Member for Cork (Mr. W. O'Brien),[38] who has taken so great an interest in land purchase and who was a party to the bargain that has been so disgracefully broken, said in relation to that speech that once the Unionists, aye, or the Liberals, got it into their heads that an Irish Parliament would produce the hell upon earth foreshadowed by Mr. Dillon there would be an end of any Home Rule Bill for years. It is not possible for me on a Motion of this kind to examine all the various proposals that have been indicated by the right hon. Gentleman. I have taken the matter in a general way. All through the Prime Minister's speech I have asked myself what are the benefits that he indicates to Irishmen, and I have not heard one. Does he think his complicated finance will make it easier to raise taxation in Ireland? Does he think the separation of the poorer and the richer country will benefit the poorer country? Does he think that in Ireland, in a country torn asunder unfortunately by religious dissension and by very grave political differences, the withdrawal of England as the arbitrator between the two will bring about a better state of things? No, Sir. I at all events represent here a minority only and I admit it, but it is a minority which has always been true to the United Kingdom.

[38] William O'Brien (1852–1928), founder of the All-for-Ireland-League, which took a conciliatory approach to the home rule question and was also concerned with land reform, was MP for Mallow in Co. Cork.

Some people say this is really a religious question. I do not see if it is that it is any less to be considered or any less important on that ground. But, Sir, it is a religious question added to various other questions. There is no doubt that the broad dividing line in Ireland in relation to this question of the Home Rule Bill can broadly be said to put on one side the Protestants, and on the other side the Roman Catholics. I know there are some Protestants, not many I think, who are Home Rulers, just as there are some Catholics, a great many I think, who are not Home Rulers. It is unfortunate that that should be the dividing line, but it is there and you cannot neglect it. The reason this is the dividing line in my opinion is an historical one. In my opinion it is the dividing line, because Protestantism has in history been looked upon as the British occupation in Ireland. It is the dividing line, because when you attempted to bring home to the people the principles of the Reformation, you did not succeed in Ireland as you did in England and in Scotland. There remains, however, the dividing line, and I would like to know when a statesman takes up a question he has to solve with that line there, what argument is there that you can raise for giving Home Rule to Ireland that you do not equally raise for giving Home Rule to that Protestant minority in the north-east province? I believe there is none. But in addition that minority which is there gives an answer to the argument of the failure of the rule of the United Kingdom Parliament in Ireland. The success of Belfast, which has grown from 15,000 or 16,000 people before the Union to a population of 400,000 or thereabouts, the success of the surrounding counties, not at all the most prolific or the most fertile in Ireland, give the lie to those who say that it is English misrule in Ireland, as they call it – though why it should be called English I do not know – that has prevented the other parts of Ireland attaining a similar state of prosperity. Those are the men at all events that I represent here – the men whom you invited into your Parliament when Pitt passed his Bill.[39]

Mr. SWIFT MACNEILL[40]
Bribery.

[39] William Pitt the Younger (1759–1806) became prime minister in 1783 and spearheaded the 1801 Act of Union.

[40] John Gordon Swift MacNeill (1849–1926), a Protestant MP for South Donegal and a member of the Irish Parliamentary Party.

Sir E. CARSON

You had better not talk of bribery. [An HON. MEMBER: 'We shall talk a great deal of it.'] I do not think there needs much to be said about bribery since the corruption of last year on the Parliament Bill, when you were prepared to buy votes for peerages. You had then a little less to say for corruption, because that was done at your bidding. The Unionist minority in Ireland were invited into your Union. Reading Mr. Gladstone's speech the other day I noticed he said that they were the men who opposed the Union. Sir, that seems to me to be the strongest reason why you should not now turn them out of the Union. You ask them into the Union and they asked to be left out. They came in and they got satisfied under your rule, and became loyal, and because they did, now you tell them to go out. Sir, that is a policy of cowardice. Where is the precedent in the whole of history for any such action by a Parliament – a Parliament turning out a community who are satisfied to stay under their rule. We used to hear of Norway and Sweden, but that argument has gone, and gone in the direction which it necessarily must go, when the tendency is for separation and not for union and co-operation.[41] We, at all events, in this matter have a plain and a ready duty before us. It is to oppose this Bill with all the energy we can at every stage and at every moment that it is before the House. That is our duty. We believe it to be an unnecessary Bill. We believe it to be a fatal Bill for our country, and an equally fatal Bill for yours, and, above all things, we believe it to be involved in the greatest series of dishonourable transactions that have ever disgraced any country.

[41] The dissolution of the Union between the Kingdoms of Sweden and Norway took place on 26 October 1905.

7 Ulster's[1]

Solemn League and Covenant[2]

Being convinced in our consciences that Home Rule would be disastrous to the material well-being of Ulster as well as of the whole of Ireland, subversive of our civil and religious freedom, destructive of our citizenship and perilous to the unity of the Empire, we, whose names are underwritten, men of Ulster, loyal subjects of His Gracious Majesty King George V., humbly relying on the God whom our fathers in days of stress and trial confidently trusted, do hereby pledge ourselves in solemn Covenant, throughout this our time of threatened calamity, to stand by one another in defending, for ourselves and our children, our cherished position of equal citizenship in the United Kingdom, and in using all means which may be found necessary to defeat the present conspiracy to set up a Home Rule Parliament in Ireland. ¶ And in the event of such a Parliament being forced upon us, we further solemnly and mutually pledge ourselves to refuse to recognise its authority. ¶ In sure confidence that God will defend the right, we hereto subscribe our names. ¶ And further, we individually declare that we have not already signed this Covenant.

The above was signed by me at ________________________
'Ulster Day', Saturday, 28th September, 1912.

__________ God Save the King. __________

[1] The hand appears in red on the original Covenant, reflecting the symbol of the red hand of Ulster.

[2] *Ulster's Solemn League and Covenant*, usually referred to as the *Ulster Covenant*, was drafted by Thomas Sinclair (1838–1914), a businessman and politician, and signed by 237,368 unionist men in protest against the third Home Rule Bill introduced by the Liberal government on 11 April 1912.

8 Ulster's[1]

Solemn League and Covenant[2]

Text of the Covenant made by the Ulster Women's Unionist Council, and which has been signed by the loyal women of Ulster in token of their unwavering hostility to Home Rule: –

We, whose names are underwritten, women of Ulster, and loyal subjects of our gracious King, being firmly persuaded that Home Rule would be disastrous to our country, desire to associate ourselves with the men of Ulster in their uncompromising opposition to the Home Rule Bill now before Parliament, whereby it is proposed to drive Ulster out of her cherished place in the Constitution of the United Kingdom, and to place her under the domination and control of a Parliament in Ireland.

Praying that from this calamity God will save Ireland, we hereto subscribe our names.

The above was signed by me at

'Ulster Day', Saturday, 28th September, 1912.

God Save the King.

1 The hand appears in red on the original Covenant, reflecting the symbol of the red hand of Ulster.

2 Usually referred to as the 'Women's Declaration'. Women were not permitted to sign the original Ulster Covenant, so this document was drafted by Thomas Sinclair (1838–1914), a businessman and politician, and sent to the Ulster Women's Unionist Council for comment. The Declaration was signed by 234,046 women.

9 Thomas M. Kettle, 'The Economics of Nationalism'*

The science of Economics is commonly held to be lamentably arid and dismal. If that is your experience of it, blame the economists. For the slice of life, with which Economics has to deal, vibrates and, so to say, bleeds with human actuality. All science, all exploration, all history in its material factors, the whole epic of man's effort to subdue the earth and establish himself on it, fall within the domain of the economist. His material consists of the ordinary man in the ordinary business of mundane life, that, namely, of getting a living. This means more than food, clothes, and shelter. The highest activities of art and religion can function only under material forms. Churches have to be paid for as well as factories; you can no more get a bar of Caruso for nothing than you can get a bar of soap for nothing.[1] Economics, moreover, is committed to an analysis not only of the production, but also of the distribution of wealth. In other words, it has to face formally the vast and dismaying problem of poverty. In the accomplishment of these tasks, moreover, the economist, preoccupied with one mode of organization among mankind, must necessarily consider the influence on it of other modes devised or evolved for other ends. Politics imposes itself on him. He can evade the political aspect of his material only by evading reality.

[1] Enrico Caruso (1873–1921), the Italian operatic tenor.

* Part of a paper read at St. Patrick's College, Maynooth, December 5, 1912. *Editorial note:* the chapter was included in Thomas M. Kettle, *The Day's Burden: Studies Literary and Political, and Miscellaneous Essays* (Dublin: Maunsel, 1918).

I

It is to a special hinterland of this last tract of territory that I wish to direct your minds to-night. Our inquiry is simple enough, and begins, as far as concerns myself, with a personal examination of conscience. Does the title National Economics amount to a contradiction in terms? If it does not, and if the nation holds a legitimate place in economic life and thought, is it that of a blessing or that of a nuisance? And if it is beneficent can we formulate an economic ideal fitted to express the self-realization of a nation which is resolute to realize itself?

A good many critics, endowed with that verbal deftness so characteristic of Irish critics, have said to me: 'You have a Chair of National Economics in your college. Have you also by any chance a Chair of National Trigonometry or National Biology?'[2] The gibe does not go home. So long as you keep to the sphere of the highly abstract sciences any limiting particularity is certainly incongruous. But as you pass from the greyness of theory to the golden-green foliage of the tree of life, to the rich and endless differentiation of concrete fact, the incongruity diminishes. A National Mathematics is absurd; a National Biology is not quite so absurd, seeing that every country has its own peculiar flora and fauna. When you come to a National Economics the incongruity has wholly disappeared. Plainly you can constitute for each nation under that title a branch of Descriptive Economics. Plainly since one nation is at one stage of growth, and another at another, and since the economy of each is, so to say, steeped and soaked in its temperament and history, your corpus of fact will in each case be strongly individual. Plainly you will have in each case a separate therapeutic. But I suggest to you that the doctrine of Nationalism in Economics goes far deeper than that.

Nationality is a principle of organization. You may regard it as ultimate and good, or as transitorial and bad, and there is no narrowly scientific test by which either view can be dismissed. But in accordance with your first standpoint your whole outlook is determined. Now, there is no doubt that the classical or English school of Political Economy did appear in its early years to be an almost irresistible solvent of Nationalism.[3] You will

[2] Kettle was appointed to a Chair in National Economics at University College Dublin in 1910.

[3] The English or 'Classical' School of political economy is normally taken to have begun with T. R. Malthus (1766–1834), James Mill (1773–1836), and David Ricardo (1772–1823) and to have continued through J. R. McCulloch (1789–1864) and J. S. Mill (1806–73).

find in Toynbee's *Industrial Revolution* two curiously similar judgments to that effect left on record by two such conflicting contemporaries as Coleridge and Napoleon.[4] The reasons are in no way mysterious. The Classicists were all for freedom – free trade, free contract, free competition – and Nationalism appeared to them under the form of restrictions on freedom. Internal tolls were disappearing: why should not the custom-house disappear? Self-contained manor and self-contained town had been fused by a long historical process into the nation: why should not the nations be fused into a world-economy? The tides seemed to be setting in that direction. Capital was becoming at once more powerful and more fluid, and there is in capital an inherent cosmopolitanism. Labour moved towards internationalism as an essential part of its 'gospel of deliverance'. What were armies and navies but the watch-dogs of the rich? What were national flags and songs but parts of a ritual which they employed to intoxicate and exploit the poor? 'The proletariat', cried out Marx in his thunderous manifesto, 'has no fatherland.'[5] The whole thought of that period is, indeed, dyed in the grain with cosmopolitanism. And then there comes that sudden upheaving renaissance, and Nationalism is there as a colossal fact. The simplest account of the change is that it was a spontaneous outgush from the deep wells of human nature, and from the overlaid but unexhausted springs of history. From that time on to our own every nation sets deliberately about the task of self-realization, material and intellectual.

The English bias towards the 'classical' economy was readily intelligible. Dominating the world she took her dominance for granted: she was unconscious of her nationality in the sense in which an entirely healthy man is unconscious of his digestion: and she devised a regime under which every other nation should be, in reference to her, a pupil and a tributary. But as the forces of growth matured and expanded in other nations they declined to Peter-Pan it to England.[6] And so effective was their refusal that if you turn to a contemporary German text-book you will find

[4] Arnold Toynbee, *Lectures on the Industrial Revolution* (London: Longmans, Green, 1884). In the first chapter, on 'Ricardo and the Old Political Economy', Toynbee cited Coleridge and Napoleon on the individualist values underpinning political economy in the Ricardian tradition.

[5] Karl Marx, *Manifest der Kommunistischen Partei* (London: J. E. Burghard, 1848), first published in English in 1850.

[6] Referring to the famous work by J. M. Barrie, which first appeared as a play in 1904 and then as a novel in 1911.

the three periods of modern economic thought formally classified as (1) Mercantilism, (2) Liberalism, and (3) Nationalism.

What is the case for Nationalism? Well, if you turn to the leaders of the revolt of which I have spoken, such as List, or Henry Carey, the Irish-American, you will find a scientific or semi-scientific statement of it.[7] If you turn to a modern leader of the revolt against what I may call Juggernaut Imperialism, such as Mr. Chesterton, you will find a better statement in terms of poetry and human nature ...[8] You will, of course, bear in mind that Mr. Chesterton is not sufficiently dull to be authoritative. Being an artist, he is ever labouring to add to an old truth the radiance of a new beauty, which compromises him with the grave and the learned ... Let me try in a less adequate way to suggest in outline the creed of Nationalism. Professor Cannan, in his recent book, *The Economic Outlook*, elaborates an antithesis between Socialism and Nationalism. And in that form the case for Nationalism is best stated.[9] His view would seem to be not that Nationalism is visibly dying, but that it can be shown to be obviously incompatible with Socialism, and that, therefore, presumably, it must die.

The stern, inevitable logic of this conclusion escapes me. The presence of the steam engine on George Stephenson's pioneer railway was incompatible with the presence of the cow, but it was not the engine that perished in the encounter. The whole tradition of Europe is for Nationalism and against Socialism. Give us deep-cutting reforms; liberate and redeem labour; bind property and service in a bond that must be respected; assume for the nation all the economic functions which in the hands of individuals degenerate into waste or tyranny; render it impossible for any man to become, by mere dead weight of money, master of his fellows, body and soul. So far we are with you. But propose to ladle us all, with all that we own and are, into your communistic hotch-pot, and, entrenched behind the ancient bulwarks of personality, family, nationality, we repel and annihilate you in the name of civilization. If too much unearned property is the grave of freedom, some earned property, with the seal of

[7] Friedrich List (1789–1846), a German-American economist; Henry Charles Carey (1793–1879), a leading American economist and son of an Irishman.

[8] G. K. Chesterton (1874–1936), English writer and lay theologian, set himself against empty cosmopolitanism and materialist gratification – for instance in his 'A Defence of Patriotism' from *The Defendant* (London: R. Brimley Johnson, 1901), where he defends the love of one's native land against 'deaf and raucous Jingoism'.

[9] Edwin Cannan was a British economist and historian of economic thought; *The Economic Outlook* (London: T. Fisher Unwin, 1912).

service on it, is the cradle of freedom. Even in Ibsen the button-moulder was able to fling back Peer Gynt into the melting-pot only because Peer had remained all his life a mere self-amorous incoherence, in the true sense, a nonentity.[10] But the nation that is a richly positive entity cannot so be dissolved and dismissed. Destroy Nationalism, and you extinguish the sacrificial flames about which the greatest nobleness of the world has gathered in abnegation. You shatter the altar vessels in which the precious wine of freedom has been passed from lip to lip.

'Cosmopolitanism', says Turgénev in *Rudin*, 'is all twaddle.... Even the ideal face must have an individual expression.'[11] This humanity, to the worship of which you are to butcher Nationalism, is too vast, too vague, too bloodless an abstraction. Our arms are not long enough to fold it in an embrace. Ireland I feel equal to, and Dublin, and that windy Atlantic cliff, straining out against the ocean and the sunset, and that farmer to whom I spoke at Tralee fair, and that publican in Tyrone, and the labourers, spoiled by unemployment, who come to me at my house nearly every day, and for whom I can get no work. But as for the world as a whole, even its geography is too large for my head, to say nothing of its problems, and its emotions are too large for my heart. What is humanity? You and I and the man round the corner, or over the sea, are humanity. And if it is the nature of us all to come to amplest self-expression by living our lives here and now, for a community which is small enough to know and to love, then by 'transcending' national categories you do not enrich, you impoverish, humanity.

Nationalism, indeed, like every other fine faith, has the misfortune to be judged less by its core of dogma than by its shell of superstition. Tariffism and militarism are its apes, not the authentic sons of its house.[12] The parallel to which appeal has been made avails here also. If I knock you down in the street, or, when you call on me, slam the door in your face, these are beyond all doubt impressive proofs of the fact that I enjoy an existence separate from yours. But there are other and better proofs, as, for instance, to buy from you, to learn from you, to feed, foster, or help

[10] A reference to the major Norwegian playwright Henrik Ibsen and his 1867 work *Peer Gynt*.

[11] The Russian novelist, playwright, and author Ivan Sergeyevich Turgenev (1818–83) published his first novel, *Rudin*, in 1856.

[12] Tariff Reform, associated with the national campaign by Liberal unionist MP Joseph Chamberlain (1836–1914) for an imperial preference on imports that would stir up popular feeling towards the Empire, became popular among Conservative grassroots from 1903.

you. There are better ways of putting heads together than banging them together. In precisely the same way a nation degrades and cancels Nationalism by choosing to identify it with isolation or aggressiveness. The first blunder is at war with the conscience of all ages: a character as Goethe says, can fashion itself only in the stream of the world.[13] The second is certainly at war with the conscience of this age. To receive hospitably, and assimilate deeply; to toil, to think, and to communicate without penury or reserve – these remain the marks of a strong nation as of a strong man. Free trade in ideas as in commodities is the desired regime of those who have attained maturity. But it is a strange altruism which bids me not only give myself, but slay myself, so that at the end of the process there is no basis left either for self-regarding or for altruistic action. I must own myself in order to give myself.

Curiously enough, it is in the writings of contemporary theorists of continental Socialism that we find the most eloquent repudiation of Professor Cannan's philosophy. Practice had preceded theory. Labour once thought – in the days of the Communist Manifesto – that its destiny centered in cosmopolitanism. On that basis it sought to construct an International, but it failed, and the failure led to a notable transformation of Marxism. To-day you have an International that possesses reality because it roots in Nationalism. We Nationalists may appeal to the authoritative words of Professor Sombart in his *Socialism and the Social Movement*: –

> Marx's opinion, 'The working-classes have no fatherland', is being replaced by another, 'If that is so, let us give them one.' … The view is gaining ground among Socialists – indeed especially among them – that all civilization has its roots in nationality, and that civilization can reach its highest development only on the basis of nationality.[14]

He goes on to quote glowing and splendid passages from David and Penestorfer, to one of which we may appeal:

> Socialism and national idea are thus not opposed to each other; they rather supplement each other. Every attempt to weaken the national idea is an attempt to lessen the precious possessions of mankind … Socialism wants to organize, and not disintegrate, humanity. But in the organisms of mankind, not individuals, but nations, are the

[13] Johann Wolfgang von Goethe (1749–1842), the famous German novelist, playwright, poet, and natural scientist.

[14] Werner Sombart, a leading German economist and socialist scientist; *Socialism and the Social Movement in the Nineteenth Century* (London: G. P. Putnam's Sons, 1898).

> tissues, and if the whole organism is to remain wholly healthy, it is necessary for the tissues to be healthy.

As for your capitalist who, in those days, was a cosmopolitan, he is now in every country a jingo. Herr Goldenberg is no sooner settled in Park Lane than you find his name heading the list of subscriptions to Lord Roberts' Conscription League.[15]

The general significance of the new politics is twofold. It substitutes an organic for the old atomistic conception of economic life. And in establishing the nation as a principle of organization it establishes it also as a principle of sacrifice, and therein provides the only basis of Protection that is not intellectually disreputable.

II

Such 'sentimentalities' will strike strangely and even harshly on the ears of those who have been bred up to believe that Political Economy began with Adam Smith and ended with John Stuart Mill, and that between 1780 and 1850 the laws underlying the business life of mankind were defined, once and for all, in immutable formulae.[16] The line of thought suggested by them is very ill represented in English text-books. There is a reason for the lacuna, as for most things, and it lies on the surface. If you want a full appreciation of the significance of health you must go not to the athlete's gymnasium, but to the hospital ward. If you want an appreciation of the value of national freedom and unity, you must go, not to the one nation which entered the Steam Age with these foundations of greatness deeply established, but to one of those which, during the nineteenth century, had to work out their salvation, political and economic, through blood and tears. During the period of crystallization of the Classical Economy the industrial hegemony of Great Britain was absolute. Her supremacy in coal, in iron, in shipping, in machinery, in

[15] Frederick Sleigh Roberts (1832–1914), 1st Earl Roberts, founded the National Service League in 1902, which campaigned for a programme of conscription. The reference to 'Herr Goldenberg' is intended to associate jingoism, capitalism, and Judaism, as popularised for instance by J. A. Hobson (1858–1940) when reporting on the Boer War.

[16] Adam Smith (1723–90), the renowned Scottish Enlightenment figure often celebrated as 'The Father of Economics', produced two classical works, *The Theory of Moral Sentiments* (1759) and *An Inquiry into the Nature and Causes of the Wealth of Nations* (1776); John Stuart Mill (1806–73), political economist, philosopher and MP, was one of the major influential thinkers in classical liberalism. His *Principles of Political Economy* appeared in 1848.

the technique of manufacture was unchallenged. On this basis the great theorists, like Ricardo, implicitly, if not deliberately, proceeded.[17] The system which they evolved was at once too English in matter, too abstract in method, and too dogmatic in tone. Protests against its exclusiveness, its insularity, could be multiplied from the pages of Continental economics. Thus Adolph Wagner, the great Austrian master, summarizing Roscher, a precursor, in his *Foundations*, writes: –

> They (the English school) have a tendency to rely solely on abstract deduction, and to exaggerate its importance …; in theory, but especially in practice, they isolate economic phenomena too radically from the other social phenomena with which they are intimately associated; they assign to economic phenomena and institutions, and to their solutions of economic questions, a character too absolute, instead of assigning only that relative and historical character which is proper to all the facts of history; their verdict on Free Trade, and its results, is in many respects erroneous, and a great deal too optimistic; they efface the State too completely, and misunderstand its rôle as regulator of the national economy.[18]

This judgment, which is not precisely a condemnation of scientific principles, but rather a methodological admonition, may now be said to be universally accepted. It is interesting to note that one of the first, and most influential, writers to propagate it in English was John Kells Ingram. Still more interesting is it to note the essential identity of the human reality behind it with that behind 'Who Fears to Speak of '98?'[19] The red fire of passion has been transmuted into the illumination of science, but here, as always, Ingram voices the revolt of the small nations against the Czarism, scientific and political, of the great. The reaction in Economics is most adequately represented by the German Historical School.[20] Of its leaders, from List and Roscher to Schmoller and Wagner, it is not too much to say that every nerve and fibre of their science

[17] David Ricardo (1772–1823), a prominent classical economist and MP.

[18] Adolph Wagner (1835–1917), economist and politician, was in fact born in Germany. Kettle is referring to his work *Grundlegung der politischen Ökonomie* (Leipzig: C. F. Winter'sche Verlagshandlung, 1892), citing Wilhelm Roscher (1817–94), a founder of the German Historical School of political economy.

[19] John Kells Ingram (1823–1907), economist and mathematician based at Trinity College Dublin. Ingram is better known for authoring this poem in honour of the 1798 Rebellion, a republican insurrection against British rule in Ireland.

[20] The School used history to explain economic matters and rejected a brand of 'theoretical' economics associated with English political economy.

quivers with Nationalism.[21] The simplest account of German history during the second generation of the nineteenth century is that it was the adolescence of a giant. It is significant of the giant's future that, during that period, he finds it most natural to call the study of business life not 'Political Economy' or merely 'Economics', but 'National Economics', *Nationaloekonomik*. From the purely scientific point of view the reaction was, undoubtedly, carried too far. If it was the fashion of the Classical School to dogmatize about everything, from a minimum of experience, it became that of the Historical School to accumulate all the experience of all time, and then to decline to dogmatize about anything. The one sect burned incense, and very often offered up human sacrifice, on the altar of inexorable laws. The other did, indeed, question from time to time the propriety of certain details of the ritual, but their dissent went very much deeper. They said simply: There are no such laws. You are worshipping the non-existent. But as spokesmen of real life against the phantasm of the intellect, which had come to be mistaken for real life, the historical economists were wholly in the right. The fruitfulness of their influences is best witnessed by a writer who does not wholly sympathize with it. Thus Professor Landry, one of the leaders of the newer generation in France, observes in his *Manuel d'Economique*: –

> It is much easier now to distinguish the Economics of one nation from that of another than it was at the beginning of the nineteenth century. This results in part from the fact that in the interval the content of Economics has been greatly enriched, and, in consequence, greatly diversified. But it is also to be explained by the development, during the nineteenth century of the spirit of Nationalism in, at all events, many parts of the civilized world. For more than a hundred years the countries in question have deliberately sought to differentiate themselves in the region of scientific research from their neighbours. Indeed, strange and deplorable as it may seem, there are even countries in which economic writers deliberately cover with contempt the productive economy of their neighbours, or else refuse to consider it at all.[22]

[21] Respectively Friedrich List (1789–1846); Wilhelm Georg Friedrich Roscher (1817–94), a German economist; Gustav von Schmoller (1838–1917), a leader of the German Historical School of Economics; and Adolph Wagner (1835–1917).

[22] Adolphe Landry (1874–1956), a French demographer, politician and author of several books on economics; *Manuel d'économique: à l'usage des facultés de droit* (Paris: V. Giard et E. Brière, 1908).

That the Historical School should also be, under another aspect, the National School, can occasion no surprise. On the one hand, if you turn to history at all the first fact that impresses itself is the colossal fact of nationality: on the other, every concrete nationality is in origin, form and tendency an historical product.

So much for what we may style the rehabilitation of the national idea. I may seem to you to have laboured it too much with something of a Falstaffian parade of erudition: if so, the explanation is obvious.[23] When you come to mix in the actual life of our contemporary Ireland, you will find everybody on the one side concerned about national self-realization, political and economic. You will find everybody on the other parroting forth the perennial nonsense that the Irish question is not political but purely economic. You will turn to some standard text-book for enlightenment – in the nature of things it will be an English text-book – and you will be confused and discouraged to find principles, which you greatly value, either cheapened or ignored. I have tried to suggest to you that there is an historical explanation for all this. Continental experience comes much closer to ours than does English experience, and Continental thought, is, as a result, a much truer source of guidance. To offer a purely economic solution for a politico-economic problem, such as ours, is futile, and even absurd. It is as if a doctor were to tell his patient, that once his lungs are brought back to health, it does not matter whether there is an aneurism in his heart or not.

It should be added that the line of criticism suggested is fully valid only as against the popularizers, not as against the masters of the English school.

III

The acceptance of the national as against the individual, of the organic as against the atomistic, point of view, transforms nearly every economic problem. Let us consider one or two of them very briefly, and first of all that of external trade policy.

I have already described what may be called platform Protectionism as intellectually disreputable. The orthodox Free Trader has no difficulty in riddling it. It is true that, theoretically in certain posited conditions,

[23] A reference to William Shakespeare's character Sir John Falstaff in *Henry IV, Part I* and *II*, and in *The Merry Wives of Windsor*, meaning fat, jolly, and indulgent.

and in one or two rare instances in practice, a tax on an import may be thrown back on to the foreign producer. But, in general, the very object of a Protective tariff is to raise prices, obtainable by the home producer, and payable by the home consumer, in the home market. If that object is not attained the tariff affords no 'Protection'. In the long run the increase of prices may, indeed, lead to the exploitation of native resources, hitherto untapped, and prices may gradually sink to their former level. But, for the time being, a tribute is, and must be, levied on the consumer. How, then, are we to describe except as impostors the Protectionists who run gaily about the country with their big and their little loaves, and all the rest of the paraphernalia, explaining that they are going to make everybody richer by adding a tax to the price of everything? So far, the Manchester stalwart is certainly entitled to the verdict as against him of Birmingham. But, when we have reached this point, the controversy is so far from being at an end that it is in truth only beginning. The advocate of taxed, as against untaxed, imports retreats to higher ground, or rather launches his charge from it. We have already quoted one great Irishman, Dr. Ingram; we now fall back on another, Professor Bastable, both of Trinity College, Dublin: –

> To understand the position taken up by the modern opponents of Free Trade [writes Professor Bastable in his *Commerce of Nations*], it is, above all, essential to recognize that the key-note of their system is nationality.... The claims of the nation as a whole are accentuated, and regarded as far more important than those of the individual, or the world at large.[24]

The nation has a continuity of existence to which none of its children can pretend. It has been from of old; it will still be long after the dust of this generation has been blown about the barren plains, or sealed within the iron hills. Given such an organism, so extended in space and time, it is reasonable to sacrifice the welfare of a part of it to that of the whole, and to sacrifice its own present to its future. The nation is held to be entitled to require from each of its citizens, even in time of peace, tax-contributions which will be spent on great public objects in which assuredly he has no bread-and-butter interest; in time of war, it will exact from him his property, his service in arms, and finally his blood. The nation does not live by bread alone, but, if its bread fails, the special type of culture of which it is

[24] Charles Francis Bastable (1855–1945), an Irish economist, Whately Professor of Political Economy and Regius Professor of Laws at Trinity College Dublin; *The Commerce of Nations* (London: Methuen, 1899).

the representative must perish. Is it not clear, then, that if the industrial and cultural strength of a people is compromised by the trend of its trade, the government of that people has the right to interfere, to impose minor economic sacrifices on this or that class, for the behoof of the community, and even to lay burdens on the whole community for the benefit of its future citizens in the same spirit in which a father will work hard, and live sparely, in order to secure for his children a place in the sun?

Such circumstances may be held to exist in three typical situations: –

(1) If the effect of foreign importation is to confine, or depress, to low-grade industries a country capable of high-grade industries.
(2) If a country is known to possess great industrial possibilities which have, nevertheless, been over-laid and annulled by the disastrous accidents of history, and by the inertia which has thus been engendered.
(3) If the development of a country has been one-sided – a predominance, let us say, of manufacture over agriculture – so as to leave it dependent on the ends of the earth for its food-supply, and so to increase enormously the perils of war.

In such instances it may be argued that the levy imposed on the consumer by a customs tariff is analogous to public expenditure on education, or on defence. I am not – let me observe – making out a case for Protection, but merely indicating a plane upon which there may be made out a case which, although it may be fallacious, is certainly very far from being a mere imposture. You will notice that the central reality from which all these arguments, economic and non-economic, radiate, the dogma which lends them their whole value and vitality, is that of sacrifice, temporary or permanent, in the name of Nationalism.

It would be misleading not to add that, on the same plane and in terms of the same creed, a policy of Free Trade, not merely for the England, but for the Ireland of 1913, may be vindicated. Here, again, the national interest, and not the interest of this or that individual, is paramount. The reply runs: –

(1) Protective duties, being a mode of indirect taxation, oppress the poor, to the advantage of the rich, and so poison the wells of national renewal.
(2) They do not evoke efficiency, but merely shelter and stereotype inefficiency.

(3) They lead to profound corruption of the national political life.
(4) If we are to subsidize experimental industries, let it be done openly through the medium of bounties or grants definitely assigned to the promoters of such enterprises to enable them to train labour.

I am myself a Free Trader, varying from the orthodox, United Kingdom type, however, in laying strong emphasis on this last rubric. That this is my view is not a matter of much importance. But it is a matter of considerable importance that it was the view of John Stuart Mill. It may, or may not, be known to those who are so fond of his 'infant industries' exception, but it is a fact that he withdrew from the position taken up in that passage. Actual observation of the pernicious effects on public life of tariff experiments in the Australian colonies, and in America, led to that withdrawal: –

> I am now [he writes, in 1868] much shaken in the opinion, which has so often been quoted for purposes which it did not warrant; and I am disposed to think that when it is advisable, as it may sometimes be, to subsidize a new industry in its commencement, this had better be done by a direct annual grant, which is far less likely to be continued after the conditions which alone justified it have ceased to exist.[25]

So much for external trade policy. Let us now turn to certain matters of internal development, bearing in mind always that we are not attempting to examine them fully on their merits, but only to construe them in terms of Economic Nationalism. The struggle in Ireland between pasture and tillage and the future of our railway system will serve as examples.

Nothing has so much compromised economic science in this country as the fact that 'the Economists' were supposed to have approved of all the clearances and consolidations which came from 1820 on, and to have greeted the cattle-jobbing grazier with a paean of applause as the first true specimen of the *homo œconomicus* vouchsafed to Ireland. In Sir Samuel Ferguson's remarkable poem, 'Inheritor and Economist', the reader will find them denounced with extraordinary vehemence on these and other scores.[26] And the pity is that although very ill-founded as affecting a great Liberal like Mill, they were very well-founded as affecting

[25] John Stuart Mill to Edward William Stafford (11 December 1868) in Francis E. Mineka and Dwight N. Lindley eds., *The Collected Works of John Stuart Mill: Volume XVI – The Later Letters, 1849–1873 Part III* (Toronto: University of Toronto Press, 1972).

[26] Samuel Ferguson (1810–86), Irish antiquarian and poet. The satire written in verse, *Inheritor and Economist*, was published in 1849.

the journalistic popularizers. When *The Times* wrote that in Ireland 'man had for long been a nuisance, and population a **drug on the market', that diagnosis was eminently orthodox. Ireland, to the popularizers, was an entirely simple case of over-population.[27] Since any one part of the earth was, to their cosmopolitanism, very much the same as any other – England and her chosen people always, of course, implicitly excepted – and since it was the nature of labour and of capital to flow to the point of maximum productiveness, the emigration of men and money was a normal, and even a beneficent, phenomenon. Indeed, McCulloch went very near saying that the drain of absentee rents was a positive advantage.[28] Moreover, with that extravagant optimism for which Wagner rebukes them, he and his friends never wavered in their faith that the line of maximum personal acquisitiveness is also the line of maximum public benefit. And so, beyond doubt, the gambler in cattle entered the rural economy of Ireland, panoplied in the 'Laws of Political Economy'.[29] Indeed, so long as we keep to the individual as against the national, to the atomistic as against the organic conception of economic life, the ranches are unassailable. It would be difficult to cite many instances in which the quotient

$$\frac{\text{net personal profit}}{\text{personal effort}}$$

is not as large, or very nearly as large, for the grass-farmer as it would be for the holder of an equal extent of land devoted to mixed farming. It is to be remembered that, in the former case, effort is reduced to a minimum, and leisure raised to a maximum. But the moment we apply the touchstone of national interest the whole aspect of the problem alters. Mixed farming will give an indefinitely larger gross output, and support a correspondingly larger number of people. Not only will it enrich the nation in point of numbers, but it will, by the greater variety and difficulty of its technique, improve them in intellectual and moral quality.

Appeal to the gospel of Economic Nationalism, and the controversy is closed: reject that gospel, fall back on what are, rather ridiculously, styled

[27] This was the view, for example, of the chief civil servant to the Treasury, Sir Charles Trevelyan (1807–86), an advocate of T. R. Malthus's argument that famine was a natural check on population growth, which framed his disastrous response to relief in Ireland during the famine of the 1840s.

[28] John Ramsay McCulloch (1789–1864), Scottish economist and author of several works on economic theory, was a follower of the Ricardian school of economists.

[29] A reference to the 'English School' of political economy generally, associated with the 'Law' that the pursuit of private advantage yields public benefits.

'purely business considerations', and there is no reason why your *latifundia* should not increase instead of disappearing.

The railway system you can similarly regard, either as a profit-earning enterprise for certain individuals, or as a fundamental instrument of national development. If you take the former view, the line of exploitation of these railways ought to be simply that of maximum dividends. You may argue, if you like, that this will also be the line of maximum public advantage, but, unless you have a singular aptitude for rose-coloured visions, you will find it hard to convince even yourself of the truth of this proposition. Take the other point of view, and it becomes your duty so to use the railways as to maximise national production. You are entitled to act on long-run instead of short-run calculations; to lose money, for the time being, instead of making money; to undertake, for the sake of the future, large expenditures by way of subsidy and re-organization which, under private enterprise, would be either impossible or else a fraud on your shareholders.

These illustrations might be almost indefinitely multiplied. But this paper has already run to inordinate length, and I must close it, leaving unanswered my own question as to the economic ideal which Ireland ought to set before herself. That must stand over for some other occasion. Had there been time to consider it, much of our discussion must have turned on the country town. That, and not the great city, is the germinal cell of industrial expansion in Ireland. In function as in name it is capable of effecting a synthesis of our two great interests, falsely supposed to be irreconcilable enemies. The country town must manufacture or perish. As capital accumulates in the hands of the new farmers, our condition of progress will be realized. As soon as they come to understand that the safest investment for it is not some oil or rubber mirage in the waste of the earth but an enterprise, associated with farming, conducted under their own eyes and their own control, the economy of Ireland will be transformed.

That is a mere suggestion. For the moment, I must be content with having unfolded to you the outline of an argument which re-establishes Nationalism, and national self-direction, as ranking among the human First Principles of material prosperity. If it helps you to join up the dreams – as yet unformulated – of the Irish nation with the intellectual tradition of Europe, then I shall not have wasted either your evening or my own.

1913

10 A. V. Dicey, from *A Fool's Paradise*[1]

Preface

A Fool's Paradise is no general dissertation on the inexpediency of granting to Ireland a separate Parliament and a separate Executive. The controversy over Home Rule has now continued for more than a quarter of a century. Any general argument or fallacy put forward, whether by Unionists or by Home Rulers, in support of their own opinions, is trite and well-worn, and hardly repays repetition. I have therefore not aimed, as I did in 1886, at setting forth in detail the general objections to the policy of Home Rule.[2]

A Fool's Paradise is a criticism upon the Home Rule Bill of 1912; but my book cannot claim to be a minute and searching criticism of the whole Bill. I have not attempted to deal with all the many and patent defects of a measure framed throughout to secure a party triumph rather than to provide a new form of government which might amend the relations between Great Britain (or, in popular language, England) and Ireland. My purpose is to achieve a much humbler end, namely, to set forth in as plain language as I can, a line of argument against the present Home Rule Bill which, if accepted, must make it impossible for any British elector

[1] Published as *A Fool's Paradise: Being a Constitutionalist's Criticism on the Home Rule Bill of 1912* (London: John Murray, 1913).

[2] Dicey originally published a critique of the first Home Rule Bill of 1886 in the form of *England's Case Against Home Rule* (London: John Murray, 1886). He then launched an attack on the second Home Rule Bill of 1893 in *A Leap in the Dark, or Our New Constitution: An Examination of the Leading Principles of the Home Rule Bill of 1893* (London: John Murray, 1893).

to support a measure which, if the House of Lords does its duty,[3] cannot pass into law before May 1914. My reasoning is contained in Chapters II. and III. of this book, and consists in the establishment of three propositions which I hold to be undoubted truths:

First, the Bill, if passed into law, will not secure to England any one of the benefits which English Home Rulers, who, from the Premier downwards, are the dupes of credulous optimism, expect or hope it will produce. The Bill will not maintain in Ireland the true supremacy of the Imperial Parliament. It will not relieve the Imperial Parliament from the burden of considering Irish affairs. It will not conciliate Ireland.

Secondly, the Bill will work great evil to England, and indeed to every part of the now United Kingdom. Hence –

Thirdly, it is the duty of Unionists, and indeed of all patriots, to make sure that the Home Rule Bill never passes into law.

The substance of this argument is contained in Chapters II. and III., and does not fill as much as a hundred pages. The Introduction to the book is an attempt to analyse from the point of view of an old Unionist of 1886 the state of opinion which alone makes it possible to pass, even through the House of Commons, a Bill which in its conception is far inferior to the Home Rule Bill of 1886, and for the most part exaggerates the patent defects of the Home Rule Bill of 1893. Chapter I. deals with arguments which, in fact, weigh with honest English Home Rulers, and apparently convince them that any Home Rule Bill, however objectionable in its details, is preferable to the refusal of something like parliamentary independence to the Irish people – by which term, in reality, is meant at most only 3,000,000 out of the 4,000,000 of the inhabitants of Ireland.[4]

Experience of something more than twenty-five years of political controversy entirely preserves me from the delusion that the force of argument, however strong, will make any converts among convinced Home Rulers. My appeal is made to that body of men, far more numerous than party managers in general believe, who are secretly alarmed at the progress of revolutionary schemes brought forward without adequate consideration, forced through the House of Commons without anything like real discussion, and intended to be driven through the House of Lords

[3] Dicey anticipates that the Lords will reject the Bill, thereby delaying it.

[4] This estimate of three million applies to the Catholics of Ireland, the remaining one million applying to Protestants.

without the assent of their Lordships, and to be enrolled on the Statute Book without any appeal to the electorate of the United Kingdom. These men may possibly give me a hearing. They will admit that, however feebly my arguments may be expressed, I rely upon the force of argument alone, and have tried to avoid the personalities which in Parliament perplex the result of what is supposed to be discussion.

As an old controversialist of 1886, I venture to refer to two points in my position which may seem open to criticism.

It may, in the first place, be said that I have not dwelt with such emphasis as heretofore on the general objections to Home Rule. My answer is that I am concerned in attacking a specific Home Rule Bill which, even if I were convinced that Home Rule must be conceded to Ireland, achieves this end by the most vicious and dangerous of all methods. I am as firmly convinced as in 1886 that there are only three policies with regard to the relation between England and Ireland which deserve consideration. The first and best is the firm maintenance of the Act of Union. The second is the boldly conferring upon Ireland colonial independence, as in New Zealand. The last is the separation of Ireland from Great Britain, or, in other words, the national independence of Ireland. Nor am I at all certain that if the Act of Union is to be virtually repealed, the independence of Ireland might not be more conducive both to the power of England and to the prosperity of Ireland itself than the concession to Irishmen of colonial independence.

It may, in the second place, be said that I regard Home Rule simply from the English, or rather the British, point of view. This is in one sense true. I am convinced that it is best that, in a great controversy, the advocate of each side should speak of the matters which he understands. I know England thoroughly. My knowledge of Ireland, though I have always had many Irish friends, is of course comparatively small. But there is another reason for my pressing forward the interest of England. It is the conviction that every scheme of Home Rule – that is, of political partnership between England and Ireland – must affect the interest of both countries. But the inhabitants of Ireland are about 4,000,000, whilst the inhabitants of Great Britain are about 40,000,000. I am an old, an unconverted, and an impenitent Benthamite.[5] I hold to the belief that where, in one State, the welfare of 40,000,000 has to be weighed against

[5] A disciple, in other words, of Jeremy Bentham (1748–1832), regarded as the founder of modern utilitarianism.

the welfare of 4,000,000, the welfare of the greater number ought to prevail, and in this case my utilitarianism is confirmed by the reflection that of the 4,000,000 residents in Ireland 1,000,000 do not demand, but on the contrary abominate Home Rule. I must on this subject speak plainly, but if any one supposes that I have ever in my life entertained a thought, or countenanced an act, of oppression, or even unfriendliness towards Ireland, he does me gross injustice. My strongest desire has always been to break down the barriers which delay the complete moral union of Great Britain and Ireland; my wish and hope are that gradually Ireland should come, like Scotland, while developing whatever is good and great in her special national character, to recognise also the claim on her allegiance of the great British nation, and the even greater British Empire. Nor am I at all disposed to place on Ireland the blame of the delayed moral unification of the United Kingdom. In the words of A. G. Richey, by far the fairest, and, had his life been prolonged, by far the greatest of Irish historians, 'A study of Irish history teaches us sympathy for all Irish parties.'[*]

For every opinion contained in this book, as for every statement of fact, I am solely responsible, but I cannot refrain from thanking friends who have helped me in the composition of a short work which was in some respects full of difficulty. To Mr. S. Rosenbaum I am deeply indebted for his suggestions as to some of the financial features in the Bill.[6] To Mr. Philip G. Cambray, whose knowledge of recent Irish politics is greater than my own, I owe much valuable information.[7]

Chapter III: The Duty of Unionists

Preliminary Observations. – At this supreme crisis, which for good or bad must affect the whole fortune of England, it will be well, before considering what may be the specific duties of Unionists, to insist upon two or three preliminary observations.

[6] Simon Rosenbaum edited *Against Home Rule: The Case for Union* (London: Frederick Warne, 1912).

[7] Philip G. Cambray was the author of numerous studies of British and Irish politics.

[*] A. G. Richey, *A Short History of the Irish People*, Introd. pp. 1–3. The noble expression of Mr. Richey's impartiality deserves a study which it has in England never as yet received. *Editorial note:* Richey published the book in 1887 (Dublin: Hodges and Figgis).

The policy of Unionists must absolutely coincide with their duty as patriots. Their one effort ought to be to preserve by every lawful means the political unity of the still United Kingdom. This was their duty and their policy in 1886 and in 1893; it is still their duty and their policy in 1913. There is no possibility of compromise between the policy of Unionism and the policy of Home Rule. Unionists themselves often find it hard to face this plain fact. They are daunted by the bold assertion, hazarded by Home Rulers or Separatists, that the Act of Union has brought no benefit whatever to the United Kingdom. This allegation is untrue. The Act of Union has brought great advantages to the whole of our common country. This Act has for now more than a century been the safeguard of Great Britain and Ireland against any rebellion even faintly resembling the savage rising of 1798, and its almost equally savage suppression.[8] The Act of Union has slowly but for ever given to all Roman Catholics, whether English or Irish, the political rights of every citizen of the United Kingdom.[9] It has secured the strenuous loyalty to the Union of every Protestant throughout Ireland and of hosts of Roman Catholics. We are called upon, especially by Home Rulers, to remember many of the traditions of Irish history which for the peace and prosperity of Ireland ought to be allowed to fall into oblivion; but an Englishman is hardly ever reminded of one circumstance which is no tradition, but an indisputable historical fact – namely, that the loyalty of Ulster has been the indubitable result of that Union with Great Britain of which in 1800 Ulstermen were the most dangerous and the most serious opponents.[10] Many of the men of Ulster had strengthened the resistance of the Thirteen Colonies to the authority of the British Parliament.[11] The terrible calamity of 1798 was, it must be remembered, the result of that misgovernment of Ireland by an Irish Parliament whereof Mr. Asquith wishes to revive the traditions.[*] But the true peril of 1798 was the possibility that the men of Ulster might

[8] The 1798 Rebellion in Ireland was a concerted uprising against British authority, organised under the banner of the United Irishmen.

[9] The final measure of Catholic Emancipation was passed by the United Kingdom parliament in 1829.

[10] Presbyterians in Ulster were staunch opponents of the Act of Union and led the United Irishmen rebellion in 1798.

[11] British colonies in North America which declared independence from Britain in 1776, later establishing the United States of America.

[*] See p. 105, *ante*.

be found ranged in the ranks of the rebels. No one can now doubt that the Ulster of 1913 demands nothing but the maintenance of the Union with Great Britain. Gladstone himself was perplexed by the question, why it was that Ulstermen whose grandfathers were the opponents of the Union had become the strongest of Unionists? He was puzzled because he refused to see that the cause of this revolution in opinion was to be found in the Act of Union itself. The true vindication, then, of that great statute is that the Act has created the loyalty of Ulster. The Act of Union has, step by step, yet certainly, removed most of Ireland's grievances.* The Act of Union has made it possible to use the credit and wealth of the whole United Kingdom for the advantage of Ireland, and thus, without the violence and injustice of revolution, turn the tenants of Ireland into the owners of the land of which they have been the occupiers.[12] This stroke of statesmanship is grounded on the Act of Union. But it is in a special sense the glory of Unionist policy. It is a joy to remember that John Bright, the most strenuous of Unionists, was almost the first English Minister whose broad good sense convinced him that the policy of the Land Purchase Acts was the fair, though indirect, answer to the demand for Home Rule or Repeal.[13] The gradual indifference of the peasant proprietors, or small land-owners, of Ireland to the cry for Home Rule, which never met their real needs, is the vindication of the Land Purchase Acts, and these statutes are the fruit of the Union between Great Britain and Ireland. A law must be judged by its results. There is no reason why any Englishman should, at this time of day, fear to speak of 1800 or of the Act of Union.

If some Unionists are discouraged by the delusion that the Act of Union has not been fruitful of good results, honest Home Rulers fail to understand why it is that, among all Unionists, the Home Rule Bill of 1912 excites intense hostility. Our enmity is caused in part by the sense

[12] Dicey is referring to the numerous Land Acts introduced between 1870 and 1909. Taken together, the Acts radically reduced the concentration of ownership of Irish land, gradually creating a class of small independent farmers.

[13] John Bright (1811–89), supporter of free trade and Liberal MP, opposed Gladstone's policy of home rule.

* Irish Home Rulers, in common with most advocates of change, whether it be desirable or undesirable, constantly confuse grievances – that is, wrongs caused by bad laws – with sufferings or misfortunes with which law has little concern. *Editorial note:* Dicey presumably has the Great Famine in mind here: a misfortune, he argues, rather than a result of deliberate legislation.

that the Home Rule Bill of 1912 is more unfair to England than were the Home Rule Bills of 1886 and of 1893. But the bitterness of our opposition is intensified by the conduct of the Coalition by whom England has the misfortune to be governed. A combination of discordant parties is attempting to drive through Parliament, without an appeal to the electors, a policy which has been twice deliberately rejected by the electorate of the United Kingdom.[14]

We detest the Home Rule Bill, moreover, because it inflicts upon Ulster an intolerable wrong; for it takes from the Protestants of that part of the United Kingdom the right to be really and directly governed by the Imperial Parliament, and by the Imperial Parliament alone. This hateful measure threatens us all with the outbreak of civil war in Ireland. This fact is one to which no Englishman, whatever his own political convictions, has the right to shut his eyes. When the Thirteen Colonies offered resistance to laws actually passed by the British Parliament there were plenty of arguments – and arguments not in themselves absurd – for making no concession to rebels. Burke's reply was summed up in the dictum that, 'No man will be argued into slavery'.[15] His words passed unheeded. But Burke, as every man now admits, was right. When I am told that Ulster ought not to object to being forced under the rule of a Government which every Ulsterman abhors and contemns, and also to being deprived of the protection of the Imperial Parliament at Westminster, to which they own allegiance, I am reminded that men will not be argued into slavery. But I do not wish for a moment to give undue prominence to the protests, however just, or the wishes, however strong, of Ulster. My whole line of reasoning, as every reader of candour must allow, is based upon the conviction, for which I tender definite reasons, that Home Rule threatens to bring ruin, not only upon Ulster, but upon Englishmen and Irishmen alike. Every loyal citizen of the United Kingdom ought in general, and as a paramount duty, to obey the law of the land, or, in other words, the clearly and indubitably expressed will of the nation. But this duty of absolute obedience is qualified by two considerations to which

[14] Dicey is referring to the results of the general elections of 1910, which left the Liberal Party dependent upon the votes of the Irish Parliamentary Party and fledgling Labour to drive through the Home Rule Bill.

[15] Edmund Burke (1729–97), the Irish philosopher and statesman; 'Speech on American Taxation', 19 April 1774, *The Writings and Speeches of Edmund Burke*, ed. Paul Langford (Oxford: Clarendon Press, 1970–2015), 9 vols., II, p. 458: 'No body will be argued into slavery.'

Unionists and Home Rulers alike must give heed. For at a crisis which gives rise to the horrible possibility of civil war laxity of thought may be the source of infinite peril. The first consideration is that such obedience can be due only when a law is the clear and undoubted expression of the will of the nation. The second is that there may exist acts of oppression on the part of a democracy, no less than of a king, which justify resistance to law, or, in other words, rebellion. It is idle to suppose that the existence or non-existence of these conditions can be determined by merely technical rules. Grave indeed is the responsibility of any one who excites rebellion; graver still is the responsibility of any man or any party of men by whom acts of oppression are, even under legal form, committed, which to the sufferers seem, not unreasonably, to justify rebellion. These are principles which I believe no Englishman, and certainly no man who, like myself, has imbibed Whig traditions, will ever deny. No doubt they are difficult of application – still I implore each of my readers to bear them in mind, for they are principles which must, to a great extent, control the action of Unionists.

Specific Duties Of Unionists.– On this matter my whole aim is to speak the truth as I see it, whether it pleases or displeases my readers. I am no politician. I have no constituency to dread or to flatter. No man of sense, I trust, will blame me if my opinion as to the conduct required at a perplexed and terrible crisis leads on some points to definite conclusions and on some other points suggests only doubt and hesitation.

First duty. – All sincere Unionists are bound to close up their ranks and stand shoulder to shoulder in resistance to the Home Rule Bill.

In this contest there should be no difference whatever between Free Traders and Tariff Reformers. The unity of the nation is at stake. We must resist Home Rule, as the Northern States of America resisted Secession.[16] Nowhere ought one Unionist candidate to be found opposing another Unionist candidate. We have paid too dear for the blunder of 1906.[17] It is for our leaders to provide the means by which differences of opinion on fiscal and other subordinate questions may best be removed. Unity, and again unity, and nothing but unity, must be the watchword of Unionism.

[16] A reference to the opposition of the North in the United States to the attempted secession of the South, leading to Civil War in 1861.

[17] The Liberal Party under Henry Campbell-Bannerman (1836–1908) won a landslide against the Conservative Party under Arthur Balfour (1848–1930) in the general election of 1906.

Second duty. – The object of all sincere Unionists should be to secure at all costs that the Home Rule Bill shall not be transformed into the Home Rule Act until the plain issue, Shall or shall not the Home Rule Bill, 1912, pass into law? has been deliberately, fairly, and squarely put before the present electorate, and has received an unmistakable answer.* One main part of this duty, as far as British Unionists are concerned, must be to spare no labour or expense in making audible to every elector throughout Great Britain the bitter cry of Ulster. But, as every Ulsterman would agree, it would be a dangerous error to allow any Home Ruler to foster the delusion that the resistance of Ulster was the sole, or even, from one point of view, the main objection to a policy of Home Rule for Ireland. The fatal objection to this policy, apart from its gross injustice to Ulster, is, that it threatens ruin to every part of the United Kingdom. I doubt not that when the clear issue, Shall or shall not the Home Rule Bill, 1912, pass into law? is laid before the present electorate, the people of Great Britain will answer, with the people of Ulster, 'We will not have Home Rule.'

At this stage of my argument I shall be met by the question, What conduct are you prepared to recommend if the electors should return to the newly elected House of Commons a majority of Home Rulers? My reply is this: I will not raise cases on the Constitution. I will not try to give an opinion upon a case which has not yet arisen and may probably never arise. The conduct of Unionists, if defeated at the next General Election, must depend upon circumstances which no human being can foresee. The proper attitude of Unionists would necessarily be dependent, for instance, upon the number, the nature, and the character of the majority by which they were defeated; how far Home Rule has been really placed before the country; whether some question – *e.g.* the position

* Of course to turn the present Cabinet out of office would, were it possible, be the best way of putting an end to the Home Rule Bill. It would obviously lead rapidly to a General Election which would make apparent to all the world whether the Home Rule Bill was or was not accepted by the electorate. It may be well to add, in order to prevent misunderstanding, that a Referendum, carried out with absolute fairness, would be a much better form of appeal to the people than even a General Election. But it is hard to believe that, in the midst of this hot party conflict, a thoroughly well considered form of Referendum could be enacted, or that we could count upon a Referendum being fairly carried out by the present Government. *Editorial note:* Dicey had originally been critical of referendums but came to defend them and define their potential role under the British constitution. See for example A. V. Dicey, 'Ought the Referendum to be Introduced into England?', *Contemporary Review*, LVII (April 1890), p. 506.

to be taken up by England in a European war – were not the matter on which the election really and substantially turned; whether the dissolution was not started upon the people by surprise without giving them time to consider the result of their vote in regard to Home Rule. These and possibly many other matters would have to be weighed and answered by an honest man called upon to determine what might be the duties of Unionists in a situation which has not yet arisen – a defeat, namely, of the Unionists on a dissolution before the Home Rule Bill shall have passed into law. This is a position of things which Ministers, to judge from their conduct, are resolved shall never arise. They are resolved, as everybody sees, that the Home Rule Bill shall, under the Parliament Act, be turned into the Home Rule Act before a General Election shall provide any sort of appeal to the people.[18] I absolutely decline, in these circumstances, to answer inquiries which are at present in strictness unanswerable. One statement alone may, I think, reasonably be made. A General Election, whilst the Home Rule Bill is nothing but a Bill, a General Election fairly conducted and in which the sole and real issue before the electors shall have been their approval or disapproval of the Home Rule Bill, would, if such an appeal to the country were answered by a return to Parliament of a large and substantial majority of Home Rulers, manifestly strengthen the case in favour of some form of Home Rule. But the occurrence of this possible calamity is highly improbable. Englishmen think and act slowly, but they have never in the long run proved deaf to the requirements of justice. There is little risk that, when the whole nature and effects of the Home Rule Bill are made clear to the mass of the electors, they will expel from the United Kingdom the most loyal of Unionists, who ask for nothing else than that they should continue to be governed, in common with Englishmen and Scotsmen, as they have been for more than a hundred and ten years, by the Imperial Parliament sitting at Westminster, and by the Imperial Parliament alone.

Third duty. – If the Government, without any dissolution of Parliament, avail themselves of the Parliament Act to transform the Home Rule Bill into the Home Rule Act, 1914, it will be in form a law but will lack all constitutional authority, and the duty of Unionists will be to treat it as a measure which lacks the sanction of the nation.

[18] The Parliament Act was passed in 1911 in response to the rejection by the House of Lords of the 1909 'People's Budget'. It had the effect of cancelling the upper chamber's veto over legislation, thereby blocking its power to stymie legislation in favour of home rule.

To this conclusion I have come advisedly and after due consideration. The grounds for it admit of a perfectly definite statement.

*I. Why the Act will lack Constitutional Authority**

(i) The Act will violate the principle that no Bill which changes the foundations of the Constitution should pass into law until it has obtained, directly or indirectly, the assent of the electors.

This principle has been tacitly but practically recognised by statesmen and by the country for at least eighty years. Let me give a few examples as illustrating its nature and application.

Take, first, the great Reform Act of 1832.[19] The leading facts, put shortly, are full of instruction. Parliament, in consequence of the death of George IV, was dissolved in 1830. The Ministry of Lord Grey, which came into office in that year, was pledged to carry Reform.[20] From March 1, 1831, when Lord John Russell introduced the first and carefully considered Reform Bill into Parliament,[21] till the passing of the Reform Act in its third form, the principles of the reforms proposed by the Whigs were known and discussed throughout the length and breadth of the United Kingdom. The Bill was carried to the watchword, 'The Bill, the whole Bill, and nothing but the Bill.' To quote Macaulay's words in 1831, an impartial observer could 'see only one question in the State – the question of Reform; only two parties – the friends of the Bill and its enemies'.†

Even in the unreformed House of Commons reformers obtained for the first reading a majority of 302 to 301. A dissolution immediately followed. In the new Parliament, still unreformed, the Bill passed the Commons by 345 to 236 votes. The Peers exerted their whole power of opposition. They rejected the second Bill on September 22, 1831, by 199 to 158. In March 1832 the third Reform Bill was passed by the Commons. Of the struggle carried on by the King, now alarmed by reform, and the House of Lords, the majority of whom thoroughly hated reform,

[19] The 1832 Representation of the People Act altered the franchise in the United Kingdom.
[20] Charles Grey (1764–1845), 2nd Earl Grey.
[21] John Russell (1792–1878), 1st Earl Russell.

* See *Rights of Citizenship*, with Preface by the Marquess of Lansdowne, K.G., chaps iv. and vi. *Editorial note:* Dicey is referring to William R. Anson et al., *Rights of Citizenship: A Survey of Safeguards for the People* (London: Warne, 1912).

† Walpole, *Hist. of England*, vol. ii. p. 656. *Editorial note:* Spencer Walpole, *A History of England from the Conclusion of the Great War in 1815* (London: Longmans, Green, 1876–86), 6 vols.

it is not necessary to state the details. The point to be noted is that the whole position of affairs was known to the whole people. A defeat of the Bill in the House of Lords, May 7, 1832, caused the resignation of the Whig Ministry. The Duke of Wellington thereupon tried, and failed, to form a Tory Ministry.[22] The King consented to the creation of Peers. The Whig Ministry returned to office. The Lords gave way, and in June 1832 the great Reform Act was passed. An impartial historian need not blame either the reformers or the anti-reformers. The Reform Act embodied an immense alteration in the Constitution. It was right that it should be carried, for it in the main corresponded to the needs of the country, and represented the indubitable will of the nation. But it was well also that a fundamental change in the Constitution should not be carried through until the will of the nation had been thoroughly ascertained. The people fully ratified the reform of 1832. To the first Reformed House of Commons there were returned 486 Liberals against 172 Conservatives. What I cannot understand is how any man can deny that the principles of the great Whig Reform Bill met with the deliberate, direct, and undoubted approval of the country.[*]

Consider, again, the Act of 1869 which disestablished the Irish Church.[23] The measure may have been wise or unwise. With this I am not concerned; the essential point, for my present purpose, is to note that Gladstone, when leader of the Opposition in 1868, laid before the House of Commons resolutions for the disestablishment of the Irish Church. Some of these resolutions were carried, and a dissolution of Parliament recommended by Mr. Disraeli, then Premier, immediately followed.[24] The Disestablishment of the Irish Church was the primary and leading question of the moment. The dissolution gave to Mr. Gladstone a decisive majority.[†] Disraeli, most rightly, at once resigned office. The Bill for the Disestablishment of the Irish Church was ultimately passed into law, though undoubtedly modified after consultation with the Conservative

[22] Arthur Wellesley (1769–1852), 1st Duke of Wellington.

[23] The Irish Church Act of 1869 separated the Church of Ireland from the Church of England, disestablishing the Irish Church in the process. Full relief from tithes came with the Act.

[24] Benjamin Disraeli (1804–81), 1st Earl of Beaconsfield.

[*] No one who gives any thought to constitutional contests can doubt that, on any matter worth discussion, the will of the electors or of the nation never represents strict unanimity. Of course there existed, during the contest over the great Reform Bill, a Tory minority of greater numbers and power than the Whig Reformers were ready to recognise.

[†] The Third Reading of the Bill in the House of Commons was carried by 362 to 247.

leaders. But it surely cannot be said that the Bill was carried without the definite assent or against the will of the electors. I take the Reform Act, 1832, and the Disestablishment of the Irish Church Act, 1869, as examples of Acts carried with the direct sanction of the electorate. But English statesmen, when at their best, try to look much less at forms than at facts, and there existed between 1830 and 1911 two processes by which it was often possible, without unfairness, to infer the assent of the electors even to Bills which had not been put directly before the people at a General Election. The assent of the electorate might, to a certain extent, and often almost necessarily, be inferred from the ultimate agreement between the leaders of two great parties as to measures to which one party, at any rate, was naturally opposed. Many critics who objected to some of the manoeuvres by which Household Suffrage was introduced into the Constitution in 1866–7 would yet, even though they were Conservatives or Moderate Whigs, assent to the statement that these measures were clearly supported by the mass of the electors.[25] This kind of indirect inference is always dangerous, but may sometimes be perfectly fair. Another mode of indirectly ascertaining the will of the electors has, for the moment, been destroyed by the work of so-called Liberals or Democrats. As long as the House of Lords had the power to necessitate a dissolution by the rejection of some Bill, say the Home Rule Bill of 1893, their hesitation to use this power afforded at least a strong presumption that their Lordships themselves doubted whether the Bill was not really supported by the electors. Here, again, this indirect inference involved some risk of mistaking the will of the people. Still, in many cases it gave effect to the wish of the nation. The plain truth is that the Parliament Act has lessened in some respects the moral authority of the House of Commons by increasing the chance that a party majority may grossly misrepresent the will of the nation.*

Let me add that the constitutional doctrine for which I am contending, though not formally admitted by the unreformed Parliament before 1832, is much older than that date. Let any fair-minded man acquainted with the history of the conflict between Pitt and the Coalition of 1783–4

[25] The Second Reform Act of 1867 extended the franchise to male property holders and lodgers who paid rent of £10 a year or more in the boroughs of the United Kingdom, doubling the electorate to two million men.

* This risk, combined with the gradual development of democracy, adds immense force to the argument that in England it is as necessary, as it is in the United States, that every great constitutional change should receive the direct sanction of the electors.

consider the causes and the justification of Pitt's triumph.[26] Such a critic will soon perceive that, according to the judgment of the greatest of Whig historians,[*] Pitt's success was due to the determination of even the unreformed electorate that the party dominant in the House of Commons should not override the will of the country.

(ii) The conduct of the Coalition of to-day proves that its members more than half believe that the Home Rule Bill is condemned by the electors. It is greatly the interest of Home Rulers that the Home Rule Bill, before it becomes an Act, should gain the undoubted support of the electorate. Till this is obtained our New Constitution will rest on a very shaky foundation. Why, then, does not Mr. Redmond press for, or even command, a dissolution of Parliament? The reason is as plain as day. He believes that the electors of England would, if once appealed to, join the Protestants of Ulster in their impassioned protest against the Home Rule Bill and the whole policy which it represents.

(iii) The Parliament Act gives no real sanction to the *coup d'état* meditated by the Coalition. That Act was intended to prevent the House of Lords from resisting the will of the people, *i.e.* of the electors. The Act was not intended to enable the majority of the House of Commons, which means, in fact, the party leaders of a majority, to resist the will of the nation. Does any one seriously maintain that the people of England are prepared to enforce Home Rule upon Ulster by means of civil war?

(iv) The attempt to transform the Home Rule Bill into a Home Rule Act without any appeal to the electors involves the following astounding and obviously unconstitutional result. Suppose that the Home Rule Bill, in virtue of the Parliament Act, becomes the Home Rule Act in May 1914. The present Parliament was summoned to meet and came into existence on January 30, 1911. It might, if the Government chose, continue in existence till, at any rate, January 29, 1916. The present Parliament might, even though it had ceased by May 1914 to represent the will of the electors, at any rate as regards Home Rule, continue in existence for a year and a half. During that period Irish Nationalists would keep urging the Government to take every step which would increase the difficulty of the repeal or modification of the Home Rule Act by the new Parliament

[26] The Fox–North Coalition was dismissed in 1783 after the defeat of the East India Bill, and replaced by George III with a government led by William Pitt the Younger (1759–1806).

[*] See 'William Pitt', Macaulay's *Writings and Speeches*, ed. 1851, p. 395.

of 1916. The Government might apply the Territorial and Reserve Forces Act to Ireland, or to the parts of Ireland where Nationalists were strongest.[27] The Government might nominate the members of the Senate. The Government might convene the Irish Parliament. The Government would, during this strange interregnum, nominate the members of the Exchequer Board. The Government might make grants to Ireland for the purchase of the buildings in which the old Parliament of Ireland was accustomed to meet. In this, and in many other ways, the Government might, without the assent of the people, throw up entrenchments, so to speak, for the protection of the new Constitution, which had never been assented to by the electorate of the United Kingdom. The very possibility of such action will be absolute proof, to many of my readers, that to pass a Home Rule Act without any appeal to the electorate violates the whole spirit of our existing constitutional government.

II. How Unionists should treat the Home Rule Act of 1914, when lacking constitutional authority

My opinion is that, in the circumstances supposed, every Unionist should go to the poll at the next General Election, after the passing of the Home Rule Act, with the avowed determination and intention to obtain by every legal means a Unionist majority, and that such a majority would not only have the legal right (which is certain), but also would be under a constitutional and moral duty to suspend, to modify, or to repeal *in toto* a Home Rule Act, passed against the will of the nation.

Of course I shall be told that this mode of proceeding is unconstitutional. It is, I admit, unusual. But when the spirit of democratic and constitutional government has been for the first time violated, the defenders of popular government are well within their rights if they set aside the practice in order to save the principles of our Constitution. But they will not, if the course I suggest be followed, in reality violate any established constitutional practice or custom. The Parliament Act may, for my purpose, be a statute as wise as I hold it to be unwise and unstatesman-like. But, whatever be its merits, it changes the whole of our constitutional usages. It logically justifies far more frequent appeals to the electorate than have hitherto been common, for it has struck away the one strong

[27] The Territorial and Reserve Forces Act (1907), also known as the Haldane Reforms after Secretary of State for War Richard Haldane (1856–1928) reformed the British Army's auxiliary forces.

security that a majority of the House of Commons shall not override the deliberate will of the nation. I shall be told, again, that I suggest reaction. So be it. No one rates the evils of a reactionary policy higher than I do. Peel set a most statesmanlike precedent when he fully accepted the results of the Reform Act, 1832.[28] His conduct was based on the clear and undoubted ratification by the nation of an immense constitutional change. It is because of this absence of national consent that I hold the Home Rule Act to be devoid of moral authority. When the attempt is made to carry through revolution by fraud, it is rightly met by reaction which at the bottom is the reassertion of the sovereignty of the nation.

My doctrine is full of encouragement to loyal Unionists in every part of the United Kingdom. The parliamentary battle will not end on the ill-omened day, if ever it should arrive, when, without the assent of the nation, the Home Rule Bill becomes the Home Rule Act, 1914. The stress of the fight will only then have begun. Every Unionist will exert himself, body and soul, to obtain a Unionist majority and destroy the Coalition. For this end no breach of law will be needed. There is nothing illegal in every Unionist throughout Ulster refusing to send a member to the Parliament at Dublin, whose moral authority we shall all deny. Nor, myself, should I see with any displeasure the peaceable non-payment of taxes at Belfast until the General Election (which could not be more than about a year distant) should give, not so much to Unionists as to the whole United Kingdom, the opportunity of repudiating legislation which would lack the moral authority which generally and rightly belongs to every established law and statute.

This is no new doctrine of my own. Lord Hartington (to use the name by which the men of 1886 knew him), was no Radical or enthusiast.[29] He was a Whig of the Whigs. Being dead he yet speaketh:

> The people of Ulster believe, rightly or wrongly, that, under a Government responsible to an Imperial Parliament, they possess at present the fullest security which they can possess of their personal freedom, their liberties, and their right to transact their own business in their own way. You have no right to offer them any inferior security to that; and if, after weighing the character of the Government which it is sought to impose upon them, they resolve that they are no longer bound to obey a law which does not give them equal

[28] Sir Robert Peel (1788–1850), Tory prime minister (1834–5 and 1841–6).

[29] Spencer Compton Cavendish (1833–1908), 8th Duke of Devonshire and styled Marquess of Hartington between 1858 and 1891.

> and just protection with their fellow subjects, who can say – how, at all events, can the descendants of those who resisted King James II say – that they have not a right, if they think fit, to resist, if they think they have the power, the imposition of a Government put upon them by force?*

Note that his language, though I do not dissent from it, goes further than anything necessary for me to lay down, for it applies to a law passed by both Houses of Parliament. In spirit, too, his lordship merely restates the old Whig doctrine that oppression, and especially resistance to the will of the nation, might justify what was technically conspiracy or rebellion. On the refusal of the House of Lords to pass the great Reform Bill, Whigs, encouraged by prominent English politicians, came to an agreement to refuse the payment of taxes till the reform of Parliament was secured,† and assuredly the story was current among those who well remembered the Reform Bill and its history, that public attention was roused by a Whig Peer bidding a collector of taxes wait and call again in a few weeks. Every one understood that his lordship was preparing, in new circumstances, to play the part of Hampden.[30] The Lords, be it remembered, throughout the battle for Reform acted strictly in accordance with their legal rights. They kept well within the forms, and even within the custom, of the Constitution; but they defied the will of the nation. This is the very offence of which the majority of the House of Commons, if they dare, in reliance on the Parliament Act, to transform the Home Rule Bill into the Home Rule Act without any appeal to the electorate, will be guilty. The language of Lord Hartington, the whole attitude of the Whigs when they fought in support of the great Reform Bill, justify every word I have used. The moral resistance which may endure for a year, or a year and a half, to the Home Rule Act will, from a constitutional point of view,

[30] John Hampden (1595–1643) was a seventeenth-century parliamentarian who opposed the arbitrary taxes imposed by Charles I at the outset of the English Civil War.

* See Bernard Holland's *Life of the Duke of Devonshire*, vol. ii. p. 250. Hear the language of John Bright in 1887. 'For myself', he wrote, 'I do not discuss the question of a little more or a little less of a Parliament in Dublin. A Parliament is a great weapon if once created and opened; not difficult to form, but dangerous to deal with and suppress.... The 2,000,000 of loyal population in Ireland are to be forgotten, and their claim to a voice in this crisis of their fate is derided and rejected.... The Liberal party is called to make this great surrender. It is to forget its noble past and to adopt a future leading to a gulf, the depth of which no one can sound' (cited in *Protest against Home Rule Bill*, Speech by the Hon. Arthur Elliot, at Freshwater, Isle of Wight, October 30, 1912, p. 11).

† See Lecky, *Leaders of Public Opinion in Ireland*, vol. ii. p. 129.

be fully justified. I do not even assert that it may not rightly be carried by Ulstermen to extreme lengths, but, in my judgment, it should for that period, at any rate, be conducted with extreme attention to the preservation of order. It is one thing for Unionists at Belfast to decline to go to the poll, or to take part in the election of any member to the so-called Parliament at Dublin; it is another thing to drive a Nationalist away by force from the polling booth. But I will not pronounce any decisive judgment upon the exact extent to which the maintenance of order and peace is incumbent upon men determined not to yield obedience to an Act of Parliament which, from the existence of very special circumstances, lacks constitutional authority, and, in my own eyes, remains little more than a Bill. Until a General Election, resistance to the so-called Home Rule Act should be carried out by legal and moral means. I am assured that such a course of action will appeal to the sympathies of every Englishman, and be crowned with success. England has always, in the long run, given a triumph to the party of morality. As I have already stated, I will not give, because I have not formed, any certain opinion as to the right course to be pursued should the British electorate sanction the monstrous iniquity of depriving the men of Ulster, who are loyal citizens of the United Kingdom, of their right to remain subject only to the Government of the Imperial Parliament at Westminster.

What are the limits within which the tyranny either of a king or of a democracy justifies civil war is not an inquiry on which I will enter. It is for the people of the United Kingdom to take care that provocation recklessly offered by the Government of the country to the most loyal of Irishmen shall not be allowed to convert a conflict which ought to be decided by free discussion, and by the vote of the nation, into a campaign to be decided by soldiers and cannon-balls. Meanwhile, I am assured that, even in the case of the oppression with which Ulster is menaced, no loyal citizen should, until all possibility of legal resistance is exhausted, have recourse to the use of arms.

The doctrine of which I am the defender contains a warning which I must press upon the attention of Nationalists. A Home Rule Bill (whether it be called a statute or not) that has not received the assent of the electorate provides no real security for the continued existence of the Irish Government and Parliament which the so-called Home Rule Bill is intended to create. A Unionist majority will, as I have insisted, be, in the case of such an Act, under the duty to modify or destroy the untoward work of parliamentary conspirators who defied the sovereignty of the nation.

Nor is this the sole insecurity to which Nationalists will be exposed. Every Unionist holds now, as every citizen of Great Britain will soon discover, that the Home Rule Bill will impose monstrously unfair burdens upon Great Britain. The labour of Unionists will assuredly tend towards freeing the inhabitants and taxpayers of Great Britain from more than one unjust burden. Assume, for the sake of argument, that it is well to grant Home Rule to Ireland, the greatest care ought to have been taken to ensure that benefit to Ireland should not work wrong to England. As regards finance, the expert Finance Committee of Home Rulers* framed a scheme which, at any rate, was intended to be just to every part of the United Kingdom, and, though it imposed heavy burdens on the predominant partner, provided that the weight of these burdens should be brought within a comparatively short period to an end. The Government deliberately rejected the proposals of their own Committee, and is forcing the predominant partner to pay for an indefinite period huge sums for the pleasure of breaking up a partnership which he does not wish to dissolve. Nor can it for a moment be supposed that millions paid willingly for the benefit of Ireland whilst she is part of the United Kingdom will, with the assent of Unionists, continue to be paid when she claims the independence without the full responsibilities of a self-governing colony.†

It is, therefore, the interest of an honest Nationalist, even more than of a strenuous Unionist, to take care that the Home Rule Bill is not passed into law in circumstances which make it possible to deny that the Act has ever gained the deliberate assent of the British electorate. An outsider would have thought that a Nationalist would even now perceive that no Home Rule Bill was worth passing unless it were studiously just to England. One thing, at least, is certain. No Home Rule Act can, in the present state of the world, permanently hold its ground which has not received

* See p. 74, *ante*. *Editorial note:* the role of expert committees was covered by Dicey in a headed section in chapter II.

† This is apparently the view of the Unionist leaders: 'So long as Ireland is an integral part of the United Kingdom there will be no difference in treatment between Ireland and any other part of the Kingdom; but if she chooses to put herself in the status of a colony, then we will give her a preference, but we shall not treat her precisely as if she were a member of the United Kingdom. I think it would be well that the people of Ireland should clearly understand that that will be the attitude, not only of the party which I represent, but I venture to say further, that if that change did actually take place, honourable gentlemen opposite will be influenced by the opinion of their own constituents, and, except to the extent of the power of forty members who are still among them, will act precisely as we will act – we shall think twice of our own people and once of them.'– Mr. Bonar Law, *Parliamentary Debates*, Oct. 17, 1912, col. 1567; see also col. 1566.

the assent, and the undoubted assent, of the vast majority of the British electorate. It is the interest of every honest Nationalist, even more than of every enthusiastic Unionist, to insist that the Home Rule Bill, 1912, shall not become the Home Rule Act until it has been without doubt submitted to the verdict of the electorate of the United Kingdom.

Fourth duty. – It is the duty of every Unionist, as indeed of any man who cares at heart for the welfare of the United Kingdom, to look facts in the face. Pessimism is folly; to suppose that every difficulty which can reasonably be foreseen in the working of an ill-prepared, incoherent, and in many respects undiscussed measure, will certainly arise argues timidity rather than foresight; but it is a still graver error when a statesman in office professes to be a 'credulous optimist'. Any indignation which I might feel at his levity is swallowed up in wonder at his momentary want of wisdom. Credulous optimism, or optimistic credulity, may possibly be natural to a Minister enjoying the power and all the other advantages of office; but it is not a condition of mind in which any man of sense should transact the serious business of the nation. Credulous optimism is, after all, merely a decent name for the delight in a paradise which is not the paradise of the wise. It is a duty of every Unionist, and of every patriot, to avoid the follies of pessimism no less than the follies of optimism, and to base his political conduct on the simple but sure rules dictated by faith in the force of common sense and of common justice.

11 Eoin MacNeill, 'The North Began'[1]

A wonderful state of things has come to pass in Ulster.[2] Three distinct parties, each too weak to be of much force in politics, have ranged themselves against Home Rule. These are the Orange industrial workers, mainly Church of Ireland Protestants; the Presbyterian rural community; and the remnant of the Feudal aristocracy. The first two elements have been drawn together by what is called the 'No-Popery' sentiment. This fact has been turned to account by the third element, and, when dual ownership, land purchase, and the abolition of Grand Jury government had apparently consigned Feudalism to the incurable ward, a combination of landlords, land-agents, land-lawyers, and their adherents, in return for conferring the stamp of 'respectability' on the 'No-Popery' sentiment, has managed to secure the control of an alliance of wage-earners and rent-payers. That this is literally true may be verified by anyone who consults the newspaper files for (1) the names of those who took the initiative in the organisation of the Ulster 'Unionist Clubs',[3] and (2) the names of the numerous *personnel* of the Ulster 'Provisional Government.'[4] To

[1] *An Claidheamh Soluis*, 1 November 1913.

[2] The Ulster Volunteers were founded in 1913 with the support of Irish Unionist leader, Edward Carson, James Craig (1871–1940), MP and a prominent Ulster unionist, and Andrew Bonar Law (1858–1923), leader of the Conservative Party, to defend Ulster from the enforcement of home rule. The militia had 100,000 members reviewed under arms on 9 April.

[3] Unionist clubs, first formed in 1893, were revived to protest against the second Home Rule Bill.

[4] The Proclamation of a Provisional Government for Ulster was publicly endorsed on 23 September 1912.

attain such an ascendancy seems almost a miracle of political adroitness, but there is another side to the picture.

The Parliament Act deprived Irish Feudalism of what hitherto had been its chief resource, the effective support of British Feudalism in the legislature.[5] Then the masters of the Ulster triple alliance decided on an extraordinary step, the enrolment of a Volunteer force manned by their 'allies', the 'Unionist' wage-earners and rent-payers. Of the three 'allied' forces, one only, the managing element, is really 'Unionist.' Intermarriage, social intercourse, and self-interest unite the decaying Feudal aristocracy of Ireland to the still opulent Feudal aristocracy of Great Britain; but history shows and observation confirms that the Orange democracy and the Presbyterian rural party are Home Rulers in principle and in essence. The loyalty of Orangemen to the 'Crown', the 'Constitution', the 'Empire', and the 'Union' arise[s] out of the notion that these entities secure them in possession of Home Rule and a little more.[6] But whenever any abatement of that little more seems likely to come from Constitutional developments, loyalty and affection instantaneously put on a different face. The Presbyterian country party, as its history shows, though slower to move and understand, is not less radically attached to Home Rule than the Orange party.[7]

The skill of the Feudal element in obtaining the lead is more than counterbalanced by their fatuity in starting among the essential Home Rulers of their present following the most decisive move towards Irish autonomy that has been made since O'Connell invented constitutional agitation. The Ulster Volunteer movement is essentially and obviously a Home Rule movement. It claims, no doubt, to hold Ireland 'for the Empire'; but really it is no matter whether Ireland is to be held for the Empire or for the empyrean, against the Pope, against John Redmond, or against the Man in the Moon. What matters is *by whom Ireland is to be held*. Lord Lansdowne, speaking recently against Home Rule, spoke

[5] The Parliament Act was passed in 1911 in response to the rejection by the House of Lords of the 1909 'People's Budget'. It had the effect of cancelling the upper chamber's veto over legislation, thereby blocking its power to stymie legislation in favour of home rule.

[6] The suggestion is that these token declarations of loyalty – to the Crown, the Empire, the constitution – mask the ambition to secure self-government.

[7] Northern Presbyterians for the most part opposed the 1801 Union in the period preceding its passage.

fine old medieval words, 'We have Ireland and we mean to keep her.'[8] The Ulster Volunteers reply, '*We* are going to hold Ireland – of course *for* your Lordships.'

The true meaning of this extraordinary development is dawning painfully on English Unionists. They are beginning to understand that Sir Edward Carson has knocked the bottom out of Unionism. To add to their comfort, a Mr. Arnold White has been proving in elaborate detail that the present available resources of the British Army are not sufficient to put down the Volunteer movement in four of the thirty-two Irish counties.[9] In any case, it appears that the British Army cannot now be used to prevent the enrolment, drilling, and reviewing of Volunteers in Ireland. There is nothing to prevent the other twenty-eight counties from calling into existence citizen forces to hold Ireland 'for the Empire'. It was precisely with this object that the Volunteers of 1782 were enrolled, and they became the instrument of establishing self-government and Irish prosperity.[10] Their disbanding led to the destruction alike of self-government and of prosperity, and the opportunity of rectifying a capital error of this sort does not always come back again to nations.[11]

The more responsible section of English Unionist opinion has taken alarm and is tentatively drawing away from the two-edged sword of 'Ulster'. But even the rashest English Unionists are clearly in great uneasiness; and while they threaten with Ulster, they are openly beseeching the other side to find them a way out of their mess. Dick Steele's creditors once sent him a deputation, as they said, 'to discuss his difficulties with him'. 'Pardon me, gentlemen', was his remark, 'your difficulties, not mine.'[12] Sir Edward Carson proclaimed that, in launching his new Ulster policy, he had not counted the cost. It looks like it.

[8] Henry Charles Keith Petty-Fitzmaurice (1845–1927), 5th Marquess of Lansdowne, became the leader of Unionists (Conservative and Liberal Unionist peers) in the House of Lords

[9] Arnold White (1848–1925) was an English journalist who wrote for *The Referee*.

[10] The 1782 Volunteers were a militia raised locally in Ireland when British soldiers were sent to fight to retain the colonies in the American Revolutionary War. The militia helped to pressurise the government into conceding further legislative independence to the Irish parliament.

[11] During the 1798 Rebellion, a failed insurrection to gain complete autonomy for the Irish parliament, many Volunteers joined the British yeomanry to fight against the rebels, who themselves had also been formerly in the Volunteers. MacNeill is referring to this division, which subsequently resulted in the 1801 Union and the abolition of the Irish parliament.

[12] Richard Steele (1672–1729), co-founder of the Tory organ, *The Spectator*.

The moral of the story is that, in public movements, every element of sham and insincerity is a mortgage given to destiny. I do not say that Sir Edward Carson is insincere. Probably he, too, like the Orangemen and Presbyterians, is at heart a Home Ruler, and thinks that the sort of Home Rule that he wants is best guaranteed by the semblance of government from outside. His English allies, however, hoped that his master-move would do effective electioneering work for them, and the fact that, since he 'drew the sword' in Ulster, he has devoted most of his energies to a political tour in Great Britain shows that he has lent himself to the game. That does not pay. In Ulster, too, the local managers, the Feudal Remnant, who have good reason not to be in earnest when they make a military array of wage-earners and rent-payers, thus mounting and loading a machine gun whose mechanism they cannot hope to control, have shown their hand and have been found evidently bluffing. Their 'Provisional Government', with its pompous detail of phantom departments, put on paper in secret session at a Belfast club, is the most ridiculous piece of political histrionics ever staged. A parcel of schoolboys would be ashamed to own it. In order to pretend strength they arranged to hold reviews in such overwhelming Nationalist districts as Omagh, Raphoe, Armagh, Newry and Kilkeel, but perhaps the crowning sham was the announcement of an insurance fund of £1,000,000. The real insurance fund for real war is fighting material, men, arms, ammunition, transport, ships, fortifications; and those who are in earnest about war will not devote a penny to any other sort of insurance. All this shows that Feudalism in Ireland is doating as well as decaying, and that the cheap cuteness that can play successfully upon religious fanaticism is no proof of any higher form of intelligence.

English Unionists realise, explicitly or instinctively, that the Ulster Volunteers have scuttled the ship; some of them, sooner than admit their discomfiture, are hankering after the separation from Ireland of what they are pleased to call 'homogeneous Ulster', namely, the four eastern counties.[13] Not a single responsible man and no assembly of men in Ireland has authorised this proposal. All Nationalist opinion and any Unionist opinion that has been expressed is strongly hostile to it. And for a very good reason. There is no 'Homogeneous Ulster'. It is impossible to separate from Ireland the city that Saint Patrick founded, the city that Saint

[13] The four north-eastern counties of Ireland had Protestant majorities. They were not, however, homogeneously Protestant.

Columba founded, or the tombs of Patrick, Brigid, and Columba.[14] They would defy and nullify the attempt. It is impossible to separate from Ireland the 'frontier town' of Newry, the men of South Down, Norman and Gael, the Gaelic stock of the Fews that hold 'the Gap of the North',[15] the glensmen of south Derry, or North Antrim. If there were any possibility of civil war, if civil war were assured, not to speak of its being insured, these districts alone would hold immovable all the resources of General – I believe – Richardson. There are besides the 100,000 Nationalist Home Rulers of Belfast, and others, Protestants, Catholic, Orange and Presbyterian, in every corner of the four counties, who under any change of government are certain to 'revert to type'. With what facility they have fallen in with the idea of holding Ireland – for the Empire!

It is evident that the only solution now possible is for the Empire either to make terms with Ireland or to let Ireland go her own way. In any case, it is manifest that all Irish people, Unionist as well as Nationalist, are determined to have their own way in Ireland. On that point, and it is the main point, Ireland is united. It is not to follow, and it will not follow, that any part of Ireland, majority or minority, is to interfere with the liberty of any other part. Sir Edward Carson may yet, at the head of his Volunteers, 'march to Cork'. If so, their progress will probably be accompanied by the greetings of ten times their number of National Volunteers, and Cork will give them a hospitable and a memorable reception. Some years ago, speaking at the Toome Féis,[16] in the heart of 'homogeneous Ulster', I said that the day would come when men of every creed and party would join in celebrating the Defence of Derry and the Battle of Benburb.[17] That day is nearer than I then expected.

[14] He is respectively referring to Armagh, Derry, and Downpatrick (Co. Down).

[15] The Fews is a former barony in Co. Armagh.

[16] A festival in Antrim.

[17] Fought on 5 June 1646 during the Irish Confederate Wars, a distinct theatre within the Wars of the Three Kingdoms, pitting Irish, Scottish, and English forces against one another.

12 Patrick Pearse, *The Coming Revolution*[1]

I have come to the conclusion that the Gaelic League, as the Gaelic League, is a spent force; and I am glad of it.[2] I do not mean that no work remains for the Gaelic League, or that the Gaelic League is no longer equal to work; I mean that the vital work to be done in the new Ireland will be done not so much by the Gaelic League itself as by men and movements that have sprung from the Gaelic League or have received from the Gaelic League a new baptism and a new life of grace. The Gaelic League was no reed shaken by the wind, no mere *vox clamantis*:[3] it was a prophet and more than a prophet. But it was not the Messiah. I do not know if the Messiah has yet come, and I am not sure that there will be any visible and personal Messiah in this redemption: the people itself will perhaps be its own Messiah, the people labouring, scourged, crowned with thorns, agonising and dying, to rise again immortal and impassible. For peoples are divine and are the only things that can properly be spoken of under figures drawn from the divine epos.

If we do not believe in the divinity of our people we have had no business, or very little, all these years in the Gaelic League. In fact, if we had not believed in the divinity of our people, we should in all probability not have gone into the Gaelic League at all. We should have made our peace with the devil, and perhaps might have found him a very decent sort; for he liberally rewards with attorney-generalships, bank balances,

1 *An Claidheamh Soluis*, 8 November 1913.

2 The Gaelic League was founded on 31 July 1893 by Douglas Hyde for the promotion of the Irish language.

3 'Voice crying out'. The medieval English poet, John Gower (1330–1408), wrote a lengthy poem with this title.

villa residences, and so forth, the great and the little who serve him well. Now, we did not turn our backs upon all these desirable things for the sake of *is* and *tá*.[4] We did it for the sake of Ireland. In other words, we had one and all of us (at least, I had, and I hope that all you had) an ulterior motive in joining the Gaelic League. We never meant to be Gaelic Leaguers and nothing more than Gaelic Leaguers. We meant to do something for Ireland, each in his own way. Our Gaelic League time was to be our tutelage: we had first to learn to know Ireland, to read the lineaments of her face, to understand the accents of her voice; to re-possess ourselves, disinherited as we were, of her spirit and mind, re-enter into our mystical birthright. For this we went to school to the Gaelic League. It was a good school, and we love its name and will champion its fame throughout all the days of our later fighting and striving. But we do not propose to remain schoolboys for ever.

I have often said (quoting, I think, Herbert Spencer) that education should be a preparation for complete living;[5] and I say now that our Gaelic League education ought to have been a preparation for our complete living as Irish Nationalists. In proportion as we have been faithful and diligent Gaelic Leaguers, our work as Irish Nationalists (by which term I mean people who accept the ideal of, and work for, the realisation of an Irish Nation, by whatever means) will be earnest and thorough, a valiant and worthy fighting, not the mere carrying out of a ritual. As to what your work as an Irish Nationalist is to be, I cannot conjecture; I know what mine is to be, and would have you know yours and buckle yourself to it. And it may be (nay, it is) that yours and mine will lead us to a common meeting-place, and that on a certain day we shall stand together, with many more beside us, ready for a greater adventure than any of us has yet had, a trial and a triumph to be endured and achieved in common.

This is what I meant when I said that our work henceforward must be done less and less through the Gaelic League and more and more through the groups and the individuals that have arisen, or are arising, out of the Gaelic League. There will be in the Ireland of the next few years a multitudinous activity of Freedom Clubs, Young Republican Parties, Labour Organisations, Socialist Groups, and what not; bewildering enterprises undertaken by sane persons and insane persons, by good men

4 That is, merely for the sake of speaking the Irish language. *Is* and *tá* are forms of the verb 'to be'.

5 Herbert Spencer (1820–1903) was a prominent Victorian social Darwinist.

and bad men, many of them seemingly contradictory, some mutually destructive, yet all tending towards a common objective, and that objective: the Irish Revolution.

For if there is one thing that has become plainer than another it is that when the seven men met in O'Connell Street to found the Gaelic League,[6] they were commencing, had there been a Liancourt there to make the epigram, not a revolt, but a revolution.[7] The work of the Gaelic League, its appointed work, was that: and the work is done. To every generation its deed. The deed of the generation that has now reached middle life was the Gaelic League: the beginning of the Irish Revolution. Let our generation not shirk *its* deed, which is to accomplish the revolution.

I believe that the national movement of which the Gaelic League has been the soul has reached the point which O'Connell's movement had reached at the close of the series of monster meetings.[8] Indeed, I believe that our movement reached that point a few years ago – say, at the conclusion of the fight for Essential Irish; and I said so at the time.[9] The moment was ripe then for a new Young Ireland Party, with a forward policy; and we have lost much by our hesitation.[10] I propose in all seriousness that we hesitate no longer – that we push on. I propose that we leave Conciliation Hall behind us and go into the Irish Confederation.

Whenever Dr. Hyde, at a meeting at which I have had a chance of speaking after him, has produced his dove of peace, I have always been careful to produce my sword; and to tantalise him by saying that the Gaelic League has brought into Ireland 'Not Peace, but a Sword.' But this does not show any fundamental difference of outlook between my leader and me; for while he is thinking of peace between brother-Irishmen, I am thinking of the sword-point between banded Irishmen and the foreign force that occupies Ireland: and his peace is necessary to my war. It is evident that there can be no peace between the body politic and a

[6] In addition to Hyde, some co-founders included: Eugene O'Growney, Eoin MacNeill and Thomas O'Neill Russell.

[7] A reference to the French social reformer François Alexandre Frédéric de La Rochefoucauld-Liancourt (1747–1827).

[8] Daniel O'Connell (1775–1847) had staged monster rallies to secure Catholic Emancipation.

[9] Pearse is referring to the Roman Catholic campaign for higher education, which culminated in the Irish Universities Act of 1908. Part of the campaign was for Irish universities to be 'distinctly Irish' and to teach the Irish language.

[10] Young Ireland was a movement of the 1840s committed to the revival of Irish culture and the pursuit of political ideals of national freedom.

foreign substance that has intruded itself into its system: between them war only until the foreign substance is expelled or assimilated.

Whether Home Rule means a loosening or a tightening of England's grip upon Ireland remains yet to be seen. But the coming of Home Rule, if come it does, will make no material difference in the nature of the work that lies before us: it will affect only the means we are to employ, our plan of campaign. There remains, under Home Rule as in its absence, the substantial task of achieving the Irish Nation. I do not think it is going to be achieved without stress and trial, without suffering and bloodshed; at any rate, it is not going to be achieved without *work*. Our business here and now is to get ourselves into harness for such work as has to be done.

I hold that before we can do any work, any *men's* work, we must first realise ourselves as men. Whatever comes to Ireland she needs men. And we of this generation are not in any real sense men, for we suffer things that men do not suffer, and we seek to redress grievances by means which men do not employ. We have, for instance, allowed ourselves to be disarmed; and, now that we have the chance of re-arming, we are not seizing it. Professor Eoin Mac Neill pointed out last week that we have at this moment an opportunity of rectifying the capital error we made when we allowed ourselves to be disarmed; and such opportunities, he reminds us, do not always come back to nations.[11]

A thing that stands demonstrable is that nationhood is not achieved otherwise than in arms: in one or two instances there may have been no actual bloodshed, but the arms were there and the ability to use them. Ireland unarmed will attain just as much freedom as it is convenient for England to give her; Ireland armed will attain ultimately just as much freedom as she wants. These are matters which may not concern the Gaelic League, as a body; but they concern every member of the Gaelic League, and every man and woman of Ireland. I urged much of this five or six years ago in addresses to the Ard-Chraobh:[12] but the League was too busy with resolutions to think of revolution, and the only resolution that a member of the League could not come to was the resolution to be a man. My fellow-Leaguers had not (and have not) apprehended that the thing which cannot defend itself, even though it may wear trousers, is no man.

[11] Eoin MacNeill proposed the formation of the Irish Volunteers on 1 November 1913.

[12] Meeting of the Gaelic League.

I am glad, then, that the North has 'begun.'[13] I am glad that the Orangemen have armed, for it is a goodly thing to see arms in Irish hands.[14] I should like to see the A. O. H. armed.[15] I should like to see the Transport Workers armed.[16] I should like to see any and every body of Irish citizens armed. We must accustom ourselves to the thought of arms, to the sight of arms, to the use of arms. We may make mistakes in the beginning and shoot the wrong people; but bloodshed is a cleansing and a sanctifying thing, and the nation which regards it as the final horror has lost its manhood. There are many things more horrible than bloodshed; and slavery is one of them.

[13] A reference to MacNeill's advocacy of the Volunteers in 'The North Began'.

[14] The Ulster Volunteers had formed as a unionist militia in 1913 to defend Ulster against the enforcement of home rule. It had 100,000 members when reviewed under arms on 9 April.

[15] Ancient Order of Hibernians, a Catholic fraternal association.

[16] The Irish Transport and General Workers' Union was a trade union founded by James Larkin (1876–1947) in 1909.

1914

13 James Connolly, 'Labour and the Proposed Partition of Ireland'[1]

The recent proposals of Messrs. Asquith, Devlin, Redmond and Co. for the settlement of the Home Rule question deserve the earnest attention of the working class democracy of this country.[2] They reveal in a most striking and unmistakeable manner the depths of betrayal to which the so-called Nationalist politicians are willing to sink. For generations the conscience of the civilised world has been shocked by the historical record of the partition of Poland;[3] publicists, poets, humanitarians, patriots, all lovers of their kind and of progress have wept over the unhappy lot of a country torn asunder by the brute force of their alien oppressors, its unity ruthlessly destroyed and its traditions trampled into the dust.

But Poland was disrupted by outside forces, its enemies were the mercenaries of the tyrant kingdoms and empires of Europe; its sons and daughters died in the trenches and on the battlefields by the thousands rather than submit to their beloved country being annihilated as a nation. But Ireland, what of Ireland? It is the trusted leaders of Ireland that in secret conclave with the enemies of Ireland have agreed to see Ireland as

1 Originally published in the *Irish Worker*, the newspaper of James Larkin's (1876–1914) Irish Transport and General Workers' Union, on 14 March 1914.

2 Herbert H. Asquith (1852–1928), Liberal prime minister. In early 1914 negotiations were under way to manage the drift towards civil war in Ireland over the Ulster question as thrown up by the prospect of devolved self-government. John Redmond (1856–1918), MP and the Irish Parliamentary Party leader, and Joe Devlin (1871–1934), MP and the Irish Parliamentary Party's northern nationalist representative, participated in the talks, which included proposals for 'Home Rule within Home Rule' for the six north-eastern counties of Ireland and the 'Temporary Exclusion' of Ulster from home rule.

3 Poland was partitioned by its powerful neighbours, the Habsburgs, Prussians, and Russian Empire, in 1772, 1793, and 1795.

a nation disrupted politically and her children divided under separate political governments with warring interests.

Now, what is the position of Labour towards it all? Let us remember that the Orange aristocracy now fighting for its supremacy in Ireland has at all times been based upon a denial of the common human rights of the Irish people; that the Orange Order was not founded to safeguard religious freedom, but to deny religious freedom, and that it raised this religious question, not for the sake of any religion, but in order to use religious zeal in the interests of the oppressive property rights of rackrenting landlords and sweating capitalists.[4] That the Irish people might be kept asunder and robbed whilst so sundered and divided, the Orange aristocracy went down to the lowest depths and out of the lowest pits of hell brought up the abominations of sectarian feuds to stir the passions of the ignorant mob. No crime was too brutal or cowardly; no lie too base; no slander too ghastly, as long as they served to keep the democracy as under.

And now that the progress of democracy elsewhere has somewhat muzzled the dogs of aristocratic power, now that in England as well as in Ireland the forces of labour are stirring and making for freedom and light, this same gang of well-fed plunderers of the people, secure in Union held upon their own dupes, seek by threats of force to arrest the march of idea and stifle the light of civilisation and liberty. And, lo and behold, the trusted guardians of the people, the vaunted saviours of the Irish race, agree in front of the enemy and in face of the world to sacrifice to the bigoted enemy the unity of the nation and along with it the lives, liberties and hopes of that portion of the nation which in the midst of the most hostile surroundings have fought to keep the faith in things national and progressive.

Such a scheme as that agreed to by Redmond and Devlin, the betrayal of the national democracy of industrial Ulster would mean a carnival of reaction both North and South, would set back the wheels of progress, would destroy the oncoming unity of the Irish Labour movement and paralyse all advanced movements whilst it endured.

To it Labour should give the bitterest opposition, against it Labour in Ulster should fight even to the death, if necessary, as our fathers fought before us.

[4] The Orange Order was founded in Armagh in 1795 to defend the Protestant interest in Ireland.

14 James Connolly, 'Our Duty in the Crisis'[1]

What should be the attitude to the working-class democracy of Ireland in face of the present crisis?[2] I wish to emphasise the fact that the question is addressed to the 'working-class democracy' because I believe that it would be worse than foolish – it would be a crime against all our hopes and aspirations – to take counsel in this matter from any other source.

Mr. John E. Redmond has just earned the plaudits of all the bitterest enemies of Ireland and slanderers of the Irish race by declaring, in the name of Ireland that the British Government can now safely withdraw all its garrisons from Ireland, and that the Irish slaves will guarantee to protect the Irish estate of England until their masters come back to take possession – a statement that announces to all the world that Ireland has at last accepted as permanent this status of a British province.[3] Surely no inspiration can be sought from that source.

The advanced Nationalists have neither a policy nor a leader. During the Russian Revolution such of their Press as existed in and out of Ireland, as well as their spokesmen, orators and writers vied with each other in laudation of Russia and vilification of all the Russian enemies

[1] Originally published in the *Irish Worker* on 8 August 1914.

[2] The First World War began on 28 July 1914 with the declaration of hostilities by Austria-Hungary against Serbia. Germany invaded Belgium on 4 August. Austro-Hungarian troops entered Serbia on 12 August.

[3] John Redmond (1856–1918), leader of the nationalist Irish Parliamentary Party, had just pledged the use of the Irish Volunteers militia in concert with the Ulster Volunteers to defend Ireland from German invasion, enabling Britain to withdraw its troops and intervene in the European crisis. Hansard, House of Commons Debates, 3 August 1914, vol. 65, cols. 1828–9.

of Czardom.[4] It was freely asserted that Russia was the natural enemy of England; that the heroic revolutionalists were in the pay of the English Government and that every true Irish patriot ought to pray for the success of the armies of the Czar. Now, as I, amongst other Irish Socialists, predicted all along, when the exigencies of diplomacy make it suitable, the Russian bear and the English lion are hunting together and every victory for the Czar's Cossacks is a victory for the paymasters of those King's Own Scottish Borderers who,[5] but the other day, murdered the people of Dublin in cold blood.[6] Surely the childish intellects that conceived of the pro-Russian campaign of nine years ago cannot give us light and leading in any campaign for freedom from the British allies of Russia today? It is well to remember also that in this connection since 1909 the enthusiasm for the Russians was replaced in the same quarter by as blatant a propaganda in favour of the German War Lord.[7] But since the guns did begin to speak in reality this propaganda had died out in whispers, whilst without a protest, the manhood of Ireland was pledged to armed warfare against the very power our advanced Nationalist friends have wasted so much good ink in acclaiming.

Of late, sections of the advanced Nationalist press have lent themselves to a desperate effort to misrepresent the position of the Carsonites, and to claim for them the admiration of Irish Nationalists on the grounds that these Carsonites were fearless Irishmen who had refused to take dictation from England.[8] A more devilishly mischievous and lying doctrine was never preached in Ireland. The Carsonite position is indeed plain – so plain that nothing but sheer perversity of purpose can misunderstand it, or cloak it with a resemblance to Irish patriotism. The Carsonites say that their fathers were planted in this country to assist in keeping the natives down in subjection that this country might be held for England. That this was God's will because the Catholic Irish were not fit for the responsibilities and powers of free men and that they

4 The Russian Revolution of 1905.

5 The Russian Empire entered the war in defence of Serbia in late July.

6 On 26 July 1914, in the aftermath of the illegal importation of arms into Ireland at Howth, a column of troops from the King's Own Scottish Borderers collided with protestors resulting in the death of four unarmed civilians at Bachelor's Walk in Dublin.

7 The German Kaiser, Wilhelm II, head of the government armed forces.

8 'Carsonites' meaning supporters of Edward Carson, the Irish Unionist leader, or Irish unionists. Carson's stand in Ulster was often identified in the Southern press as a militant stand against the British, exemplified as early as 1913 by Eoin MacNeill's 'The North Began'.

are not fit for the exercise of these responsibilities and powers till this day. Therefore, say the Carsonites, we have kept our side of the bargain; we have refused to admit the Catholics to power and responsibility; we have manned the government of this country for England, we propose to continue to do so, and rather than admit that these Catholics – these 'mickies and teagues'[9] – are our equals, we will fight, in the hope that our fighting will cause the English people to revolt against their government and re-establish us in our historic position as an English colony in Ireland, superior to, and unhampered by, the political institutions of the Irish natives.

How this can be represented as the case of Irishmen refusing to take dictation from England passeth all comprehension. It is rather the case of a community in Poland, after 250 years colonisation, still refusing to adopt the title of natives, and obstinately clinging to the position and privileges of a dominant colony. Their programme is summed up in the expression which forms the dominant note of all their speeches, sermons and literature:

> We are loyal British subjects. We hold this country for England. England cannot desert us.

What light or leading then can Ireland get from the hysterical patriots who so egregiously misrepresent this fierce contempt for Ireland as something that ought to win the esteem of Irishmen?

What ought to be the attitude of the working-class democracy of Ireland in face of the present crisis?

In the first place, then, we ought to clear our minds of all the political cant which would tell us that we have either 'natural enemies' or 'natural allies' in any of the powers now warring.[10] When it is said that we ought to unite to protect our shores against the 'foreign enemy' I confess to be unable to follow that line of reasoning, as I know of no foreign enemy of this country except the British Government and know that it is not the British Government that is meant.

In the second place we ought to seriously consider that the evil effects of this war upon Ireland will be simply incalculable, that it will cause untold suffering and misery amongst the people, and that as this misery and

[9] Derogatory terms for the Irish. Teague comes from the Irish first name, Tadhg.

[10] A reference to the political rhetoric surrounding the war which accompanied the creation of the Allied forces and Central Powers. Connolly is disputing the validity of categorising Germany as an 'enemy' of Ireland.

suffering have been brought upon us because of our enforced partisanship with a nation whose government never consulted us in the matter, we are therefore perfectly at liberty morally to make any bargain we may see fit, or that may present itself in the course of events.

Should a German army land in Ireland tomorrow we should be perfectly justified in joining it if by doing so we could rid this country once and for all from its connection with the Brigand Empire that drags us unwillingly into this war.

Should the working class of Europe, rather than slaughter each other for the benefit of kings and financiers, proceed tomorrow to erect barricades all over Europe, to break up bridges and destroy the transport service that war might be abolished, we should be perfectly justified in following such a glorious example and contributing our aid to the final dethronement of the vulture classes that rule and rob the world.

But pending either of these consummations it is our manifest duty to take all possible action to save the poor from the horrors this war has in store.

Let it be remembered that there is no natural scarcity of food in Ireland. Ireland is an agricultural country, and can normally feed all her people under any sane system of things. But prices are going up in England and hence there will be an immense demand for Irish produce. To meet that demand all nerves will be strained on this side, the food that ought to feed the people of Ireland will be sent out of Ireland in greater quantities than ever and famine prices will come in Ireland to be immediately followed by famine itself. Ireland will starve, or rather the townspeople of Ireland will starve, that the British army and navy and jingoes may be fed. Remember, the Irish farmer like all other farmers will benefit by the high prices of the war, but these high prices will mean starvation to the labourers in the towns. But without these labourers the farmers' produce cannot leave Ireland without the help of a garrison that England cannot now spare. We must consider at once whether it will not be our duty to refuse to allow agricultural produce to leave Ireland until provision is made for the Irish working class.

Let us not shrink from the consequences. This may mean more than a transport strike, it may mean armed battling in the streets to keep in this country the food for our people. But whatever it may mean it must not be shrunk from. It is the immediately feasible policy of the working-class democracy, the answer to all the weaklings who in this crisis of our country's history stand helpless and bewildered crying for guidance, when they are not hastening to betray her.

Starting thus, Ireland may yet set the torch to a European conflagration that will not burn out until the last throne and the last capitalist bond and debenture will be shrivelled on the funeral pyre of the last war lord.

15 James Connolly, 'A Continental Revolution'[1]

The outbreak of war on the continent of Europe makes it impossible this week to write to *Forward* upon any other question.[2] I have no doubt that to most of my readers Ireland has ere now ceased to be, in colloquial phraseology, the most important place on the map, and that their thoughts are turning gravely to a consideration of the position of the European socialist movement in the face of this crisis.

Judging by developments up to the time of writing, such considerations must fall far short of affording satisfying reflections to the socialist thinker. For, what is the position of the socialist movement in Europe to-day? Summed up briefly it is as follows:

For a generation at least the socialist movement in all the countries now involved has progressed by leaps and bounds, and more satisfactory still, by steady and continuous increase and development.

The number of votes recorded for socialist candidates has increased at a phenomenally rapid rate, the number of socialist representatives in all legislative chambers has become more and more of a disturbing factor in the calculations of governments. Newspapers, magazines, pamphlets and literature of all kinds teaching socialist ideas have been and are daily distributed by the million amongst the masses; every army and navy in Europe has seen a constantly increasing proportion of socialists amongst its soldiers and sailors, and the industrial organisations of the working class have more and more perfected their grasp over the economic machinery of society, and more and more moved responsive to the socialist

[1] Originally published on 15 August 1914 in *Forward*, the newspaper of the Independent Labour Party in Britain.

[2] Referring to the First World War, which began in late July 1914.

conception of their duties. Along with this, hatred of militarism has spread through every rank of society, making everywhere its recruits, and raising an aversion to war even amongst those who in other things accepted the capitalist order of things. Anti-militarist societies and anti-militarist campaigns of socialist societies and parties, and anti-militarist resolutions of socialist and international trade union conferences have become part of the order of the day and are no longer phenomena to be wondered at. The whole working-class movement stands committed to war upon war – stands so committed at the very height of its strength and influence.[3]

And now, like the proverbial bolt from the blue, war is upon us, and war between the most important, because the most socialist, nations of the earth. And we are helpless!

What then becomes of all our resolutions; all our protests of fraternisation; all our threats of general strikes; all our carefully-built machinery of internationalism; all our hopes for the future? Were they all as sound and fury, signifying nothing? When the German artilleryman, a socialist serving in the German army of invasion, sends a shell into the ranks of the French army, blowing off their heads; tearing out their bowels, and mangling the limbs of dozens of socialist comrades in that force, will the fact that he, before leaving for the front 'demonstrated' against the war be of any value to the widows and orphans made by the shell he sent upon its mission of murder? Or, when the French rifleman pours his murderous rifle fire into the ranks of the German line of attack, will he be able to derive any comfort from the probability that his bullets are murdering or maiming comrades who last year joined in thundering 'hochs' and cheers of greeting to the eloquent Jaurès, when in Berlin he pleaded for international solidarity?[4] When the socialist pressed into the army of the Austrian Kaiser, sticks a long, cruel bayonet-knife into the stomach of the socialist conscript in the army of the Russian Czar, and gives it a twist

[3] Prominent figures within the Second International (1889–1916) had suggested that a strike might foil the war plans of capitalist powers. Earlier resolutions had condemned colonialism (Stuttgart Congress, 1907) and opposed militarism (Copenhagen Congress, 1910). However most socialist parties in Europe in the end supported their respective national governments from the outset of the First World War. Sections of national parties did however split into internationalist and defencist factions.

[4] Jean Jaurès (1859–1914) led the French Socialist Party from 1902. He was a prominent anti-militarist in the run up to the war, trying to organise general strikes in France and Germany to force governments to negotiate, but he was assassinated on his way to an international conference on 31 July 1914.

so that when pulled out it will pull the entrails out along with it, will the terrible act lose any of its fiendish cruelty by the fact of their common theoretical adhesion to an anti-war propaganda in times of peace? When the socialist soldier from the Baltic provinces of Russia is sent forward into Prussian Poland to bombard towns and villages until a red trail of blood and fire covers the homes of the unwilling Polish subjects of Prussia, as he gazes upon the corpses of those he has slaughtered and the homes he has destroyed, will he in his turn be comforted by the thought that the Czar whom he serves sent other soldiers a few years ago to carry the same devastation and murder into his own home by the Baltic Sea?

But why go on? Is it not as clear as the fact of life itself that no insurrection of the working class; no general strike; no general uprising of the forces of Labour in Europe, could possibly carry with it, or entail a greater slaughter of socialists, than will their participation as soldiers in the campaigns of the armies of their respective countries? Every shell which explodes in the midst of a German battalion will slaughter some socialists; every Austrian cavalry charge will leave the gashed and hacked bodies of Serbian or Russian socialists squirming and twisting in agony upon the ground; every Russian, Austrian, or German ship sent to the bottom or blown sky-high will mean sorrow and mourning in the homes of some socialist comrades of ours. If these men must die, would it not be better to die in their own country fighting for freedom for their class, and for the abolition of war, than to go forth to strange countries and die slaughtering and slaughtered by their brothers that tyrants and profiteers might live?

Civilisation is being destroyed before our eyes; the results of generations of propaganda and patient heroic plodding and self-sacrifice are being blown into annihilation from a hundred cannon mouths; thousands of comrades with whose souls we have lived in fraternal communion are about to be done to death; they whose one hope it was to be spared to cooperate in building the perfect society of the future are being driven to fratricidal slaughter in shambles where that hope will be buried under a sea of blood.

I am not writing in captious criticism of my continental comrades. We know too little about what is happening on the continent, and events have moved too quickly for any of us to be in a position to criticise at all. But believing as I do that any action would be justified which would put a stop to this colossal crime now being perpetrated, I feel compelled to express the hope that ere long we may read of the paralysing of the internal transport service on the continent, even should the act of paralysing necessitate the erection of socialist barricades and acts of rioting by socialist soldiers and sailors, as happened in Russia in 1905.[5] Even an unsuccessful attempt at social revolution by force of arms, following the paralysis of the economic life of militarism, would be less disastrous to the socialist cause than the act of socialists allowing themselves to be used in the slaughter of their brothers in the cause.

A great continental uprising of the working class would stop the war; a universal protest at public meetings will not save a single life from being wantonly slaughtered.

I make no war upon patriotism; never have done. But against the patriotism of capitalism – the patriotism which makes the interest of the capitalist class the supreme test of duty and right – I place the patriotism of the working class, the patriotism which judges every public act by its effect upon the fortunes of those who toil. That which is good for the working class I esteem patriotic, but that party or movement is the most perfect embodiment of patriotism which most successfully works for the conquest by the working class of the control of the destinies of the land wherein they labour.

To me, therefore, the socialist of another country is a fellow-patriot, as the capitalist of my own country is a natural enemy. I regard each nation as the possessor of a definite contribution to the common stock of civilisation, and I regard the capitalist class of each nation as being the logical and natural enemy of the national culture which constitutes that definite contribution.

Therefore, the stronger I am in my affection for national tradition, literature, language, and sympathies, the more firmly rooted I am in my opposition to that capitalist class which in its soulless lust for power and gold would bray the nations as in a mortar.

Reasoning from such premises, therefore, this war appears to me as the most fearful crime of the centuries. In it the working class are to be sacrificed that a small clique of rulers and armament makers may sate their lust for power and their greed for wealth. Nations are to be obliterated, progress stopped, and international hatreds erected into deities to be worshipped.

[5] Peasants, workers, and sections of the military that had mutinied took part in the 1905 Russian Revolution, which resulted in the formation of the multi-party State Duma and Constitution of 1906.

16 John Redmond, 'Speech on the Suspensory Bill'[1]

The right hon. Gentleman who has just spoken, and who has since left the Chamber, has said many bitter things and many violent things.[2] He said many unjust things and many ungenerous things. But I do not propose to waste my time and the time of the House by replying to statements of that sort. The only controversial thing I will say about that speech is that, having told the world that the Government of this Empire is made up of men devoid of honour, devoid of truth, devoid of decency, he wound up his speech by saying that his one desire in life was to support the Government in this crisis. Let me say with reference to one, and, indeed, the main theme of the right hon. Gentleman, that for my part – and in this I am sure I speak for all my Friends – we entirely dispute the statement that out of what has occurred, and out of the proposals of the Government, we gain any advantage whatever in consequence of the War. I have said more than once in the House that we had no desire to gain any advantage from what has taken place in connection with the War.[3] All that we asked was that we should not be damnified. When the War broke out, as the Prime Minister has so powerfully explained, we had what was the practical certainty of the enactment of the Home Rule Bill.[4] We had won a long

1 Hansard, House of Commons Debates, 15 September 1914, vol. 66, cols. 905–12.

2 Andrew Bonar Law (1858–1923), leader of the Conservative opposition, who had just spoken in response to the Liberal Prime Minister Henry Asquith (1852–1928).

3 Referring to the First World War, which began in late July 1914.

4 The third Home Rule Bill was introduced into the Commons on 11 April 1912. During the course of its passage through parliament it was rejected twice by the Lords. It passed its third reading in the Commons on 25 May 1914. Under the 1911 Parliament Act, in being rejected a third time by the Lords, their veto was overridden and the Bill was ready

and hard Parliamentary battle, a battle which had been carried on for a generation and more outside the walls of Parliament, and which for the last few years had been carried on laboriously within the walls of Parliament, and we had won that Parliamentary battle.

It is true, as the Leader of the Opposition said, that an Amending Bill was upon the stocks. We hoped, and no one hoped more sincerely than I did, that in that Amending Bill might be found the means of placating those fellow countrymen of ours in Ulster who were in violent opposition to the policy of Home Rule. But we knew that, Amending Bill or no Amending Bill, at the end of this Session the Home Rule Bill must, under the Parliament Act, receive the Royal Assent, not only that it would receive the Royal Assent, but that it would immediately pass into operation. Under the plan of the Government, the Bill is immediately to pass into law, but it is not to become operative for a year or more. The idea of anyone pretending that out of a proposal of that kind we are snatching an advantage from the state of things caused by the War seems to me absolutely absurd. I certainly do not regard this settlement of the difficulty as a party triumph for my Friends or myself, and I shall certainly not represent it as a party triumph either in this House or in Ireland. It is nothing of the kind. It inflicts a severe disadvantage upon us. But at the same time I must declare my opinion that, under all the circumstances of the case, this moratorium which the Government propose is a reasonable one.[5] Of course, when everybody is preoccupied by the War, and when everyone is endeavouring – and the endeavour will be made as enthusiastically in Ireland as anywhere else in the United Kingdom – to bring about the creation of an Army,[6] the idea is absurd, and cannot be entertained by any intelligent man, that under these circumstances a new Government and a new Parliament could be erected in Ireland.

Let me say further, and I am not at all sure that this moratorium may not in the end be found, as was indicated in one part of the speech of the Prime Minister, to be of great good to Ireland. The Amending Bill

to be submitted for royal assent at the end of the session. During this interval, on 23 June 1914 an Amending Bill to deal with arrangements for the temporary or permanent exclusion of Ulster from the jurisdiction of a home rule parliament in Southern Ireland was introduced by the government in the Lords. Before a resolution was reached, the First World War intervened.

[5] The moratorium was in substance a proposal to suspend the operation of the Act for the duration of the war.

[6] Redmond is referring to Secretary of State Lord Kitchener's proposal to create 'New Armies' of volunteers.

is still on the stocks – that is to say, an Amending Bill. The Government have pledged themselves, within the period of suspension now provided, to introduce next Session an Amending Bill. That is a pledge which for my part I entirely accept. I believe this delay, this moratorium may lead – and I pray and hope that it will – to an Amending Bill very different from that about which we have been quarrelling in the past. There are two things that I care most about in this world of politics. The first is that the system of autonomy which is to be extended to Ireland shall be extended to the whole country, and that not a single sod of Irish soil and not a single citizen of the Irish nation shall be excluded from its operation. Let me say – and this may perhaps surprise some hon. Members, but it has honestly been my view all through – that the second thing that I most earnestly desire is that no coercion shall be applied to any single county in Ireland to force them against their will to come into the Irish Government.[7] At this moment, as everybody knows, these two things are unfortunately incompatible. Will they be incompatible after an interval of some months, as those months will be occupied by the Irish people at home? No, Sir, I do not believe they will. During that interval, Catholic Nationalist Irishmen and Protestant Unionist Irishmen from the North of Ireland will be fighting side by side on the battlefields on the Continent, and shedding their blood side by side; and at home in Ireland, Catholic Nationalists and Protestant Ulstermen will, I hope and believe, be found drilling shoulder to shoulder for the defence of the shores of their own country.

The result of all that must inevitably be to assuage bitterness, and to mollify the hatred and misunderstanding which have kept them apart, and I do not think I am too sanguine when I express my belief that, when the time has arrived for the Government to introduce their Amending Bill, we may have been able by this process in Ireland to come to an agreement amongst ourselves whereby we can suggest to the Government an Amending Bill which they can easily accept and ratify, a Bill which will be a real Amending Bill, not a Bill for emasculation or exclusion, but a Bill based upon very different and more hopeful lines. In my opinion it

7 Redmond is referring to Ulster unionist claims that Ulster will be 'coerced' if home rule were passed and that unionists would defend Ulster against the imposition of Irish self-government. Before Redmond rose to speak, Bonar Law had directed the following remark at him: 'The hon. Member for Waterford has made a great mistake. Ulster never can be coerced; she can only be won.' See Hansard, House of Commons Debates, 15 September 1915, vol. 66, col. 903.

will be the highest duty of every Irish Nationalist – and I shall say so to my fellow-countrymen when I go home – during that interval to cultivate sedulously the spirit of conciliation, to suppress the voice of faction, sectarian strife and hatred, and to unite, as I hope we will be able to unite, all the sons of Ireland in the great task which this War imposes upon our Nation.

An allusion has been made to recruiting in Ireland. A rather ungenerous and unjust allusion was made by the Leader of the Opposition to a speech which I made about a month ago.[8] He said that that speech was an offer of conditional loyalty. It was nothing of the kind! That speech was an appeal. I venture to recall – not in any spirit of controversy at all, but really in the spirit of self-defence – the attention of the House to the fact that that speech of mine was a double appeal. It was an appeal to the Ulster Volunteers to allow us – I used the phrase 'to allow us' – to have the honour, shoulder to shoulder with them, of engaging in the defence of our country, and it was an appeal, at the same time, to the Government and the War Office to enable the National Volunteers to fulfil that duty. I made no condition of any sort or kind, and – if hon. Members will only think of it – it would have been an absurdity for me to have made it a condition that the Bill should go on the Statute Book, because all through we had the certainty that it was going on the Statute Book. I would like to say this – if the Prime Minister will allow me – that all through these negotiations, conversations, and so on, that I have had with him, all through on every occasion that I had any dealings with him about this matter, he has assured me that it was the intention of the Government to put this Bill on the Statute Book this Session. From that he never wavered, and it would have been an utter absurdity for me, under these circumstances, to have made the putting of the Bill on the Statute Book a condition with reference to my offer of the Irish Volunteers.

As the matter has been mentioned, may I be allowed to say this further: That double appeal I made has met with no response. I deeply regret it. I appealed to the Volunteers of Ulster to allow us, shoulder to shoulder with them, to enter on the defence of our country. I have got no response. The appeal still stands – indeed, I repeat it now. The appeal I made to

[8] The intervention by Redmond referred to was in the House of Commons on 10 August 1914. Bonar Law noted Redmond's statement in his Speech of 15 September 1914, construing his original request to Asquith to take 'advantage' of the Volunteers as a statement of 'conditional loyalty'. See Hansard, House of Commons Debates, 10 August 1914, vol. 65, col. 2265 and Hansard, House of Commons Debates, 15 September 1914, col. 902

the Government has met with no response. I must say on this question of recruiting that if the advice I gave, and if the appeal I made to them had been met, and if they had done something to arm, drill, and equip a certain number, at any rate, of the National Volunteers, the recruiting probably would have been faster than it has been. As the question of recruiting has been mentioned, and as some very offensive cries reached my ears from those benches on the subject, will you allow me to say this: That the proportion of the population of Ireland who are at the present day in the Army, and who have been in it for a very long time past, is larger than the proportion of the people of Great Britain. I have the figures here. From the days of the Peninsular War and Waterloo, right up to last year, the Irish people have furnished a larger quota by far, in proportion to their population, than the people of England or Scotland.[9] According to the figures the number per thousand of the male population from twenty to forty-five years of age who joined the Regular Army and the Special Reserve was, in the year 1885: Irish born, 76; British born, 42; 1893: Irish born, 75; British born, 47; 1903: Irish born, 69; British born, 44. In the latest figures for 1913 the Irish born per thousand number 42, and the British born 32.

It is impossible, at any rate impossible for Irishmen, in speaking on this point of recruiting, not to look back with sorrow and with indignation at that long course of history which had the effect in seventy years of reducing the population of Ireland from 8,000,000 to 4,000,000.[10] That is the record of Ireland in relation to the Army in the past when the Nationalist sentiment of the country was undoubtedly out of touch with this country. What, I ask you, will be the record now that the sentiment of the whole Irish people undoubtedly is with you in this War? And what material it is! I have been moved, and I dare say every man in this House has been moved, by some of the war stories that have come back from the seat of war. There is the story of the Munster Fusiliers, who stood by their guns all day, and in the end dragged them back to their lines themselves.[11] There was, too, the story in yesterday's papers from the lips of the wounded French soldiers, who described how the Irish Guards charged

[9] The conflict fought by Portugal and Spain against France from 1807 to 1814, assisted by the United Kingdom, and the Battle of Waterloo in 1815.

[10] He is referring to the seventy-year period since the Great Famine of 1845–52.

[11] The Royal Munster Fusiliers were an Irish regiment of the British Army. Redmond is likely referring to their heavy losses at Etreux in September 1914.

with the bayonet three regiments of German Cavalry.[12] As the wounded French soldier said, they charged singing 'a strange song that I have never heard before'. The newspaper man asked the wounded soldier what were the words, and the answer was, 'I cannot tell you what the words were, but it was something about God saving Ireland.'[13] I saw these men marching through London on their way to the station. They marched here past this building singing 'God save Ireland'. It is unnecessary for me to tell this House of the magnificent material that the country has at its disposal in the Irish soldier, and the sneers that we have heard are a little too hard on us. The *Times*, in an article to-day, says: – 'Nationalist Ireland still disowns her gallant soldiers, flaunts placards against enlistment, and preaches sedition in her newspapers.' That is a cruel libel on Ireland. The men who are circulating hand-bills against enlistment – the men who are publishing little wretched rags once a week or once a month which none of us ever see – who are sending them by some mysterious agency through the post in this country, and day by day to Members – these are the little group of men who never belonged to the National Constitutional party at all, but who have been all through, and are to-day, our bitterest enemies.[14] If you take up these wretched rags you will find praises of the Emperor of Germany in the same sentence as are denunciations of my colleagues and myself. For the first time – certainly for over one hundred years – Ireland in this War feels her interests are precisely the same as yours. She feels, she will feel, that the British democracy has kept faith with her. She knows that this is a just War. She knows, she is moved in a very special way by the fact that this War is undertaken in the defence of small nations and oppressed peoples. Belgium! gallant Belgium! there is not a heart in Ireland that is not stirred with admiration for her defence, and with it a desire to give her succour.[15] Alsace! which has the whole sympathy of the Irish people in desiring to come back to its

[12] He is probably referring to the Battle of the Marne, which took place from 6 to 12 September.

[13] 'God Save Ireland' was a patriotic anthem that achieved quasi-official status between 1867 and 1916.

[14] The *Times* is referring to the Irish Parliamentary Party, largely deemed to be the constitutional expression of Irish nationalism, as opposed to more radical movements.

[15] Catholic Ireland had historic links with Catholic Belgium, and the Irish clergy played an important role in mobilising Catholic support for the plight of Belgium, bolstering the wider UK discourse that the conflict was one for 'small nations' like Belgium and Serbia.

ancient nationality.[16] And Poland! which the other day received the magnificent gift of Home Rule from the Czar, and on whose side the whole sympathy of the Irish people has been, not to-day or yesterday, but for many a long generation.[17]

I say nothing about France, the old friend of Ireland! France, the champion of democratic freedom, which has done so much for the freedom of America, as well as of Europe! I say that the manhood of Ireland will spring to your aid in this War. Speaking personally for myself, I do not think it is an exaggeration to say that on hundreds of platforms in this country during the last few years I have publicly promised, not only for myself, but in the name of my country, that when the rights of Ireland were admitted by the democracy of England, that Ireland would become the strongest arm in the defence of the Empire. The test has come sooner than I, or anyone, expected. I tell the Prime Minister that that test will be honourably met. I say for myself, that I would feel myself personally dishonoured if I did not say to my fellow countrymen, as I say today to them here, and as I will say from the public platform when I go back to Ireland, that it is their duty, and should be their honour, to take their place in the firing line in this contest. The right hon. Gentleman the Prime Minister has announced that he is going to address a meeting in Dublin.

Let me beg of him to come soon. I hope to have the honour of standing upon the platform beside him. I can promise him here to-night that he will get an enthusiastic reception, and that there will be an enthusiastic response to his appeal. The whole world has been struck by the spectacle of unity in the Empire – in India, Canada, Australia, New Zealand, and last, but not least, in South Africa and Ireland. No one could have read unmoved the magnificent speeches of General Botha and General Smuts, and no one could have read unmoved the declaration of that old veteran General De Wet, who, old as he is, is organising a regiment to be led by himself to the front on the Continent of Europe.[18] Just as Botha and Smuts have been able to say in the speeches which were published three days ago that the concession of free institutions to South Africa has

[16] Alsace was annexed by Germany after the Franco-Prussian War of 1871. A degree of autonomy was conceded in 1911.

[17] The Polish National Committee was formed in the Russian partition at the start of the war with a view to establishing an autonomous kingdom.

[18] Louis Botha (1862–1919) was the first prime minister of the Union of South Africa; Jan Smuts (1870–1950) was a South African statesman who became prime minister in 1919; Christiaan Rudolf de Wet (1854–1922) was a South African politician. These men had served on the Boer side in the conflict of 1899–1901.

changed the men who but ten or a little more years ago were your bitter enemy in the field into your loyal comrades and fellow citizens in the Empire, just as truthfully can I say to you that by what of recent years has happened in this country with the democracy of England, Ireland has been transformed from what George Meredith described a short time ago as 'the broken arm of England' into one of the strongest bulwarks of the Empire.[19]

[19] George Meredith (1828–1909) was a novelist, poet, and nominee for the Nobel Prize for Literature.

1915

17 James Connolly, 'A War for Civilization'[1]

We are hearing and reading a lot just now about a war for civilization.[2] In some vague, ill-defined manner we are led to believe that the great empires of Europe have suddenly been seized with a chivalrous desire to right the wrongs of mankind, and have sallied forth to war, giving their noblest blood and greatest measures to the task of furthering the cause of civilization.

It seems unreal, but it may be possible. Great emotions sometimes master the most cold and calculating individuals, pushing them on to do that which in their colder moments they would have sneered at. In like manner great emotions sometimes master whole communities of men and women, and nations have gone mad, as in the Crusades, over matters that did not enter into any scheme of selfish calculation.[3]

But in such cases the great emotions manifested themselves in at least an appropriate manner. Their actions under the influence of great emotions had a relation to the cause or the ideal for which they were ostensibly warring.

In the case of the war for civilization, however, we look in vain for any action which in itself bears the mark of civilization. As we count civilization it means the ascendancy of industry and the arts of industry over the reign of violence and pillage. Civilization means the conquest by ordered law and peaceful discussion of the forces of evil, it means the exaltation

[1] Originally published on 30 October 1915 in *Workers' Republic*, the newspaper of the Irish Socialist Republican Party.

[2] Connolly is referring to the First World War, framed by the Allies in its early years as a 'war for civilisation'.

[3] The Crusades were a series of religious wars between 1096 and 1271.

of those whose strength is only in the righteousness of their cause over those whose power is gained by a ruthless seizing of domination founded on force.

Civilization necessarily connotes the gradual supplanting of the reign of chance and muddling by the forces of order and careful provision for the future; it means the levelling up of classes, and the initiation of the people into a knowledge and enjoyment of all that tends to soften the natural hardships of life and to make that life refined and beautiful.

But the war for civilization has done none of those things – aspires to do none of these things. It is primarily a war upon a nation whose chief crime is that it refuses to accept a position of dependence, but insists instead upon organizing its forces so that its people can co-operate with nature in making their lives independent of chance, and independent of the goodwill of others.

The war for civilization is a war upon a nation which insists upon organizing its intellect so as to produce the highest and best in science, in art, in music, in industry; and insists moreover upon so co-ordinating and linking up all these that the final result shall be a perfectly educated nation of men and women.[4]

In the past civilization has been a heritage enjoyed by a few upon a basis of the brutalization of the vast multitude; that nation aims at a civilization of the whole resting upon the whole, and only made possible by the educated co-operation of an educated whole.

The war for civilization is waged by a nation like Russia, which has the greatest proportion of illiterates of any European power, and which strives sedulously to prevent education where it is possible, and to poison it where prohibition is impossible.

The war for civilization is waged by a nation like Britain which holds in thrall a sixth of the human race, and holds as a cardinal doctrine of its faith that none of its subject races may, under penalty of imprisonment and death, dream of ruling their own territories. A nation which believes that all races are subject to purchase, and which brands as perfidy the act of any nation which, like Bulgaria, chooses to carry its wares and its arms to any other than a British market.

This war for civilization in the name of neutrality and small nationalities invades Persia and Greece, and in the name of the interests of

[4] The nation is Germany.

commerce seizes the cargo of neutral ships, and flaunts its defiance of neutral flags.[5]

In the name of freedom from militarism it establishes military rule in Ireland, battling for progress it abolishes trial by jury, and waging war for enlightened rule it tramples the freedom of the press under the heel of a military despot.[6]

Is it any wonder then that that particular war for civilization arouses no enthusiasm in the ranks of the toiling masses of the Irish nation?

But there is another war for civilization in which these masses are interested. That war is being waged by the forces of organized labour.

Civilization cannot be built upon slaves; civilization cannot be secured if the producers are sinking into misery; civilization is lost if they whose labour makes it possible share so little of its fruits that its fall can leave them no worse than its security.

The workers are at the bottom of civilized society. That civilization may endure they ought to push upward from their poverty and misery until they emerge into the full sunlight of freedom. When the fruits of civilization, created by all, are enjoyed in common by all, then civilization is secure. Not till then.

Since this European war started the workers as a whole have been sinking. It is not merely that they have lost in comfort – have lost a certain standard of food and clothing by reason of the increase of prices – but they have lost in a great measure, in Britain at least, all those hard won rights of combination and freedom of action, the possession of which was the foundation upon which they hoped to build the greater freedom of the future.[7]

From being citizens with rights the workers were being driven and betrayed into the position of slaves with duties. Some of them may have been well-paid slaves, but slavery is not measured by the amount of oats in the feeding trough to which the slave is tied. It is measured by his loss of control of the conditions under which he labours.

[5] Connolly is referring to the Persian Campaign, when the British and Russian Empires invaded parts of the neutral Middle East from the end of 1914 to fight the Ottoman Empire. Greece was neutral upon the war's outbreak. Its neutrality was broken by France and Britain when they invaded Athens in September 1915.

[6] The Defence of the Realm Act (1914) was passed four days after the UK declared war on Germany and gave the government wide-ranging emergency powers that replaced ordinary law.

[7] The Munitions War Act of 2 July 1915 placed severe restrictions on labour, including outlawing strikes and lockouts.

We here in Ireland, particularly those who follow the example of the Irish Transport and General Workers Union, have been battling to preserve those rights which others have surrendered; we have fought to keep up our standards of life, to force up our wages, to better our conditions.[8]

To that extent we have been truly engaged in a war for civilization. Every victory we have gained has gone to increase the security of life amongst our class, has gone to put bread on the tables, coals in the fires, clothes on the backs of those to whom food and warmth and clothing are things of ever pressing moment.

Some of our class have fought in Flanders and the Dardanelles; the greatest achievement of them all combined will weigh but a feather in the balance for good compared with the achievements of those who stayed at home and fought to secure the rights of the working class against invasion.

The carnival of murder on the continent will be remembered as a nightmare in the future, will not have the slightest effect in deciding for good the fate of our homes, our wages, our hours, our conditions. But the victories of labour in Ireland will be as footholds, secure and firm, in the upward climb of our class to the fulness and enjoyment of all that labour creates, and organized society can provide.

Truly, labour alone in these days is fighting the real war for civilization.

[8] Connolly became acting secretary of the trade union, the Irish Transport and General Workers Union, from 1914, in effect succeeding James Larkin (1876–1947) who departed for the US in that year.

18 James Connolly, from *The Re-Conquest of Ireland*[1]

Chapter IX: Re-Conquest – A Summing Up

Recent events in Ireland have gone far to show that the old lines of political demarcation no longer serve to express any reality in the lives of the people. The growth of unrest in the industrial field, the bitterness of industrial conflict, the manner in which employers of the most varying political and religious faiths combine against the workers in the attempt to starve them into submission, and the marked increase in the fraternal feelings with which all classes of Labour regard each other all serve to indicate that there is preparing in our midst the material for a new struggle on a national scale – a struggle fierce enough, deep enough, and enduring enough to completely obliterate all the old landmarks carried over from past political struggles into the new conditions.

In the great Dublin lock-out of 1913–1914 the manner in which the Dublin employers, overwhelmingly Unionist, received the enthusiastic and unscrupulous support of the entire Home Rule Press was a fore-taste of the possibilities of the new combinations with which Labour in Ireland will have to reckon.[2] The semi-radical phrases with which the middle class Home Rule Press and politicians so often duped the public (and sometimes themselves) were seen to have no radical feeling behind them.

1 James Connolly, *The Re-Conquest of Ireland* (Dublin: Trade Union Labour, 1915), ch. 9.

2 The Dublin lockout was a major industrial dispute, centring on the right to unionise, that took place in Dublin between 26 August 1913 and 18 January 1914. By the 'Home Rule Press', Connolly is referring to national newspapers, such as *The Freeman's Journal* and *The Irish Independent* (the latter was owned by business magnate William Martin Murphy, Dublin's leading employer who in the end broke the strikes).

Sham battle cries of a sham struggle they were hurriedly put out of sight the moment the war cries of a real conflict rose upon the air.

From this lesson, as from the others already mentioned in this book, Labour must learn that the time has come for a new marshalling of forces to face the future. As the old political parties must go so must many of the old craft divisions in the ranks of Labour.[3] We have learned the value of the sympathetic strike, and must no longer allow craft divisions to fetter our hands and keep us from helping our brother or sister when they are attacked by the capitalist enemy. We must pursue the idea to its logical conclusion and work for the obliteration of all division of the forces of Labour on the industrial field.

The principle of complete unity upon the Industrial plan must be unceasingly sought after; the Industrial union embracing all workers in each industry must replace the multiplicity of unions which now hamper and restrict our operations, multiply our expenses and divide our forces in face of the mutual enemy. With the Industrial Union as our principle of action branches can be formed to give expression to the need for effective supervision of the affairs of the workshop, shipyard, dock or railway; each branch to consist of the men and women now associated in Labour upon the same technical basis as our craft unions of to-day. Add to this the concept of one Big Union embracing all, and you have not only the outline of the most effective form of combination for industrial warfare to-day, but also for Social Administration of the Co-operative Commonwealth of the future.[4]

A system of society in which the workshops, factories, docks, railways, shipyards, &c., shall be owned by the nation, but administered by the Industrial Unions of the respective industries organised as above seems best calculated to secure the highest form of industrial efficiency combined with the greatest amount of individual freedom from state despotism. Such a system would, we believe, realise for Ireland the most radiant hopes of all her heroes and martyrs.

Concurrently with the gradual shaping of our industrial activities towards the end of industrial union Labour must necessarily attack the political and municipal citadels of power.

[3] Connolly is arguing for industrial in opposition to craft unionism.

[4] The concept of One Big Union had been spearheaded in the US by the Industrial Workers of the World (IWW) with the aim of advancing industrial trade unionism and revolutionary socialism.

Every effort should be made to extend the scope of public ownership. As democracy invades and captures public powers, public ownership will of necessity be transformed and infused with a new spirit. As Democracy enters Bureaucracy will take flight. But without the power of the Industrial Union behind it Democracy can only enter the State as the victim enters the gullet of the Serpent.

Therefore political power must for the working classes come straight out of the Industrial battlefield as the expression of the organised economic force of Labour; else it cannot come at all. With Labour properly organised upon the Industrial and political field each extension of the principle of the public ownership brings us nearer to the re-conquest of Ireland by its people; it means the gradual resumption of the common ownership of all Ireland by all the Irish – the realisation of Freedom.

Not the least of the many encouraging signs given to the world during the great Dublin Labour dispute just mentioned was the keen and sympathetic interest shown by the 'intellectuals' in the fortunes of the workers.[5] In itself this was a phenomenon in Ireland. Until then there had been discovered no means of bridging the gap between the Irish workers who toiled as ordinary day labourers and those other workers whose toil was upon the intellectual plane, and whose remuneration kept them generally free from the actual pressure of want.

In other European countries the Socialist movement had brought these two elements together in organised defensive and aggressive warfare against the brutal regime of the purse, but in Ireland the fight for national freedom had absorbed the intellect of the one, and prevented the development of the necessary class-consciousness on the part of the other.

But when the belief that some form of national freedom was about to be realised spread in Ireland, and consequently the minds of all began to turn to consideration of the uses to which that freedom might be put, the possibility of co-operation between these two classes became apparent to the thoughtful patriot and reformer.

The incidents accompanying the great Labour struggle furnished just the necessary common denominator to establish relations between the two.

[5] For example George Russell (Æ) (1867–1935), the writer and mystic, who at personal cost took a stand in support of Irish workers during the Irish industrial dispute resulting in the 1913 lockout.

We have no doubt that it will be found in Ireland, as it has already been found in Italy, that the co-operation of the wage labourers and their intellectual comrades will create an uplifting atmosphere of social helpfulness of the greatest benefit in the work of national regeneration. We have in Ireland, particularly outside of the industrial districts of the North, a greater proportion of professional, literary and artistic people than is to be found in any European country, except Italy, and without enquiring too closely into the cause of this undue proportion it may be predicted that its existence will serve the cause of Labour in Ireland.

Arising out of the same struggle what may yet develop into a perfect understanding and concert of action was opened up between the Urban labourers and the apostles of co-operation amongst the agricultural population of Ireland. The great genius and magnetic personality of Mr. Russell, editor of the *Irish Homestead*, brought to the long-neglected toilers of Dublin a new conception – viz., that the co-operative societies which had been so long and so successfully propagating themselves throughout the agricultural areas of the country might yet be linked up with the fortunes of the industrial workers in such a manner that, each serving the other's temporary needs, they could between them lay the groundwork of a new social order.[6]

Almost throughout all historic periods there has been a latent antagonism between town and country; the Socialist has predicted that the Socialist state of the future will put an end to that antagonism by bringing the advantages of the city to the toiler in the country; Mr. Russell foresees, however, a co-operation in which the city and the country shall merge in perfecting methods of fraternal production and distribution that shall serve first to enable each to combat capitalism and finally to supplant it. Such a development of co-operative effort between the workers of town and country would be a great achievement, and we can at least bespeak for the effort the constant support of every friend of progress in Ireland.

In conclusion we may say that this hope of co-operation between the town and country for the purpose of common regeneration is typical of the hopes and possibilities now opening up to the workers of Ireland.

[6] Russell worked for the Irish Agricultural Organisation Society (IAOS) established in the wake of the pioneering co-operative activities of Horace Plunkett (1854–1932). He edited the *Irish Homestead*, the journal of the IAOS, from 1905 to 1923. Connolly first met Russell at a demonstration held at the Royal Albert Hall in November 1913. Russell sympathised with the cause of labour during the lockout.

Everywhere we see friends where formerly we met only suspicion and distrust, and we realise that the difference in the attitude with which Labour is regarded now to what it met formerly, is the difference with which the world at large treats those who simply claim its pity, and those who are strong and self-reliant enough to enforce its respect.

Labour in Ireland tends to become more and more self-reliant and in its self-reliance it discovers its strength. Out of such strong self-reliance it develops a magnetism which will draw to it more and more support from all the adherents of all the causes which in their entirety make for a regenerated Ireland.

The Gaelic Leaguer realises that capitalism did more in one century to destroy the tongue of the Gael than the sword of the Saxon did in six;[7] the apostle of self-reliance amongst Irishmen and women finds no more earnest exponents of self-reliance than those who expound it as the creed of Labour; the earnest advocates of co-operation find the workers stating their ideals as a co-operative commonwealth; the earnest teacher of Christian morality sees that in that co-operative commonwealth alone will true morality be possible, and the fervent patriot learns that his hopes of an Ireland re-born to National life are better stated and can be better and more completely realised in the Labour movement for the Re-Conquest of Ireland.

Our readers will help forward the purpose of this book, and hasten the coming of the good results that should flow from the happy synchronising of facts just alluded to if they will always remember that the objective aimed at is to establish in the minds of the men and women of Ireland the necessity of giving effective expression, politically and socially, to the right of the community (all) to control for the good of all the industrial activities of each, and to endow such activities with the necessary means.

This, historically speaking, will mean the enthronement of the Irish nation as the supreme ruler and owner of itself, and all things necessary to its people – supreme alike against the foreigner and the native usurping ownership, and the power dangerous to freedom that goes with ownership.

7 Connolly is referring to the dramatic decline of the Irish language. The Gaelic League was founded in 1893 by Douglas Hyde to promote the use of Gaelic in everyday life.

19 Patrick Pearse, 'O'Donovan Rossa: Graveside Panegyric'[1]

A Ghaedheala,
Do hiarradh orm-sa labhairt indiu ar son a bhfuil cruinnighthe ar an láthair so agus ar son a bhfuil beo de Chlannaibh Gaedheal, ag moladh an leomhain do leagamar i gcré annso agus ag gríosadh meanman na gcarad atá go brónach ina dhiaidh.

A cháirde, ná bíodh brón ar éinne atá ina sheasamh ag an uaigh so, acht bíodh buidheachas againn inar gcroidhthibh do Dhia na ngrás do chruthuigh anam uasal áluinn Dhiarmuda Uí Dhonnabháin Rosa agus thug sé fhada dhó ar an saoghal so.

Ba chalma an fear thu, a Dhiarmuid. Is thréan d'fhearais cath ar son cirt do chine, is ní beag ar fhuilingis; agus ní dhéanfaidh Gaedhil dearmad ort go bráth na breithe.

Acht, a cháirde, ná bíodh brón orainn, acht bíodh misneach inar gcroidhthibh agus bíodh neart inar gcuirleannaibh, óir cuimhnighimís nach mbíonn aon bhás ann nach mbíonn aiséirghe ina dhiaidh, agus gur-ab as an uaigh so agus as na huaghannaibh atá inar dtimcheall éireochas saoirse Gheadheal.[2]

1 Delivered 1 August 1915 at Glasnevin Cemetery in Dublin.

2 'Irish People, I was asked to speak on behalf of those gathered at this place and of all who are alive of the Irish Family, to praise the lion we lay in the soil today and to offer encouragement to those who are sad because he is gone. ¶ Friends, let nobody standing at this grave be sad, but give heartfelt thanks to the God of Grace who created the noble beautiful soul of Diarmuid Ó Donnabháin Rosa and who gave him such a long life. ¶ You were a fine stalwart man Diarmuid. In your strong manly struggle for the rights of your

It has seemed right, before we turn away from this place in which we have laid the mortal remains of O'Donovan Rossa, that one among us should, in the name of all, speak the praise of that valiant man, and endeavour to formulate the thought and the hope that are in us as we stand around his grave.[3] And if there is anything that makes it fitting that I, rather than some other, I rather than one of the grey-haired men who were young with him and shared in his labour and in his suffering, should speak here, it is perhaps that I may be taken as speaking on behalf of a new generation that has been re-baptised in the Fenian faith, and that has accepted the responsibility of carrying out the Fenian programme. I propose to you then that, here by the grave of this unrepentant Fenian, we renew our baptismal vows; that, here by the grave of this unconquered and unconquerable man, we ask of God, each one for himself, such unshakable purpose, such high and gallant courage, such unbreakable strength of soul as belonged to O'Donovan Rossa.

Deliberately here we avow ourselves, as he avowed himself in the dock, Irishmen of one allegiance only. We of the Irish Volunteers, and you others who are associated with us in to-day's task and duty, are bound together and must stand together henceforth in brotherly union for the achievement of the freedom of Ireland. And we know only one definition of freedom: it is Tone's definition,[4] it is Mitchel's definition,[5] it is Rossa's definition. Let no man blaspheme the cause that the dead generations of Ireland served by giving it any other name and definition than their name and their definition.

We stand at Rossa's grave not in sadness but rather in exaltation of spirit that it has been given to us to come thus into so close a communion with that brave and splendid Gael. Splendid and holy causes are served by

race you suffered much; and the Irish will never ever forget you. ¶ But friends, let us not be sorrowful but rather let us have courage in our hearts and let us have strength in our limbs, as we remember that no death occurs that is not followed by a resurrection, and that out of this grave and from the graves surrounding us will Irish freedom rise.'

[3] Jeremiah O'Donovan Rossa (1831–1915) was a Fenian leader and member of the paramilitary organisation, the Irish Republican Brotherhood (IRB). The Fenians were a revolutionary nationalist organisation in Ireland and North America that staged unsuccessful insurrections against the British government. O'Donovan Rossa's body had been returned to Ireland from the United States where he had been since 1870 on the basis of an amnesty granted by the United Kingdom government. From his base in New York he had been at the forefront of organising the republican dynamite campaign of the 1880s.

[4] Theobald Wolfe Tone (1763–98), a founder member of the United Irishman, played a leading role in the 1798 Rebellion.

[5] John Mitchel (1815–75) was a prominent Young Irelander and nationalist agitator. Exiled in 1848, he entered the United States in 1853 where he became a partisan of the Southern secessionist cause.

men who are themselves splendid and holy. O'Donovan Rossa was splendid in the proud manhood of him, splendid in the heroic grace of him, splendid in the Gaelic strength and clarity and truth of him. And all that splendour and pride and strength was compatible with a humility and a simplicity of devotion to Ireland, to all that was olden and beautiful and Gaelic in Ireland, the holiness and simplicity of patriotism of a Michael O'Clery or of an Eoghan O'Growney.[6] The clear true eyes of this man almost alone in his day visioned Ireland as we of to-day would surely have her: not free merely, but Gaelic as well; not Gaelic merely, but free as well.

In a closer spiritual communion with him now than ever before or perhaps ever again, in a spiritual communion with those of his day, living and dead, who suffered with him in English prisons, in communion of spirit too with our own dear comrades who suffer in English prisons to-day, and speaking on their behalf as well as our own, we pledge to Ireland our love, and we pledge to English rule in Ireland our hate. This is a place of peace, sacred to the dead, where men should speak with all charity and with all restraint; but I hold it a Christian thing, as O'Donovan Rossa held it, to hate evil, to hate untruth, to hate oppression, and, hating them, to strive to overthrow them. Our foes are strong and wise and wary; but, strong and wise and wary as they are, they cannot undo the miracles of God who ripens in the hearts of young men the seeds sown by the young men of a former generation. And the seeds sown by the young men of '65 and '67 are coming to their miraculous ripening to-day.[7] Rulers and Defenders of Realms had need to be wary if they would guard against such processes. Life springs from death; and from the graves of patriot men and women spring living nations. The Defenders of this Realm have worked well in secret and in the open.[8] They think that they have pacified Ireland. They think that they have purchased half of us and intimidated the other half. They think that they have foreseen everything, think that they have provided against everything; but the fools, the fools, the fools! – they have left us our Fenian dead, and while Ireland holds these graves, Ireland unfree shall never be at peace.

[6] Michael O'Clery (1590–1643) was an Irish chronicler and antiquary; Eugene (Eoghan) O'Growney (1863–99) was a priest and scholar, and a figure in the Gaelic revival.

[7] The Fenians started preparations for a rising in 1865, leading in that year to the arrest of much of its leadership, including O'Donovan Rossa, John O'Leary (1830–1907), Thomas Clarke Luby (1822–1901), and James Stephens (1825–1901). In 1867 a series of risings organised by the IRB were carried out in Ireland and abroad.

[8] A reference to British Crown forces and their intelligence networks.

1916

20 James Connolly, 'What Is a Free Nation?'[1]

We are moved to ask this question because of the extraordinary confusion of thought upon the subject which prevails in this country, due principally to the pernicious and misleading newspaper garbage upon which the Irish public has been fed for the past twenty-five years.

Our Irish daily newspapers have done all that human agencies could do to confuse the public mind upon the question of what the essentials of a free nation are, what a free nation must be, and what a nation cannot submit to lose without losing its title to be free.

It is because of this extraordinary newspaper-created ignorance that we find so many people enlisting in the British army under the belief that Ireland has at long last attained to the status of a free nation, and that therefore the relations between Ireland and England have at last been placed upon the satisfactory basis of freedom.[2] Ireland and England, they have been told, are now sister nations, joined in the bond of Empire, but each enjoying equal liberties – the equal liberties of nations equally free. How many recruits this idea sent into the British army in the first flush of the war it would be difficult to estimate, but they were assuredly numbered by the thousand.

[1] Originally published on 12 February 1916 in the *Workers' Republic*.

[2] Connolly is referring to the fact that home rule was placed on the statute book in September 1914, therefore guaranteeing the implementation of self-government in Ireland. The Irish Parliamentary Party (IPP) used this as evidence that Ireland was now participating in the war as a free and independent nation. The Act was in fact placed on statute with a clause delaying its implementation until the period of one year or until the end of the War, whichever was longer, and actually never came into operation in the form in which it had been passed.

The Irish Parliamentary Party, which at every stage of the Home Rule game has been outwitted and bulldozed by Carson and the Unionists, which had surrendered every point and yielded every advantage to the skilful campaign of the aristocratic Orange military clique in times of peace, behaved in equally as cowardly and treacherous a manner in the crisis of war.[3]

There are few men in whom the blast of the bugles of war do not arouse the fighting instinct, do not excite to some chivalrous impulses if only for a moment. But the Irish Parliamentary Party must be reckoned amongst that few. In them the bugles of war only awakened the impulse to sell the bodies of their countrymen as cannon fodder in exchange for the gracious smiles of the rulers of England.[4] In them the call of war sounded only as a call to emulate in prostitution. They heard the call of war – and set out to prove that the nationalists of Ireland were more slavish than the Orangemen of Ireland, would more readily kill and be killed at the bidding of an Empire that despised them both.

The Orangemen had at least the satisfaction that they were called upon to fight abroad in order to save an Empire they had been prepared to fight to retain unaltered at home;[5] but the nationalists were called upon to fight abroad to save an Empire whose rulers in their most generous moments had refused to grant their country the essentials of freedom in nationhood.[6]

Fighting abroad the Orangeman knows that he fights to preserve the power of the aristocratic rulers whom he followed at home; fighting abroad the nationalist soldier is fighting to maintain unimpaired the

[3] The IPP was the leading nationalist party; Sir Edward Carson (1854–1935) was the Irish Unionist leader; by the 'Orange military clique' he is referring to the Orange Order, a Protestant fraternal association which had connections with both Tory MPs and senior British military personnel.

[4] On 3 August 1914, John Redmond, the IPP leader, committed the Irish Volunteers militia to the defence of Ireland. On 21 September, he told them to go 'wherever the firing line extends', encouraging them to serve abroad with the British Forces, in part because home rule was now on the statute book.

[5] Unionists had formed the Ulster Volunteer Force militia in 1913 and were prepared to fight the British Army in order to defend Ulster from the implementation of Irish self-government.

[6] Britain's grant of freedom amounted to the third Home Rule Bill, which had passed on its third reading in 1914, but which was now in suspension, with an Amending Bill to be agreed. Connolly objected to the original provision itself as a mere simulacrum of freedom.

power of those who conspired to shoot him down at home when he asked for a small instalment of freedom.

The Orangeman says: 'We will fight for the Empire abroad if its rulers will promise not to force us to submit to Home Rule.' And the rulers say heartily: 'It is unthinkable that we should coerce Ulster for any such purpose.'

The Irish Parliamentary Party and its press said: 'We will prove ourselves fit to be in the British Empire by fighting for it, in the hopes that after the war is over we will get Home Rule.'[7] And the rulers of the British Empire say: 'Well, you know what we have promised Carson, but send out the Irish rabble to fight for us, and we will, ahem, consider your application after the war.'[8] Whereat, all the Parliamentary leaders and their press call the world to witness that they have won a wonderful victory!

James Fintan Lalor spoke and conceived of Ireland as a 'discrowned queen, taking back her own with an armed hand'.[9] Our Parliamentarians treat Ireland, their country, as an old prostitute selling her soul for the promise of favours to come, and in the spirit of that conception of their country they are conducting their political campaign.

That they should be able to do so with even the partial success that for a while attended their apostasy was possible only because so few in Ireland really understood the answer to the question that stands at the head of this article.

What is a free nation? A free nation is one which possesses absolute control over all its own internal resources and powers, and which has no restriction upon its intercourse with all other nations similarly circumstanced except the restrictions placed upon it by nature. Is that the case of Ireland? If the Home Rule Bill were in operation would that be the case of Ireland? To both questions the answer is: no, most emphatically, NO!

A free nation must have complete control over its own harbours, to open them or close them at will, or shut out any commodity, or allow it to enter in, just as it seemed best to suit the well-being of its own people, and

[7] The main journalistic support for the IPP came from *The Freeman's Journal*. The *Cork Examiner* was also sympathetic. Among provincial newspapers, organs like the *Tuam Herald* and the *Frontier Sentinel* similarly toed the IPP line.

[8] The promise to unionism was special treatment for Ulster, the nature of which had yet to be agreed.

[9] James Fintan Lalor (1809–49) was a writer and revolutionary member of the Irish nationalist movement of the 1840s, Young Ireland. See his 'The Faith of a Felon' in *The Writings of James Fintan Lalor* (Dublin: T. G. O'Donoghue, 1895), p. 100, originally published in *The Irish Felon*, 24 June 1848. The phrase was in fact 'decrowned Queen'.

in obedience to their wishes, and entirely free of the interference of any other nation, and in complete disregard of the wishes of any other nation. Short of that power no nation possesses the first essentials of freedom.[10]

Does Ireland possess such control? No. Will the Home Rule Bill give such control over Irish harbours in Ireland? It will not. Ireland must open its harbours when it suits the interests of another nation, England, and must shut its harbours when it suits the interests of another nation, England; and the Home Rule Bill pledges Ireland to accept this loss of national control for ever.

How would you like to live in a house if the keys of all the doors of that house were in the pockets of a rival of yours who had often robbed you in the past? Would you be satisfied if he told you that he and you were going to be friends for ever more, but insisted upon you signing an agreement to leave him control of all your doors, and custody of all your keys? This is the condition of Ireland today, and will be the condition of Ireland under Redmond and Devlin's precious Home Rule Bill.[11]

That is worth dying for in Flanders, the Balkans, Egypt or India, is it not?

A free nation must have full power to nurse industries to health, either by government encouragement or by government prohibition of the sale of goods of foreign rivals. It may be foolish to do either, but a nation is not free unless it has that power, as all free nations in the world have today. Ireland has no such power, will have no such power under Home Rule. The nourishing of industries in Ireland hurts capitalists in England, therefore this power is expressly withheld from Ireland.

A free nation must have full power to alter, amend, or abolish or modify the laws under which the property of its citizens is held in obedience to the demand of its own citizens for any such alteration, amendment, abolition, or modification. Every free nation has that power; Ireland does not have it, and is not allowed it by the Home Rule Bill.

It is recognized today that it is upon the wise treatment of economic power and resources, and upon the wise ordering of social activities that the future of nations depends. That nation will be the richest and happiest which has the foresight to marshal the most carefully its natural resources to national ends. But Ireland is denied this power, and will

[10] Under the proposal, Ireland's ports would still be owned and controlled by Westminster.

[11] Joseph Devlin (1871–1934) was a northern nationalist MP for the IPP at Westminster and a prominent supporter of home rule. He sided with John Redmond in support of recruitment in Ireland for the Allied war effort.

be denied it under Home Rule. Ireland's rich natural resources, and the kindly genius of its children, are not to be allowed to combine for the satisfaction of Irish wants, save in so far as their combination can operate on lines approved of by the rulers of England.

Her postal service, her telegraphs, her wireless, her customs and excise, her coinage, her fighting forces, her relations with other nations, her merchant commerce, her property relations, her national activities, her legislative sovereignty – all the things that are essential to a nation's freedom are denied to Ireland now, and are denied to her under the provisions of the Home Rule Bill. And Irish soldiers in the English Army are fighting in Flanders to win for Belgium, we are told, all those things which the British Empire, now as in the past, denies to Ireland.[12]

There is not a Belgian patriot who would not prefer to see his country devastated by war a hundred times rather than accept as a settlement for Belgium what Redmond and Devlin have accepted for Ireland. Have we Irish been fashioned in meaner clay than the Belgians?

There is not a pacifist in England who would wish to end the war without Belgium being restored to full possession of all those national rights and powers which Ireland does not possess, and which the Home Rule Bill denies to her. But these same pacifists never mention Ireland when discussing or suggesting terms of settlement. Why should they? Belgium is fighting for her independence, but Irishmen are fighting for the Empire that denies Ireland every right that Belgians think worth fighting for.

And yet Belgium as a nation is, so to speak, but a creation of yesterday – an artificial product of the schemes of statesmen. Whereas, the frontiers of Ireland, the ineffaceable marks of the separate existence of Ireland, are as old as Europe itself, the handiwork of the Almighty, not of politicians. And as the marks of Ireland's separate nationality were not made by politicians so they cannot be unmade by them.

As the separate individual is to the family, so the separate nation is to humanity. The perfect family is that which best draws out the inner powers of the individual, the most perfect world is that in which the separate existence of nations is held most sacred. There can be no perfect Europe in which Ireland is denied even the least of its national rights; there can

[12] The First World War was standardly presented as a war for the rights of small nations. Belgium was the favoured example. As reported in the *Times* on 7 August 1914, Asquith declared at the outset of the war that Britain was 'fighting to vindicate the principle … that small nationalities are not to be crushed in defiance of international good faith by the arbitrary will of a strong and overmastering power'.

be no worthy Ireland whose children brook tamely such denial. If such denial has been accepted by soulless slaves of politicians then it must be repudiated by Irish men and women whose souls are still their own.

The peaceful progress of the future requires the possession by Ireland of all the national rights now denied to her. Only in such possession can the workers of Ireland see stability and security for the fruits of their toil and organization. A destiny not of our fashioning has chosen this generation as the one called upon for the supreme act of self-sacrifice – to die if need be that our race might live in freedom.[13]

Are we worthy of the choice? Only by our response to the call can that question be answered.

[13] Connolly was at this point involved in advanced preparations for the Easter 1916 Rebellion.

21 Proclamation of the Republic[1]

POBLACHT NA H ÉIREANN.

THE PROVISIONAL GOVERNMENT OF THE

IRISH REPUBLIC

TO THE PEOPLE OF IRELAND.

IRISHMEN AND IRISHWOMEN: In the name of God and of the dead generations from which she receives her old tradition of nationhood, Ireland, through us, summons her children to her flag and strikes for her freedom.

Having organised and trained her manhood through her secret revolutionary organisation, the Irish Republican Brotherhood, and through her open military organisations, the Irish Volunteers and the Irish Citizen Army,[2] having patiently perfected her discipline, having resolutely waited for the right moment to reveal itself,[3] she now seizes that moment, and

[1] The Proclamation of the Irish Republic was read outside the general post office in Dublin by Patrick Pearse (1879–1916), the leader of the insurrection, on the first day of the Easter Rising of 24–9 April 1916.

[2] The Irish Citizen Army (ICA) was a volunteer paramilitary organisation comprising trained trade union activists formed by James Larkin, James Connolly, and Jack White (1879–1946) on 23 November 1913; 220 members of the ICA participated in the 1916 Rebellion.

[3] A secret faction within the clandestine Irish Republican Brotherhood (IRB) which had joined the Irish Volunteers orchestrated the Rebellion.

supported by her exiled children in America and by gallant allies in Europe,[4] but relying in the first on her own strength, she strikes in full confidence of victory.

We declare the right of the people of Ireland to the ownership of Ireland, and to the unfettered control of Irish destinies, to be sovereign and indefeasible. The long usurpation of that right by a foreign people and government has not extinguished the right, nor can it ever be extinguished except by the destruction of the Irish people.[5] In every generation the Irish people have asserted their right to national freedom and sovereignty; six times during the past three hundred years they have asserted it in arms.[6] Standing on that fundamental right and again asserting it in arms in the face of the world, we hereby proclaim the Irish Republic as a Sovereign Independent State, and we pledge our lives and the lives of our comrades in arms to the cause of its freedom, of its welfare, and of its exaltation among the nations.

The Irish Republic is entitled to, and hereby claims, the allegiance of every Irishman and Irishwoman. The Republic guarantees religious and civil liberty, equal rights and equal opportunities to all its citizens, and declares its resolve to pursue the happiness and prosperity of the whole nation and of all its parts, cherishing all of the children of the nation equally, and oblivious of the differences carefully fostered by an alien government, which have divided a minority from the majority in the past.[7]

Until our arms have brought the opportune moment for the establishment of a permanent National Government, representative of the whole people of Ireland and elected by the suffrages of all her men and women, the Provisional Government, hereby constituted, will administer the civil and military affairs of the Republic in trust for the people.

We place the cause of the Irish Republic under the protection of the Most High God, Whose blessing we invoke upon our arms, and we pray that no one who serves that cause will dishonour it by cowardice,

[4] The IRB had extensive organisational networks within the United States. The 'gallant allies' refers essentially to Germany.

[5] National destiny cannot be revoked by an act of choice since a mere aggregate of individuals has no right to choose against the more fundamental right to existence of a people.

[6] Various armed campaigns against British governance were orchestrated in 1688–91, 1798, 1803, 1848, 1867 and 1881–5.

[7] This paragraph refers to the 'divide and rule' thesis: that the British government had fostered political and religious divisions between the majority Catholics and minority Protestants across Ireland and particularly in Ulster.

inhumanity, or rapine. In this supreme hour the Irish nation must, by its valour and discipline and by the readiness of its children to sacrifice themselves for the common good, prove itself worthy of the august destiny to which it is called.

Signed on behalf of the Provisional Government,[8]

THOMAS J. CLARKE.	
SEAN Mac DIARMADA.	THOMAS MacDONAGH.
P. H. PEARSE.	EAMONN CEANNT.
JAMES CONNOLLY.	JOSEPH PLUNKETT.

[8] In addition to Connolly and Pearse, the signatories to the Proclamation, all executed in May 1916 for their part in the insurrection, were: Thomas J. Clarke (1858–1916), an IRB leader who joined the organisation in 1878 and became a Fenian dynamiter in the 1880s; Seán Mac Diarmada (John MacDermott) (1883–1916), a manager of *Irish Freedom* and member of the military committee of the IRB; Thomas MacDonagh (1878–1916), a poet and playwright who joined the Irish Volunteers and then the IRB in 1915; Éamonn Ceannt (Edward Kent) (1881–1916), a trade unionist who worked for Dublin Corporation, joined the IRB in 1912 and became its director of communications; and Joseph Plunkett (1887–1916), a journalist and poet who joined the IRB in 1915 and became a member of its military committee.

22 Patrick Pearse, *The Sovereign People*[1]

I

National independence involves national sovereignty. National sovereignty is twofold in its nature. It is both internal and external. It implies the sovereignty of the nation over all its parts, over all men and things within the nation; and it implies the sovereignty of the nation as against all other nations. Nationality is a spiritual fact; but nationhood includes physical freedom, and physical power in order to the maintenance of physical freedom, as well as the spiritual fact of nationality. This physical freedom is necessary to the healthy life, and may even be necessary to the continued existence of the nation. Without it the nation droops, withers, ultimately perhaps dies; only a very steadfast nation, a nation of great spiritual and intellectual strength like Ireland, can live for more than a few generations in its absence, and without it even so stubborn a nation as Ireland would doubtless ultimately perish. Physical freedom, in brief, is necessary to sane and vigorous life; for physical freedom means precisely control of the conditions that are necessary to sane and vigorous life. It is obvious that these things are partly material, and that therefore national freedom involves control of the material things which are essential to the continued physical life and freedom of the nation. So that the nation's sovereignty extends not only to all the material possessions of the nation, the nation's soil and all its resources, all wealth and all wealth-producing processes within the nation. In other words, no private right to property is good as against the public right of the nation. But the nation is under

[1] *The Sovereign People* was the last of four political pamphlets written by Pearse between December 1915 and March 1916.

a moral obligation so to exercise its public right as to secure strictly equal rights and liberties to every man and woman within the nation. The whole is entitled to pursue the happiness and prosperity of the whole, but this is to be pursued exactly for the end that each of the individuals composing the whole may enjoy happiness and prosperity, the maximum amount of happiness and prosperity consistent with the happiness and prosperity of all the rest.

One may reduce all this to a few simple propositions:

1. The end of freedom is human happiness.
2. The end of national freedom is individual freedom; therefore, individual happiness.
3. National freedom implies national sovereignty.
4. National sovereignty implies control of all the moral and material resources of the nation.

I have insisted upon the spiritual fact of nationality; I have insisted upon the necessity of physical freedom in order to the continued preservation of that spiritual fact in a living people; I now insist upon the necessity of complete control of the material resources of the nation in order to the completeness of that physical freedom. And here I think I give what has been called ‘the material basis of freedom’ its proper place and importance. A nation’s material resources are not the nation, any more than a man’s food is the man; but the material resources are as necessary to the nation’s life as the man’s food to the man’s life.

And I claim that the nation’s sovereignty over the nation’s material resources is absolute; but that obviously such sovereignty must be exercised for the good of the nation and without prejudice to the rights of other nations, since national sovereignty, like everything else on earth, is subject to the laws of morality.

Now, the good of the nation means ultimately the good of the individual men and women who compose the nation. Physically considered, what does a nation consist of? It consists of its men and women; of all its men and women, without any exceptions. Every man and every woman within the nation has normally equal rights, but a man or a woman may forfeit his or her rights by turning recreant to the nation. No class in the nation has rights superior to those of any other class. No class in the nation is entitled to privileges beyond any other class except with the consent of the nation. The right and privilege to make laws or to administer laws does not reside in any class within the nation; it resides in the whole nation, that is, in the whole people, and can be lawfully exercised only by those to whom it is delegated by the whole people. The right to the control of the material resources of a nation does not reside in any individual or in any class of individuals; it resides in the whole people and can be lawfully exercised only by those to whom it is delegated by the whole people, and in the manner in which the whole people ordains. Once more, no individual right is good as against the right of the whole people; but the people, in exercising its sovereign rights, is morally bound to consider individual rights, to do equity between itself and each of the individuals that compose it as well as to see that equity is done between individual and individual.

To insist upon the sovereign control of the nation over all the property within the nation is not to disallow the right to private property. It is for the nation to determine to what extent private property may be held by its members, and in what items of the nation's material resources private property shall be allowed. A nation may, for instance, determine, as the free Irish nation determined and enforced for many centuries, that private ownership shall not exist in land; that the whole of a nation's soil is the public property of the nation.[2] A nation may determine, as many modern nations have determined, that all the means of transport within a nation, all its railways and waterways, are the public property of the nation to be administered by the nation for the general benefit. A nation may go further and determine that all sources of wealth whatsoever are the property of the nation, that each individual shall give his service for the nation's good, and shall be adequately provided for by the nation, and that all surplus wealth shall go to the national treasury to be expended on national purposes, rather than be accumulated by private persons. There is nothing divine or sacrosanct in any of these arrangements; they are matters of purely human concern, matters for discussion and adjustment between the members of a nation, matters to be decided upon finally by the nation as a whole; and matters in which the nation as a whole can revise or reverse its decision whenever it seems good in the common interests to do so. I do not disallow the right to private property; but I insist that all property is held subject to the national sanction.

[2] Picking up on the arguments of Alice Stopford Green, *The Making of Ireland and Its Undoing, 1200–1600* (London: Macmillan, 1908), to the effect that communal property in land characterised social relations in pre-Norman Ireland.

And I come back again to this: that the people are the nation; the whole people, all its men and women; and that laws made or acts done by anybody purporting to represent the people but not really authorised by the people, either expressly or impliedly, to represent them and to act for them do not bind the people; are a usurpation, an impertinence, a nullity. For instance, a Government of capitalists, or a Government of clerics, or a Government of lawyers, or a Government of tinkers, or a Government of red-headed men, or a Government of men born on a Tuesday, does not represent the people, and cannot bind the people, unless it is expressly or impliedly chosen and accepted by the people to represent and act for them; and in that case it becomes the lawful government of the people, and continues such until the people withdraw their mandate. Now, the people, if wise, will not choose the makers and administrators of their laws on such arbitrary and fantastic grounds as the possession of capital, or the possession of red heads, or the having been born on a Tuesday; a Government chosen in such a manner, or preponderatingly representing (even if not so deliberately chosen) capitalists, red-headed men, or men born on a Tuesday will inevitably legislate and govern in the interests of capitalists, red-headed men, or men born on a Tuesday, as the case may be. The people, if wise, will choose as the makers and administrators of their laws men and women actually and fully representative of all the men and women of the nation, the men and women of no property equally with the men and women of property;[3] they will regard such an accident as the possession of 'property', 'capital', 'wealth' in any shape, the possession of what is called 'a stake in the country', as conferring no more right to represent the people than would the accident of possessing a red head or the accident of having been born on a Tuesday. And in order that the people may be able to choose as a legislation and as a government men and women really and fully representative of themselves, they will keep the choice actually or virtually in the hands of the whole people; in other words, while, in the exercise of their sovereign rights they may, if they will, delegate the actual choice to some body among them, *i.e.*, adopt a 'restricted franchise', they will, if wise, adopt the widest possible franchise – give a vote to every adult man and woman of sound mind.[4] To

[3] The phrase 'men of no property' derives from Wolfe Tone (1763–98). See *The Autobiography of Theobald Wolfe Tone, 1763–98*, ed. R. Barry O'Brien (Dublin: Maunsel, 1910), 2 vols., I, p. 38.

[4] Since virtual representation is permissible if unwise, the franchise is not an absolute but a conditional right. It is conditional on the national will.

restrict the franchise in any respect is to prepare the way for some future usurpation of the rights of the sovereign people. The people, that is, the whole people, must remain sovereign not only in theory, but in fact.

I assert, then, the divine right of the people, 'God's grant to Adam and his poor children for ever', to have and to hold this good green earth. And I assert the sovereignty and the sanctity of the nations, which are the people embodied and organised. The nation is a natural division, as natural as the family, and as inevitable. That is one reason why a nation is holy and why an empire is not holy. A nation is knit together by natural ties, ties mystic and spiritual, and ties human and kindly; an empire is at best held together by ties of mutual interest, and at worst by brute force. The nation is the family in large; an empire is a commercial corporation in large. The nation is of God; the empire is of man – if it be not of the devil.

II

The democratic truths that I have just stated are implicit in Tone and in Davis, though there was this difference between the two men, that Tone had a manly contempt for 'the gentry (as they affect to call themselves)', while Davis had a little sentimental regard for them.[5] But Davis loved the people, as every Nationalist must love the people, seeing that the people are the nation; his nationalism was not mere devotion to an abstract idea, it was a devotion to the actual men and women who make up this nation of Ireland, a belief in their rights, and a resolve to establish them as the owners of Ireland and the masters of all her destinies. There is no other sort of nationalism than this, the nationalism which believes in and seeks to enthrone the sovereign people. Tone had appealed to 'that numerous and respectable class, the men of no property', and in that gallant and characteristic phrase he had revealed his perception of a great historic truth, namely, that in Ireland 'the gentry (as they affect to call themselves)' have uniformly been corrupted by England, and the merchants and middle-class capitalists have, when not corrupted, been uniformly intimidated, whereas the common people have for the most part remained unbought and unterrified. It is, in fact, true that the repositories of the Irish tradition, as well the spiritual tradition of nationality as the

[5] Thomas Davis (1814–45) was a writer and leading figure within the 1840s radical nationalist movement Young Ireland, who co-founded *The Nation* with Charles Gavan Duffy (1816–1903) and John Blake Dillon (1814–66).

kindred tradition of stubborn physical resistance to England, have been the great, splendid, faithful, common people – that dumb multitudinous throng which sorrowed during the penal night, which bled in '98, which starved in the Famine;[6] and which is here still what is left of it – unbought and unterrified. Let no man be mistaken as to who will be lord in Ireland when Ireland is free. The people will be lord and master. The people who wept in Gethsemane, who trod the sorrowful way, who died naked on a cross, who went down into hell, will rise again glorious and immortal, will sit on the right hand of God, and will come in the end to give judgment, a judge just and terrible.[7]

Tone sounded the gallant *réveille* of democracy in Ireland. The man who gave it its battle-cries was James Fintan Lalor.[8] Lalor was a fiery spirit, as of some angelic missionary, imprisoned for a few years in a very frail tenement, drawing his earthly breath in pain; but strong with a great spiritual strength and gifted with a mind which had the trenchant beauty of steel. What he had to say for his people (and for all mankind) was said in a very few words. This gospel of the Sovereign People that Fintan Lalor delivered is the shortest of the gospels; but so precious is it, so pregnant with meaning in its every word, that to express its sense one would have to quote it almost as it stands; which indeed one could do in a tract a very little longer than this. No one who wrote as little as Lalor has ever written so well. In his first letter he laments that he has never learned the art of literary expression; in 'The Faith of a Felon' he says that he has all his life been destitute of books.[9] Commonly, it is by reading and writing that a man learns to write greatly. Lalor, who had read little and written nothing, wrote greatly from the moment he began to write. The Lord God must have inspired the poor crippled recluse, for no mortal man could of himself have uttered the things he uttered.

6 The 'penal night' refers to the eighteenth-century penal era during which the political and civil rights of Roman Catholics were radically curtailed by legislation. The reference to 1798 is to the United Irishmen's Rebellion of that year. The Great Irish Famine was a period of mass starvation, disease and death between 1845 and 1852 during which the potato crop successively failed.

7 Christ underwent his agony and was arrested the night before his crucifixion in the Garden of Gethsemane at the foot of the Mount of Olives in Jerusalem.

8 James Fintan Lalor (1809–49) was an influential writer and activist who played a prominent part in the 1848 Rebellion in Ireland.

9 Lalor contributed to the newspaper *The Irish Felon* from June 1848, including 'What is to be Done', 'The Faith of a Felon', 'Resistance', and 'Clearing the Decks'.

James Fintan Lalor, in Duffy's phrase, 'announced himself' in Irish politics in 1847, and he announced himself 'with a voice of assured confidence and authority'.[10] In a letter to Duffy, which startled all the Young Irelanders and which set Mitchel's heart on fire, he declared himself one of the people, one who therefore knew the people: and he told the young men that there was neither strength nor even a disposition among the people to carry on O'Connell's Repeal, but that there was strength in the people to carry national independence if national independence were associated with something else.[11]

> A mightier question is in the land – one beside which Repeal dwarfs down to a petty parish question; one on which Ireland may not alone try her own right but try the right of the world; on which she would be not merely an asserter of old principles, often asserted, and better asserted before her, an humble and feeble imitator and follower of other countries – but an original inventor, propounder, and propagandist, in the van of the earth, and heading the nations; on which her success or her failure alike would never be forgotten by man, but would make her for ever a lodestar of history; on which Ulster would be not '"on her flank"' but at her side, and on which, better and best of all, she need not plead in humble petitions her beggarly wrongs and how beggarly she bore them, nor plead any right save the right of her MIGHT....[12]
>
> Repeal may perish with all who support it sooner than I will consent to be fettered on this question, or to connect myself with any organised body that would ban or merge, in favour of Repeal or any other measure, that greatest of all our rights on this side of heaven – God's grant to Adam and his poor children for ever, when He sent them from Eden in His wrath and bid them go work for their bread. Why should I name it?[13]

[10] Charles Gavan Duffy, journalist and poet, was another leading Young Irelander.

[11] John Mitchel (1815–75) was a writer, journalist, and activist involved with Young Ireland, sentenced in 1848 to penal transportation for advocating resistance to exactions by landlords. Daniel O'Connell (1775–1847) led the campaign for Catholic Emancipation followed by agitation for the Repeal of the Union conducted under the auspices of the Repeal Association, set up in 1830.

[12] He is referring to Protestants in Ulster – often synonymised with Ulster throughout the nineteenth and twentieth centuries – and their contemporary resistance to repeal of the Union.

[13] James Fintan Lalor, 'To Charles Gavin Duffy, Editor of the "Nation"', 11 January 1847 in *The Writings of James Fintan Lalor* (Dublin: 1895), pp. 3–5.

His proposals as to means thrilled the young orators and debaters as the ringing voice of an angel might thrill them:

> As regards the use of none but legal means, any means and all means might be made illegal by Act of Parliament, and such pledge, therefore, is passive obedience. As to the pledge of abstaining from the use of any but moral force, I am quite willing to take such pledge, if, and provided, the English Government agree to take it also; but 'if not, not'. Let England pledge not to argue the question by the prison, the convict-ship, or the halter; and I will readily pledge not to argue it in any form of physical logic. But dogs tied and stones loose are no bargain. Let the stones be given up; or unmuzzle the wolf-dog. ...[14]

At Duffy's invitation Lalor developed his doctrines in two letters to the *Nation*, one addressed to the landlords and one to the people. To the landlords he spoke this ominous warning:

> Refuse it [to be Irishmen], and you commit yourself to the position of paupers, to the mercy of English Ministers and English members; you throw your very existence on English support, which England soon may find too costly to afford; you lie at the feet of events; you lie in the way of a people and the movement of events and the march of a people shall be over you.[15]

The essence of Lalor's teaching is that the right to the material ownership of a nation's soil co-exists with the right to make laws for the nation and that both are inherent in the same authority, the Sovereign People. He held in substance that Separation from England would be valueless unless it put the people – the actual people and not merely certain rich men – of Ireland in effectual ownership and possession of the soil of Ireland; as for a return to the *status quo* before 1800, it was to him impossible and unthinkable.[16] When Mitchel's *United Irishman* was suppressed in 1848, Martin's *Irish Felon*, with Lalor as its standard-bearer and spokesman, stepped into the breach; and in an article entitled 'The Rights of Ireland' in the first issue of that paper (June 24, 1848) Lalor delivered the

[14] Ibid., pp. 5–6.

[15] James Fintan Lalor, 'A New Nation: Proposal for an Agricultural Association Between the Landowners and the Occupiers' in *The Writings of James Fintan Lalor*, p. 22.

[16] This entails a critique of the idea of repealing the Union on the understanding that repeal would mean a return to the restricted franchise that operated in the eighteenth century.

new gospel.[17] A long passage must be quoted in full; but it can be quoted without any comment, for it is self-luminous:

> Without agreement as to our objects we cannot agree on the course we should follow. It is requisite the paper should have but one purpose; and the public should understand what that purpose is. Mine is not to repeal the Union, or restore Eighty-two.[18] This is not the year '82, this is the year '48. For repeal I never went into 'Agitation', and will not go into insurrection. On that question, I refuse to arm, or to act in any mode; and the country refuses. O'Connell made no mistake when he pronounced it not worth the price of one drop of blood; and for myself, I regret it was not left in the hands of Conciliation Hall, whose lawful property it was, and is. Moral force and repeal, the means and the purpose, were just fitted to each other – *Arcades ambo*, balmy Arcadians both. When the means were limited, it was only proper and necessary to limit the purpose. When the means were enlarged, that purpose ought to have been enlarged also. Repeal, in its vulgar meaning, I look on as utterly impracticable by any mode of action whatever; and the constitution of '82 was absurd, worthless, and worse than worthless. The English Government will never concede or surrender to any species of moral force whatsoever; and the country-peasantry will never arm and fight for it – neither will I. If I am to stake life and fame, it must assuredly be for something better and greater, more likely to last, more likely to succeed, and better worth success. And a stronger passion, a higher purpose, a nobler and more needful enterprise is fermenting in the hearts of the people. A mightier question moves Ireland to-day than that of merely repealing the Act of Union. Not the constitution that Wolfe Tone died to abolish, but the constitution that Tone died to obtain – independence; full and absolute independence for this island, and for every man within this island. Into no movement that would leave an enemy's garrison in possession of all our lands, masters of our liberties, our lives, and all our means of life and happiness – into no such movement will a single man of the greycoats enter with an armed hand, whatever the town population may do. On a wider fighting field, with stronger positions and greater resources than are

[17] The first number of John Mitchel's (1815–75) *United Irishman* appeared on 12 February 1848. The paper was suppressed after sixteen editions were published. Its mission was continued by John Martin (1812–75), assisted by Lalor, in the form of *The Irish Felon*, the first edition of which appeared on 24 June 1848.

[18] That is, the programme was a rejection of the indeterminate O'Connellite plan to repeal the Union and thereby re-establish Grattan's Parliament, or the 'Constitution of 1782'.

> afforded by the paltry question of Repeal, must we close for our final struggle with England, or sink and surrender.
>
> Ireland her own – Ireland her own, and all therein, from the sod to the sky. The soil of Ireland for the people of Ireland, to have and hold from God alone who gave it – to have and to hold to them and their heirs for ever, without suit or service, faith or fealty, rent or render, to any power under Heaven … When a greater and more ennobling enterprise is on foot, every inferior and feebler project or proceeding will soon be left in the hands of old women, of dastards, imposters, swindlers, and imbeciles. All the strength and manhood of the island – all the courage, energies, and ambition – all the passion, heroism, and chivalry – all the strong men and strong minds – all those that make revolutions will quickly desert it, and throw themselves into the greater movement, throng into the larger and loftier undertaking, and flock round the banner that flies nearest the sky. There go the young, the gallant, the gifted, the daring; and there, too, go the wise. For wisdom knows that in national action *littleness* is more fatal than the wildest rashness; that greatness of object is essential to greatness of effort, strength, and success; that a revolution ought never to take its stand on low or narrow ground, but seize on the broadest and highest ground it can lay hands on; and that a petty enterprise seldom succeeds. Had America aimed or declared for less than independence, she would, probably, have failed, and been a fettered slave to-day.
>
> Not to repeal the Union, then, but the conquest – not to disturb or dismantle the empire, but to abolish it utterly for ever – not to fall back on '82, but act up to '48 – not to resume or restore an old constitution, but found a new nation and raise up a free people, and strong as well as free, and secure as well as strong, based on a peasantry rooted like rocks in the soil of the land – this is my object, as I hope it is yours; and this, you may rest assured, is the easier, as it is the nobler and more pressing enterprise.[19]

Lalor proceeds to develop his teaching as to the ownership of the soil of Ireland by its people:

> The principle I state, and mean to stand upon, is this: that the entire ownership of Ireland, moral and material, up to the sun and down to the centre, is vested of right in the people of Ireland; that they, and

[19] James Fintan Lalor, 'The Rights of Ireland' in *The Writings of James Fintan Lalor* (Dublin: T. G. O'Donoghue, 1895), pp. 62–6, originally published in *The Irish Felon*, 24 June 1848. The phrase 'Arcades ambo' is from Virgil's seventh eclogue: *Ambo florentes aetatibus, Arcades ambo* ('Both in the flower of youth, Arcadians both').

> none but they, are the land-owners and law-makers of this island; that all laws are null and void not made by them, and all titles to land invalid not conferred or confirmed by them; and that this full right of ownership may and ought to be asserted by any and all means which God has put in the power of man. In other, if not plainer words, I hold and maintain that the entire soil of a country belongs of right to the entire people of that country, and is the rightful property, not of any one class, but of the nation at large, in full effective possession, to let to whom they will, on whatever tenures, terms, rents, services, and conditions they will; one condition, however, being unavoidable and essential, the condition that the tenant shall bear full, true, and undivided fealty and allegiance to the nation, and the laws of the nation whose lands he holds, and owe no allegiance whatsoever to any other prince, power, or people, or any obligation of obedience or respect to their will, orders, or laws. I hold, further, and firmly believe, that the enjoyment by the people of this right of first ownership of the soil is essential to the vigour and vitality of all other rights, to their validity, efficacy, and value; to their secure possession and safe exercise. For let no people deceive themselves, or be deceived by the words, and colours, and phrases, and forms of a mock freedom, by constitutions, and charters, and articles, and franchise. These things are paper and parchment, waste and worthless. Let laws and institutions say what they will, this fact will be stronger than all laws, and prevail against them – the fact that those who own your lands will make your laws, and command your liberties and your lives. But this is tyranny and slavery; tyranny in its widest scope and worst shape; slavery of body and soul, from the cradle to the coffin – slavery with all its horrors, and with none of its physical comforts and security; even as it is in Ireland, where the whole community is made up of tyrants, slaves, and slave-drivers. ...[20]

As to the question of dealing with land-owners, Lalor re-echoes Tone and Davis:

> There are, however, many landlords, perhaps, and certainly a few, not fairly chargeable with the crimes of their order; and you may think it hard they should lose their lands. But recollect the principle I assert would make Ireland, *in fact*, as she is *of right*, mistress and queen of all those lands; that she, poor lady, had ever a soft heart and grateful disposition; and that she may, if she please, in reward of allegiance,

[20] Ibid., pp. 67–9.

> confer new titles or confirm the old. Let us crown her a queen; and then – let her do with her lands as a queen may do.
>
> In the case of any existing interest, of what nature soever, I feel assured that no question but one would need to be answered. Does the owner of that interest assent to swear allegiance to the people of Ireland, and to hold in fee from the Irish nation? If he assent he may be assured he will suffer no loss. No eventual or permanent loss I mean; for some temporary loss he must assuredly suffer. But such loss would be incidental and inevitable to any armed insurrection whatever, no matter on what principle the right of resistance should be resorted to. If he refuses, then I say – away with him – out of this land with him – himself and all his robber rights and all the things himself and his rights have brought into our island – blood and tears, and famine, and the fever that goes with famine.[21]

In the issue of the *Irish Felon* for July 8, Lalor, expecting suppression and arrest, wrote 'The Faith of a Felon' – a statement which, ill-framed and ill-connected though he knew it to be, he firmly believed to 'carry the fortunes of Ireland', and sent 'forth to its fate, to conquer or be conquered'.[22] It was conquered for the time, but, like such immortal things, it was destined to rise again. In it Lalor re-affirmed his principles and re-stated his programme. The idea of the ownership of the soil by the whole people, which is his essential contribution to modern political thought, was in this statement put more clearly even than before:

> What forms the right of property in land? I have never read in the direction of that question. I have all my life been destitute of books. But from the first chapter of Blackstone's second book, the only page I ever read on the subject, I know that jurists are unanimously agreed in considering 'first occupancy' to be the only true original foundation on the right of property and possession of land.
>
> Now, I am prepared to prove that 'occupancy' wants every character and quality that could give it moral efficacy as a foundation of right. I am prepared to prove this, when 'occupancy' has first been *defined*. If no definition can be given, I am relieved from the necessity of showing any claim founded on occupancy to be weak and worthless.
>
> To any plain understanding the right of private property is very simple. It is the right of man to possess, enjoy, and transfer the

[21] Ibid., p. 70.

[22] James Fintan Lalor, 'The Faith of a Felon' in *The Writings of James Fintan Lalor*, p. 93, originally published in *The Irish Felon*, 8 July 1848.

> substance and use of whatever HE HAS HIMSELF CREATED. This title is good against the world; and it is the *sole* and *only* title by which a valid right of absolute private property can possibly vest.
>
> But no man can plead any such title to a right of property in the substance of the soil.
>
> The earth, together with all it *spontaneously* produces, is the free and common property of all mankind, of natural right, and by the grant of God – and all men being equal, no man, therefore, has a right, to appropriate exclusively to himself any part or portion thereof, except with and by the *common consent* and *agreement* of all other men.
>
> The sole original right of property in land which I acknowledge to be morally valid, is this right of common consent and agreement. Every other I hold to be fabricated and fictitious, null, void, and of no effect.[23]

As for Lalor's programme of action, it was in brief:

1. To refuse all rent and arrears beyond the value of the overplus of harvest remaining after due provision for the tenants' subsistence for twelve months.
2. To resist eviction under the English law of ejection.
3. To refuse all rent to the usurping proprietors, until the people, the true proprietors, had decided in national congress what rents were to be paid, and to whom.
4. That the people should decide that rents should 'be paid to *themselves*, the people, for public purposes, and for behoof and benefit of them, the entire general people'.[24]

Lalor saw clearly that this programme might, and almost certainly would, lead to armed revolution. If so –

> Welcome be the will of God. We must only try to keep our harvest, to offer a peaceful, passive resistance, to barricade the island, to break

[23] Ibid., pp. 101–3. Lalor is referring to William Blackstone, *Commentaries on the Laws of England in Four Books* (London: A. Strahan, for T. Cadell and W. Davies, 1809), 2 vols., I, ch. 16: 'Occupancy is the taking possession of those things which before belonged to nobody. This, as we have seen, is the true ground and foundation of all property …' For Blackstone, however, as for theorists of natural rights in general, first occupancy is an original right which can be trumped by other rights, for instance, as Blackstone and Hume argued, by prescription.

[24] Lalor, 'The Faith of a Felon' in *The Writings of James Fintan Lalor*, pp. 96–7.

> up the roads, to break down the bridges – and, should need be, and favourable occasions offer, surely we may venture to try the steel. …
>
> It has been said to me that such a war, on the principles I propose, would be looked on with detestation by Europe. I assert the contrary. I say such a war would propagate itself throughout Europe. Mark the words of this prophecy: – The principle I propound goes to the foundations of Europe, and, sooner or later, will cause Europe to outrise. Mankind will yet be masters of the earth. The rights of the people to make the laws – this produced the first great modern earthquake, whose latest shocks, even now, are heaving in the heart of the world. The right of the people to own the land – this will produce the next. Train your hands, and your son's hands, gentlemen of earth, for you and they will yet have to use them. I want to put Ireland foremost, in the van of the world, at the head of the nations – to set her aloft in the blaze of the sun, and to make her for ages the lodestar of history. Will she take the path I point out – the path to be free, and famed, and feared, and followed – the path that goes sunward? …[25]

A fortnight later, in the *Irish Felon* for July 22, Lalor wrote the article 'Clearing the Decks', which was intended to declare the revolution. It was worthy of a braver response than it received:

> If Ireland be conquered now – or what would be worse – if she fails to fight, it will certainly not be the fault of the people at large, of those who form the rank and file of the nation. The failure and fault will be that of those who have assumed to take the office of commanding and conducting the march of a people for liberty without, perhaps, having any commission from nature to do so, or natural right, or acquired requisite. The general population of this island are ready to find and furnish everything which can be demanded from the mass of a people – the members, the physical strength, the animal daring, the health, hardihood, and endurance. No population on earth of equal amount would furnish a more effective military conscription. We want only competent leaders – men of courage and capacity – men whom nature meant and made for leaders. … These leaders are yet to be found. Can Ireland furnish them? It would be a sheer and absurd blasphemy against nature to doubt it. The first blow will bring them out. …
>
> In the case of Ireland now there is but *one fact* to deal with, and *one question* to be considered. The *fact* is this – that there are at present in occupation of our country some 40,000 armed men, in the livery

[25] Ibid., pp. 98–9.

> and service of England; and the *question* is how best and soonest to kill and capture these 40,000? ...
>
> Meanwhile, however, remember this – that somewhere, and somehow, and by somebody, a beginning must be made. Who strikes the first blow for Ireland? Who wins a wreath that will be green for ever?[26]

That was Lalor's last word. The issue containing the article was seized, the *Irish Felon* suppressed, and Martin and Lalor arrested. In a few months Lalor was released from prison a dying man. From his sick bed he tried to rally the beaten forces; he actually went down into North Munster and endeavoured to lead the people.[27] This effort – the almost forgotten rising of 1849 – failed. Lalor died in Dublin a few weeks after. But his word has marched on, conquering.

III

The doctrine and proposals of Fintan Lalor stirred John Mitchel profoundly. Mitchel was not a democrat by instinct, as Tone and Lalor were; he was not a revolutionary by process of thought, as Tone and Lalor were; he was not from the beginning of his public life a believer in the possibility and desirability of physical force, as Tone and Lalor were.[28] He became all these things; and he became all these things suddenly. It was as if revolutionary Ireland, speaking through Lalor, had said to Mitchel, 'Follow me', and Mitchel, leaving all things followed. Duffy and others were amazed that the most conservative of the Young Irelanders should become the most revolutionary. They ought not to have been amazed. That deep and passionate man could not have been anything by halves. As well expect a Paul or a Teresa or an Ignatius Loyola to be a 'moderate' Christian as John Mitchel, once that 'Follow me' had been spoken, to be a 'moderate' Nationalist. Mitchel was of the stuff of which the great prophets and ecstatics have been made. He did really hold converse with God; he did really deliver God's word to man, delivered it fiery-tongued.

Mitchel's is the last of the four gospels of the new testament of Irish nationality, the last and the fieriest and the most sublime. It flames with

[26] James Fintan Lalor, 'Clearing the Decks' in *The Writings of James Fintan Lalor*, pp. 107–12. The paragraphs in the original appear in another order.

[27] The most southernly of the four provinces in Ireland.

[28] Mitchel became a staunch supporter of the pro-slavery Southern secessionist cause in America after he escaped there in 1853 from having been exiled in 'Van Diemen's Land' (i.e., Tasmania).

apocalyptic wrath, such wrath as there is nowhere else in literature. And it is because the man loved so well that his wrath was so terrible. It is foolish to say of Mitchel, as it has been said, that his is a gospel of hate, that hate is barren, that a nation cannot feed itself on hate without peril to its soul, or at least to the sanity and sweetness of its mind, that Davis, who preached love, is a truer leader and guide for Ireland than Mitchel, who preached hate.

The answer to this is – first, that love and hate are not mutually antagonistic but mutually complementary; that love connotes hate, hate of the thing that denies or destroys or threatens the thing beloved: that love of good connotes hate of evil, love of truth hate of falsehood, love of freedom hate of oppression; that hate may be as pure and good a thing as love, just as love may be as impure and evil a thing as hate; that hate is no more ineffective and barren than love, both being as necessary to moral sanity and growth as sun and storm are to physical life and growth. And, secondly, that Mitchel, the least apologetic of men, was at pains to explain that his hate was not of English men and women, but of the English thing which called itself a government in Ireland, of the English Empire, of English commercialism supported by English militarism, a thing wholly evil, perhaps the most evil thing that there has ever been in the world. To talk of such hate as unholy, unchristian, barren, is to talk folly or hypocrisy. Such hate is not only a good thing, but is a duty.

When Mitchel's critics (or his own Doppelganger, who was his severest critic) objected that his glorious wrath was merely destructive,[29] a thing splendid in slaying, but without any fecundity or life-giving principle within it, Mitchel's answer was adequate and conclusive:

> … Can you dare to pronounce that the winds, and the lightnings, which tear down, degrade, destroy, execute a more ignoble office than the volcanoes and subterranean deeps that upheave, renew, recreate? Are the nether fires holier than the upper fires? The waters that are above the firmament, do they hold of Ahriman, and the waters that are below the firmament, of Ormuzd?[30] Do you take up a reproach against the lightnings for that they only shatter and shiver, but never

[29] A reference to the dialogue between the Ego and its Doppelganger in John Mitchel, *Jail Journal, or Five Years in British Prisons* (New York: The Office of The "Citizen", 1854), ch. 5.

[30] Ahriman is the ancient evil spirit in Zoroastrianism, the early Iranian religion. Ahriman is the source of human strife, confusion, and disappointment. It exists in opposition to Ormuzd, the good or bright spirit.

construct? Or have you a quarrel with the winds because they fight against the churches, and build them not? In all nature, spiritual and physical, do you not see that some powers and agents have it for their function to abolish and demolish and derange – other some to construct and set in order? But is not the destruction, then, as natural, as needful, as the construction? – Rather tell me, I pray you, which is construction – which destruction? This destruction is creation: Death is Birth and

'The quick spring like weeds out of the dead.'

Go to – the revolutionary Leveller is your only architect.[31] Therefore, take courage, all you that Jacobins be,[32] and stand upon your rights, and do your appointed work with all your strength, let the canting fed classes rave and shriek as they will – where you see a respectable, fair-spoken Lie sitting in high places, feeding itself fat on human sacrifices – down with it, strip it naked, and pitch it to the demons; whenever you see a greedy tyranny (constitutional or other) grinding the faces of the poor, join battle with it on the spot – conspire, confederate, and combine against it, resting never till the huge mischief come down, though the whole 'structure of society' come down along with it. Never you mind funds and stocks; if the price of the things called *Consols* depend on lies and fraud, down with them, too.[33] Take no heed of 'social disorganisation'; you cannot bring back chaos – never fear; no disorganisation in the world can be so complete but there will be a germ of new order in it; sans-culottism, when she hath conceived, will bring forth venerable institutions. Never spare; work joyfully, according to your nature and function; and when your work is effectually done, and it is time for the counter operations to begin, why, then, you can fall a-constructing, if you have a gift that way; if not, let others do *their* work, and take your rest, having discharged your duty. Courage, Jacobins! for ye, too, are ministers of heaven. …

I do believe myself incapable of desiring private vengeance; at least, I have never yet suffered any private wrong atrocious enough to stir up that sleeping passion. The vengeance I seek is the righting of my country's wrong, which includes my own. Ireland, indeed, needs

[31] The Levellers were a political movement during the English Civil War (1642–51) committed to popular sovereignty, religious tolerance, and equality before the law. Equal natural rights were at the heart of Leveller thought.

[32] The Jacobins were the most influential political club in revolutionary France that advocated republican ideals. Mitchel presents a positive conception of their goals in opposition to more negative verdicts focused on the Jacobin Reign of Terror from 1793.

[33] Consols is a term for consolidated stock in the form of government bonds.

> vengeance; but this is public vengeance – public justice. Herein England is truly a great public criminal. England! all England, operating through her Government; through all her organised and effectual public opinion, press, platform, pulpit, Parliament, has done, is doing, and means to do, grievous wrong to Ireland. She must be punished; that punishment will, as I believe, come upon her by and through Ireland; and so will Ireland be *avenged*.[34]

This denunciation of woe against the enemy of Irish freedom is as necessary a part of the religion of Irish nationality as are Davis's pleas for love and concord between brother Irishmen. The Church that preaches peace and goodwill launches her anathemas against the enemies of peace and goodwill. Mitchel's gospel is part of the testament, even as Davis's is; it but reveals a different facet of the truth. A man must accept the whole testament; but a man may prefer Davis to Mitchel, just as a man may prefer the gospel according to St. Luke, the kindliest and most human of the gospels, to the gospel of St. John.

Mitchel's teaching contains nothing that is definitely new and his. He accepted Tone; he accepted Davis; he accepted in particular Lalor; and he summed up and expressed all their teaching in a language transfigured by wrath and vision. Tone is the intellectual ancestor of the whole modern movement of Irish nationalism, of Davis, and Lalor, and Mitchel, and all their followers; Davis is the immediate ancestor of the spiritual and imaginative part of that movement, embodied in our day in the Gaelic League; Lalor is the immediate ancestor of the specifically democratic part of that movement, embodied to-day in the more virile labour organisations; Mitchel is the immediate ancestor of Fenianism, the noblest and most terrible manifestation of this unconquered nation.

And just as all the four have reached, in different terms, the same gospel, making plain in turn different facets of the same truth, so the movements I have indicated are but facets of a whole, different expressions, and each one a necessary expression, of the august, though denied, truth of Irish Nationhood; nationhood in virtue of an old spiritual tradition of nationality, nationhood involving Separation and Sovereignty, nationhood resting on and guaranteeing the freedom of all the men and women of the nation and placing them in effective possession of the physical conditions necessary to the reality and to the perpetuation of their freedom, nationhood declaring and establishing and defending

[34] Ibid., pp. 110–11.

itself by the good smiting sword. I who have been in and of each of these movements make here the necessary synthesis, and in the name of all of them I assert the forgotten truth, and ask all who accept it to testify to it with me, here in our day and, if need be, with our blood.

At the end of a former essay I set that prophecy of Mitchel's as to the coming of a time when the kindred and tongues and nations of the earth should give their banners to the wind; and his prayer that he, John Mitchel, might live to see it, and that on that great day of the Lord he might have breath and strength enough to stand under Ireland's immortal Green. John Mitchel did not live to see it. He died, an old man, forty years before its dawning. But the day of the Lord is here, and you and I have lived to see it.[35]

And we are young. And God has given us strength and courage and counsel. May He give us victory.

[35] Pearse is characterising the present time, just over forty years after Mitchel's death, as a quasi-millenarian moment.

1917

23 Hanna Sheehy-Skeffington, 'State of Ireland'[1]

Ireland is still under martial law, threatened with famine and with conscription; death by hunger or in the trenches.[2] But Ireland's spirit was never stronger, never was it more clearly shown that no nation can be held by force, that the aspiration after liberty cannot be quelled by shot or shell.

The Volunteers

A word as to the Irish Republicans. 'Treason doth never prosper. What is the reason? When treason prospers, none dare call it treason.' When the United States of America set up its republic it declared its independence of Great Britain, it happily won, and maintained its independence. But if it had lost – would its leaders find quicklime graves? Surely.

I know the Irish Republican leaders, and am proud to call Connolly, Pearse, Macdonagh, Plunkett, O'Rahilly and others friends[3] – proud to

1 This document makes up the concluding section of Hanna Sheehy-Skeffington's *British Militarism as I Have Known It* (New York: The Donnelly Press, 1917), first delivered as a lecture but published together with Francis Sheehy-Skeffington's (1878–1916) *A Forgotten Nationality: Ireland and the War*, which had originally appeared separately in *Century Magazine* in February 1916.

2 The Defence of the Realm Act was introduced on 8 August 1914 and subsequently amended six times, drastically curtailing numerous civil freedoms. Under this amendment, martial law was imposed in parts of Ireland in the aftermath of the Easter Rising and was only lifted in mid-1917. Presumably Skeffington is referring to the possibility of severe food shortages as a result of German U-boat warfare around the coastlines of Ireland. Conscription was finally introduced in April 1918 in Ireland, which had avoided the measure when first implemented in January 1916.

3 Thomas MacDonagh (1878–1916), Joseph Plunkett (1887–1916), and Michael Joseph O'Rahilly (1875–1916). MacDonagh and Plunkett were executed for their role in the Easter Rebellion. O'Rahilly had been a founding member of the Irish Volunteers. Although

have known them and had their friendship. They fought a clean fight against terrible odds – and terrible was the price they had to pay. They were sober and God-fearing, filled with a high idealism. They had banks, factories, the General Post Office, the lower courts, their enemies' strongholds for days in their keeping, yet bankers, merchants and others testified as to the scrupulous way in which their stock was guarded.[4] A poet truly said, 'Your dream, not mine, / And yet the thought, for this you fell, / Turns all life's water into wine.'[5] Their proclamation gave equal citizenship to women – beating all records – except that of the Russian Revolutionists.[6]

It is the dreamers and the visionaries that keep hope alive and feed enthusiasm – not the statesmen and politicians. Sometimes it is harder to live for a cause than to die for it. It would be a poor tribute to my husband if grief were to break my spirit.[7] It shall not do so. I am not here just to harrow your hearts by a passing thrill, to feed you on horrors for sensation's sake. I want to continue my husband's work so that when I meet him some day in the Great Beyond, he will be pleased with my stewardship.

The lesson of the Irish Rising and its suppression is that our small nation, Ireland, has a right also to its place in the sun. We look to the United States particularly to help us in this matter. The question of Ireland is not, as suggested by England, 'A domestic matter'. It is an international one, just as the case of Belgium, Serbia and other small nationalities is. We want our case to come up at the Peace Conference, if not before – to the international tribunal for settlement.[8]

he originally opposed the Rebellion, he joined the Rising nonetheless and was killed in a charge on a British machine gun post.

4 She is referring to the fact that most of the locations used for the Rising were chosen for their theatrical rather than strategic importance. Many were epicentres of civic life.

5 The lines are taken from George Russell's poem 'Salutation', subtitled 'To the memory of some I knew who are dead and who loved Ireland'. The passage quoted is about Patrick Pearse.

6 A reference to the Easter 1916 Proclamation of the Irish Republic. In July 1917 women over the age of twenty were given the right to vote and hold public office in Russia in the aftermath of the February Revolution.

7 Francis Sheehy-Skeffington, a pacifist, was killed after intervening to stop looting during the 1916 Rebellion. The pamphlet from which this section is taken is largely concerned with the circumstances of his execution by firing squad while in custody after his arrest.

8 The Paris Peace Conference would sit from 1919 to 1920 under the auspices of the Allies who won the First World War. At this conference, nationalists like Skeffington sought to make a case for Ireland's independence from Britain.

The United States Government has declared that it is entering this war for the democratization of Europe.[9] We do not want democracy to stop short of the Irish sea, but to begin there. If Great Britain is in good faith in this matter, she can begin now, by freeing our small nation, and this can be done without the shedding of a single drop of American blood, and the whole world would applaud the deed.

We look, therefore, to America to see that her allies live up to their professions and that the end of the war will see all small nations of Europe free. As my husband said, in an article in the Century Magazine, February, 1916, on a 'Forgotten Small Nationality', 'Shall peace bring freedom to Belgium, to Poland, perhaps to Finland and Bohemia, and not to Ireland?'[10] It is for America to see that Ireland is not excluded from the blessings of true democracy and freedom. In this respect America will be but paying back the debt she owes to Ireland. In the day of her struggle for independence, before she set up her republic, she was aided by Irish citizens – many of whom gave their lives for her freedom.[11] And in the Civil War thousands of Irishmen died that your negroes might be free men. The record of the Fighting 69th of New York is famous in your history;[12] it was a regiment of Roman Catholic Irish who were wiped out so that the regiment disappeared for a time till it could be practically recruited entirely afresh, and to-day it is allowed to keep its name of (the 69 N. Y. N. G.) in parenthesis after the new name given it in drafting it into the Federal army for service in France, the 165th Infantry of the N. Y. National Guard Army. It is for their descendants, the beneficiaries of those old wars of yours for freedom in '76 and 1861,[13] now to pay back that debt, and to help us set up an Irish republic, as independent of Great Britain as is your own.

At the end of the war we hope to see a 'United Europe' on the model of your own United States, where each state is free and independent, yet

[9] The US finally entered the War on the side of the Allies in April 1917.

[10] Francis Sheehy-Skeffington, *A Forgotten Nationality: Ireland and the War* (New York: The Donnelly Press, 1917), p. 16.

[11] Considerable numbers of Irish men assisted both the revolutionaries and the British Army during the American Revolutionary War. Skeffington is referring to those who assisted the revolutionaries.

[12] The 69th Infantry Regiment was originally known as the 'Fighting Sixty-Ninth'. Allegedly so named by Robert E. Lee during the Civil War, it was commonly known as the 'Fighting Irish' and was at the time training for overseas service in the world war.

[13] Referring to the 1776 Declaration of Independence and the start of the American Civil War in 1861.

all are part of a great federation. We want Ireland to belong to this united Europe, and not to be a vassal of Great Britain, a province of the British Empire, governed without consent. Unless the United States is as wholeheartedly in favor of the freedom of Ireland as she is for the emancipation of Belgium, she cannot be true to her own principles. Her honor is involved and we look particularly to the Irish in America to remember the claims of the land of their fathers, when the day of reckoning comes.

I shall conclude by quoting from William Rooney's poem, 'Dear Dark Head', which embodies in poetic form Ireland's lifelong dream for freedom.[14] Speaking of the men who died for Ireland, he says:

> And though their fathers' fate be theirs, shall others
> With hearts as faithful still that pathway tread
> Till we have set, Oh Mother Dear of Mothers,
> A nation's crown upon thy Dear, Dark Head?[15]

[14] William Rooney (1873–1901) was a poet and Irish nationalist who had co-founded the Celtic Literary Society with Arthur Griffith and Denis Devereux.

[15] The lines are taken from Rooney's love poem, 'Ceann Dubh Dílis', roughly translated as 'Black Haired Darling'.

24 Horace Plunkett, 'A Defence of the Convention'[1]

MR. CHAIRMAN, LADIES AND GENTLEMEN,

This is the first time in over fifteen years that I have stood on a platform which could be called political, and I daresay there are many others here who leave party politics severely alone. But to-day Ireland, in common with many another country, is passing through a crisis unprecedented in its history, and the call has come for men of no party to work together with men of all parties in the field of politics. For, whether we wish it or not, changes are about to be made in our system of government which must profoundly affect us all. These changes are to be discussed in a National Convention, which the leader of over four-fifths of our Parliamentary representatives has himself declared should be composed mainly of non-partisan Irishmen.[2] To these latter, therefore, I desire chiefly to speak, as one of them, upon our political duty at this time.

[1] Horace Plunkett, 'A Defence of the Convention' in George Russell, Horace Plunkett, and John Quinn, *The Irish Home Rule Convention* (New York: Macmillan, 1917). Plunkett's defence was first delivered as a speech at Dundalk on 25 June 1917.

[2] The Irish Convention was proposed in May 1917 and sat in Dublin from 25 July until April the following year under the chairmanship of Horace Plunkett. Comprising a range of party and non-party representatives, it was charged with discussing the prospective enactment of self-government for Ireland. The provision of home rule had been in suspension for the duration of the War, the 1916 Rising had occurred during the interval, and the settlement of the Ulster question was still outstanding. Attempts to resolve the issue in the summer of 1916 ended in failure, coinciding with major losses to Irish divisions at the Battle of the Somme. In response, the British Prime Minister, Lloyd George (1863–1945), now presiding over a new coalition government, proposed the establishment of the Convention to John Redmond.

The Convention and its Critics

A great majority of the Irish people have already decided that an attempt should be made at once in Ireland by Irishmen to come to some agreement, and have welcomed the plan offered for our acceptance by the Government. But voices are heard denying that the Convention gives us any real opportunity of attaining the end in view.[3] So strongly is this felt that a body of opinion, of unknown numerical strength but of unquestioned sincerity and of great determination, is urging upon us a wholly different plan. Ireland is to appear before the Peace Conference and to demand that her government shall be brought into accord with the principles for which the Allies profess to be fighting.[4] These men who reject, and others who accept, the Convention make two objections to it: they say, first, that it is not in any true sense representative, and secondly, that it has no power to get legislative effect given to its decision, no matter by how large a majority its wishes may be declared. The best contribution I can make to your deliberations will be to examine, briefly, the alternative which has been suggested, to answer, as far as I can, the two damaging criticisms of the Convention itself, and then to give my reason for holding that we should accept the offer of the Government.

Ireland at the Peace Conference

It would not be fair to criticize the Peace Conference proposal in its details, because the time has not come to work these out; but it is quite necessary to discuss the plan in its broad outlines, since it is advocated as a better way than that which most of us wish to take. I submit, then, that if the Conference were to meet to-morrow, Ireland could not be represented at it, for the obvious reason that there would be no agreement as to who were to be her plenipotentiaries. But, if this difficulty were surmounted – and in an atmosphere which makes it almost impossible to find an Irish Chairman for our Convention it is a big 'if' – what is it that our plenipotentiaries are going to ask of the assembled representatives of the war-worn nations? They will have to admit that the people of Ireland are not

[3] Sinn Féin, along with William O'Brien's (1852–1928) All-For-Ireland-League and the Irish Labour Party, refused to attend the conference.

[4] This was a Sinn Féin proposal. The party won a number of by-elections in the run-up to the Convention and proposed bringing Ireland's case for independence before the anticipated Peace Conference which would happen upon the conclusion of the war.

unanimous as to the kind of government they require. Some prefer the *status quo*; others desire devolution within the United Kingdom; a much larger section favour government within the British Commonwealth of self-governing nations, but differ considerably as to the precise position Ireland should occupy in it; and yet another group desire to make their country an independent sovereign State. Worse still, there is the Ulster difficulty, which three short years ago brought us to the verge of civil war. What, again, I ask, would our plenipotentiaries at the peace conference propose, assuming – and it is a large assumption – that the Conference admitted them to its councils and did not tell them to try first a conference at home? Is it likely that the representatives of the nations, having to discover the means to be taken to prevent further attempts to disturb the world's peace and the practicable limitations of militarism and navalism, having to decide vast questions of restitution and reparation, having to allay the fiercest racial antagonisms of the Near East – to mention but a few of their problems – will welcome the task of settling the Irish question not only in its old and well-understood Anglo-Irish significance, but in its later development of Irish disagreement? How many minorities is a peace conference to be asked to coerce, to say nothing of the coercion of Great Britain which any settlement agreeable to the advocates of this plan would involve? I cannot help feeling that this method of settlement, which, no doubt, will appeal to the imagination and stir the pride of many Irishmen, would provoke more violent opposition than any that has yet been proposed. So let us turn to the Convention, and see whether that bird in the hand does not offer a better solution than this doubtful bird in a distant bush.

The Alleged Unrepresentative Character of the Convention

I come now to the main criticism of the Convention – its constitution. It is not ideally representative – that may be admitted at once.[5] It is widely felt that the only satisfactory plan would be to let the democracy choose its delegates as it chooses its Parliamentary representatives. But there are several objections to any popular election just now. The Parliamentary register is out of date, and it would take a long time to revise it. The country is in a state of considerable unrest, which we all hope the Convention

[5] Appointment to the Convention was by public nomination rather than popular election.

will allay. In the circumstances, if we were to have a hundred fights over the selection of the delegates, the birthpangs of the Convention might be fatal to the spirit in which it can alone succeed. There is a very strongly felt objection to having any election while a large number of Irishmen are fighting abroad. No body of citizens has a better right to be heard than those soldiers, who, apart from other claims, are very likely to have gained some wide points of view. I fully realize that the *Sinn Féin* group have a grievance in the large representation of local government bodies elected before they gained their present numerical strength; but it is notorious that the great bulk of that party – which rose phoenix-like out of the ashes of the rebellion – consists of recent converts. Has their doctrine failed to commend itself to a full proportion of the chairmen of county and county-borough councils and to the urban district nominees who will be delegates under the Government's plan? Theirs is not the only grievance. The Nationalists in the six Ulster counties claiming exclusion are also unrepresented, and other bodies make similar complaints. Of all these I would ask: does the basis of representation very much matter? Surely the equal balance of parties is far less important than a comprehensive representation of Irish interests, and this is more easily reached by nomination than by election. As the Convention, which, as many have pointed out, would be more properly called a Conference, is constituted, every considerable section of Irishmen should find in it some competent advocate of its views. One essential point is that, if the Convention agrees upon a scheme which does not clearly meet with popular favour, it will unquestionably be submitted by *referendum* or otherwise for popular approval. Lastly, consider the constructive work the Convention has to do. While every delegate will be competent to criticize its report, those who will have the necessary special knowledge for drafting a bill will be exceeding few. One Alexander Hamilton would do the whole job.[6] No one who knows the way such work has to be done would be surprised either by a good report from a bad Convention or a bad report from a good Convention.

The Case for an All-Ireland Support

The conclusion, then, that I reach is that, in times of great difficulty, the Government have made an honest attempt to enable us to settle the

[6] Alexander Hamilton (1755/7–1804), an American lawyer, publicist and statesman. He was secretary of the US Treasury from 1789 to 1795.

political question for ourselves. They have striven to bring together a body of Irishmen sufficiently representing the main currents of Irish opinion to bespeak favourable consideration for decisions as to which they are unanimous, and to make a strong case for those at which they arrive by a substantial majority. It has been suggested, I know, that it is nothing more than a clever trick to put Ireland in the wrong by proving to the world that, in the words of Lord Dufferin's joke at our expense, 'the Irish don't know what they want, and won't be happy till they get it'.[7] The suggestion comes from those who foster that undying hatred of England which, if it does not exclude, most assuredly renders barren their love for Ireland. To such I would say the England of the war is wholly unlike any England that has ever been – as unlike as is the Lloyd George Government from any of its predecessors. It is dominated by labour. Little time has the British democracy just now to think of Ireland, but I am convinced it wants to do justly by Ireland for its own sake, for Ireland's sake, and out of regard to the opinion of its Allies, especially America and Russia. But, if this view cannot be taken by those I am now addressing, I have another answer. If they really think England is an insidious foe, seeking our destruction, why, in the name of common sense, should they fall into the trap which they plainly see when, by simply taking counsel together, the Irish have it in their power to hoist the enemy with his own petard? What, however, concerns us here is that the Convention will meet, and we wish it Godspeed. Far the best service this meeting can do is to appeal to those Irishmen who have determined to remain aloof to reconsider their decision.

An Appeal to Those who have Refused Co-operation

To those of our countrymen upon whose willingness to make some sacrifice of individual opinions, the full success of the Convention will depend, I beg leave to address a few friendly words. Of all the abstentions, that of Mr. William O'Brien is to me the most pathetic. When I accepted the invitation to come here to-day and plead for unity, I had hoped that his mantle would fall upon me, but never dreamed that he would himself cast it off. No man has more consistently stood for the coming together

[7] Frederick Temple Hamilton-Temple-Blackwood (1826–1902), 1st Marquess of Dufferin and Ava, was a British diplomat who served as Governor General of Canada and then as Viceroy of India.

of Irishmen to try and compose their differences, and at least, I looked to him to tell us to make the best of a bad Convention. I can well believe in the 'poignant personal sorrow' with which he made his great refusal, and I hope he will see in this meeting a direct appeal to him to reconsider it. He will thus render the greatest service of a life devoted to Ireland.[8]

The abstention of the *Sinn Féiners* is, in a sense, more regrettable, because they are more numerous. In some respects, theirs is the most interesting political party in Irish history. Most other parties depend for their strength upon organization, and this is the weakness of *Sinn Féin.* Its strength is in its idealism, the central idea being the concentration of all Irish thought and action upon exclusively Irish service. That idea, in some of its implications, leads, unhappily, to extreme courses, but none will question the nobility of an aspiration for which many fine young Irishmen have laid down their lives.[9] But around this central idea seethes every kind of discontent, and it seems to me that the one thing the cool-headed leaders should see their party requires at the moment – indeed, the condition precedent of the realization of any of its aims – is to find its place in the national life. This can only be done by meeting face to face, under conditions favourable to frank discussion, every section of the community to which, in common with every other political party, it aspires to commend its policy. They, I should have thought, would see that the one gleam of hope which has in modern times brightened the political prospect in Ireland is the recognition by England that the settlement of the Irish question must come from Ireland – from ourselves alone.[10] They, of all Irishmen, should not lightly reject a Convention which, whatever its defects, has at least the merit of being Irish.

I regret, too, more than I can say, the abstention of labour.[11] Irish policies, owing, no doubt, to the domination of the land question, have notably disregarded the workers of both town and country. In a constitutional Convention the voice of those who toil and spin, must be heard. Three capable and authorized spokesmen would do as well as a hundred. All that is wanted is that a watching brief should be held for labour.

[8] O'Brien declined to participate on the grounds that a Convention with over one hundred members could not be expected to deliberate constructively.

[9] Sinn Féin was associated in the public mind with the 1916 Rising, though in fact it did not participate.

[10] The standard translation of Sinn Féin is 'Ourselves Alone'.

[11] The Irish Labour Party was established on 28 May 1912 as the political wing of the Irish Trades Union Congress by James Larkin, James Connolly, and William O'Brien.

Ireland's Difficulty, Ulster's Opportunity

Strange as it may seem, the solvent for all these discords lies just across the borders to the North. So here, North of the Boyne, and in sight of the Ulster hills, may we not appeal to those Unionists who have earned our respect by agreeing to meet us, to help the cause of peace and goodwill in Ireland by listening with an open mind to any fresh arguments which may be offered to them on this first opportunity for a free and unfettered interchange of view upon the Irish question? Their position in Ireland is to the foreign observer the most anomalous. On the one hand, they appear as a minority claiming to dictate to the majority. I dismiss that charge. They do not want to interfere with us. They have their own version of *Sinn Féin* – they, too, want to be left to themselves alone.[12] On the other hand, they claim, and they rightly claim, that they have to their credit certain solid achievements, the result of certain solid qualities. There is not a thinking Irishman but admits the achievements and regards the qualities as absolutely indispensable to any prosperous and progressive Ireland in the future. But of all the misunderstandings which curse our unhappy country, the worst is the conviction among these Ulstermen that we of the South and West bear them no good will, and that we so little understand their industrial and commercial activities, that, even with the best intentions in the world, we should inevitably embark upon schemes of legislation and practise methods of administration fatal to their interests. Personally, I think we have neglected the duty of trying to allay – much that we have done has tended to confirm – these fears.

For this reason, when the Ulster crisis was most acute, I elaborated a plan for the temporary inclusion of Ulster in an all-Ireland government for an experimental period, with the right guaranteed by all parties to withdraw if, after a fair trial, the plan did not work, or at any time, if a competent impartial tribunal decided that serious harm was being done to Ulster interests.[13] I thought it most auspicious that Nationalist Ireland seemed willing to accept the compromise, and that fact makes me believe that Ulster Unionists will be astonished at the reception they will get in the Convention. There they will find an honest and unanimous desire not to coerce, but to win, them. All the alternative schemes for the future

[12] The Ulster Unionist Council, founded in 1905, sought to resist the inclusion of Ulster under a devolved Irish government and thus to be left 'alone'.

[13] Horace Plunkett, *A Better Way: An Appeal to Ulster not to Desert Ireland* (Dublin: Hodges, Figgis, 1914).

government of Ireland will be discussed in turn, and discussed in their severely practical, as well as in their sentimental, aspects. Unless I am greatly mistaken, partition in the last analysis may prove to be administratively and financially as distasteful to the North-East as it is for other reasons to the rest of Ireland. And in the course of these practical discussions I confidently believe that a better understanding of the South by the North will inevitably result. It will be seen that our hearts and minds are shown at their worst in a public life dominated by the grievance of its unsettled Question. Other men and other methods will prevail in a self-governing Ireland if only Ulster will play its part.

The real feeling of Southern Ireland to the Northern Province is well expressed in the words of a song which I remember was very popular some forty years ago, called 'Strangers Yet'. Two whom God had joined together were unnaturally kept apart. One asks:

> Must it ever more be thus –
> Spirits still impervious?
> Can we never fairly stand
> Soul to soul, as hand in hand?
> Are the bounds eternal set
> To retain us strangers yet?[14]

If at the Convention Ulster answers these questions as the whole world hopes she will, she will have saved the country at a critical moment, and done herself lasting honour which Ireland will never forget. The Unionists in three predominantly Nationalist counties of Ulster throughout the South and West, the Nationalists in the six Ulster Unionist counties, and to my personal knowledge, the people of the United States, would all be relieved of not unwarranted misgivings. To the *Sinn Féiners* a shining example would be set, while the Nationalist Party, who, at any rate, have repudiated the idea of coercing Ulster, would feel that those strong, determined men had bent down to place a wreath on the grave of Willie Redmond, who went over the top with a United Ireland as his heart's desire.[15]

[14] From the fifth stanza of 'Strangers Yet!' by Richard Monckton Milnes (1809–85), 1st Baron Houghton.

[15] William Redmond (1861–1917), brother of John Redmond, died after being wounded at the Battle of Messines Ridge in Flanders on 7 June 1917.

1918

25 Louie Bennett, *Ireland and a People's Peace*[1]

We are all conscious of a stir of new life in Ireland in these past few years manifesting itself in various reformative progressive tendencies, and in considerable mental activity and independent thinking. Much discussion has centred round this new spirit in our national life. And all of us, whatever be our political creed, are keenly anxious to direct it into channels which may lead to the harmonizing of the discordant elements in the National Being. But until we trace its origin and visualize its goal, we shall not find that common platform upon which Irishmen of different creeds and politics can meet in a common desire for the welfare of the Irish people. That common platform cannot be found in artificial compromises. It will only be found in some conception larger and more comprehensive than Irish Nationalism or Imperial loyalties; in some concrete expression of ideals and principles which are essential to the welfare of humanity as a whole. The thought and sympathies of modern man, pushing out towards ever larger conceptions of life, are gradually extending the purposes of Nationalism so as to bring it into harmony with the larger ideals of Internationalism. For a century and more, a new vision of civilization, new, though springing from old and deep sources, has been subtly penetrating the mind of man, subtly shaping the course of the eternal struggle of humanity towards higher levels of life. If the new spirit in Ireland be sound and permanent, we shall find its inspiration in that vision, and perceive its goal to be the common goal of humanity – a finer and nobler order of civilization.

[1] Louie Bennett, *Ireland and a People's Peace* (Dublin: Maunsel, 1918) was originally read as a paper to a joint meeting of the Irishwomen's International League and the Irish section of the Union of Democratic Control on 27 February 1918.

To-day a revolutionary ferment is stirring in the bewildered minds of the European nations, kindling a blaze of idealism in the hearts of the peoples before which the vices of Imperialism must presently shrink abashed, and drawing from the welter of the war the conception of an association of nations co-operating for the good of all.[2] In this revolutionary ferment we divine the birth of a new civilization. And however passionately self-centred Nationalist Ireland may seem to be, however remote from any conscious alliance with this ferment, it becomes increasingly obvious that her fate is inextricably linked with it, and that the freedom and happiness of her people hang upon the ultimate triumph of the principles it strives to make articulate. For the moment, democratic nationalism in Ireland gropes for an outlet, but it must eventually win its way to the light, and our ideal will rise from 'Ireland a Nation' to 'Ireland a Nation amongst Nations', Ireland a co-operative factor in that International League which is to realize the new and far-reaching conceptions of civilization now growing in men's minds.[3] As James Connolly has been at pains to point out in his book, *Labour in Ireland*, Ireland has always reacted to the ferment of revolution in Europe.[4] The present time is no exception. Now, as in the past, the spirit of Ireland shows itself instinctively, if unconsciously, international, responsive to the bugle call of freedom from whatever land it may come. We in Ireland, in common with other peoples, are confusedly aware to-day of the emergence of new perspectives, new ideals, new theories of life, and are turning to them with the desperate hope of horror-stricken souls. But it is not possible to point out the methods by which they may be attained either in our own

[2] Bennett is referring to the Inter-Parliamentary Union (IPU), which had been formed by the peace activists William Randal Cremer (1828–1908) and Frédéric Passy (1822–1912) in 1889. Theodore Roosevelt (1858–1919) called for a world league to enforce peace in his Nobel Peace Prize address of 1910, and affirmed the concept in 1914. In 1899 and 1907 the international Hague Conventions governing rules of war and the peaceful settlement of international disputes were promulgated. Goldsworthy Lowes Dickinson (1862–1932), a British political scientist, coined the term 'League of Nations' in 1914, drafting a scheme for its organisation. Within weeks of the opening of the First World War numerous women's organisations, from the US to Hungary, campaigned for international co-operation. In the aftermath of the collapse of the Second International, V. I. Lenin (1870–1924) inaugurated a movement directed against the 'imperialist war' at the Zimmerwald Conference in Switzerland on 5–8 September 1915.

[3] The film *Ireland a Nation*, narrating the country's history since 1798, was released in the US on 23 September 1914. It was shown for the first time in Dublin at the Rotunda Picture House on 8 January 1917.

[4] She is actually referring to James Connolly, *Labour in Irish History* (Dublin: Maunsel, 1910).

land or elsewhere until we understand what are the forces which have led mankind to this new vision of the world's objectives.

I wish now to suggest a line of thought which may illuminate Ireland's place in the revolutionary movement of to-day, and show how, through it, she may achieve independence and full self-expression, and find a common national purpose in the promotion of the democratic ideals which have become the hope of an agonized world.

The passion for freedom, so powerful a factor in human life, is a symptom of growth, the inspiration of progress. The desire for freedom is far from being purposeless: it is intrinsically synonymous with the human instinct to find fuller development of powers and aptitudes. Its methods of expression may often be crude, violent, morally unjustifiable; but it nevertheless constitutes man's highest goal. In trying to trace, therefore, the growth of real civilization, we trace the progress of the ideal of freedom. But it is of primary importance to note that all progress towards freedom involves the subordination of lesser liberties as a means to the attainment of the higher. We mount to freedom on the ladder of law. The individual consents to the control and limitation of his personal freedom for sake of the greater freedom of the community: the community yields for the nation: the nation for humanity. *To-day the struggle for freedom centres round the problem of national or imperial concessions in the interests of humanity.*

Each age makes its struggle for freedom in its own way. In our modern age the struggle has found its inspiration in two great principles – Nationality and Democracy. These principles cannot be considered apart from each other. They are interdependent. One cannot exist without the other. Democratic institutions within a subject nation are inconceivable. And only from a democracy can we hope for the honest application of the principle of Nationality. Each has a similar aim – freedom for self-determination and self-development. But democracy has already found its watchwords – international solidarity, international co-operation – whereas Nationality is only to-day beginning to appreciate the vital significance of Interdependence, and to perceive that the freedom of nations can only be maintained under some form of International government animated by the spirit of co-operation.

Nationality and Democracy emerged as the most immediate objectives of human progress towards the close of the eighteenth century. Subject nations and subject classes began then to define their desires in terms definite enough to give pause to the forces of tyranny and aggression. And from that time the struggle for freedom has continued unceasingly, sometimes subtly and unperceived, sometimes in violent upheaval. Imperialism and Capitalism have marched together from one obvious triumph to another: but all the while the twin spirits of Nationality and Democracy have been subtly undermining their strongholds just as a stream running secretly through a bed of limestone fatally saps its foundations. The War of American Independence gave reality to the theory of the right of every people to determine their own destiny. The French Revolution threw out the great banner of 'Liberty, Fraternity, Equality'. The Revolution failed, but its ideal persisted and has been as yeast in the minds of men. The kings and diplomats who presided over the Congress of Vienna chose to ignore the claims of Nationality and Democracy; they parcelled out Europe as it best pleased them, regardless of national or human aspirations, and thus laid up a heritage of wars and revolts dear in cost to life and treasure.[5] But the love of freedom drew new life from sacrifice. Those twin principles proved themselves unconquerable forces, and as the nineteenth century progressed they drew to their allegiance many different minds, many different movements, and found expression in various and unexpected forms. Even from the ranks of the reactionaries many groups and individuals, swayed by the thrilling appeal of socialism, of humanitarianism, or of nationalism, came half way to meet those who were struggling fiercely for their 'rights'. Thus at the beginning of the present century it was possible to conceive of a gradual and peaceful social revolution through the absorption of new ideals into the mind and conscience of the people and a consequent pressure upon dominant forces which should compel extensions of national and human liberty on all sides. Through trade unionism, socialism, and the co-operative movement, the proletariats were winning their own emancipation, helped not a little by science, education, and the spread of humanitarian ideas. Imperial powers were beginning to show a half-hearted recognition of the rights of peoples to determine their own destiny – most notably perhaps in the British Empire, where the slow conversion of colonies into dominions, of empire into federation, was most advanced.[6] And, at the outbreak of the war, the substitution of reason for force in international affairs (as shown, for instance, in the increasing practice of conferences, arbitration and arbitration treaties) had become sufficiently usual for liberal Statesmen to

[5] The 1814–15 Congress of Vienna reconfigured the map of Europe in the aftermath of the fall of Napoleon.

[6] This principally refers to Canada, Australia, and South Africa, which, having been colonies, were granted dominion status and later federated their territories.

look forward to the gradual enthronement of public right as a governing factor in interstate relations.

Looking back over the past century, when men were rushed along the road of material progress too rapidly to allow of the adjustment of facts with ideas, of methods with purpose, it is strange to note how education and science, by creating innumerable methods of intercourse and bonds of common interest among the peoples, were making some sort of co-operative League of Nations an imperative necessity, from the moral, the intellectual, and the practical point of view. We must despair of a League of Nations were it merely a moral conception (for it is, in fact, an outcome of morality's long groping towards the elimination of force in human relationships); but, like so many human ideals that are primarily moral, this one, too, is more and more clearly seen to be based on practical necessity, created by the powers of destruction which science is placing in the hands of man.[7] And we may, in fact, fairly claim it to be the ultimate object of the great struggle for freedom which has centred round the problems of Nationality and Democracy.

But whilst this gradual building up of the foundations of a new civilization proceeded, the forces of reaction were not idle. It was possible for them to draw immense reinforcements from all the educational, scientific, and industrial developments of the last century. Whilst the ideals of co-operation and fraternity were creeping into life, competition, aggression and exploitation still dominated the world, and the votaries of power were too preoccupied with their mutual antagonisms to foresee that the new social forces might become their most dangerous foe. Their only fear was of each other; their main concern, to meet schemes of Imperialistic and commercial aggressions with counter-schemes; and meantime small nationalities would remain powerless against the mailed fist, and the under-dog of democracy could always be kept quiet with a bone.

It was inevitable that an International system devoid of morality, which acknowledged no fundamental principle of liberty or public right, and

[7] The Bryce Group, a loose organisation within the British Liberal Party, had made proposals for a league of nations that were adopted by the British League of Nations Society, founded in 1915. In the United States, the Century Association in New York City developed an international peace plan of its own. Lord Robert Cecil (1864–1958) recommended the establishment of a committee to draft a covenant for a future league in December 1916. A committee was finally appointed in February 1918. The US President Woodrow Wilson (1856–1924) at that point proceeded with his own preferred scheme, later collaborating at the 1919 Paris Peace Conference with Cecil and Jan Smuts (1870–1950) to draft a new covenant.

made of life a game of grab played by diplomacy or force, should end in some violent cataclysm such as the war of to-day. And so entangled are all the interests and activities of mankind that on the outbreak of war in 1914, democrats and the friends of liberty were all alike caught up in the vortex; and for a time it seemed as if all the new, growing ideals had been swept away. But a few faithful held fast, showing a quite remarkable insight as to the essential issues of the crisis. And, in the course of time, by a strange combination of circumstances, the principles of Nationality and Democracy have been swept up to the surface of a struggle which is fundamentally Imperialistic, and have become the battle-cries of the belligerents: reactionaries pay lip-service at their shrine, and herald them as dominant factors in a 'reconstructed' world. It remains for the workers of the world to carry the process of compulsory conversion from profession to action.

These big words, Nationality and Democracy, now so lightly tossed about, raise tremendous issues. It must prove a formidable task to translate them into realities, to apply them in particular cases.

Our hope of ultimately achieving this lies in the fact that there exists in every country a section of the people who are agreed on certain fundamental points as essential to any regeneration of our social system, and who are organized to make them the controlling factors of the Peace Settlement.

These points are: –

1. The right of all nations to determine their own destiny.
2. The right of the people in every nation to control (through Parliament) their government in foreign and home affairs, and to be kept informed of the treaties to which they are pledged. In a word, democratic control.
3. The application of the principle of International Co-operation in the form of a League of Free Nations, existing to promote the well-being of humanity as a whole, and to conduct International affairs by methods of negotiation, conciliation, and arbitration.
4. The substitution of reason for force as the basis of government, in fact as well as theory, by the gradual reduction and elimination of armaments.
5. The establishment of the practice of justice in the economic relations of peoples, so as to ensure the equal rights of all peoples to a share in the earth's treasures, and a system of mutual interchange of essential products.

Obviously, the world programme outlined under these headings, rests upon the principles of Nationality and Democracy, and it is, in fact, a proclamation of a political and economic moral code which must be carried right through all human affairs before we can attain a pacific civilization.

Ireland has ever been in the current that makes for freedom. The Irish people have proved passionate lovers of liberty, neither to be bought nor terrified. Our country has been a centre of the long struggle of Nationality and Democracy; and, although the national issue has inevitably dominated the situation, almost all our great political leaders, from Wolfe Tone to Pearse and Connolly, have been democrats, have coupled the freedom of the nation with the freedom of the men and women who constitute the nation. And it has been the peasants, the common people, who have always most selflessly, most loyally, and most persistently upheld the national cause. In fact, it may be said that the cause of Nationalism in Ireland has been the cause of the common people, for, throughout the nineteenth century, the Irish capitalist class was bound to England by a multitude of ties, and joined issue with England against the Nationalist element. In the period which can most aptly be compared with the present day, the period of the American War of Independence and the French Revolution, Wolfe Tone was promulgating Republican principles, and North and South, Protestant and Catholic, were fighting a common foe, the oppressive rule of a capitalistic foreign government.[8] The great democratic upheaval which convulsed Europe at the end of the eighteenth century, had its reverberation in Ireland, and gave a common cause to the Irish people, whether in Ulster or Connaught.[9] And so when men talk to-day of a new spirit in Ireland, they are surely in error to suppose it purely insular, a product of yesterday's Rising or of an intermixture of race. This new spirit is Ireland's expression of the universal, liberating movement which has been at work in the world for more than a century. And it is worth noting that, whilst in France, England, and Germany, this movement has manifested itself chiefly in industrial struggles and social reforms, in Ireland it bloomed out in an efflorescence of art, literature, and drama, in the development of a Celtic culture, and in the conscious

[8] The United Irishmen, in which Theobald Wolfe Tone (1763–98) was a leading figure, campaigned for Irish liberty and ultimately for independence, in due course spearheading the 1798 Rebellion.

[9] The 1798 Rebellion was concentrated in Wexford, the West, and the North.

building up of a National Being materially and intellectually strong.[10] Ireland was unique amongst the nations at the beginning of the present century: whilst other peoples toiled towards emancipation along the dull road of reform, the soul of Ireland soared up into freedom on a flame of national genius.

It is futile now to discuss the folly or the wisdom, the crime or the heroism, of events in this country during the past few years. But it is immensely important to prove that the Irish people, in their errors, follies, heroisms or virtues have been instinctively true to the principle of freedom in so far as they understand it. What they have done, they have done for the sake of freedom. And here it is that they may take their place beside all lovers of liberty, beside all those who have consistently upheld their vision of liberty against reactionary forces, whether in their own country or another. For they have not been guilty of standing aside from that fundamental struggle of ideas which cuts across the outward conflict of armies, goes on in spite of it, and bids fair now to control it. This is the one great struggle that really matters – this struggle of ideas. In the sense in which it is merely a conflict of Great Powers, the actual war matters not at all. It matters only in so far as it may be made to serve the purposes of freedom. And when the forces of destruction have spent themselves, when the influence of reason is once more felt, and men look out on their shattered world with vision sharpened by terrible experience, Ireland's part in the deeper struggle of justice and liberty against materialism will be more clearly perceived.

To-day issues face her demanding more purposeful thinking, more consciously international action. If she is to win real freedom, she must range herself with the forces of Internationalism and Democracy, and make their programme hers. 'Without Internationalism in spirit and in practice', says Mr. Charles Trevelyan, 'there is no future for democracy.'[11] And we would add: Without democracy in spirit and in practice there is no future for nationality. The Peace Conference will determine world

[10] Bennett is referring to assorted cultural movements focused on literature, the Irish language, and sports devoted to promoting the principle of nationality. These included the Gaelic League, the Irish Literary Society, the National Literary Society, the Irish Literary Theatre, Inghinidhe na hÉireann (Daughters of Ireland), and the Gaelic Athletic Association.

[11] Charles Trevelyan (1870–1958) was a Liberal Party MP who converted to the cause of Labour. He resigned from the government in 1914 in opposition to Britain's entry into the First World War. In the same year he founded the Union of Democratic Control, an all-party organisation rallying opposition to the war.

conditions for the coming generation. *Therefore the character of that Conference is the first vital issue to be fought by lovers of liberty.* If the world is to be made safe for democracy and for the weaker nations, democracy's programme must control the Peace Conference.[12]

The programme is before us. How far can it be Ireland's programme?

Even if the issues of civilization did not concern Ireland, and her whole interests were really centred on the attainment of independence, she must still for that one issue alone rely on the triumph of democracy at the Peace Conference. For the measure of independence granted her and the measure of her future security, will be proportionate to the influence of democracy's programme at that Conference. It is, therefore, more vitally essential for Nationalist Ireland to help in making the Conference truly democratic than to secure the representation of her own delegates.[13] *The cause of Ireland must be incorporated with the cause of International Democracy.* It would be futile to send delegates from Ireland in the simple rôle of Nationalists; if they go there they must go as the advocates of the new International Code. Therefore Ireland should adopt as her own the five principles already cited, and organize a movement to promote them.

It was never more urgent than now that the progressive parties should be alert and watchful. The Imperialists may easily outwit a halting antagonist. They still hold the cards; they are growingly apprehensive of their new peril, and may negotiate peace terms whilst Democracy is still mobilizing its forces. It is just here that the danger of secret diplomacy becomes markedly apparent, and the wisdom of those who have consistently opposed it finds justification. For if the peace terms are hatched in secret, then the Imperialists will assuredly play into each others' hands as they have done in the past, bargaining with nations and peoples and building walls round the interests and privileges of capitalists and financiers against which Democracy may batter in vain for another generation.

There has been a tendency in Ireland to disregard the principle of democratic control of foreign policy as being outside her present sphere of interest and influence. It is, however, a point of vital importance to her. The results of secret diplomacy might well, at such a crisis as the present, prove fatal to her freedom and happiness, for Ireland will surely be used as a pawn in the diplomatic game if the settlement is controlled only by

[12] On 2 April 1917, Woodrow Wilson had gone before a joint session of Congress to seek a Declaration of War against Germany in order that the world 'be made safe for democracy'.

[13] This is intended as a criticism of Sinn Féin policy which was to seek representation at any peace conference that might succeed the War.

Government Ministers and Bureaucrats. The people of this country must be as firm in their stand for truth and candour as in their stand for the rights of nationalities. '*Diplomacy shall proceed frankly in the public view.*' '*Open covenants of peace openly arrived at.*' President Wilson has given us the phrases.[14] But only the democracies will give us the realities.

This principle of democratic control is the keynote of our whole programme, and has a particularly important bearing upon the proposal for a League of Nations. For such a League could be no more successful than the Holy Alliance if it were free from the control of an informed and undeceived public opinion. *For Ireland the initiation of a League of Nations based on sound principles is not one whit less essential than the recognition of the rights of small nationalities. No small nation can maintain an independent existence in security until some International Council has been set up whose function it will be to ensure justice towards all peoples.* The Sinn Féin programme shows weakness in its failure to perceive that Ireland cannot stand alone in a world such as our modern world, whose component parts are drawn ever more closely together by innumerable ties, material and spiritual. Sinn Féin should have preached the gospel of Interdependence as persistently as that of Nationality, and coupled the claim for a League of Nations with the claim for national independence. This would have placed Ireland unmistakably in line with the democratic forces of the world, and secured for her their entire and unhesitating support. As it is, Sinn Féin sets Ireland as an isolated plaintiff at the bar of the nations instead of making her an active partner in the great democratic alliance which aims at the common uplift of all subject elements in human society to a higher level of freedom. Sinn Féin has suffered, as other political parties suffer, from the vice of compromise. They had not the vision nor the courage to throw expediency to the winds and stand firm upon bedrock principles. They overlooked the new factor of Internationalism just as they shrank from uncompromising alliance with Democracy. James Connolly was the one leader who followed with sympathy and understanding the new orientation of world affairs, and might have brought Ireland more definitely and boldly into line with International Democracy. For he clearly saw how all the intricate developments and expansions of modern life were drawing the two factors of Nationalism and Internationalism into ever closer co-operation: saw, too, that the ideal

[14] These formulations are taken from the first principle presented in Woodrow Wilson's Fourteen Point Peace Plan, outlined on 8 January 1918.

implicit in their co-operation can only be translated into reality by the power of Democracy. The theories he flung out to an uncomprehending public must eventually dominate civilized Ireland.

The primary aim of Democracy is economic justice. It must also become the primary aim of Nationalists and Internationalists if nations are ever to live in security, or the world to be freed from exterminating wars and the crushing burden of militarism. Whilst the economic basis of society is unjust and non-moral, nations as well as individuals will be subject to exploitation and tyranny. Fundamentally, the source of national wrongs is economic: the source of war and militarism is also economic. But the system must be attacked at the roots. It will be impossible to establish a code of economic morality amongst nations until that code has been established amongst individuals. When economic justice prevails within communities, it will inevitably pervade international relationships. Imperialists, capitalists, financiers, cannot be expected to envisage such a code with open or unwarped minds. Only the democracies have in any sense won the vision of freedom which grants full opportunities of self-development to nation, class, and individual. Only the democracies have from harsh experience learned something of the true meaning and value of the principles of freedom of opportunity and co-operation, and recognize them as fundamental to communal morality. But obviously these are also the principles which must be the pillars of any stable society of nations. Therefore, the friends of Internationalism are looking to Democracy for the achievement of their ends.

It is interesting to note how the thinkers who first formulated this programme have gradually been driven back to fundamentals and forced to realize that the rights of nations will never be acknowledged by communities which refuse freedom of life and opportunity to individuals; and that until we have ousted commercial competition by a system of industrial co-operation, the exploitation of weaker peoples will continue, free trade will remain a mirage, and a pacific civilization impossible. The perception of this truth is drawing the thinkers into ever closer association with the workers, and the men of ideas are relying upon the men of tools to realize their ideas. This coalition of brain and manual workers is one of the most significant and fertile signs of the times. It gives substance to the conception of human society as a community of co-operative commonwealths united in the service of humanity under some form of international government. A conception which sounds Utopian. But in these days of rapid and extraordinary changes, what idea may be dismissed as merely Utopian? The pressure of material necessities created by the war, the instinct of self-preservation which modern war methods must surely arouse, and the new alliance of intellect and labour may carry us more rapidly than we now anticipate to the realization of many Utopian conceptions.

At first sight one might say that to substitute co-operation for competition in commercial and industrial life – to open up the world's markets for the equal benefit of all – to give to every nation the right of self-determination – to bring the nations together into conclave for the joint settlement of disputes and joint deliberation on international affairs – would eliminate causes for serious quarrel and leave the sword to rust in its scabbard. But this revolution in human thought and purpose cannot be attained without a prolonged struggle against old-established forces. We have to escape from a series of vicious circles. The system of armaments with its many ramifications – such as complex financial interests, the restless energy of scientists and inventors, the subtle social influences of army and navy, the vast industrial army employed in the trade – would be used by the reactionaries to block all the reforms which threatened its existence.

Plainly therefore, *Ireland must adopt the full programme of Democracy.* It is on the tide of International Democracy that she will eventually be swept to freedom. As long ago as 1907, a writer in a weekly paper run by Kettle and Sheehy-Skeffington wrote:– 'It is to Ireland's final gain to keep herself in touch with the democracies of Europe, to share their enthusiasms and hopes, to assimilate the spirit of a growing humanism which is uniting the peoples of the world, in spite of all the tawdry Imperialisms, and which promises more for human well-being in the end than all the Jingoes in their narrow hearts could ever dream of'.[15] That is still more true to-day than ten years ago. It is to Ireland's final individual gain to act in unity with these progressive forces, for in so doing she may attain unity within her own borders. Arguments and compromise will never achieve harmony. Our need is for a common purpose, large enough to draw to it men of various religious and political creeds. The great ideas now stirring men's minds cannot leave either Nationalist or Imperialist Ireland unchanged. The new vision emerging now upon the

[15] Francis Sheehy-Skeffington (1878–1916) and Thomas Kettle (1880–1916) worked together on *The Nationist* in the first decade of the twentieth century. The newspaper supported home rule and women's suffrage, and agitated in support of labour. It was sceptical about Sinn Féin and critical of the Gaelic League.

world's horizon does in fact suggest a solution for the 'Ulster Problem'.[16] For this big conception of nations co-operating for the good of all, of an International Council existing to safeguard the rights of the weaker peoples and of minorities, must gradually lift the whole Irish question into a freer atmosphere in which old problems will be freshly illuminated. The outlook of the most bigoted elements of Ulster as of the most extreme Sinn Féiner must eventually, sensibly or insensibly, be modified by these ideas; and it is inconceivable that the mass of workers in Ulster will for long stand aside from the rising tide of freedom and remain the bondservants of Imperialism and Capitalism. To toiling proletariats the appeal of an economic revolution must prove irresistible. And as in the past, the people of Ulster joined with the people of the other three Provinces to fight a common wrong, so now they may all stand together for the common cause of International Democracy.

And that common cause itself needs the allegiance of Ireland. We of this country can make a valuable contribution to its real success. The history and circumstances of the Irish people have deepened in them the characteristics of unworldliness, of idealism, of capacity for self-sacrifice; and these qualities, coupled with a strong religious sense, have given them something of the Russian people's aptitude for revolutionary thinking and revolutionary action.[17] Again, the National struggle, by creating a bond of sympathy amongst men and women of all classes, has saved Irish workers from narrow and embittered concentration upon the class struggle: and they may therefore well serve the cause of Democracy by bringing to it a broader conception of its range. (For assuredly the proletariats cannot make the world safe for themselves or for any other class by limiting their interests to their own particular needs.) Further, our comparative freedom from the commercialism and industrialism which breeds materialism in England, and from the mechanical system of organization which fosters militarism in Germany, has left us a larger measure of idealism and hopefulness with which to approach the formidable task of reconstruction. In fine, the gift of Ireland to 'the growing humanism which is uniting the peoples of the world' is 'a sprig of poetry'. The cause of Democracy is the cause of life. And life without poetry is joyless and meaningless.

[16] Referring to Ulster's opposition to Irish home rule.

[17] Referring to the February and October Revolutions of the previous year.

We who preach these doctrines will be reproached as visionaries. But it is time we ceased to fear idealism. For see what a world has been created by our subservience to expediency and compromise! And in these last few terrible years so many scoffed at ideals have been accepted as 'practical' that we have grounds for reasserting our faith in such theories as the freedom of nations, economic justice, co-operation, fraternity. It is our task to-day to uphold ideas against materialism. The power of ideas is immeasurable. Men and movements and revolutions rise and fall, but the ideas which inspired them, in so far as they are pure, are imperishable. The Russian Revolution may fail; the Bolsheviks may be overwhelmed: but the ideas for which they have stood will persist and come to fulfilment, if not in this generation, then in the next. President Wilson may be proved a reactionary, faithless to democracy and liberalism: but the ideas he has made articulate in arresting phrases will not be degraded nor permanently denied. From Russia and America the basic principles of the new civilization have been proclaimed. All that materialism can do by force or intrigue to destroy them will assuredly be done. But we to whom they have come home with conviction are bound to do battle for them unflinchingly, and to take our part, however small, in making them the dominant factors of the world's life. Each of us has some power to mould and direct public opinion; and it is public opinion which will give the impetus to the translation of our principles into concrete expression.

We who call ourselves Democrats are aiming at a social revolution. But we must first effect a revolution in thought. No revolution is permanently achieved by violence: such violence, even in the name of freedom, is tyranny. We do not aspire to the freedom which disclaims law, but to the freedom which has assimilated and transcended law. Therefore our immediate task is to spread far and wide in Ireland the principles of International Democracy.

26 Alice Stopford Green, *Loyalty and Disloyalty: What it Means in Ireland*[1]

A GREAT Frenchman, 150 years ago, wondered that the world had not for ever condemned the most evil of all forms of Government – the rule of a Nation by a Nation. Such a rule is, indeed, the most tyrannous and the most intolerable, leaving the people under it more helpless for resistance and more emptied of hope than any other system. Government by a Nation is, so to speak, eternal in its monotony. Emperor or King may die, and his authority pass to a successor of other views: a nation never dies, nor departs from its fundamental character. There can be no change of outlook on its own special interests, which have been created by its situation; and from age to age its pre-occupations remain the same, only increasing in intensity. A single ruler and his personal advisers may hear an appeal to reason; it is another matter to convince a nation made up of millions of private wills and of thousands of jealous interests, not to speak of ignorances and prejudices. The passions of the crowd rise in flood to a torrent uncontrollable and irresistible. Even tyrant kings are compelled for their own safety to follow and yield to public opinion within reasonable time. There is no such necessity for a nation, which in its long collective life can afford to turn away from appeals of a subject race – in prosperity through indifference and disdain, in adversity through panic. It can neglect the verdict of mankind, for the greater its reputation for will to power and the strength of its arms, the less it cares to court the

1 Alice Stopford Green, *Loyalty and Disloyalty: What it Means in Ireland* (Dublin: Maunsel, 1918).

good opinion of the external world. In the rule of one nation by another all natural safeguards for the governed are in effect swept away.

It is this obnoxious type of government to which Ireland has been subjected for over 250 years. As, however, the form of Irish subjection in its complete and latest expression, its final stage of evolution, is without precedent or parallel in politics, it is profitable for the student of history to trace its development.

In earlier times of English rule, government had been formally carried on by a 'Lord' or a 'King' of Ireland, with two Houses of Parliament sitting in the Pale, and representing the Norman, French, and English invaders. Heavy sufferings were inflicted on the people. But amid all evil there was some hope for the future. The position of Ireland was not wholly without dignity. It was a distinct Kingdom co-ordinate with that of England, and was possessed consequently of rights which, as they occurred to it in its character of a separate sovereignty, may in a manner be conveniently regarded as national rights. However foreign it may have been in its origins and in its first ideals, a Parliament in Ireland did in truth provide a groundwork and some conditions of the possibility of a later national life: in fact, under the Tudor Kings this Parliament of settlers who began to call themselves 'Ireland-men', showed itself capable of courage and zeal in defending the claims of Ireland to liberty and justice. The Kings, moreover, who coveted from Ireland a revenue to maintain their Imperial state, and an army at their own bidding to increase their power, needed a prosperous and well-peopled island; and the royal policy was to encourage trade and manufacture, and to favour the towns.

A decisive change, carrying with it tremendous consequences to Ireland, began with Cromwell, when the Commonwealth Parliament, after beheading the King in Whitehall, took on themselves his business and authority.[2] Dominion passed to the English Nation, which now took control of the Irish Lords and Commons, and of Ireland itself. The Parliament of England claimed supreme control and arrogated power to pass laws for Ireland over the head of the Irish Parliament.

The Kingdom of Ireland was thus suddenly degraded from the high status of a co-ordinate part of the King's dominions to a strictly

[2] The execution of Charles I (1600–49), the Stuart King of England, Scotland, and Wales, on 20 September 1649. Once the monarchy had been overthrown, England briefly became a republic or 'Commonwealth' under Oliver Cromwell (1599–1658), who brought Ireland into an 'incorporating' union with Britain in the aftermath of the military conquest of the island, which took place between 1649 and 1653.

subordinated position. Its inhabitants became a subject people under the English Parliament. Nor did they, in becoming English citizens, secure in return the privileges of English citizenship. The Irish Parliament was now cast into abject submission to the Parliament of another nation. The new authority could compel assent to its widened powers from the foreign sovereigns, William III., who held his place solely by their election, and the Hanoverian Kings, also dependent on a parliamentary title.[3] With the remembrance of one monarch beheaded and another deposed, they were of necessity wholly subdued by degrees to the constitutional system which had established their own power.

Under this rule Ireland suffered the utmost humiliation. The legislation of a multitude swayed by the fury of religious passion and trade bigotries opened a new era – the era of the penal laws for the degradation of Irish Catholics, and commercial laws for the deliberate destruction of Irish industries.[4]

The Irish Parliament meanwhile lived on in obscure slavery to the Parliament at Westminster, till the American War of Independence gave it the excuse and the opportunity of a less ignoble life.[5] Roused by the spirit of the country to revive its ancient state, it forced from the English Government in 1782 a statute declaring that (as in old times) the King, Lords, and Commons of Ireland could alone make laws for that nation, without interference from the English Parliament.[6] With its new independence the country awoke to new life. The traveller in Ireland can still see in every small town traces of activity and prosperity that followed the work of a legislature established in the country, and interested to secure the welfare of their own people.

3 William III of England (1650–1702), popularly known as William of Orange. The Hanoverian Kings she refers to began with the reign of George I in 1714 and ended with that of Queen Victorian upon her death in 1901.

4 The Penal (or Popery) Laws were passed between 1695 and 1719. Irish trade was subject to commercial restrictions from 1663; limitations were progressively extended in 1671, 1681, 1696 and 1699, and gradually repealed in the eighteenth century.

5 Poynings's Law of 1494 provided that Irish legislation was subject to approval by Westminster, the English Privy Council, and English monarch. The Declaratory Act of 1719 conferred the right on the British Parliament to pass laws for the Kingdom of Ireland, and gave the British House of Lords jurisdiction for Irish court cases. In 1782, in the aftermath of the American Revolution, restraints on Irish legislation were lifted with the establishment of Grattan's Parliament and then the passage of the Renunciation Act in 1783.

6 Referring to the Constitution of that year which freed the Irish Parliament of English restrictions.

The revolt and brief revival of the Parliament from 1782 to 1800 were crushed out by the Union, and from this time the rule of the English nation became absolute. It was in a period of the darkest political reaction, when in the 'Great War' the military spirit and the terror of democratic liberties were at their height, that the English Parliament established its own dominion, more powerful than of old since there was not even an apparent intermediary to stand for the rights of the subject country.[7] Of its three Estates of the Realm, all were traditionally hostile to Ireland. The House of Lords was, in fact, a purely English assembly, for if it held a minority of absentee Irish Peers, these were of their own caste by descent and marriage alliances, by tradition and prejudice. In the House of Commons the Irish Members, with 100 votes against 570, were in a position of permanent inferiority to the representatives of the English people – and were held as a negligible quantity, except in cases where it suited English convenience to use them in party strife as make-weights in the balance of power. The complaint of Irish Members to-day – that their presence in the English Parliament is a mockery, since they are not consulted on the gravest Irish questions, nor their advice even listened to in the most momentous legislation – is but a repetition of similar protests throughout the whole of the nineteenth century. The island was tossed like a football from one English party to another in the cynical game of politics. English interests were inevitably the supreme concern at Westminster. One of England's Prime Ministers alone has visited Dublin on two occasions, for one day or two.[8] No one – King, Lords, or Commons – doubted that Ireland must take a second place and subserve the welfare of the ruling nation. 'How will it affect England?' was the invariable question of the English people, of their Parliament, of their Cabinet, and of the rulers sent to Dublin Castle. These officials, with their eyes fixed on the London Parliament and the shifting balance of votes there, could give little attention to the realities of Irish life.

As for the Crown, ever since English monarchs had assumed the title of 'Kings of Great Britain and Ireland', they had in mind and act remained sovereigns of England, concerned about her special interests first and last, with Ireland as an outlying and alien dependency of ill repute. During six and a half centuries five English monarchs crossed to Ireland

[7] The 1801 Act of Union passed against the background of the French Revolutionary Wars. By the 'Great War' she is referring to the Napoleonic Wars of 1803–15.

[8] Herbert H. Asquith (1852–1928) visited Ireland in 1914 and 1916.

on war and conquest expeditions.[9] Two brief visits of State parade were made in the nineteenth century.[10] Three have reached as far as Dublin in the last eighteen years.[11] No single occasion can be recalled when the King in power considered it either a right or a duty as Sovereign of Ireland to mitigate the oppression of the Irish people, or to interfere for their protection against civil or religious tyranny; the royal influence was never used even to discountenance social prejudice and contempt. In every conflict or calamity the Sovereign was the defender of English superiority, and no Irish petition could reach the throne. It was not only the English legislature but the English monarchy which through all the centuries looked on the Irish with indifference, if not with marked hostility. The desperate effort of O'Connell to overcome a chilling disapproval by lavish faith and loyalty to the sovereign as ruler of Ireland is remembered by the Irish for its utter failure.[12]

During the nineteenth century, moreover, when England fully developed her own form of national life, the Crown became of necessity the mere expression of the will of the Prime Minister of Great Britain. With the growth of the representative system it was recognised that the Sovereign's public conduct should be entirely controlled by the Head of the Cabinet.[13] The evolution of this system of constitutional government, admirably suited to the English people who had succeeded in bringing the royal action into complete obedience to their will, had in Ireland a very different result. It finally shut out from the Irish people all hope that their case, no matter what the urgency, could be submitted to the King of Ireland, save as a matter of party politics in England. All chance of his mediation with the English nation on behalf of his Irish subjects was completely barred out. In spite of the retention of the title, 'King of Ireland', the King was King only as King of England, and reigned under

[9] Henry II (1133–89) arrived in Ireland in 1171 to assist in the conquest of the country. King John (1166–1216) arrived in 1210, Richard II (1367–1400) in 1394 and 1399, James II (1622–1701) in 1689, William III (1650–1702) in 1691.

[10] George IV (1762–1830) visited Ireland on 17 August 1821 as did Queen Victoria (1819–1901) in 1849, 1853, and 1861.

[11] Queen Victoria visited Ireland in 1900 while Edvard VII (1841–1910) visited in 1903 and George V (1865–1936) in 1911.

[12] Daniel O'Connell (1775–1847), politician and leader of the Irish Catholic majority in the early nineteenth century, was profuse in his declarations of loyalty to the crown, not least during the visit of George IV when he presented him with a laurel crown at Dún Laoghaire, although the King would oppose Catholic Emancipation in 1829.

[13] She is referring to the progressive changes between the 'dignified' and the 'efficient' which reduced the power of the monarchy in the making of British legislation.

the absolute direction of an English Premier. According to that constitutional maxim, 'the King reigns but does not govern', Parliament assumed the functions of government, and the royal independence is so circumscribed in actual practice that for 'the King' we must now substitute the 'Prime Minister'. And so under the rule of the English nation, the loyalty demanded from Ireland to the King of Great Britain and Ireland became transmuted into 'loyalty' to successive English Premiers changing at the popular convenience of the British people. The diversity of situation of necessity creates a diversity of national emotion. To England the National Anthem is the jubilant expression of closer alliance of King and people, an alliance made by the people after their own liking. To Ireland, by the facts of her position and history, a different experience has been reserved.

The relation of Ireland to the Crown in the United Kingdom of Great Britain and Ireland is one of the unconsidered results of the Act of Union. England, intent on her own development as a single State, and encouraged by her statesmen and her writers to regard her Constitution as the most transcendent achievement of human genius, failed to consider some natural effects of absorbing Ireland into her system. What suited her, she confidently believed, must perforce suit any State so absorbed, and should result in profit. She rejected the warning of her Imperial statesman, Chatham, and untroubled by imagination or foresight went doggedly ahead.[14] The Act of Union was the triumph of provincialism over imperialism. For a hundred years the resultant struggle between them has followed its riotous course.

As the power of the English Parliament advanced, and that of the Crown decayed, so much the heavier fell the weight of the English nation on Ireland. When the Colonies with one accord refused to submit to the unnatural control of one nation by another, Ireland was left alone as a monument of the evils of such a form of government.

The government of Ireland by the Union Parliament had, in fact, all the faults of the old system. Instead of a United Kingdom, one nation remained completely subordinate to the other. The Parliament of the ruling and capitalist classes had no vision of a well-peopled, strong, and prosperous Ireland as a true security for the idea of an Imperial Confederation of free peoples. Still less had they any sense of obligation for the dignity, freedom, and wealth of the nation at their side. During that

[14] William Pitt (1708–78), Prime Minister from 1766 to 1768, was elevated to become Earl of Chatham in 1766.

century, Ireland was governed by Coercion Acts, Crimes Acts, and Suspensions of the Habeas Corpus Act, such as no government ever ventured to enact for Great Britain after 1817.[15] The results of such a conception of the rule of a nation by a nation have been the depopulation and the grave economic jeopardy of Ireland. But there has been another consequence – the profound determination of Irishmen to realise their own national life, and in self-government to find a rule more worthy of their ancient history, and more adapted to their intellectual powers and their national needs. The force of this national demand of to-day is greater than any that has yet been known in this country.

The experiment of government by the English nation, under its various forms, has been given a long and complete trial. From the first its results were inevitable. History shows universally that in governments where, by the very necessity of the case, there is no appeal to reason possible, and no hope of change in the governing mind, the aggrieved subject rapidly becomes an active malcontent, and resorts to violence as the only agency of reform. So it was in Ireland. No demand for remedy was heard across the water till it was enforced by leagues of desperate men driven to extremity and by outbreaks of popular fury. It was a dreary and gloomy road, but there was none other. We can all remember the hurricane of indignation that swept over England some dozen years ago at the saying of an Irish Under-Secretary that Ireland ought to be governed by Irish ideas.[16] When Major Redmond died with such gallantry the other day, the English parties at Westminster vied with one another in his praise, but neither Tory nor Liberal whispered that each party of them in its turn had flung him into prison.[17]

It is obvious that it is not the 'Irish Question' which confronts us in Ireland. Our problem is 'the English Question'. It is that in one form or

[15] Numerous coercion acts were passed during the period, for instance in 1870, 1871, and 1881. The Criminal Law and Procedure (Ireland) Act of 1887 was introduced by Arthur Balfour to give greater law enforcement power to the authorities in the context of the Land War. Habeas Corpus was suspended in Ireland on several occasions, for example in 1848, 1849, 1866, 1868, and 1869.

[16] Antony MacDonnell (1844–1925), who was Permanent Under-Secretary to the Lord Lieutenant of Ireland from 1902 to 1908.

[17] Willie Redmond (1861–1917), MP was the brother of the Nationalist leader John Redmond and was killed at the Battle of Messines Ridge on 7 June 1917. He had been imprisoned in 1882 alongside the former Irish Nationalist leader Charles Stewart Parnell, allegedly because he possessed seditious literature relating to the Irish National Land League, which was agitating for land reform using both constitutional and radical methods. He was again imprisoned in 1888 and 1902.

another which meets us at every turn, and which has now, among other matters, raised fundamental problems of government, even the discussion of Monarchy *versus* Republic. We cannot think it surprising, given the actual conditions, that there should be Irishmen who can see no ready way of adapting the present English constitutional system to the necessities of Ireland: even those who view with bitter enmity the appearance of a party agitating for a Republican State in Ireland must, in reason, admit that these reformers can only be understood and judged in relation to the history of the government of the Irish nation by the English nation, under a constitutional system devised by the English to suit their own national needs. It is no wonder that there are some to whom a republic seems the only outlet. It must be remembered that when this question of Republic or Monarchy engages the mind of an Irishman, it arises not as an abstract academic comparison between the advantages of monarchy and republic, but as the practical and pressing question of how to secure such self-government for his country as shall safeguard her from the dangers that follow the dominion of one nation over another. The lessons learned by the methods of corrupting and of closing the Irish Parliament which were employed by the ruling English Parliament, and were pursued for the Act of Union, cannot be forgotten. Nor can the Irish be expected to centre their hopes on any dream of a royal sympathy (the first time in 700 years) with the griefs of the Irish people: for the way of access to the Crown has been finally barred, and the keeper of the gate is England's Prime Minister, always changing, yet always the same. The fact of Sinn Féin cannot be put aside by mere abuse of Republics and Republican conceptions; nor can the difficulties which its actual being creates for British 'managing' politicians be surmounted by bribing a cohort of placemen to sing the National Anthem of England with lusty simulation of sincerity. Some deeper understanding of the realities of the Irish problem is now demanded, and a loftier intelligence to find the remedy of so great a need. Every fresh enquiry demonstrates the hazardous state of the country, where the economic conditions afford no sound basis for the people's life, where a population, by nature extremely robust, is enfeebled beyond measure by poor living and disease, by a high death-rate and a lamentable birth-rate, by late marriages, by emigration, by every evidence of insecure national existence. The Irish contribution to England, measured by taxable capacity, was reckoned in 1895 at one-sixteenth of what Great Britain can afford: economists now estimate it at one-thirty-second. On all sides Irishmen see grave outward signs of the failure of rule by one nation over another. To all the world the evidence is clear of a people haunted in their own land by sorrow, unrest, and indignation – a people who everywhere else prove active and contented citizens. The call of America to freedom is again heard after a hundred and fifty years, a call to the 'universal dominion of right by a consent of free peoples', to a 'world safe for democracy, its peace planted on the trusted foundation of political liberty', to 'the rights of nations great and small, and the privileges of men everywhere to choose their way of life and obedience'.[18] In such a world the rule of one democracy by another is unthinkable. If self-government is to be won for the Irish nation under a monarchy, there must be a new relation of the Crown and the Irish nation. If there is to be a Commonwealth of peoples, it must be everywhere based on that equality of rights from which alone friendship and alliance can spring, and a conception of government must arise which rejects all idea of the subjection of a nation to a nation.

[18] The quotations come from Woodrow Wilson's (1856–1924) 'War Message' delivered before Congress on 2 April 1917.

27 Alice Stopford Green, *Ourselves Alone in Ulster*[1]

In a speech delivered on December 14, 1917, Mr. Lloyd George spoke of 'a definite and clear line of action, intelligible in consciences of a certain quality' – 'Ourselves first, ourselves last, ourselves all the time, and ourselves alone.' 'It is pretty mean', he added, 'but there are in every country men built that way, and you must reckon with them in the world.'[2]

A subtle question of casuistry could be raised as to how great a number of people must be united to make this motto either a despicable or an honourable one. It would doubtless be thought very creditable in an Empire. How about a United Kingdom – a Nation – or half a Province of a nation?[3]

This problem was decided without difficulty by north-east Ulster. The superiority of its wealth, the vigour of its creed, the self-confidence of its men – there were its sufficient credentials for a policy of 'ourselves first and last, ourselves all the time'. North-east Ulster had no wrongs or sufferings to proclaim to the human conscience. The only trouble was a story as old as the world, that in its proud prosperity it fell into those fearful apprehensions that haunt the way of the wealthy, driving them in every age to multiply safeguards and shelters for their riches and power. North-east Ulster required, in a changing world, that the guarantees of

[1] Alice Stopford Green, *Ourselves Alone in Ulster* (Dublin: Maunsel, 1918).

[2] In actual fact, only the Lords sat on 14 December 1917, but Lloyd George did deliver a speech at Gray's Inn in London in which he famously pressed the view that there 'is no half-way house between victory and defeat'. Reported in the *Times* 15 December 1917.

[3] The implication is that Ulster unionism was more narrowly 'Sinn Féin' (Ourselves Alone) than the Sinn Féin party.

its commercial interests should remain unchanged.[4] To secure this fixity of position rebellion under arms might be allowed.[5] If an illegal form of government, as near high treason as could be, could assure material safety, the only question was how to perfect scientific organization, with sufficient finances to withstand every strain.[6] Rebellion would be justified in one way only, by success. In the three phases of the northern movement it has preserved its character unchanged, and adhered to its first purpose.

I

The first phase of organized resistance was in response to the demand of three-fourths of Ireland for a grant of Home Rule to be enacted by the King and Parliament of the United Kingdom. In the heated controversies of 1910 the Right Hon. Thomas Andrews, P.C., Hon. Secretary of the Unionist Council, sounded his note of defiance by declaring that he, and he believed his colleagues, would rather be governed by Germany than by Patrick Ford and John Redmond and Company.[*] It was a time when the foreign policy of the Kaiser was a subject of the gravest alarm in England, and English anxieties were diligently exploited by the leaders of Unionism in Ulster.[7] Captain Watt, at a meeting of Londonderry Orangemen in August 1910, gave his warning to the new King just entered on his inheritance: 'It has been said that we want another King William the Third. Well, take care that the present King is not to be another King James, but I ask you to give King George a chance before you come to any

[4] North-east Ulster was one of the few regions in Ireland that had benefited from the Industrial Revolution. One of the arguments made against home rule was the loss of economic benefits by leaving the United Kingdom.

[5] She is referring to the militarisation of Ulster loyalists in 1913 who formed the Ulster Volunteer Force militia.

[6] In September 1912 the Ulster Unionist Council endorsed the creation of an illegal provisional government for Ulster in the event that home rule would come to pass.

[7] She is referring to the so-called 'naval race' between Britain and Germany prior to the First World War.

[*] Leaflet published by Ulster Liberal Association, *The Kaiser's Ulster Friends. Editorial note:* Thomas Andrews (1843–1916) was President of the Ulster Liberal Unionist Association (ULUA) between 1892 and 1916. The ULUA advocated home rule for Ulster. *The Kaiser's Ulster Friends: Pro-German Speeches by Prominent Carsonites* was a four-page document issued to highlight pro-German statements made by Ulster unionists during the home rule crisis. Patrick Ford (1837–1913) was an Irish American journalist, land reformer, and activist who founded the influential Irish American newspaper the *Irish World*. John Redmond (1856–1918) was the leader of the Irish Parliamentary Party which agitated for home rule.

decision.'* In January 1911, before the King was crowned, Captain Craig, M.P., warned England from his personal knowledge that Germany and the German Emperor would be preferred of the rules of John Redmond, Patrick Ford, and the Molly Maguires.† The year was one of continued excitement. The coronation in June was quickly followed by the 'Agadir' alarm in July.[8] It will be remembered that war with Germany was thought inevitable; officers were ready for their marching orders, and the fleet lay with sealed orders, waiting the signal to set sail. The close of the grave railway strike in England was determined by the extreme danger of the foreign situation, and the pressure which the Cabinet, under such perilous conditions, brought to bear on industrial magnates in England.[9] But the Government eschewed controversy with imperialists of the north-east Ulster quality. Rebellious incitements were freely carried on by 'Ourselves first and last'. In August Sir Edward Carson stated that the passing of the Home Rule Bill would be resisted by force‡ – a threat of civil war. 'If Home Rule were granted', said Mr. C. C. Craig, M.P., on October 17, 1911, 'it would not matter a row of pins whether they were separated from Great Britain or whether they were not.'§

From words they passed to deeds. The Ulster Unionist Council of four hundred members, representing Unionist Associations in Ulster constituencies, met under the Marquis of Londonderry in Belfast on September 25, 1911, and then resolved:# – (1) That it was their imperative duty to make arrangements for a Provisional Government of Ulster; and (2) That they hereby appointed a Commission which, in

8 The Agadir Crisis was sparked by the deployment of a force of French troops in the interior of Morocco in April 1911. Germany responded by sending a gunboat on 1 July.

9 A national two-day railway strike was organised in Britain in 1911.

* *Ib. Editorial note:* William III of England (1650–1702), popularly known as William of Orange, who defeated the Catholic King James II of England and Ireland in the Battle of the Boyne in 1690. The battle ensured the continuation of the Protestant ascendancy across the islands.

† *Ib. Editorial note:* the Molly Maguires were a secret society active in Ireland, Liverpool, and parts of the United States from the nineteenth century. In Ireland, they engaged in agrarian violence. It isn't clear if Green is referring to Captain James Craig (1st Viscount Craigavon) (1871–1940), the prominent Unionist businessman and politician who became first Prime Minister of Northern Ireland, or Captain Charles Craig discussed below.

‡ *Hansard*, Vol. 29, *p.* 988 (Speech in House, Aug. 8, 1911).

§ *Northern Whig*, Oct. 20, 1911. *Editorial note:* Charles Curtis Craig (1869–1960) was an Irish Unionist and later Ulster Unionist politician and MP for County Antrim from 1903 to 1929.

Northern Whig, Sept. 26, 1911. *Editorial note:* Charles Stewart Henry Vane-Tempest-Stewart (1878–1949), 7th Marquess of Londonderry.

consultation with Sir Edward Carson, should frame and submit a constitution for this Provisional Government. A silence of sixteen months followed; but the Council and secret Commission were not idle. An invigorated north-east Ulster declared its will to suppress all freedom of speech – even on the part of Ministers of the Crown – with regard to the government of Ireland. The Liberals had engaged the Ulster Hall in February 1912, for Mr. Winston Churchill, First Lord of the Admiralty, to address Belfast citizens on the subject of Home Rule.[10] The Harbour Board refused to allow Mr. Churchill a reception as First Lord. The Hall, as the property of the whole body of citizens, was up to that time open for all forms of discussion, Tory, Liberal, Labour, and Nationalist, as represented by Mr. Redmond and Mr. Dillon.[11] Now, however, the Orangemen seized the Hall, and held possession for a week before the meeting. No Nationalist, they declared, should sully the Ulster Hall by his presence; and to cries of 'Ulster will fight and Ulster will be right' the Unionists drove the Government representative to hold his meeting in a football ground, the Celtic Park.[*] By this first outrage they demonstrated to a humiliated Cabinet that Ulster Protestants could do as they liked.

With the second reading of the Home Rule Bill in April 1912, the education of north-east Ulster in rebellion became even more emphatic. The Rev. T. Walmesley spoke on August 13, of the prospect of the Sovereign coming one day for the ceremony of re-opening the Parliament of a free and reconciled Ireland.[†] 'If', he declared, 'our King should be there of his own free will, then I for one will feel myself justified in no longer regarding him as my King.' There were excited ceremonies, at which Sir Edward Carson was presented with a blackthorn stick adorned with the Orange and Freemason colours; and with the banner under which William III had gone to victory on the Boyne.[‡] Public emotion culminated on 'Ulster Day', September 28, 1912, when the 'Covenant' was signed by

[10] Winston Churchill (1874–1965) had visited Belfast to make a pro-home rule speech to nationalists in west Belfast and was threatened and nearly attacked by unionist mobs.

[11] John Dillon MP (1851–1927) was a leading member of the Irish Parliamentary Party.

[*] *Northern Whig*, Feb. 7, 1912. *Editorial note:* the phrase 'Ulster will fight and Ulster will be right' is attributed to Randolph Churchill (1849–95), Winston's father, after a famous anti-home rule speech in the Ulster Hall in 1886.

[†] Leaflet published by The Ulster Liberal Association, *The Kaiser's Ulster Friends*, *p.* 4.

[‡] *Annual Register*, Sept. 1912, *p.* 210

218,206 men, and 228,991 women in Ulster – 447,197 persons out of a population (counting those over 16) of 1,074,000.[12]

The proceedings of the Ulster Unionist Council meanwhile were carried on in private. Nothing more was publicly heard of the 'Special Commission' of 1911 till the third reading of the Home Rule Bill in January 1913. Then on January 31 the Council announced the passing by them of a notable resolution:[*] – 'We ratify and confirm the further steps so far taken by the Special Commission, and approve of the draft resolutions and articles of the Ulster Provisional Government this day submitted to us, and appoint the members of the Special Commission to act as the Executive thereunder.' The work of the Commission remained secret. No hint of the terms of the articles and resolutions was permitted to leak out. The Council was, in fact, a close corporation, the members of which were selected from classes prominent in the older fights for dominance and committed to the tradition of Ascendancy – peers, land-owners, militia officers, ecclesiastics, and by degrees capitalists and employers. There was no pretence of representation as generally understood. Members were not chosen by the working-classes, nor even by public bodies over which Unionists had control, such as boards of guardians, urban councils, or the like; and in counties such as Cavan, Monaghan, and Donegal, which were strongly represented, not one of the members could have been openly elected by the people on his merits. A cynic might have suggested that it was a last bid of the aristocratic and superior classes, lay and ecclesiastical, in alliance with English Tories, to guide the people for their good. The *Times* on May 9, 1913, justified the high purpose of their aristocratic and religious mission. 'The occasion has been used to strengthen the conservatism of Ulster – I do not use the word in a party sense. By disciplining the Ulster democracy, and by teaching it to look up to them as its natural leaders, the clergy and gentry are providing against the spread of Revolutionary doctrine and free thought.'

So efficient and well-drilled a scheme of establishing the superior classes in control secured, in fact, the utmost sympathy among the English nobility and clergy, expressed in vast sums of money. The English upper classes recognized the wholesome influence of the 'natural leaders' of Belfast, that vast industrial city where labour had been long accustomed

[12] The Covenant was signed by 237,368 men and the accompanying Women's Declaration by 234,046 women.

[*] *Northern Whig*, Feb. 1, 1913.

to no representation; unless of late years when Protestant Unionist workers found themselves forced to invoke in any special distress the aid of a Catholic Nationalist member of Parliament. In north-east Ulster might be seen the model of discipline by the clergy and gentry, its natural leaders.

Loyalty to the Crown was no part of the new conservative mission, except on terms that the Crown accepted the decisions of the north-east Ulster Unionists. 'If Home Rule is passed I would not care whether the British Empire went to smash or not', said the Rev. Chancellor Hobson on Easter Monday, 1913.* The threat of Germany was still freely used. Mr. James Chambers, M.P. for South Belfast, suggested it to his constituents on May 23, 1913.† 'As regards the future, what if a day should come when Ireland would be clamouring for independence complete and thorough from Great Britain? … What side would they take then? (A voice: "Germany".) He (Mr. Chambers) bound no man to his opinions. They owed to England allegiance, loyalty, and gratitude; but if England cast them off then he reserved the right as a betrayed man to say "I shall act as I have a right to act. I shall sing no longer 'God save the King'" … He said there solemnly that the day England cast him off and despised his loyalty and allegiance, that day he would say: "England, I will laugh at your calamity, I will mock when your fear cometh."' *The Irish Churchman* on November 14, 1913,‡ gave prominence to a letter addressed to it: 'It may not be known to the rank and file of Unionists that we have the offer of aid from a powerful Continental monarch who, if Home Rule is forced on the Protestants of Ireland, is prepared to send an army sufficient to release England of any further trouble in Ireland by attaching it to his dominion, believing, as he does, that if our King breaks his Coronation Oath by signing the Home Rule Bill he will, by so doing, have forfeited his claim to rule Ireland. And should our King sign the Home Rule Bill the Protestants of Ireland will welcome this Continental deliverer as their forefathers, under similar circumstances, did once before.' 'Can King George sign the Home Rule Bill?' ran an open letter to Mr. Asquith in the leading Unionist paper in Mr. Barrie's constituency in July 1913.§ 'Let him

* *Portadown News*, March 29, 1913.

† *Belfast Newsletter*, May 24, 1913. *Editorial note:* James Chambers (1863–1917) was an Irish barrister and ardent Unionist politician.

‡ Letter signed 'H.G'. in *Irish Churchman*, Nov. 14, 1913.

§ Open letter to Mr. Asquith in Coleraine Constitution, July 1913. *Editorial note:* Herbert H. Asquith (1852–1928), Liberal MP and Prime Minister from 1908 to 1916. Hugh T. Barrie (1860–1922) was a Scottish-born businessman and politician who served as MP for North Londonderry.

do so, and his Empire shall perish as true as God rules Heaven … Therefore let King George sign the Home Rule Bill – he is no longer my King.' Such phrases were repeated on all sides in full security. Unionists had, and rightly, no apprehension of blame. They have long known that public opinion in England can never be roused to alarm or indignation by any Protestant propaganda, whatever be its purpose or the violence of its methods. An unquestioning trust has always rewarded Orange Lodges.

Inspirited by uninterrupted success and the applause of English Tories, the party of north-east Ulster opened a further enterprise. The Unionist Council met on September 24, 1913, in the Ulster Hall, to decree itself the Central Authority of the Provisional Government, and its Standing Committee of seventy-six was declared to be the Executive Committee of the Provisional Government of Ulster.* Sir Edward Carson was appointed head of the Central Authority, with a multitude of Committees and Boards under him. There were the Executive Committee, Military Council, Ulster Volunteer Committee, Volunteer Advisory-Board, Personnel Board, Supply Board, Medical Board, Finance and Business Committee, Legal Committee, Education Committee, Publication and Literary Committee, Customs and Excise Committee, Post Office Committee. Chaplains were appointed, and an Assessor. Power was given to Committees to co-opt a member or members of the Ulster Women's Unionist Council.

No statement was made as to the powers and functions of either the central authority or subordinate boards and committees. These, the public were told, 'shall be as defined hereafter'. Sir Edward Carson was chairman of every committee and board, the only link between them so far as outsiders knew. Not one working man was selected in this one-sided State – no representative of Labour, Democracy, or Liberalism. Ministers of religion might find a place by virtue of high office in Freemason or Orange bodies. All members of the various committees were local Unionist leaders, arbitrarily appointed without consulting popular opinion. It was Dublin Castle over again without even the pretence of a Westminster Parliament as the final authority.

This Provisional Government was ready to be called into full working order at the command of Sir Edward Carson. For the present it exerted a complete authority as the organized Unionist Council. It found a home in the old City Hall of Belfast, heavily subsidized by the Corporation. The leaders, familiar with the old habit of the diplomatic craft by which States

* *Northern Whig*, Sept. 25, 1913.

are led, exploited (with their allies) all the chances of secret politics, and spent their unlimited resources with rich freedom and equal dexterity. From time to time public meetings were held to announce the general decisions of the new Ulster Government, while the administration was skilfully carried out in camera. Fiery denunciations of the King and Parliament of England, and of all the rest of Ireland, along with the Pope, were addressed to the public. The immense funds at the disposal of the governing body made it easy to arrange exhilarating festivals and gatherings for the encouragement of the people. The State had been cemented by a sworn Covenant, and the attendant religious ceremonies emphasized the doctrine of a peculiar people, chosen by a special Deity. 'O God', ran the prayer of one of the greatest Presbyterian assemblies in a chief centre of Covenanters, who had met on the great day of signing to consecrate their work, 'O God, remember that Thou art not a God like other gods.'* The naturally militant and aggressive character of a 'chosen people' was emphasized by a multitude of sermons in which, so far as we can judge from those printed in the papers, the texts were invariably taken from the warlike incitements of Old Testament warriors and prophets, while only two verses were adopted by the leading preachers from the New Testament of the Christian faith: 'I am not come to send peace but a sword': 'He that hath no sword let him sell his cloak and buy one.' In such a temper the *Times* saw a spiritual hope. 'The Covenant', it wrote on May 3, 1913, 'was a mystical affirmation. … Ulster seemed to enter into an offensive and defensive alliance with the Deity.' Ministers of the various creeds, after long severance, found their meeting-place in a common political faith – the faith which was expressed later by the Protestant potentate who was to them the spiritual heir of the pious William of the Boyne: 'The German people has in the Lord of Creation above an unconditional and avowed Ally on whom it can absolutely rely.'

To complete the attributes of a self-contained State an army was needed. Unionist Clubs had long been formed throughout the country, whose members were easily ranged into corps of Volunteer soldiers. They were said to number 60,000 when reviewed by the new Ulster Provisional Government. It was now held necessary to replace Volunteers with wooden rifles and cannon by troops armed for active service with modern weapons. The creation of such an army was certainly illegal. But mere illegality was not an obstacle to stop the march of Ulster. In June 1913, a large

* Heard by the writer. Sir E. Carson was described at a luncheon of the Nonconformist Unionist Association in London, as the best embodiment, at that moment, of the ancient spirit of Nonconformity. – *Annual Register*, 1913, *p.* 206.

consignment of arms was imported to Belfast as 'electrical plant'.* Sir Edward Carson already anticipated 'Der Tag'. 'I like', he said on August 3, 1913, 'to get nearer the enemy.† I like to see the men are preparing for what I call the Great Day'. A Volunteer Force numbering according to report 100,000, or presently 200,000 men, was equipped by the Ulster Provisional Government on a very sumptuous scale, with khaki uniforms, military boots, motor-cycles, rifles, machine-guns, and all other necessaries. A couple of Germans assisted in their training.‡ An indemnity fund of £1,000,000 was announced, to indemnify Volunteers for loss of life and property. Ambulances and nurses were provided.§ Sir Edward Carson stated that to his personal knowledge 'The forces of the Crown were already dividing into hostile camps'.# Imperialist and Unionist Ulster set no limits to its defiance of the Imperial Government, encouraged by their English friends. Sir Edward Carson's lieutenant, the 'Galloper' F. E. Smith, speaking in County Antrim on September 21, said if war began in Ulster 'From that moment we hold ourselves absolved from all allegiance to this Government. From that moment we on our part will say to our fellows in England: "To your tents, O Israel." From that moment we shall stand side by side with you refusing to recognise any law.'~ Friends

* An action was brought by Belfast gunsmiths against the port officials for detaining arms consigned to the plaintiffs at Hamburg, on Dec. 18, 1913. *Annual Register*, March 1914, *p.* 66. In May and June 1914, the *Northern Whig* records that two hundred and forty sacks of cartridges were found in a cargo of cement, and Mauser rifles and ammunition to the value of £1,200 concealed in a furniture van with sides of false sheeting. They were entering into a 'very extreme course', Sir E. Carson allowed later, 'a course which could only be justified because we were being singled out for exceptional treatment of betrayal'. – *Irish Times*, Feb. 4, 1918.

† 'I like to get near the enemy. We are coming near them in the near future, and I like to see that men are preparing for what I call the great day.' – *Northern Whig*, Aug. 4, 1913.

‡ Leaflet published by Ulster Liberal Association, *The Kaiser's Ulster Friends*, *p.* 3.

§ *Annual Register*, 1913, *p.* 205. *Times*, Sept. 27, 1913.

\# *Northern Whig*, Sept. 25, 1913. In accepting office as head of the Provisional Government, Sir E. Carson declared that Government policy would have a disastrous effect on the forces of the Crown, since he knew from his correspondence that these were already dividing into hostile camps. Speaking at Manchester he stated that since the army must obey lawful orders politicians must see that the passing of the Bill should not be enforced. – *Times*, Dec. 3, 1913. *Annual Register*, 1913, *p.* 249.

~ *Northern Whig*, Sept. 21, 1913. 'If I were an Ulster Protestant I would rather be ruled from Constantinople, by the Sultan of Turkey, than by a politician like Mr. Devlin.' Belfast, July 12, 1912. Leaflet published by Ulster Liberal Association, *The Kaiser's Ulster Friends*. *Editorial note:* F. E. Smith refers to Frederick Edwin Smith (1872–1930), 1st Earl of Birkenhead, a prominent Conservative and critic of Irish nationalism. The quotation is taken from 1 Kings 12:16. Joseph Devlin (1871–1934) was a leading Nationalist MP in the Irish Parliamentary Party and represented the northern nationalists.

in England proposed by the help of Ulster to smash the Territorials, who were afterwards to play so great a part in the war. *The Observer* of November 30, 1913, 'urged that all Unionist Lords Lieutenant should resign their position as heads of the County Territorial Associations', that 'every Unionist should prepare to leave the Territorials'; and that 'the whole of Unionist influence throughout the country ought to be used to prevent recruits from joining so long as there is the slightest threat of coercing Ulster'. In defence of Protestant Unionism, Sir Edward Carson declared himself ready to break all laws.* He professed scorn and defiance of anything done 'down in a little place called Westminster'. His insolences were studied: 'I saw', he declared in the Ulster Hall, 'Mr. Lloyd George in his robes as Chancellor of the Exchequer, and I almost mistook him for a gentleman.' Carson's followers blatantly announced their preference for a Protestant German ruler who would revive the glorious and immortal memory of an older William.[13] Mr. Chambers, Solicitor-General for Ireland, gave it to be understood that he was in negotiation with the German Chancellor for the transfer of Ulster if necessary, owing to its resolve to be attached to a strictly Protestant Power. When he proclaimed in the high street of his constituency in Belfast, that if English George signed the bill he was for the German William, the vaunt was repeated on all sides.

An ignoble form of north-east Ulster bigotry manifested itself in a common cry that Catholics were all very well in their place as hewers of wood and drawers of water,† but under the Ulster Provisional Government no Catholic should be employed in Belfast. The battle in the ship-yards is well remembered with its Catholic boycott and violent expulsion of the Catholic workingmen. All Catholics, in fact, fled or were withdrawn from the ship-yards for many months, to protect them from

[13] I.e. William III of Orange.

* At the Women's Amalgamated Unionist and Tariff Reform Association, London, June 24, 1912 (as quoted by leaflet Ulster Liberal Association, *The Kaiser's Ulster Friends*), Sir E. Carson stated – 'regarding the pronouncement of policy of the Government in relation to Ulster, he intended when he went over there to break every law that was possible. Let the Government take their own course. He was not a bit afraid of them, for a more wretched, miserable, time-serving opportunist lot never before sat in Parliament.' 'If it is illegal we don't mind that.' – *Northern Whig*, Aug. 5, 1912.

'For his own part he knew nothing of legality or illegality … All he thought of was his Covenant. His Covenant to him was the text and the foundation of what was illegality and what was legality, and everything that was necessary to carry out his Covenant he believed in his conscience he was under Heaven entitled to do.' – *Northern Whig*, July 14, 1914.

† See Redmond's speech, at Manchester, quoting the *Belfast Newsletter*. *Annual Register*, 1913, *p*. 234.

the violence of the Protestant mob. Sir Edward Carson said no word in condemnation of this brutality, nor did any minister of religion, though Belfast never failed in denouncing outrages in the South and West.*

In fact the Government of the half-province justified the boast that it was ready to break all laws of the United Kingdom. A Royal Proclamation had in December, 1913, forbidden the importing of arms. Sir Edward Carson admitted no such control. The departure of the *Fanny* from Hamburg, in 1914, laden with arms for the new army was foreshadowed in the papers three weeks before its arrival at Larne in April 1914.† All the Volunteers were called out. They guarded Belfast, where a decoy-boat was sent in to mislead the police. They surrounded Larne and Bangor and shut them out from 'the enemy'. At the famous gun-running into the Irish harbour the Provisional Government took possession of the King's high-roads, ran telegraph wires to earth, confined the police to barracks, seized harbours, locked up officials of the customs, rounded up suspected Nationalists and locked them in a barn, and generally broke the public laws of sea and land. Admirals, generals, officials of the coast-guard, of police, of the post-office, and telegraph service, all connived at the lawless deeds. Public law was suspended. Evidently at Larne the Provisional Government not merely claimed but exercised the right to rebel. The fact was emphasized on April 29 in a speech by Major Crawford, the captain of the *Fanny*, to a Unionist Club in County Down: 'If they were put out of the Union … he would infinitely prefer to change his allegiance right over to the Emperor of Germany, or any one else who had got a proper and stable government.'‡

England was startled. Her Prime Minister in Parliament formally denounced the whole proceeding at Larne, as 'an unprecedented outrage'.§ The answer of the north-east Ulster Government to English tremors was

* In July 1912. See legal proceedings following the onslaught on Catholic workingmen; *Northern Whig*, Jan. 13 and 16, 1913; and *Evening Telegraph*, Nov. 1912; April 1913. (McCotter and others *v. Evening Telegraph.*) The Catholics have not even yet been restored to Workman and Clark's in their old numbers.

† Sir Edward Carson's letter to the papers asked for funds in view of a 'more forward movement', 'the climax of all we have been aiming at', 'involving action almost unprecedented'. – *Northern Whig*, March 14, 1914. The gun-running is described in the *Irish Volunteer*, May 2, 1914, *p.* 9.

‡ *North Down Herald*, May 3, 1912.

§ The words were 'this grave and unprecedented outrage'. The Government promised to undertake, without delay, appropriate steps to vindicate the authority of the law, and protect officers and servants of the King, and His Majesty's subjects in the exercise of their duty, and in the enjoyment of their legal rights. It was admitted that a coastguardsman died in the performance of his duty. – *Hansard*, Vol. 61, *p.* 1348.

unhesitating. Captain Craig, M.P., on July 9, 1914, read for the first time openly the preamble to the Constitution of the Ulster Provisional Government. The people, it stated, of the counties and places represented in the Ulster Unionist Council undertook to resist to the utmost the powers to be exercised over them by a Nationalist Government, and resolved if Home Rule was set up to ignore the Irish Parliament, and to assume and exercise all powers necessary for the government of Ulster, pending the restoration of direct Imperial government.[*] Fresh military preparations were made for the army, now said to have reached 200,000 men. Machine guns were landed, and rest stations arranged for refugees flying from the threatened civil war. A resolution was proposed by Lord Londonderry, stating that preparations would be made to resist by force and every other method decrees of any Nationalist Parliament that might be established.[†] At Larne, on July 11, Sir Edward Carson first announced the name of the pirate hero of the *Fanny*, expounded the lesson of Larne, lauded the organizers of the gun-running, classing himself among them, and directed the volunteers to be ready, 'if not for peace with honour, for war with honour'.[‡] The Government was again flouted in the Belfast celebration of the glorious Twelfth of July.[14] The black pirate flag was hoisted on the gate of the chief gun-runner, and as the procession passed in its multitudinous glory, Sir Edward Carson, called on to salute the lawless emblem, rose in his carriage laden with orange lilies, and more than once bowed low, to tumultuous cheers, amid flags of the Brethren and the 'open Bibles' of wood borne aloft by the Orange Lodges in testimony of their rigid creed.[§] He led the march to Drumbeg of 70,000 men, where he boasted of the army mutiny and the Larne triumph.[#] There was a series of reviews. Among the forty reporters said to be gathered in Belfast for the display, three or four Germans watched the proceedings, and Baron von Kuhlmann, of the German Embassy, now the German Secretary for Foreign Affairs, arrived quietly, without information given to the Press, as an

[14] The victory of William III over James II was secured at the Battle of the Boyne on 12 July 1690 and has been celebrated by Irish Protestants since the early eighteenth century.

[*] *Annual Register*, 1914, *p.* 152.

[†] The resolution was proposed at a meeting on July 11, the Twelfth being a Sunday. See *Northern Whig*, July 11–13, 1914.

[‡] *Northern Whig*, July 13, 1914.

[§] Not mentioned in the Press. Witnessed by the writer.

[#] He defied the Government to prosecute them, and charged it with plots to arrest some of them as a sop to John Redmond and his cattle-drivers and boycotters. *Northern Whig*, July 14, 1914. *Editorial note:* Drumbeg is a small village in Co. Down.

honoured guest, to view the magnitude of the Protestant preparations for Civil War.[*] According to the boast of the Covenanting Government, the force raised to defy the Government at Westminster was so furnished and drilled as to be ready at any moment to take the field. English generals and English Press-men proclaimed aloud that the troops exceeded any army in training, appearance and equipment. Their defiant quality was shown the day after the Conference at Buckingham Palace had broken up, when on July 25 the Provisional Government of Ulster organized a parade through Belfast of 5,000 men in khaki, with bands, rifles, and machine-guns, all traffic in the streets being held up officially for the display.[†]

Sensational public shows, on however costly a scale of European advertisement, were but the decorative ornaments of methodical and hard-cut business. The English War Office, moved by some natural fears that the new 'Army' might be tempted in the interests of Ulster to appropriate some of the military stores collected in certain mobilization centres, had before these events proposed to send military guards to protect their own material, and had thought it prudent to appoint General Sir Neville MacCready to Belfast as military governor in reserve, in case the magistrates refused to perform their duty.[15] He was received with shouts of 'Butcher MacCready'.[‡] Cries of agonised terror resounded, 'The English Government had planned a "pogrom"', 'There was to be a massacre of Protestants.' The country was blazing with excitement when the Provisional Government sprang to the rescue. It possessed unexploited resources in certain lofty connexions, and the wide-spread influences of Orange and Freemason propaganda in high circles were available to organize a secret conspiracy throughout the British Army and Navy, and even the Air Force, that they should stand on the side of north-east Ulster in all eventualities, and refuse to act against her. To their temporary annoyance the plot was accidently revealed early in 1914 by the notorious 'Curragh mutiny',[§] when the illegal complicity of generals and officers

[15] Major General Sir Cecil Frederick Nevil Macready (1862–1946) was a senior British Army officer appointed to the rank of General following the 'Curragh Incident'.

[*] See *Northern Whig*, March 23, 1917.

[†] Guns which had been distributed over the country were systematically collected from all parts to add to the formidable show of force. *Northern Whig*, July 27, 1914.

[‡] Sir E. Carson used the words 'pogrom plot' in his speech on Ulster Day 1914. – *Northern Whig*. For 'pogrom' to make 'the red blood flow' see leading article, *Ib.*, July 27, 1914.

[§] March 20. See *Annual Register*, 1914, *p.* 55–66, 69, which gives a summary and references. For questions in the House see *Hansard*, Vol. 61, *p.* 1347. Mr. Asquith took charge of the War Office from March 30 to August 5.

became known, whose military discipline had been degraded at the bidding of faction cries, and whose larger outlook had been eclipsed by the glamour of old ascendancies.[16] The Prime Minister took charge of the War Office. But the discomfiture of the Provisional Government was only momentary. The Prime Minister returned to his usual position. Before the scientific organization and the warlike threats of the Unionist Council, the Government of the United Kingdom, over-awed and intimidated, succumbed and laid down all opposition.

II

The outbreak of war opened the second scene in the drama of the Provisional Government. The Council of the half-province, professing an undying loyalty to the Imperial Government which it had vanquished, became the Mayor of the Palace to the defeated powers of Westminster. It consented to fill the chief places of the Law, and to guide the Imperial Cabinet according to the Ulster formulae. Sir Edward Carson and Mr. F. E. Smith undertook as Attorney and Solicitor-General to deal in England with any rebellious-minded persons less successful than themselves; and Mr. Campbell and Mr. William Moore were in due time made Lord Chief Justice and Judge of the High Court in Ireland.[17] The Higher Policy was thus proclaimed identical with the Higher Law, to the confusion of all objectors. In course of affairs Sir Edward Carson passed to the War Cabinet, the Admiralty, and finally to the political Propaganda, by which foreign nations were instructed as to what was or was not laudable 'rebellion' in Ireland.[*]

All this implied no change in Sir Edward Carson's views, as north-east Ulster might see when on a visit to Ireland as Minister of the Crown, he gracefully accepted the gift of a silver model of the *Fanny*.[†] Meanwhile

[16] The Curragh Mutiny, or Curragh Incident, occurred on 20 March 1914 when senior officers at the main British military base in Ireland indicated their refusal to be used to tackle the Ulster Volunteers in the event of their resistance to home rule.

[17] Sir William Moore (1864–1944) was a Unionist member of the House of Commons from Antrim and a judge.

[*] Sir E. Carson was Attorney-General in the Government of 1915; First Lord of the Admiralty in the next Government of 1916. *Editorial note:* the first government (from May 1915) was a wartime coalition led by Liberal prime minister, Herbert H. Asquith. The second was a smaller and largely Unionist war cabinet created in December 1916 and was led by Liberal Prime Minister David Lloyd George.

[†] The presentation of the model of the notorious gun-running privateer of the Provisional Government was made in the Ulster Volunteer Hospital in the presence of Lady Londonderry.

in Belfast itself the Ulster Provisional Government was maintained in full force, and the second stage of the north-east movement was not less efficiently directed than the first. The Orange and Unionist Press maintained their policy of threats. The *Northern Whig* on August 24, reminded 'three-fourths of the people of Ulster' (an amazing calculation) that if the Home Rule Bill became an Act they 'must become either traitors to the Covenant which they have solemnly signed or rebels to the Crown'. On the next day the *Belfast Evening Telegraph* commented on the suggestion to put the Home Rule Bill upon the Statute Book with a time reservation: 'To do that would create a serious position. It would drive Ulster Loyalists into this position, that much as they desire to assist Britain's armed forces abroad at this juncture, and much as their help in that direction is needed, they would be compelled, through the Government's action, to remain here for the defence of their hearths and homes against an enemy no less deadly and embittered.' The Unionist Council meanwhile undertook no recruiting for the war.* There was a good deal of local effort, on natural and liberal lines, where Protestants and Catholics enlisted together, and sent out men to fight and die at Suvla Bay – all this apart from any direction of Sir Edward Carson.[18] Recruiting

[18] Suvla Bay was on the Aegean coast of the Gallipoli peninsula and was the location chosen for an amphibious landing, beginning on 6 August 1915, by British imperial forces. It aimed to knock the Ottoman Empire out of the war and open supply routes to Russia. The disastrous campaign resulted in heavy casualties, not least for Irish Protestant and Catholic volunteers who had joined the 10th (Irish) Division.

* A leader in the *Northern Whig* stated that there had been little recruiting in Ulster, for which the Government policy was to blame. Sept. 2, 1914. A meeting was held in Belfast, August 1914, to consider the war problem. Sir E. Carson wrote they would show 'without any bartering of conditions, that the cause of Great Britain is our cause ... and that we will make common cause, and suffer all sacrifices'. Captain J. Craig stated that he, with Sir E. Carson, were arranging the best terms that could be fixed for the Volunteer Force to offer its services. They were ready to go forward at any length, 'trusting in the first instance to Sir E. Carson to preserve their political heritage'. – *Northern Whig*, Aug. 8, 1914. Observe Sir E. Carson's statement on Feb. 3, 1918: 'Let those who talk of Ulster's unreasonableness remember this – that the distinct promise *we got from the Prime Minister of the day, and by the House of Commons*, was that the question of Home Rule should stand over until the war was ended. *Then we got up our splendid Ulster Division.*' – *Irish Times*, Feb. 4, 1918. The Volunteer Force was said to number 80,000 drilled and armed men. – *Northern Whig*, Aug. 12. There was a parade of 300 who offered for foreign service, and 700 for home defence. – *Ib.*, Aug. 17. Appeals were made constantly for contributions to the Prince of Wales' Fund. – *Ib.*, Aug. 14, 15, 18, 22, 28. A letter from Sir E. Carson commending the Ulster Defence Fund for 'our efforts to maintain our position in the United Kingdom' was inserted twice. – *Ib.*, Aug. 13, 25.

was in fact officially frowned on until the leader had given the word.[19] A letter written by Captain Arthur O'Neill from the front urging men to enlist was refused by a Unionist paper, because Sir Edward Carson had made no pronouncement. In Tyrone, one who was urgent in calling for recruits was accused of 'spoiling the game' before his leader had spoken. Covenanters declared that if the Home Rule Bill was signed there would not be a single man sent from Ulster to the war. Strange scenes of excitement were reported. Sir Edward Carson arrived unannounced in Belfast on September 1[*] to explain the bargain he had completed with the War Office before authorizing the use of Ulster troops. After some days of private negotiations he stated the terms on September 4, at a meeting of the Unionist Association, and afterwards at a public meeting. The Volunteers were to form a separate division, under their old officers, and to have back any of their officers who had had to mobilize. As for the fear of danger at home, he told them from 20,000 to 30,000 soldiers could hold Ulster, and the Volunteer force at home would be kept efficient to repel those who would try to invade their country.[†] At Larne he renewed this assurance: 'I am proud of the men in the Ulster Volunteers – not only those who are enlisting, *but those who are staying at home*, to save us from a tyranny to which we will never submit.'[‡] His first promise was a division maintained as a separate and complete unit, without being attached

[19] Contrary to the myth that Ulster Protestants rallied to the flag from the outset of the conflict, there was considerable hesitancy in early months to leave Ulster in case home rule were suddenly implemented.

[*] The *Northern Whig* announced that Sir Edward Carson had arrived to offer the Ulster Unionist Association 'a scheme sanctioned by the War Office, whereby the members of the Ulster Volunteer Force may be able to assist in defending their country in the present great crisis'. 'If the Ulster Volunteers agree to fight for the King and the Empire now, afterwards they will, if necessary, also fight for Ulster, and with this intention they must go on strengthening their organization and increasing their numbers.' – *Northern Whig*, Sept. 2, 1914.

[†] At the parade of the North Belfast Regiment, Sir E. Carson promised: 'I and those who remain behind will take care that Ulster is no invaded province'. – *Northern Whig*, Sept. 4, 5, 1914. Sir E. Carson, in justifying his resignation from the Cabinet, laid stress on his position: 'I am a Covenanter.' This placed him in a dual capacity, for while trying to make out the best course the Government ought to adopt, on the other hand he would be thinking how that was to affect his Covenant and his pledges to the people of Ulster. He was enabled to remain in the Government as long as he did because 'I was perfectly well aware that those with whom I had Covenants in this province would wish, above all things, that I should put aside all questions of local interest.' He repudiated the idea of being 'a traitor to Ulster and a breaker of my Covenant'. – *Irish Times*, Feb. 4, 1918.

[‡] *Northern Whig*, Sept. 8, 1914.

to any other division. The second pledge was an assurance that the policy of the Ulster Provisional Government and the Covenant would suffer no slightest injury: 'I promise you that I will reorganize the Volunteers, and that when you come back you will not find Home Rule in Ulster.' By these emphatic pledges the policy was confirmed of ourselves first, ourselves last, ourselves all the time.

The War Office kept to its pledge of a separate unit. The Ulster Volunteer Force were allowed, contrary to army rules, to retain their special cap badges, and flags worked for their use. But the essential bond of union lay in the signing of the Covenant, which was enforced on every member who joined the new division. In compelling the War Office to admit a separate and complete unit bound by a special political oath – a course unfamiliar in modern armies since Cromwell's time – Sir Edward Carson had won a notable victory for the Provisional Government of north-east Ulster.[20] The triumph over the unity of the King's Imperial forces had indeed its natural effect on discipline, as may be illustrated by the Inniskillings, whose battalions, like the Irish Rifles, are divided between the Ulster Division and the Irish Division in the army.[21] It was the Covenanting Inniskillings, under the protection of the Provisional Government, who felt at liberty to riot through Enniskillen trampling under foot and insulting Irish emblems.[*] Meanwhile in Ulster no time was lost in affirming Sir Edward Carson's second pledge as to the security of the Volunteers and of the Covenanters. On the anniversary of Ulster Day, September 28, 1914, he in Belfast made clear to his followers the purpose of the Provisional Government. 'What I propose to do' (that is after the war) 'is to summon the Provisional Government and repeal the Home

[20] Oliver Cromwell (1599–1658) brought Ireland into an 'incorporating' union with Britain in the aftermath of the military conquest of the island, which took place between 1649 and 1653.

[21] The Royal Inniskilling Fusiliers was an Irish regiment of the British Army between 1881 and 1968. The Royal Irish Rifles was an infantry rifle regiment likewise created in 1881. It became the Royal Ulster Rifles in 1921.

[*] The covenanters added the usual curses for the Pope. The outrage was on October 16, 1917. The account given in the long correspondence of Archdeacon Keown with Sir Bryan Mahon was not published till December 15, 1917. It is there stated that Catholics of Enniskillen had made a larger contribution to the fighting force of the war than all other religious denominations of the town combined. – *Irish Times*, Dec. 15, 1917. *Editorial note:* there is a discrepancy in the original text regarding what point this note refers to, but it seems likely to refer to this point, hence it has been moved here. Archdeacon Patrick Keown was a parish priest in Enniskillen, a town in Co. Fermanagh, from 1909 to 1919. Bryan Mahon (1862–1930) commanded the 10th (Irish) Division in the Great War.

Rule Bill, and I propose in the same act to enact that it is the duty of the Volunteers to see that the Act shall never have effect in Ulster ... Our Volunteers who cannot go abroad will go on with the work at home. We have plenty of guns, and we are going to keep them. We are afraid of nothing.'*

Discipline was enforced with a stern hand. Even Mr. F. E. Smith, 'the Galloper', was sternly rebuked by the *Northern Whig* for a temporary lapse, in his imperial enthusiasm, from the pure doctrine of the 'natural leaders' of Ulster arrayed against 'the spread of Revolutionary doctrine and free thought'. He was accused of attempting to recruit for the British army without strict adherence to the tactics of Sir Edward Carson, by addressing a recruiting meeting at Liverpool along with leading Radicals. His intention was condemned by 'the opinion of leading Unionists as to the impropriety of his conduct', and his apology was rejected. 'We hope he will reconsider his decision, and that no other leading Unionists will be found on the platforms with Radicals.'† Sir Edward Carson for his part refused to stand with Mr. Redmond at a recruiting meeting in Newry.‡ All necessary steps were taken to reinforce the militant Covenanters. Unionists over military age, or not inclined to join the army, were encouraged to take on Ulster Volunteer Force uniform and equipment, and fill up the ranks. While it was understood that the outgoing troops would on their return be used to enforce all the demands of the Covenanters – the more efficiently, as Sir Edward Carson explained, from actual experience and discipline in war – the home army was kept in being with its arms, ammunition, and equipment. The able head of the cycle corps was retained in Belfast in a good position, at a time when advertisements were posted for weeks at all the cinemas in Dublin and elsewhere calling

* The words of Sir Edward Carson to Unionist Council were: – 'And I propose if necessary... that their first Act shall be to repeal the Home Rule Act as regards Ulster. And I propose in the same Act to enact that it is the duty of the Volunteers to see that no Act, or no attempt at an Act, under that Bill shall ever have effect in Ulster.' At a public meeting he promised that he and the other leaders would devote themselves 'heart and soul to maintaining the organization intact, so that we may repel any invader who dares to come and try to interfere with us'. He repeated the words: 'We have got the men, we have got the guns – and we are going to keep the guns – and therefore what have we to be afraid of?' – *Northern Whig*, Sept. 29, 1914.

† Mr. F. E. Smith spoke at Liverpool on Sept. 21, along with Mr. T. P. O'Connor. In view of the recent co-operation of these two speakers in America, the *Northern Whig* objection is interesting. – *Northern Whig*, Sept. 17, 1914. *Editorial note:* Thomas Power O'Connor (1848–1929) was the Irish Parliamentary Party MP for Liverpool.

‡ The meeting was not held, as Sir E. Carson did not see any need for Mr. Redmond's proposal. It was commented on in the papers early in 1915.

for motor cyclists for the Ulster Division. When the War Office was in distress for supplies, if the Covenanters released to it some of their vast stores of khaki uniforms, etc., it was at prices which were no disadvantage to themselves. By the aid of a submissive Cabinet at Westminster all who had connived at the Larne 'outrage' from generals downwards were given military promotion. As the correspondent of the *Manchester Guardian* pointed out on January 17, 1917, the Larne gun-running won as many titles, honours, and offices for its organizers and patrons as if it had been an incident in the first battle of Ypres.[22] The major who had brought the *Fanny* into harbour was raised to the rank of Colonel, retained at the centre of action in Belfast, and made head of the Commissariat. In recognition of the unparalleled outrage not only the military but all other consenting officials were well provided for; not one was left derelict.[*] There was thus in the numerous and lucrative administrative posts at home an organization ready for future emergencies. The Protestant Primate illustrated the unity of the Ulster Volunteer Force at home and abroad, which he said could not be better described than in the words of Holy Writ: 'There were some that went forth to the battle, and others that tarried with the stuff.' The troops who remained at home were carefully linked with their comrades who had joined the army. Practically all the Volunteer officers had immediately obtained army commissions, without further question, as their indubitable right. The roll of honour gave not only the soldier's place in the British army, but his rank in the Ulster Volunteers. The Volunteers at home were as before commended to the good offices of the English army of the old intrigue. Their friends of the Curragh Mutiny were not forgotten, and in view of future emergencies special Christmas boxes of cigarettes, with encouraging mottoes and remembrances, were sent from Belfast to the officers and privates concerned.[†] A leading Liberal paper in England refused to allow any information of this incident lest it should be accused of breaking the 'truce'

[22] The Battle of Ypres (19 October – 22 November 1914) involved a series of engagements around the Belgian city between the German Army and Allied forces.

[*] Among numerous instances one may be given as an illustration. The 'Competent Military Authority' in Belfast is Brigadier-General Hackett Pain, who before the war was Chief of the Staff of the Ulster Force, which had been illegally organized and armed with rifles from Germany for the purpose of resisting His Majesty's forces. He is now commanding the Northern District Irish command, and orders prohibiting meetings and the like are issued by him to those who, in the speeches of the Ulster leaders, were always alluded to as 'the enemy' whom 'we loathe'.

[†] Seen by the writer.

which had been proclaimed – a truce which the Covenanters were so cheerfully defying. In Belfast, however, the event was widely advertised; and thus by silence abroad, and advertisement at home, Belfast enjoyed its well organized double triumph.

There was no lack meanwhile of sermons to glorify the unchanging fixity of the Provisional Government and the Covenant. The ladies of the movement were also useful in upholding the doctrine of ourselves first and last and all the time. In the Hospital War Supplies and in the supply of comforts for prisoners of war their object was to draw Ulster into a separate organization for the work of mercy from the rest of Ireland.[23]

III

The third stage of the Provisional Government opened on May 21, 1917, with the proposal of a Convention to effect a settlement of the Irish question.[24] 'The Government have therefore decided', said the Premier, 'to invite Irishmen to put forward their own proposals for the government of their country. We propose that Ireland should try her own hand at hammering out an instrument of government for her own people. The experiment has succeeded in other parts of the British Empire. It succeeded in Canada; it succeeded in South Africa. What was accomplished in South Africa, in Australia, and in Canada, I cannot help believing is achievable in Ireland ... No proposal on any side for the better government of Ireland can be shut out from discussion under the terms of reference.' The only limitation was 'within the Empire'.* The Covenanters saw their isolation threatened, and hastened to assert their independent position. Sir John Lonsdale protested against any steps being taken to bring pressure on Ulster, relying on

[23] Early in the war the Ulster Women's Unionist Council (UWUC) declared that it would not join with Dublin in the organisation of supplies for the war effort but would instead maintain its independence.

[24] The Irish Convention was proposed in May 1917 and sat in Dublin from 25 July until April the following year under the chairmanship of Horace Plunkett. Comprising a range of party and non-party representatives, it was charged with discussing the prospective enactment of self-government for Ireland. The provision of home rule had been in suspension for the duration of the war, the 1916 Rising had occurred during the interval, and the settlement of the Ulster question was still outstanding. Attempts to resolve the issue in the summer of 1916 ended in failure, coinciding with major losses to Irish divisions at the Battle of the Somme. In response, the British Prime Minister, Lloyd George (1863–1945), now presiding over a new coalition government, proposed the establishment of the Convention to John Redmond.

* These terms were fundamentally altered by the Prime Minister on Feb. 23, 1918.

Mr. Asquith's promise that 'Ulster should not be coerced.'[25] 'The people of Ulster', he said, 'are a democratic community, and they possess in the Ulster Unionist Council' (a council of peers, capitalists, and employers) 'a thoroughly representative organization. All that we – their representatives in this House – can do is to lay the government proposals before them.' Mr. Asquith noted that the leader of Ulster Members of Parliament could not assent without referring to the Ulster Unionist Council (*i.e.* Provisional Government) for their decision. 'If the Convention fails', he said, 'Heaven help us – I will not take that despondent, I may say, desperate view.' Sir Edward Carson, then First Lord of the Admiralty, insisted on the absolute independence and authority of the Provisional Government. 'Whether the Unionist Council will accept the invitation, or whether it will not, I am sure I do not know. Of one thing I am certain: no threats will have the slightest effect upon them. Whatever decision they take, and I hope they will take a wise one, I will be with them to the end.'[*]

The scientific organization of north-east Ulster was equal to the strain. The new business was taken in hand by the Provisional Government with the same single eye and the same efficiency of control as ever. Having already a pledge-bound party, their first step was to create a pledge-bound British Government. They took the precaution of immediately insisting in Parliament on an open and unmistakable pledge that the half-province should not be outvoted by the whole of the rest of Ireland. The matter was carried through by Mr. Ronald McNeill and Mr. Bonar Law, both Sir Edward Carson's lieutenants in the Ulster militant campaign.[26] On May 24, Mr. Ronald McNeill asked the Prime Minister whether his statement, that in the event of the Convention coming to a 'substantial agreement', the Government would introduce legislation to give effect to such agreement, is to be taken as in any degree affecting his previous pledge that under no circumstances shall Ulster be coerced into submitting to the jurisdiction of an Irish Parliament: and Mr. Bonar Law answered that 'There could not be "substantial agreement" in the circumstance suggested by my hon. Friend's question.'[*] It was clearly understood that the

[25] John Brownlee Lonsdale (1850–1924), 1st Baron Armaghdale, was elected MP for Mid-Armagh in February 1900 and sat until 1918.

[26] Ronald John McNeill, 1st Baron Cushendun, PC (1861–1934), was a Conservative MP from Ulster. Andrew Bonar Law (1858–1923) was also a Conservative MP of Scottish and Ulster-Scots descent. He served as Prime Minister of the United Kingdom from 1922 to 1923.

[*] *Hansard*, Vol. 93, *p.* 2020.

object of question and answer was to nullify any conclusion come to by the Convention which is not agreed to by representatives of Ulster, so that north-east Ulster should absolutely hold the fate of Ireland in its hands. A safe position being thus secured, Sir Edward Carson on June 11, stated in Parliament that he had presided in Belfast over a conference of 500 Covenanters and advised them to consent to the Convention.[†]

'Substantial agreement' became the fixed and mysterious phrase for all later ministerial pronouncements – vague and ominous. In the negotiations the Sinn Féinidhthe of the South naturally saw a direct menace to the freedom and dignity of the Convention, and a new pledge for the dominance of north-east Ulster, nor is it wonderful that they should refuse to enter a conference so trammelled before it was allowed to exist.[27] On the other hand the Provisional Government, in its newly assured security, could devise methods adapted to the free position of Belfast and its dependencies. Members were selected for the Convention and a deliberative Committee of the Council was appointed, to whom they should report privately, and take their secret directions, without power themselves to vote or intimate the eventual intentions of the Council behind them. According to the *Manchester Guardian* of January 16, 1918, the Standing Committee maintained a strict control; and the *Northern Whig* closely identified with the Council, told the Convention when it visited Belfast that whatever scheme of government it might fashion would find its way to the waste-paper basket. It is easy to understand the dangers of such a system, with its inevitable hindrances and delays to serious work, and the hopelessness of bringing the general interests of Ireland into equal discussion with the claims of 'Ourselves first and last'. The English government had already learned in past years that any appeal to Imperial necessities, and necessary sacrifices to meet them, has been met by the Provisional Government with its fixed interpretation of Imperial policy and obligations. The Covenanters will accept an Empire that is fashioned according to their own formulae, and pledged to protect their special privileges and industrial interests, in the manner which they themselves dictate. Otherwise in preparation for civil war they retain their own State policy, their government, their army; while beyond these they look to their continued alliance with the British army, and the spreading influence of

[27] 'Sinn Féinidhthe' means Sinn Féiners.

* *Ib.* Vol. 93, *p.* 2473.

† *Ib.* Vol. 94, *p.* 619.

Orange Lodges and Freemasonry in military circles.* While the rank and file change, the engineers of the Curragh mutiny grasp more firmly than ever supreme control of the entire army organization and policy.

Having proved their power of intimidating the government of England, north-east Ulster again showed its activity in what was thought by many to be a new unparalleled outrage, flung this time at the Convention. A demand was made for a redistribution of seats in Ireland to come into operation in case the Convention (which north-east Ulster, as it believed, had the pledged power to ruin) should fail in its task; and Sir John Lonsdale, representing in Parliament the policy of the Unionist Council, prepared a plan of redistribution, which would add strength to his party for the conflict at the end of the war. Once more the House of Commons was scandalized at the surrender of the Government.† But the compromise allowed to it was but a matter of details, leaving the principle untouched. Sir John Lonsdale, in virtue (according to the ominous comment of the *Times*)‡ of 'his strong and respected views on the Irish situation', with Colonel Craig and the Mayor of Derry, as men whom the Government delighted to honour, accepted a peerage, a baronetcy, and a knighthood, and the public wait to see whether the service recognized is the breaking or the saving of the Convention. Whatever it be, their reward is secured in advance. So the Government drives the State with even keel over the turbulent waters, with Orange and Freemason destroyers on either side to mark the path of safety.

It must be noticed that nowhere in Ireland is there so stern a resistance to conscription as in Ulster.[28] The numbers of those who enlisted in the

[28] Conscription was introduced in Britain in January 1916. In April 1918 the government moved to impose conscription on Ireland whilst extending the measure throughout Britain in order to meet the German Spring Offensive with an increase in the supply of troops to the Western Front. Opposition was concerted by trade unions, nationalist parties, and the Roman Catholic clergy. The measure passed into law but was never put into effect, although it nonetheless galvanised Irish separatism.

* In Sir E. Carson's opinion it would be 'indecent' in any wise to interfere with the 'meditations' of the Convention. If by 'settlement, settlement, settlement … I am never done hearing of the word now – if by settlement people have in their minds surrender, well then there will be no settlement.' – *Irish Times*, Feb. 4, 1918. See his earlier statement, 'He would fight no one if they were allowed to take their own course, and keep their own taxes.' – *Times*, Dec. 5. *Annual Register*, 1913, *p.* 251. An Orange Military Lodge was started in the camp at Ballykinlar.

† The Boundary Commission was appointed in October, 1917, while the Convention was sitting, and the Redistribution Bill passed by the Lords, Feb. 5, 1918. The *Freeman's Journal* and Hansard show the feeling aroused in and outside Parliament.

‡ In the announcement of New Year's Honours, 1918.

first period of the war* (August 2, 1914, to January 8, 1916), when recruiting was most active, show that outside the military recruiting area of Belfast, where the figures are high, the counties of the North fell behind those of the South. In Donegal, Derry, Fermanagh, Tyrone, the percentage to population was 1.03; in Armagh, Cavan, Louth, and Monaghan, 1.1; in Antrim and Down, the very centre of 'loyal' and Imperial enthusiasm, 1.36. In Carlow, Kildare, and Wicklow, on the other hand, the percentage was 1.57; in King's and Queen's Counties, Longford, Meath, and Westmeath, 1.53; in Cork, 1.66; in Kilkenny, Tipperary, Waterford, and Wexford, 1.7. Only along the western coast where land disputes have of old raged, and where great tracts are being gradually reclaimed from the most extreme poverty by the Congested Districts Board, have the percentages fallen to .97 and .16. During the course of the war recruiting has generally ceased. The *Irish News*, of April 30, 1917, reported a meeting of the engineers in Belfast when an amendment was submitted calling upon the Government to apply conscription to Ireland as a means of relieving the demand upon the services of skilled artisans in England. Out of a meeting of fifteen hundred men, mostly Unionists, only eleven voted for conscription. The attitude of the farmers is said to be yet stronger. In the year 1916–17, according to the annual report of the Vice-Chancellor for the Queen's University in Belfast, 440 men and 203 women had been enrolled – a record for the University, while the appended report of the Officers' Training Corps gives the number of cadets who have enlisted as 14. Attempts to recruit have failed from the fact that the majority of the students before entering were pledged by their fathers not to enlist. Yet in politics these people, or nine-tenths of them, are emphatic Carsonites.† Even now the reason is alleged that the Covenanters are needed at home to protect their women and their farms from 'the enemy'. Apart from the grossness of the libel on their Catholic fellow-countrymen, this argument takes no account of the 70,000 or more English troops detained to keep order in Ireland. A second reason advanced in various occupations is the fear of the employed men that their Unionist masters might if they were absent fill up their places with Nationalist working-men – a reason which

* The numbers enlisted are taken from official figures in the Viceroy's Report of Jan. 14, 1916. The Ulster Volunteer Division was not sent into battle till the summer of 1916.

† On February 3 Sir E. Carson stated that he had always wished that conscription should be applied to Ireland. 'We never asked that it should not.' He himself had proposed an amendment to that effect. He added: 'I am not going into the question of whether that is a possible policy now or not. The lapse of time makes great differences.' In his own province he avoided the responsibility of advising conscription. – *Irish Times*, Feb. 4, 1918.

implies considerable distrust of the political loyalty of the employers. These magnates in fact have been known to allege a preference for Catholic workmen, as they were not infected with Marxian Socialism, while the Protestant workmen were riddled with it; and that once Home Rule and Rome Rule were settled these Protestants would turn anti-capitalist and renounce the 'natural leaders' of democracy. It is not impossible that the attitude of Ulster has had a more determining effect upon the Government in delaying conscription than that of the Southern Irishman; on whom, however, all the blame is publicly thrown.

North-east Ulster evidently remains the supreme example of the policy defined by the Prime Minister, 'Ourselves first, ourselves last, ourselves all the time, and ourselves alone'. It is a characteristic enlargement of the 'Sinn Féin' of the rest of Ireland, words which are more truly translated 'We ourselves', and carry the simple lesson that indeed it is to the diligent efforts of only ourselves that we must look to mend our position. Ulster has made its own peculiar form of 'Sinn Féin', and organized it scientifically. In this external organization alone lies its triumph. There is nothing novel in its aim of material success and reservation of the natural leaders of the democracy. If therefore the Provisional Government of the north lifts a voice of shocked indignation at 'rebellion' by southern Sinn Féin, it can with justice only reprove it for a single reason, its inferior success in coercing the Imperial Government. The indignation of the Covenanters cannot rest on any ground of principle, since they have not only claimed but asserted the right to define their own view of imperial duties, and to break all laws and rise in civil war in defence of that view – 'Belfast *contra mundum*'.[29] North-east Ulster, however, cannot expect to be the final judge in all causes for all time, and so practical a community (leaving out the Pope for the moment) will allow that regard for ourselves first, ourselves last, ourselves all the time, ourselves alone, has for its sanction but one final test – that of Success. The northerners must naturally repudiate with sincere contempt a movement less highly organized and financed than their own, and lacking all its advantages for victorious intrigues. Ulster aptitude and Ulster business instinct have materialized what south Ireland has dreamed of. Their leaders have been more methodical, and with their special privileges of position, riches, and allies, they have done better than the men of the south; why should they spare their contempt? The only danger they have to fear lies hidden in the secrets of the future.

[29] Meaning 'Belfast against the world'.

In due time it will be revealed whether a rigid present can be bound to a rigid past by ropes of steel – even by pledges and by 'mystical' Covenants with an offensive and defensive alliance which shall secure an everlasting and unchanging protection for Belfast's industrial wealth under the 'God who is not as other Gods'. Once again in the world's history it will be discovered how long men or provinces can live by organization, and the power to do what they will with their own; or whether the force of the spirit may not yet again break ancient moulds to reach a larger life. We shall learn, in due time, whether the rickety shelters guaranteed by an old statecraft will stand against rising floods, and whether the bravest men are not those who advance under the open heavens to new horizons.[30]

[30] Green appended a note at the conclusion of her endnotes in the original pamphlet: '*N.B.* – The question of the support of English Unionism to civil war in Ireland has not been dealt with here. One quotation will illustrate the defiance to the Government, and the incitements to north-east Ulster, which English politicians did not scruple to use. We have the contribution to high statesmanship of Mr. Bonar Law on Nov. 28, 1913, in Dublin: "I have said on behalf of the party that if the Government attempt to coerce Ulster before they have received the sanction of the electors, *Ulster will do well to resist them and we will support resistance to the end.*"

"I wonder whether you have tried to picture in your own minds what civil war means … it is a prospect from which I shrink in horror, and for which I wish to avoid, if I can, any responsibility … But really we must try to think what the effect of bloodshed and civil war would be on our Parliamentary institutions, on the army, on the Empire as a whole. It would not mean anarchy; it would mean literally red ruin and the breaking up of law. It would produce results from which our country would not recover in the lifetime of any one of those whom I am addressing."

This was the high emprise upon which Mr. Bonar Law encouraged north-east Ulster to embark, and for which he promised them the support of his party "to the end".

The resistance which Mr. Bonar Law thus commended to Ulster Unionists will be recalled to mind by Irishmen in his own identical terms.'

1920

28 Robert Lynd, 'Ulster: The Facts of the Case'[1]

Ulster's fear of Home Rule or any other form of national government is a much simpler and more intelligible thing than is sometimes admitted. What the Ulsterman fears most of all is that under Home Rule he will not enjoy self-government. He is sometimes painted as a person who is determined at all costs not to surrender a position of ascendancy for one of equality. But that is hardly fair to the average Ulsterman. He has usually allowed himself to be led by men who believed in the gospel of the top-dog and did their best to live up to it; but there have also always been tens of thousands of Ulstermen who were instinctively democrats, and who would never have opposed Home Rule but for the dread that it would mean not the reign of equality but the reign of a new sort of ascendancy. What men of this kind fear is that in an Irish Parliament they will be given laws they do not want, like a subject people.

Oddly enough, they argue that the Irishman enjoys equality in the 'United Kingdom' because he has a vote and is allowed to send representatives to the Parliament in London. They fail to see that according to this argument the Ulsterman must enjoy equality in a self-governed Ireland because he will have a vote and be able to send representatives to the Parliament in Dublin. As a Nationalist, I naturally hold that freedom consists in something more than the right to send representatives to somebody else's Parliament. But the point that has just been made is worth making as a reminder to the Ulsterman that, even were the worst to come to the worst, an Ulster Party in a Dublin Parliament would be

[1] Robert Lynd, 'Ulster: The Facts of the Case' was published in Lynd's *Ireland a Nation* (New York: Dodd, Mead, 1920).

proportionately far larger and more powerful than an Irish Party in the present British House of Commons. An Ulster Party could easily wreck any Irish Parliament that attempted injustice to Ulster.

It may be worth inquiring, however, whether there are any grounds for the fear of the moderate Ulsterman – I use the word 'Ulsterman', of course, in the customary political sense – that he will not enjoy self-government in a self-governed Ireland.[2] He has been legislated for to some extent by Irish Nationalists in the past. Which of the laws demanded and won by Irish Nationalists in the last fifty years has been contrary to the wishes of the ordinary Ulsterman? Land Act after Land Act has been gained.[3] Who can deny that the Land Acts represent the wishes of the Presbyterian farmers of County Antrim as well as of the Catholics of County Galway? Orange tenants, again, are as quick to take advantage of the Town Tenants Act as if they lived in Tipperary and went to Mass.[4] It would be impossible, I think, to name a single law agitated for and won by Nationalist Irishmen in the last fifty years which the ordinary Ulster Protestant really would like to see repealed. The Ulsterman's quarrel with the Nationalist is not with the laws they have made or compelled to be made. It is with the laws he imagines they would like to make if they dared. His terror of Nationalism is not based on the legislative record of Nationalism (which consists of Land Acts, the Town Tenants Act, Acts about trade-marks, harbours, local government and education), but on some such fantastic theory as that if he marries a Catholic (whom he does not, except in a very rare instance, want to marry) an Irish Parliament will declare the marriage invalid.[5] He thinks of Nationalists chiefly as people who desire to penalize him. He thinks, too, that even if they would not penalize him through vindictiveness, they would ruin him through incompetence.

[2] He means the definition of an Ulsterman which had been made synonymous with Protestantism and unionism, rather than a man from Ulster who could be of any background.

[3] The Land Acts passed by the Westminster legislature were designed to reform tenancy rights and proprietorship in Ireland and passed between 1870 and 1909.

[4] The Town Tenants (Ireland) Act of 1906 granted new entitlements to tenants of business holdings, together with the right, on the falling in of leases, to claim compensation for disturbance as well as improvements.

[5] A reference to the *Ne Temere* decree of 10 August 1907 issued under Pope Pius X regulating the canon law of the Church regarding mixed marriages to the detriment of Protestants.

The worst of illusions of this kind is that they are so difficult to destroy. They have the strength of principles, not of arguments. Reason is almost powerless against them. All the same, one is bound to go on reasoning. It is necessary to keep on asking the Unionist Ulsterman to mention any one point in regard to which the legislative ideals of North and South have clashed in the past. If Ulster had enjoyed complete self-government in the past, would she have passed the laws for which Nationalists have been responsible, or would she have been content with the laws which satisfied the Ulster Tory leaders? It is one of the paradoxes of the Irish situation that in most matters the Ulsterman has been far more in sympathy with the legislative policy of the Nationalists than with that of his own leaders. Lord Londonderry and Col. Saunderson had his vote, but Parnell and Davitt represented his ideals, so far at least as the land was concerned.[6] The division between Ulster and the South has for the most part not been a division of interests, but a division of political leaders.

As regards the future, also, our interests are at one. Ireland as a whole is an undeveloped country. Ulster and Munster are developed in a sense in which Connaught is not. But it is broadly true of the whole country, North and South, that its resources, intellectual and material, have been left in a state of neglect, and that even the richest parts of Ulster are not rich according, say, to English and Scottish standards. The modern world is setting new standards of efficiency and education, and no people that does not take its own problems in hand and devote its united energies to solving them can expect to take its place among civilized and successful peoples. Even if Ulster did not come into an Irish Parliament she would have to learn to manage her own affairs. England has no longer time to manage Ulster land and Ulster education. All she can do is to place matters of this kind in the hands of a board. With the war over she has less time than ever to devote to the solution of the special problems of Ulster or of any other part of Ireland. If the Ulsterman wants to find eager allies in the work of draining the Bann, he will find them among the Irish Nationalists, not among even the best-intentioned English members. To the Englishman, the Bann drainage is a question of as little interest as

[6] Charles Stewart Henry Vane-Tempest-Stewart (1878–1949), 7th Marquess of Londonderry, was politically active in the cause of Ulster unionism; Edward James Saunderson (1837–1906) led the Irish Unionist Alliance between 1891 and 1906; Charles Stewart Parnell (1846–91) led the Irish Parliamentary Party from 1882 to 1891; Michael Davitt (1846–1906) pioneered co-operation across the extremes of Irish politics over the land question and became an MP in the 1890s.

the drainage of a district in China or Australia.[7] To every Irishman it is a home problem, a thing about which one can get excited. It is a fact of human nature that problems can only be solved by those who are sufficiently interested in them to get excited about them.

The chief function of an Irish Parliament will be to focus the national mind on the various national problems. The Ulsterman may protest that Ulster problems are not the same as Irish problems. But the fact that Ulstermen have consentingly lived for so many years past under Irish laws, not English laws, as regards land, education, temperance, etc., suggests that what Ulster wants in all these matters is more like what Ireland wants than like what England wants. Had Ulster felt herself to be a part of Great Britain rather than of Ireland, she would long ago have insisted on being excluded from all this specially Irish legislation. By remaining without protest under Irish laws she has, it seems to me, confessed her unity of interests with the rest of Ireland.

The only matter in regard to which I can imagine any serious difference of ideal between Ulster and the rest of Ireland is education. And in regard to education it seems to me obvious that Ulster can obtain complete provincial autonomy if she wishes it. The encouragement of industrial life, however, the discovery of new methods of increasing the food supply, the raising of the level of health and wealth and happiness for all the people – these are objects upon which the best brains of all the four provinces can concentrate, without any clash of principle. In regard to these objects, indeed, I hold that Ulster can only realize herself fully if she is willing to play her part in the general resurrection of Ireland. Outside Ireland she would merely be a backward and outlying province of Great Britain, with all her best sons emigrating to some happier soil. As part of the Irish nation, she will be the pioneer province of a country with immense untapped resources of every kind – a country which will attract the young and the enterprising instead of frightening them away. She will enjoy self-government because she will not – she does not even now – feel that her interests demand different laws from the interests of the rest of Ireland, and she will have a full share in making those laws. Judging by the way in which Ulster has lived under Irish law up till the present, she can never possibly feel a stranger, a nuisance, a bore, a bottom dog, a mere hostile element with different needs, in the Dublin Parliament, as Ireland

7 The River Bann flows from the south-east corner of Ulster to the north-west coast. The Bann Drainage Bill was debated in the House of Commons on 24 June 1889.

has so often felt in the British House of Commons. Ulster is an integral part of Ireland to a degree to which Ireland has never been an integral part of the 'United Kingdom'. She has never objected to Irish laws, but only to an Irish Parliament. She will have no objection to an Irish Parliament either, as soon as she realizes that it will be, not an instrument for her subjection, but an instrument for the expression of her desires, her energies and her ideals. Most people outside Ulster take it for granted that Ulster is much more likely to dominate an Irish Parliament than to be dominated by it. One thing is certain. She will be able to impress her will on Dublin far more powerfully and effectively than Lancashire impresses her will on London. Can self-government go further than that?

1921

29 Erskine Childers, *Is Ireland a Danger to England?*[1]

The Strategical Question Examined

Why does England refuse freedom to Ireland?

A host of evasive and contradictory answers have been given to this question in the past. But the last two years have cleared the ground of unreal controversies and fictitious issues. There survives but one answer to the eternal question, and that answer is that it would be 'unsafe' for England to do otherwise.[2]

All the recent utterances of responsible British statesmen, including the Prime Minister, have narrowed the question to this single point. 'An independent Ireland on our flank', they have repeated again and again, 'would be a military and strategical danger to us.'[3]

[1] Erskine Childers, *Is Ireland a Danger to England? The Strategical Question Examined* (Dublin: Irish Bulletin, 1921) originally appeared in the *Irish Bulletin*, 29 July 1921, and was then revised for publication as a pamphlet by Dáil Éireann.

[2] Britain had been at war with separatist forces in Ireland since January 1919, escalating from November of that year. After two bloody years, conflict began to be scaled down on 6 June 1921. George V (1865–1936) made a conciliation speech in Belfast, part-drafted by Jan Smuts (1870–1950), pleading for an era of peace and goodwill on 22 June. On 24 June the British coalition cabinet proposed peace talks with Sinn Féin. Terms for a truce were agreed on 9 July and implemented three days later.

[3] During debate in the Commons on the Government of Ireland Act (1920), Prime Minister David Lloyd George sought to illustrate the danger posed by Ireland to Britain with reference to the recent world war: 'If Ireland had been a separate unit, with a separate Parliament', a 'hostile republic' would have rendered the Allied cause acutely vulnerable. See Hansard, House of Commons Debates, 22 December 1919, vol. 123, cols. 1173–4.

In the negotiations begun in July, this again has been the one dominating issue.[4] The naval and military conditions imposed upon Ireland under the British proposals of July 20th were justified by Mr. Lloyd George on the ground that 'the geographical propinquity of Ireland to the British Isles is a fundamental fact.' (Letter of August 13th.)[5]

Ireland, simply because she is so near to England, is alleged to be a danger to England, and to guard against this danger England claims for ever to rule Ireland, whatever the rights and wishes of the Irish people.

That is the proposition: a brutally frank proposition, proclaimed without hypocrisy and seemingly without a suspicion that it amounts to a denial of all international morality, and violates the principle in the name of which Europe was drenched with blood for four years.[6] For if England can say this to Ireland any state in the world can say it to any adjoining state, and with greater force; for whereas Ireland is an island, most states are actually contiguous to their neighbours.

But whether the proposition be morally right or wrong, is it true? Would an independent Ireland in fact be a danger to England?

An Appeal for Clear Thinking

The difficulty is to place this important theme upon the plane of reasonable discussion. The supposed danger, for those who believe in it, is usually not a matter of argument but of unreasoning fear, while the trained strategists, accustomed to regard the world as a battle-field and humanity as cannon-fodder, take it for granted that every country, even an island, must be military danger to its neighbours.

Yet it is a shocking and unconscionable thing that men should fight with passion for an empty delusion, above all in a war which, at the time when hostilities were suspended, was threatening to become a veritable war of extermination upon the Irish people, and which, if peace were not to result, might resume that terrible complexion.

We appeal, while there is still time, for a cool and thoughtful consideration of the subject.

4 Lloyd George (1863–1945) wrote to Éamon de Valera (1882–1975), the president of Dáil Éireann, with an offer of peace talks on 24 June 1921.

5 See Lloyd George to de Valera, 13 August 1921, Lloyd George Papers F/14/6/15, House of Lords Library.

6 That is, the 'rights of small nations'.

The Choice before England

In the first place let us have it clear that for England the question is not one simply of safety, but of contrasting the relative safety of two opposite courses. Is she safer with an Ireland under her military control, as at present, than she would be with an independent Ireland? A violently hostile Ireland is undoubtedly a danger to her, and, in the larger sense of the word 'strategy', a strategical danger. It chains to the costly and odious task of coercion a large army which might at any moment be needed for vital work elsewhere. It requires a money outlay far exceeding any money profit derived from the possession of Ireland. It involves England in a war of a kind which is damaging to her prestige and admits of no finality because the objective is an unconquerable abstraction, the soul and spirit of the people. Lastly, it makes England bitter enemies among the Irish race throughout the world, with results, especially in America, which are an embarrassment to her imperial policies.

These facts are unquestioned. Those who say that Irish independence would be a danger to England are bound to prove that the danger would be greater than it is now.

Mr. Lloyd George's View

Mr. Lloyd George, in a speech at Carnarvon, on October 9th of last year, came nearer to a reasoned strategical argument than any statesman in recent days, and the reasons he gave for the military subjection of Ireland will serve as a basis for discussion.[7]

He made two points, not merely against an Irish Republic but against 'Dominion Home Rule'. The first was that England would be forced to have conscription because 'you could not have an army of 500,000 or 600,000 men in Ireland and only an army of about 100,000 men here'.

The second point was that 'they (the Irish) need not build a navy. You do not need to spend much on submarines. They are vicious little craft but they are not expensive.'

Here are two assertions with which we can grapple. The danger to England is alleged to come from an Irish army and Irish submarines.

[7] Lloyd George had spoken at his constituency in Carnarvon on 9 October 1920 defending the policy of reprisals in outlining the strategic position of Britain in relation to Ireland.

Mr. Lloyd George spoke as if Ireland, single-handed, could make these menaces effective, and the simplest plan is to begin by following him in this assumption because the underlying strategic principles will thus emerge most clearly. Afterwards we can suppose that Ireland had an ally or allies or that her neutrality, like that of Belgium, was violated.

The Supposed Danger from an Irish Army

Let us take the Army first and, passing by the rhetorical use of some rather startling figures, get to the point. The only rational meaning to be attached to Mr. Lloyd George's proposition is that the Irish Army would in some way threaten England. The same fear is expressed in the second of the six conditions attached to the peace offer made to Ireland by the British Government on July 30th, 1921. Now let us suppose that little Ireland with her 4½ millions of people and her revenue, screwed to the highest point by exorbitant taxation, of only 50 million, were really to form the insane ambition of menacing with military force her mighty neighbour, Britain, with 42 millions of people, a revenue of 1,000 millions, and an army potentially 5 millions strong. How is the threat to be carried out?

The small Irish army could certainly be used up to the limit of its strength for defending Irish soil. But defence is not a menace. For offence it must be transported over-seas on ships which would have to be protected by a navy capable of defeating the British Navy and securing the permanent and undisputed command of the sea; for it is an accepted axiom of strategy that an over-sea invasion is not possible without the secure maintenance of sea-communications. Germany with the largest army in the world and the second navy in the world, was not able to land a man in England in the recent war.[8] England, thanks to her command of the sea was able to land millions of troops continuously upon the continent, place them upon the battle-front and eventually throw them into Germany.

Ireland then, starting without a single naval ship to her credit, must in order to menace England with her army, first become a naval power greater than England. Now it certainly is not reasonable to refuse Ireland independence on the ground that this prodigious inversion of relative

[8] He is referring to the First World War.

positions might by a miracle come to pass in the far future. It is hardly necessary to add that all the small nations of Europe could legitimately be extinguished to-morrow by their great military neighbours if the principle applied to Ireland were to be sanctioned by the opinion of the world.

Governing Strategical Facts

Some governing strategical facts are now becoming clear: –

1. Ireland and Britain are islands.
2. Their offensive and defensive power in war depend therefore primarily on naval strength.
3. Ireland is immeasurably weaker than Britain not only in naval but in military resources, and cannot begin to approach equality within any foreseeable period.

The Submarine Peril

An appreciation of these governing facts, ignored by Mr. Lloyd George, should dissipate the submarine peril also – a peril with a peculiar appeal to nervous and unreflecting minds. It is so easy to conjure up pictures of these mysterious little craft, 'vicious', and 'not expensive', issuing from a small nation's ports to paralyse the fleets and commerce of a mighty enemy. But is this really possible? Observe Mr. Lloyd George's words. 'They (the Irish) need not build a navy.' But we have seen in reality they must build the greatest navy in the world in order to threaten England with their army. The same condition applies to their use of submarines.

The Conditions of a Submarine Offensive

Submarines to be of the smallest use in modern war, are, of course, not cheap. They must be large, numerous and costly out of all proportion to the slender revenues of Ireland. Germany built 400, lost 200 and failed in her objective. But their cost is a minor matter. The bases from which they operate must be secure, and, with a hostile power like England in command of the neighbouring seas, the Irish submarine bases would have to be impregnably secure against attack by sea, air and land. They must be secure from sea and air attack because naval bombardment, with aerial observation, or aerial bombardment from aircraft carried on warships can destroy unprotected dockyards and submarines on the surface – and they must be on the surface in and approaching port – can prevent the establishment of protective minefields and play havoc with the auxiliary surface craft which are indispensable to submarine bases. But protection by sea and air would itself be wholly wasted without protection by land, because the command of the sea would enable England to throw into Ireland at selected points armies capable of enveloping and destroying the submarine bases, or at any rate of rendering them strategically untenable by cutting their communications with the Irish military centres. A submarine base cannot exist in the air.

The Analogy from the World-War

The strategic conditions in the North Sea during the world-war supply a vivid illustration of these facts. Germany with her vast resources and the second navy in the world was just able, by immense outlay in men and money upon protective air-squadrons, ferro-concreted dockyard protection (including a colossal bomb proof shelter for submarines at Bruges, which is one of the wonders of the world), numerous squadrons of destroyers, minelayers and minor surface-craft, to maintain against naval and aerial attack her advanced submarine base, Bruges, with its sea-port, Zeebrugge, until near the close of the war. Ostend became useless owing to naval bombardment. In April, 1918, an assault on Zeebrugge closed access to Bruges, which lies nine miles inland, for several weeks and might, if repeated, have closed it permanently. But, whether this happened or not, the existence of the Bruges base depended on uninterrupted communication with the military and industrial centres of Germany. When the Allied armies began to break the battle front in Belgium in October, Bruges, Zeebrugge and Ostend, threatened with envelopment, were instantly evacuated. This was the final result of England's command of the sea, enabling her, in spite of fleets of German submarines, to maintain the transport of her growing army across the channel for more than four years.

Throwing Money into the Sea

An Irish Minister of War, therefore, asked to prepare estimates for a naval establishment, with or without submarines, capable of threatening England, or even for providing an adequate defence against English aggression, would refuse or resign at the first survey of the facts. He would say that he was asked, literally, to throw money into the sea. The utmost he, like the Naval Minister, of any other small country, would sanction, would be a small outlay, purely for defensive purposes, on small vessels of war, strictly for fishery, coast and harbour protection, together with a modest air-defence, mainly for reconnaissance.

Ireland's Defensive Power against England

From the purely defensive standpoint, these provisions would be useless in the last resort against an attack by a strong naval and air power though they could cause delay and necessitate some additional output of strength in the enemy's offensive. This in the last resort, though with a marked difference of degree is all that Ireland's main line of defence, her Army, could do to prevent a resolute invasion by so great a power as England. We cannot now by sheer military force expel the British armies, and we could not prevent them from re-entering, if they were inflexibly determined to do so. In the final reckoning we must face the fact that our resistance depends upon moral right.

But from England's standpoint that moral right and the resistance founded upon it is an insurmountable obstacle now. Unsatisfied, with the far-reaching results flowing from its refusal, it is her strategical danger. Satisfied, it would be her strategical safeguard.

England's Interest in the Freedom of Ireland

For it is not to England's interest that Ireland, her best, and indeed, her indispensable food-supplier and market, should be under the control of a hostile power. A free Ireland would be her strongest guarantee against any such eventuality. For a free Ireland would fight to the death against any kind of foreign control.

Other Possibilities

This plain inference from ordinary human motives, taken with the root strategical facts, should be a sufficient answer to the fears expressed about the other contingencies we have to consider – the alliance of Ireland with some other power or powers, or the forced violation of her neutrality.

The Violation of a Neutral Ireland

We have already disposed by implication of the latter case. Leaving aside for the moment the naval possibility of a forced landing in a neutral Ireland by a foreign power, the military defence of the island, supposing the landing were effected, could not be in better hands than that of an Irish army fighting with vehemence to defend its own soil. An English army of occupation, with an Irish rebel army upon its back, perhaps in actual sympathy with the invader, would be paralysed from the first.

An Alliance against England? Ireland's Motives to the Contrary

The contingency of a hostile Ireland, allied with another power, must in justice be considered, though it is one that hardly comes within the scope of reasonable discussion; and without some little tincture of reason all discussion is futile. What could be the motive for such an alliance? Ireland has and would have no continental entanglements or colonial ambitions, no land-frontiers, no irredenta, nothing to covet or intrigue for. To win her freedom from England has been the single object of her policy for seven hundred years. To retain it when won would be her supreme object in the future. She cannot retain it without the good-will of England. The instinct of self-preservation, if nothing else, would dictate the friendly relations of a small neutral nation with a powerful neighbour. There would also be cogent motives of economic and commercial interest. Ireland would not profit from the destruction of England, she would be at a heavy loss.

What Possible Allies?

So much for motives. But for the sake of argument credit Ireland with the lunacy of deserting her safest role – the only safe role for any small nation – that of strict neutrality, and of entering into some joint design against England, based, one must suppose, upon a senseless spirit of revenge for wrongs already righted. The strategic facts demand that her alliance must be with a naval power or powers. The combined navies of Europe are negligible beside the British Navy and are likely to remain so for further than we can see. Japan? A war between England and Japan, waged in European waters, is not a possible contingency and an alliance between Ireland and Japan raises a smile. America? The independence of Ireland would itself remove the main obstacle to friendly co-operation between England and America and would render war between them, a most unnatural and unlikely event in any case, practicably unthinkable. If it did take place, it would not be fought in waters where Ireland could be a strategic factor. America is too distant; her communications too long. It would be a colonial and economic struggle.

The First Consequences of an Alliance

Nevertheless, to shirk no issue, let us suppose this alliance or any other, however unlikely, to be entertained by Ireland, what would be the result? At the first glimpse of preparation for it – and the preparation could not be concealed – perhaps at the first wind of it, an ultimatum from England, with all the fearful perils involved. Suppose, even so, that the war actually came to pass. Ireland would certainly be the first to suffer, and heavily, from England. But could she be of any practical assistance to her ally?

Strategic Conditions of an Alliance

None, if the governing principles of naval strategy be remembered. Her only contribution to the war would be to offer her shores as a foothold to the armies of her ally and her ports as a shelter for her ships. But neither of these offers could take effect until the English navy had been destroyed or driven finally from the seas. Until that happened no hostile power could land a man in Ireland or derive any appreciable advantage from the use of Irish ports. The idea that submarines can be based surreptitiously on the ports of a little country without a navy and in direct defiance of an enemy power holding the local command of the sea is a delusion born of the tittle-tattle of scare-mongers.

But let us make the final supposition; that England did in fact lose the command of the sea. In that case there would be no need for her enemy to land a man in Ireland or to use Irish ports. England's economic position is such that her loss of the command of the sea means starvation and defeat.

That is undoubtedly a fact, and it is a fact which in this Irish question deeply influences the minds even of the most reasonable and well-disposed Englishman. But to the inferences drawn from it that Ireland must be subject to England is false and unworthy of thinking men.

Conclusion

Where does England's true strategic interest lie? In antagonizing Ireland or conciliating her? There can be but one reasonable answer. It is her interest to recognize our independence. To contest it to the last point in a war of extermination would be not only shameful but ruinous to her.

30 Arthur Griffith, 'Debate on Treaty'[1]

It is not a question of courtesy; it is not a question of the rules of procedure; it is a question of the lives and fortunes of the people of Ireland. While I shall so far as I can respect President de Valera's wish, I am not going to hide from the Irish people what the alternative is that is proposed. I move the motion standing in my name –

> That Dáil Éireann approves of the Treaty between Great Britain and Ireland, signed in London on December 6th, 1921.[2]

Nearly three months ago Dáil Éireann appointed plenipotentiaries to go to London to treat with the British Government and to make a bargain with them.[3] We have made a bargain. We have brought it back. We were to go there to reconcile our aspirations with the association of the

[1] Dáil Éireann debate, Monday, 19 December 1921, vol. T, no. 6.

[2] Dáil Éireann is the 'Assembly of Ireland', the lower house of its legislature, created in January 1919 following the 1918 general election in the UK when Sinn Féin won a landslide victory. The First Dáil sat between 1919 and 1921, abstained from Westminster, ratified the Proclamation of the Irish Republic issued at the 1916 Easter Rising, and adopted a provisional constitution. Griffith is speaking in the Second Dáil which sat from 16 August 1921 until 8 June 1922, consisting of members elected in 1921. Its task now was to ratify the 'Articles of Agreement for a Treaty Between Great Britain and Ireland' usually referred to simply as 'The Treaty'.

[3] The Irish plenipotentiaries dispatched to negotiate the Treaty were: Arthur Griffith (1871–1922), Michael Collins (1890–1922), Robert Barton (1881–1975), Eamonn Duggan (1878–1936), and George Gavan Duffy (1882–1951). These five plenipotentiaries had the authority to negotiate a Treaty without reference back to their superiors. The Treaty negotiations lasted from 11 October until 6 December 1921. Erskine Childers (1870–1922) attended as a secretary to the Irish delegation.

community of nations known as the British Empire.[4] That task which was given to us was as hard as was ever placed on the shoulders of men. We faced that task; we knew that whatever happened we would have our critics, and we made up our minds to do whatever was right and disregard whatever criticism might occur. We could have shirked the responsibility. We did not seek to act as the plenipotentiaries; other men were asked and other men refused.[5] We went. The responsibility is on our shoulders; we took the responsibility in London and we take the responsibility in Dublin. I signed that Treaty not as the ideal thing, but fully believing, as I believe now, it is a treaty honourable to Ireland, and safeguards the vital interests of Ireland.[6]

And now by that Treaty I am going to stand, and every man with a scrap of honour who signed it is going to stand. It is for the Irish people – who are our masters ['Hear, hear.'] not our servants as some think – it is for the Irish people to say whether it is good enough. I hold that it is, and I hold that the Irish people – that 95 per cent of them believe it to be good enough. We are here, not as the dictators of the Irish People, but as the representatives of the Irish people, and if we misrepresent the Irish people, then the moral authority of Dáil Éireann, the strength behind it, and the fact that Dáil Éireann spoke the voice of the Irish people, is gone, and gone for ever. Now, the President – and I am in a difficult position – does not wish a certain document referred to read.[7] But I must

[4] Prime Minister David Lloyd George (1863–1945) wrote to Éamon de Valera (1882–1975), president of Dáil Éireann, on 29 September 1921 setting out the terms of the prospective negotiations as seeking 'to ascertain how the association of Ireland with the community of nations known as the British Empire can best be reconciled with Irish national aspirations'. A week earlier he had underlined that since June he had affirmed 'that we looked to Ireland to own allegiance to the Throne, and to make her future as a member of the British Commonwealth. That was the basis of our proposals, and we cannot alter it'.

[5] De Valera, accorded the status of president on 26 August 1921, declined to attend the negotiations.

[6] Under the terms of the Treaty, Southern Ireland was to become a self-governing dominion of the British Empire, a status shared by Australia, Canada, Newfoundland, New Zealand, and the Union of South Africa. Northern Ireland, founded under the 1920 Government of Ireland Act, was entitled to opt out of the Treaty, a right it duly exercised. A Boundary Commission was established to finalise its border. Ireland was therefore neither a republic nor unified and so the arrangement was not 'ideal' from the perspective of Sinn Féin.

[7] This is usually referred to as 'Document 2', de Valera's preferred resolution of the difference between the Irish and British negotiators. The document proposed a form of 'external association' between Ireland and the British Commonwealth whereby the Irish state would 'associate with' but not be under the British Empire, now for the first time described as a Commonwealth. The British monarch was to be head of the association. De Valera declined at this point to have his proposal tabled.

refer to the substance of it. An effort has been made outside to represent that a certain number of men stood uncompromisingly on the rock of the Republic – the Republic, and nothing but the Republic. It has been stated also here that the man who made this position, the man who won the war – Michael Collins – compromised Ireland's rights.[8] In the letters that preceded the negotiations not once was a demand made for recognition of the Irish Republic. If it had been made we knew it would have been refused. We went there to see how to reconcile the two positions, and I hold we have done it.[9] The President does not wish this document to be read. What am I to do? What am I to say? Am I to keep my mouth shut and let the Irish people think about this uncompromising rock?[10]

What we have to say is this, that the difference in this Cabinet and in this House is between half-recognising the British King and the British Empire, and between marching in, as one of the speakers said, with our heads up. The gentlemen on the other side are prepared to recognise the King of England as head of the British Commonwealth.[11] They are prepared to go half in the Empire and half out. They are prepared to go into the Empire for war and peace and treaties, and to keep out for other matters, and that is what the Irish people have got to know is the difference. Does all this quibble of words – because it is merely a quibble of words – mean that Ireland is asked to throw away this Treaty and go back to war?[12] So far as my power or voice extends, not one young Irishman's life shall be lost on that quibble. We owe responsibility to the Irish people. I feel my responsibility to the Irish people, and the Irish people must know, and know in every detail, the difference that exists between us, and the Irish people must be our judges. When the plenipotentiaries came back they were sought to be put in the dock. Well, if I am going to be tried, I am going to be tried by the people of Ireland. ['Hear, hear.'] Now this Treaty has been attacked. It has been examined with a microscope to find its defects, and this little thing and that little thing has been pointed

8 Michael Collins had been Director of Intelligence for the Irish Republican Army (IRA) during the War of Irish Independence, becoming a Teachta Dála (TD) or member of the Irish parliament in 1919 and Minister for Finance in the First Dáil.

9 That is, the position set out by the British side and Irish aspirations.

10 De Valera intervened here declaring: 'I will make my position in my speech quite clear.'

11 Under de Valera's proposal in Document 2, George V was to be recognised as the Head of the Association of Ireland and the British Commonwealth but not Head of the British Commonwealth of which Ireland was a member.

12 Lloyd George is reported to have threatened the Irish delegation with 'terrible and immediate war' if they rejected the terms of the Treaty as negotiated in December 1921.

out, and the people are told – one of the gentlemen said it here – that it was less even than the proposals of July.[13] It is the first Treaty between the representatives of the Irish Government and the representatives of the English Government since 1172 signed on equal footing.[14] It is the first Treaty that admits the equality of Ireland. It is a Treaty of equality, and because of that I am standing by it. We have come back from London with that Treaty – Saorstát na hÉireann recognised – the Free State of Ireland.[15] We have brought back the flag; we have brought back the evacuation of Ireland after 700 years by British troops and the formation of an Irish army. [Applause.] We have brought back to Ireland her full rights and powers of fiscal control. We have brought back to Ireland equality with England, equality with all nations which form that Commonwealth, and an equal voice in the direction of foreign affairs in peace and war.[16] Well, we are told that that Treaty is a derogation from our status; that it is a Treaty not to be accepted, that it is a poor thing, and that the Irish people ought to go back and fight for something more, and that something more is what I describe as a quibble of words. Now, I shall have an opportunity later on of replying to the very formidably arranged criticism that is going to be levelled at the Treaty to show its defects. At all events, the Irish people are a people of great common sense. They know that a Treaty that gives them their flag and their Free State and their Army [Cheers.] is not a sham Treaty, and the sophists and the men of words will not mislead them, I tell you. In connection with the Treaty men said this and said that, and I was requested to get from Mr. Lloyd George a definite statement covering points in the Treaty which some gentlemen misunderstood. This is Mr. Lloyd George's letter:

> 10, Downing Street, S.W. 1
> *13th December*, 1921.
> Sir, – As doubts may be expressed regarding certain points not specifically mentioned in the Treaty terms, I think it is important that their meaning should be clearly understood.

[13] That is, the opening British position before the negotiations got under way.

[14] King Henry II landed in Ireland in 1171 to assert his authority, marking the beginning of the conquest and subordination of the island as represented in nationalist historiography at the time.

[15] Saorstát na hÉireann is the Irish for 'Irish Free State'.

[16] Under the terms of the Treaty crown forces were to be withdrawn from Ireland though Britain would retain control of specified ports and Ireland would be a member of the Commonwealth with the king as the head of the Irish state.

The first question relates to the method of appointment of the Representatives of the Crown in Ireland. Article III. of the Agreement lays down that he is to be appointed 'in like manner as the Governor-General of Canada and in accordance with the practice observed in the making of such appointment'. This means that the Government of the Irish Free State will be consulted so as to ensure a selection acceptable to the Irish Government before any recommendation is made to his Majesty.

The second question is as to the scope of the Arbitration contemplated in Article V. regarding Ireland's liability for a share of War Pensions and the Public Debt. The procedure contemplated by the Conference was that the British Government should submit its claim, and that the Government of the Irish Free State should submit any counter-claim to which it thought Ireland entitled.

Upon the case so submitted the Arbitrators would decide after making such further inquiries as they might think necessary; their decision would then be final and binding on both parties. It is, of course, understood that the arbitrator or arbitrators to whom the case is referred shall be men as to whose impartiality both the British Government and the Government of the Irish Free State are satisfied. The third question relates to the status of the Irish Free State. The special arrangements agreed between us in Articles VI., VII., VIII. and IX., which are not in the Canadian constitution, in no way affect status. They are necessitated by the proximity and interdependence of the two islands – by conditions, that is, which do not exist in the case of Canada.

They in no way affect the position of the Irish Free State in the Commonwealth or its title to representation, like Canada, in the Assembly of the League of Nations. They were agreed between us for our mutual benefit, and have no bearing of any kind upon the question of status. It is our desire that Ireland shall rank as co-equal with the other nations of the Commonwealth, and we are ready to support her claim to a similar place in the League of Nations as soon as her new Constitution comes into effect.[17]

The framing of that Constitution will be in the hands of the Irish Government, subject, of course, to the terms of Agreement, and to the pledges given in respect of the minority by the head of the Irish Delegation. The establishment and composition of the Second Chamber is, therefore, in the discretion of the Irish people. There is

[17] The League of Nations was an international organisation founded in the aftermath of the First World War whose primary aim was to maintain world peace.

nothing in the Articles of Agreement to suggest that Ireland is in this respect bound to the Canadian model.

I may add that we propose to begin withdrawing the Military and Auxiliary Forces of the Crown in Southern Ireland when the Articles of Agreement are ratified.

I am, Sir,
Your obedient Servant,
D. LLOYD GEORGE.

Various different methods of attack on this Treaty have been made. One of them was they did not mean to keep it. Well, they have ratified it, and it can come into operation inside a fortnight. We think they do mean to keep it if we keep it. They are pledged now before the world, pledged by their signature, and if they depart from it they will be disgraced and we will be stronger in the world's eyes than we are today. During the last few years a war was waged on the Irish people, and the Irish people defended themselves, and for a portion of that time, when President de Valera was in America, I had at least the responsibility on my shoulders of standing for all that was done in that defence, and I stood for it. [Applause.] I would stand for it again under similar conditions. Ireland was fighting then against an enemy that was striking at her life, and was denying her liberty, but in any contest that would follow the rejection of this offer Ireland would be fighting with the sympathy of the world against her, and with all the Dominions – all the nations that comprise the British Commonwealth – against her.

The position would be such that I believe no conscientious Irishman could take the responsibility for a single Irishman's life in that futile war. Now, many criticisms, I know, will be levelled against this Treaty; one in particular, one that is in many instances quite honest, it is the question of the oath.[18] I ask the members to see what the oath is, to read it, not to misunderstand or misrepresent it. It is an oath of allegiance to the Constitution of the Free State of Ireland and of faithfulness to King George V. in his capacity as head and in virtue of the common citizenship of Ireland with Great Britain and the other nations comprising the British Commonwealth. That is an oath, I say, that any Irishman could take with honour. He pledges his allegiance to his country and to be faithful to this

[18] Members of the Dáil were required under the Treaty to take an Oath of Allegiance to the Irish Free State which included a supplementary pledge to 'be faithful to His Majesty King George V, His heirs and successors by law, in virtue of the common citizenship'.

Treaty, and faithfulness after to the head of the British Commonwealth of Nations. If his country were unjustly used by any of the nations of that Commonwealth, or its head, then his allegiance is to his own country and his allegiance bids him to resist. ['Hear, hear.']

We took an oath to the Irish Republic, but, as President de Valera himself said, he understood that oath to bind him to do the best he could for Ireland. So do we. We have done the best we could for Ireland. If the Irish people say 'We have got everything else but the name Republic, and we will fight for it', I would say to them that they are fools, but I will follow in the ranks. I will take no responsibility. But the Irish people will not do that. Now it has become rather a custom for men to speak of what they did, and did not do, in the past. I am not going to speak of that aspect, except one thing. It is this. The prophet I followed throughout my life, the man whose words and teachings I tried to translate into practice in politics, the man whom I revered above all Irish patriots was Thomas Davis.[19] In the hard way of fitting practical affairs into idealism I have made Thomas Davis my guide. I have never departed in my life one inch from the principles of Thomas Davis, and in signing this Treaty and bringing it here and asking Ireland to ratify it I am following Thomas Davis still.

Later on, when coming to reply to criticism, I will deal with the other matters. Thomas Davis said.–

> Peace with England, alliance with England to some extent, and, under certain circumstances, confederation with England; but an Irish ambition, Irish hopes, strength, virtue, and rewards for the Irish.

That is what we have brought back, peace with England, alliance with England, confederation with England, an Ireland developing her own life, carving out her own way of existence, and rebuilding the Gaelic civilisation broken down at the battle of Kinsale.[20] I say we have brought you that. I say we have translated Thomas Davis into the practical politics of the day. I ask then this Dáil to pass this resolution, and I ask the people of Ireland, and the Irish people everywhere, to ratify this Treaty, to end this bitter conflict of centuries, to end it for ever, to take away that poison that

[19] Thomas Davis (1814–45) was a writer and publicist and a chief inspirational figure within the Young Ireland movement, a political and cultural movement during the 1840s.

[20] Irish forces were defeated by the army of Elizabeth I (1533–1603) at the Battle of Kinsale in 1601.

has been rankling in the two countries and ruining the relationship of good neighbours. Let us stand as free partners, equal with England, and make after 700 years the greatest revolution that has ever been made in the history of the world – a revolution of seeing the two countries standing not apart as enemies, but standing together as equals and as friends. I ask you, therefore, to pass this resolution. [Applause.]

1922

31 Ronald McNeill, from *Ulster's Stand for Union*

The Ulster Standpoint[1]

Like all other movements in human affairs, the opposition of the Northern Protestants of Ireland to the agitation of their Nationalist fellow-countrymen for Home Rule can only be properly understood by those who take some pains to get at the true motives, and to appreciate the spirit, of those who engaged in it. And as it is nowhere more true than in Ireland that the events of to-day are the outcome of events that occurred longer ago than yesterday, and that the motives of to-day have consequently their roots buried somewhat deeply in the past, it is no easy task for the outside observer to gain the insight requisite for understanding fairly the conduct of the persons concerned.

It was Mr. Asquith who very truly said that the Irish question, of which one of the principal factors is the opposition of Ulster to Home Rule, 'springs from sources that are historic, economic, social, racial, and religious'.[2] It would be a hopeless undertaking to attempt here to probe to the bottom an origin so complex; but, whether the sympathies of the reader be for or against the standpoint of the Irish Loyalists, the actual events which make up what may be called the Ulster Movement would be wholly unintelligible without some introductory retrospect.[3] Indeed,

[1] Ronald McNeill, 'The Ulster Standpoint' forms the Introduction to McNeill's *Ulster's Stand for Union* (London: John Murray, 1922).

[2] Prime Minister Herbert Henry Asquith (1852–1958) introduced the third Home Rule Bill into the House of Commons in 1912.

[3] Irish 'loyalists' essentially means unionists supportive of the parliamentary Union between Great Britain and Ireland, who were thus loyal to Britain and the Crown and opposed to incorporation into an all-Ireland home rule jurisdiction or, as it became, a southern Irish Dominion. Most unionists were concentrated in the north-east portion

to those who set out to judge Irish political conditions without troubling themselves about anything more ancient than their own memory can recall, the most fundamental factor of all – the line of cleavage between Ulster and the rest of the island – is more than unintelligible. In the eyes of many it presents itself as an example of perversity, of 'cussedness' on the part of men who insist on magnifying mere differences of opinion, which would be easily composed by reasonable people, into obstacles to co-operation which have no reality behind them.

Writers and speakers on the Nationalist side deride the idea of 'two nations' in Ireland, calling in evidence many obvious identities of interest, of sentiment, or of temperament between the inhabitants of the North and of the South.[4] The Ulsterman no more denies these identities than the Greek, the Bulgar, and the Serb would deny that there are features common to all dwellers in the Balkan peninsula;[5] but he is more deeply conscious of the difference than of the likeness between himself and the man from Munster or Connaught. His reply to those who denounced the Irish Government Act of 1920 on the ground that it set up a 'partition of Ireland', is that the Act did not 'set up', but only recognised, the partition which history made long ago, and which wrecked all attempts to solve the problem of Irish Government that neglected to take it into account.[6] If there be any force in Renan's saying that the root of nationality is 'the will to live together', the Nationalist cry of 'Ireland a Nation' harmonises ill with the actual conditions of Ireland north and south of the Boyne.[7] This dividing gulf between the two populations in Ireland is the result

of the province of Ulster comprising six counties which were now generally referred to generically (especially by Unionists) as Ulster. Ulster in this sense had its own parliament conferred upon it under the 1920 Government of Ireland Act, creating Northern Ireland, and so loyalty in the first instance involved allegiance to the devolved government of partitioned Ulster.

4 The idea of two nations occupying the island of Ireland was first advocated by Thomas Macknight in his *Ulster as it Is; or, Twenty-Eight Years' Experience as an Irish Editor* (London: Macmillan, 1896), 2 vols.

5 The cases are chosen to illustrate instances of the nationalities question that emerged at the outset and in the aftermath of the First World War, leading to the break-up of assorted empires from the Ottoman to the Austro-Hungarian.

6 The Government of Ireland Act of 1920 was in effect a fourth Home Rule Act intended for the island of Ireland, which was superseded in the South by the 1921 Treaty but which continued to apply to Northern Ireland.

7 Ernest Renan (1823–92) was a French Orientalist and Semitic scholar who published a theory of nationality in 1882 under the title *Que'est-ce qu'une nation?* in the context of the ongoing dispute over Alsace-Lorraine. The 'Boyne' refers to the River Boyne which flows from Co. Kildare to Drogheda.

of the same causes as the political dissension that springs from it, as described by Mr. Asquith in words quoted above. The tendencies of social and racial origin operate for the most part subconsciously – though not perhaps less powerfully on that account; those connected with economic considerations, with religious creeds, and with events in political history enter directly and consciously into the formation of convictions which in turn become the motives for action.

In the mind of the average Ulster Unionist the particular point of contrast between himself and the Nationalist of which he is more forcibly conscious than of any other, and in which all other distinguishing traits are merged, is that he is loyal to the British Crown and the British Flag, whereas the other man is loyal to neither. Religious intolerance, so far as the Protestants are concerned, of which so much is heard, is in actual fact mainly traceable to the same sentiment. It is unfortunately true that the lines of political and of religious division coincide; but religious dissensions seldom flare up except at times of political excitement; and, while it is undeniable that the temper of the creeds more resembles what prevailed in England in the seventeenth than in the twentieth century, yet when overt hostility breaks out it is because the creed is taken – and usually taken rightly – as *prima facie* evidence of political opinion – political opinion meaning 'loyalty' or 'disloyalty', as the case may be. The label of 'loyalist' is that which the Ulsterman cherishes above all others. It means something definite to him; its special significance is reinforced by the consciousness of its wearers that they are a minority;[8] it sustains the feeling that the division between parties is something deeper and more fundamental than anything that in England is called difference of opinion. This feeling accounts for much that sometimes perplexes even the sympathetic English observer, and moves the hostile partisan to scornful criticism. The ordinary Protestant farmer or artisan of Ulster is by nature as far as possible removed from the being who is derisively nicknamed the 'noisy patriot' or the 'flag-wagging jingo'. If the National Anthem has become a 'party tune' in Ireland, it is not because the loyalist sings it, but because the disloyalist shuns it; and its avoidance at gatherings both political and social where Nationalists predominate, naturally makes those who value loyalty the more punctilious in its use. If there is a profuse display of the Union Jack, it is because it is in Ulster not

[8] Unionists were a minority on the island of Ireland but formed a majority in the six-counties of the newly established Northern Ireland.

merely 'bunting' for decorative purposes as in England, but the symbol of a cherished faith.

There may, perhaps, be some persons, unfamiliar with the Ulster cast of mind, who find it hard to reconcile this profession of passionate loyalty with the methods embarked upon in 1912 by the Ulster people.[9] It is a question upon which there will be something to be said when the narrative reaches the events of that date. Here it need only be stated that, in the eyes of Ulstermen at all events, constitutional orthodoxy is quite a different thing from loyalty, and that true allegiance to the Sovereign is by them sharply differentiated from passive obedience to an Act of Parliament.[10]

The sincerity with which this loyalist creed is held by practically the entire Protestant population of Ulster cannot be questioned by anyone who knows the people, however much he may criticise it on other grounds. And equally sincere is the conviction held by the same people that disloyalty is, and always has been, the essential characteristic of Nationalism. The conviction is founded on close personal contact continued through many generations with the adherents of that political party, and the tradition thus formed draws more support from authentic history than many Englishmen are willing to believe. Consequently, when the General Election of 1918 revealed that the whole of Nationalist Ireland had gone over with foot, horse, and artillery, with bag and baggage, from the camp of so-called Constitutional Home Rule, to the Sinn Féiners who made no pretence that their aim was anything short of complete independent sovereignty for Ireland, no surprise was felt in Ulster.[11] It was there realised that nothing had happened beyond the throwing off of the mask which had been used as a matter of political tactics to disguise what had always been the real underlying aim, if not of the parliamentary leaders, at all events of the great mass of Nationalist opinion throughout the three southern provinces. The whole population had not with one consent changed their views in the course of a night; they had merely rallied to support the first leaders whom they had found prepared to

[9] This refers to unionist opposition to home rule culminating in the drafting and signing of the Ulster League and Covenant in September 1912.

[10] Loyalty to the Crown as the link between Northern Ireland and Britain trumped obedience to parliament, which was seen as the agent responsible for the Home Rule Bill.

[11] The 1918 British general election saw the overwhelming defeat of the Irish Parliamentary Party (IPP) with Sinn Féin securing nearly 70 per cent of the seats in contention. Unionists secured 20 per cent and the IPP just 5 per cent.

proclaim the true objective. Curiously enough, this truth was realised by an English politician who was in other respects conspicuously deficient in insight regarding Ireland. The Easter insurrection of 1916 in Dublin was only rendered possible by the negligence or the incompetence of the Chief Secretary; but, in giving evidence before the Commission appointed to inquire into it, Mr. Birrell said: 'The spirit of what to-day is called Sinn Féinism is mainly composed of the old hatred and distrust of the British connection … always there as the background of Irish politics and character'; and, after recalling that Cardinal Newman had observed the same state of feeling in Dublin more than half a century before, Mr. Birrell added quite truly that 'this dislike, hatred, disloyalty (so unintelligible to many Englishmen) is hard to define but easy to discern, though incapable of exact measurement from year to year'.[12] This disloyal spirit, which struck Newman, and which Mr. Birrell found easy to discern, was of course always familiar to Ulstermen as characteristic of 'the South and West', and was their justification for the badge of 'loyalist', their assumption of which English Liberals, knowing nothing of Ireland, held to be an unjust slur on the Irish majority.

If this belief in the inherent disloyalty of Nationalist Ireland to the British Empire did any injustice to individual Nationalist politicians, they had nobody but themselves to blame for it. Their pronouncements in America, as well as at home, were scrutinised in Ulster with a care that Englishmen seldom took the trouble to give them. Nor must it be forgotten that, up to the date when Mr. Gladstone made Home Rule a plank in an English party's programme – which, whatever else it did, could not alter the facts of the case – the same conviction, held in Ulster so tenaciously, had prevailed almost universally in Great Britain also; and had been proclaimed by no one so vehemently as by Mr. Gladstone himself, whose famous declarations that the Nationalists of that day were 'steeped to the lips in treason', and were 'marching through rapine to the dismemberment of the Empire', were not so quickly forgotten in Ulster as in England, nor so easily passed over as either meaningless or untrue as soon as they became inconvenient for a political party to remember.[13] English

[12] Augustine Birrell (1850–1933) was Chief Secretary to Ireland from 1907 to 1916, when he resigned as a result of the 1916 Easter Rising. John Henry Newman (1801–90) was an Anglican theologian who converted to Catholicism and founded the Catholic University of Ireland, which later became University College Dublin.

[13] William Ewart Gladstone (1809–98) converted to the cause of home rule for Ireland in 1885 and duly made it a plank of Liberal Party policy, ultimately splitting the party.

supporters of Home Rule, when reminded of such utterances, dismissed with a shrug the 'unedifying pastime of unearthing buried speeches'; and showed equal determination to see nothing in speeches delivered by Nationalist leaders in America inconsistent with the purely constitutional demand for 'extended self-government'.

Ulster never would consent to bandage her own eyes in similar fashion, or to plug her ears with wool. The 'two voices' of Nationalist leaders, from Mr. Parnell to Mr. Dillon, were equally audible to her;[14] and, of the two, she was certain that the true aim of Nationalist policy was expressed by the one whose tone was disloyal to the British Empire. Lookout was kept for any change in the direction of moderation, for any real indication that those who professed to be 'constitutional Nationalists' were any less determined than 'the physical force party' to reach the goal described by Parnell in the famous sentence, 'None of us will be … satisfied until we have destroyed the last link which keeps Ireland bound to England.'[15]

No such indication was ever discernible. On the contrary, Parnell's phrase became a refrain to be heard in many later pronouncements of his successors, and the policy he thus described was again and again propounded in afteryears on innumerable Nationalist platforms, in speeches constantly quoted to prove, as was the contention of Ulster from the first, that Home Rule as understood by English Liberals was no more than an instalment of the real demand of Nationalists, who, if they once obtained the 'comparative freedom' of an Irish legislature – to quote the words used by Mr. Devlin at a later date – would then, with that leverage, 'operate by whatever means they should think best to achieve the great and desirable end' of complete independence of Great Britain.[16]

This was an end that could not by any juggling be reconciled with the Ulsterman's notion of 'loyalty'. Moreover, whatever knowledge he possessed of his country's history – and he knows a good deal more, man for man, than the Englishman – confirmed his deep distrust of those whom, following the example of John Bright, he always bluntly described as 'the rebel party'.[17] He knew something of the rebellions in

[14] Charles Stewart Parnell (1846–91) was the leader of Irish nationalists in the House of Commons from 1882 while John Dillon (1851–1927) was a prominent politician in the IPP and MP for East Mayo.

[15] Parnell uttered the statement during his tour of the US in 1880.

[16] Joseph Devlin (1871–1934) was an IPP MP who represented northern nationalists.

[17] John Bright (1811–89) was a Liberal statesman who opposed home rule.

Ireland in the seventeenth, eighteenth, and nineteenth centuries, and was under no illusion as to the design for which arms had been taken up in the past. He knew that that design had not changed with the passing of generations, although gentler methods of accomplishing it might sometimes find favour. Indeed, one Nationalist leader himself took pains, at a comparatively recent date, to remove any excuse there may ever have been for doubt on this point. Mr. John Redmond was an orator who selected his words with care, and his appeals to historical analogies were not made haphazard. When he declared (in a speech in 1901) that, 'in its essence, the national movement to-day is the same as it was in the days of Hugh O'Neill, of Owen Roe, of Emmet, or of Wolfe Tone', those names, which would have had but a shadowy significance for a popular audience in England, carried very definite meaning to the ears of Irishmen, whether Nationalist or Unionist.[18] Mr. Gladstone, in the fervour of his conversion to Home Rule, was fond of allusions to the work of Molyneux and Swift, Flood and Grattan; but these were men whose Irish patriotism never betrayed them into disloyalty to the British Crown or hostility to the British connection.[19] They were reformers, not rebels. But it was not with the political ideals of such men that Mr. Redmond claimed his own to be identical, nor even with that of O'Connell, the apostle of repeal of the Union,[20] but with the aims of men who, animated solely by hatred of England, sought to establish the complete independence of Ireland by force of arms, and in some cases by calling in (like Roger Casement in our own day) the aid of England's foreign enemies.[21]

In the face of appeals like this to the historic imagination of an impressionable people, it is not surprising that by neither Mr. Redmond's fol-

[18] The statement was in fact made by George Clark MP in the House of Commons in a debate to which John Redmond also contributed. See Hansard, House of Commons Debates, 30 March 1908, vol. 187, col. 183. Hugh O'Neill (1550–1616), Owen Roe O'Neill (1585–1649), Robert Emmet (1778–1803), and Theobald Wolfe Tone (1763–98) had all 'resisted' English or British governance in Ireland.

[19] William Molyneux (1656–98), Jonathan Swift (1667–1745), and Wolfe Tone (1763–1798) had all been Protestant 'Patriot' critics of the British government. Each sought to secure the authority of the subordinate Irish Parliament, though Tone argued and fought for independence.

[20] Daniel O'Connell (1775–1847) pursued the cause of 'repealing' the Union after the achievement of Catholic Emancipation in 1829.

[21] Roger Casement (1864–1916) was tried for treason for attempting to import arms into Ireland by consorting with Germany during the war and was hanged at Pentonville Prison.

lowers nor by his opponents was much account taken of his own personal disapproval of extremes both of means and ends. His opponents in Ulster simply accepted such utterances as confirmation of what they had known all along from other sources to be the actual facts, namely, that the Home Rule agitation was 'in its essence' a separatist movement; that its adherents were, as Mr. Redmond himself said on another occasion, 'as much rebels as their fathers were in 1798'; and that the men of Ulster were, together with some scattered sympathisers in the other Provinces, the depositaries of the 'loyal' tradition.

The latter could boast of a pedigree as long as that of the rebels. If Mr. Redmond's followers were to trace their political ancestry, as he told them, to the great Earl of Tyrone who essayed to overthrow England with the help of the Spaniard and the Pope, the Ulster Protestants could claim descent from the men of the Plantation, through generation after generation of loyalists who had kept the British flag flying in Ireland in times of stress and danger, when Mr. Redmond's historical heroes were making England's difficulty Ireland's opportunity.[22]

There have been, and are, many individual Nationalists, no doubt, especially among the more educated and thoughtful, to whom it would be unjust to impute bad faith when they professed that their political aspirations for Ireland were really limited to obtaining local control of local affairs, and who resented being called 'Separatists', since their desire was not for separation from Great Britain but for the 'union of hearts', which they believed would grow out of extended self-government. But the answer of Irish Unionists, especially in Ulster, has always been that, whatever such 'moderate', or 'constitutional' Nationalists might dream, it would be found in practice, if the experiment were made, that no halting-place could be found between legislative union and complete separation. Moreover, the same view was held by men as far as possible removed from the standpoint of the Ulster Protestant. Cardinal Manning, for example, although an intimate personal friend of Gladstone, in a letter to Leo XIII, wrote: 'As for myself. Holy Father, allow me to say that I consider a Parliament in Dublin and a separation to be equivalent

[22] A reference to the Tyrone Rebellion prosecuted between 1593 and 1603 by Hugh O'Neill (1550–1616). There was a series of plantations in Ireland during the sixteenth and seventeenth centuries, including the Laois-Offaly Plantation (1556–76), the Munster Plantation (from 1583), the Ulster Plantation (from 1606), and plantations in the context of the Wars of the Three Kingdoms after 1640 and the Glorious Revolution after 1688.

to the same thing. Ireland is not a Colony like Canada, but it is an integral and vital part of one country.'*

It is improbable that identical lines of reasoning led the Roman Catholic Cardinal and the Belfast Orangeman and Presbyterian to this identical conclusion; but a position reached by convergent paths from such distant points of departure is defensible presumably on grounds more solid than prejudice or passion. It is unnecessary here to examine those grounds at length, for the present purpose is not to argue the Ulster case, but to let the reader know what was, as a matter of fact, the Ulster point of view, whether that point of view was well or ill founded.

But, while the opinion that a Dublin Parliament meant separation was shared by many who had little else in common with the Ulster Protestants, the latter stood alone in the intensity of their conviction that 'Home Rule meant Rome Rule'.[23] It has already been mentioned that it is the 'disloyalty' attributed rightly or wrongly to the Roman Catholics as a body that has been, in recent times at all events, the mainspring of Protestant distrust. But sectarian feeling, everywhere common between rival creeds, is, of course, by no means absent. Englishmen find it hard to understand what seems to them the bigoted and senseless animosity of the rival faiths in Ireland. This is due to the astonishing shortness of their memory in regard to their own history, and their very limited outlook on the world outside their own island. If, without looking further back in their history, they reflected that the 'No Popery' feeling in England in mid-Victorian days was scarcely less intense than it is in Ulster to-day; or if they realised the extent to which Gambetta's 'Le cléricalisme, voila l'ennemi' continues still to influence public life in France, they might be less ready to censure the Irish Protestant's dislike of priestly interference in affairs outside the domain of faith and morals.[24] It is indeed remarkable that Nonconformists, especially in Wales, who within living memory have displayed their own horror of the much milder form of sacerdotalism to be found in the Anglican Church, have no sympathy apparently with the Presbyterian and the Methodist in Ulster when the latter kick against the

[23] The phrase was originally coined by John Bright (1811–89), a Quaker, radical Liberal, and free trader.

[24] A reference to an anti-clerical statement by the French statesman Léon Gambetta (1838–82) in the Chambre des Députés on 4 May 1877.

* *Henry Edward Manning*, by Shane Leslie, p. 406. *Editorial note:* the full details are: Shane Leslie, *Henry Edward Manning: His Life and Labours* (London: Burns, Oates, and Washbourne, 1921).

encompassing pressure of the Roman Catholic priesthood, not in educational matters alone, but in all the petty activities of every-day life.

Whenever this aspect of the Home Rule controversy was emphasised Englishmen asked what sort of persecution Irish Protestants had to fear from a Parliament in Dublin, and appeared to think all such fear illusory unless evidence could be adduced that the Holy Office was to be set up at Maynooth, equipped with faggot and thumbscrew. Of persecution of that sort there never has been, of course, any apprehension in modern times. Individual Catholics and Protestants live side by side in Ireland with fully as much amity as elsewhere, but whereas the Catholic instinctively, and by upbringing, looks to the parish priest as his director in all affairs of life, the Protestant dislikes and resists clerical influence as strongly as does the Nonconformist in England and Wales – and with much better reason. For the latter has never known clericalism as it exists in a Roman Catholic country where the Church is wholly unrestrained by the civil power. He has resented what he regards as Anglican arrogance in regard to educational management or the use of burying-grounds, but he has never experienced a much more aggressive clerical temper exercised in all the incidents of daily life – in the market, the political meeting, the disposition of property, the amusements of the people, the polling booth, the farm, and the home.

This involves no condemnation of the Irish priest as an individual or as a minister of his Church. He is kind-hearted, charitable, and conscientious; and, except that it does not encourage self-reliance and enterprise, his influence with his own people is no more open to criticism than that of any other body of religious ministers. But the Roman Catholic Church has always made a larger claim than any other on the obedience of its adherents, and it has always enforced that obedience whenever it has had the power by methods which, in Protestant opinion, are extremely objectionable. In theory the claim may be limited to affairs concerned with faith and morals; but the definition of such affairs is a very elastic one. Cardinal Logue not many years ago said: 'When political action trenches upon faith or morals or affects religion, the Vicar of Christ, as the supreme teacher and guardian of faith and morals, and as the custodian of the immunities of religion, has, by Divine Right, authority to interfere and to enforce his decisions.'[25] How far this principle is in practice carried beyond the limits so defined was proved in the famous Meath elec-

[25] Michael Logue (1840–1924) served as Archbishop of Armagh and Primate of All Ireland from 1887 until his death.

tion petition in 1892, in which the Judge who tried it, himself a devout Catholic, declared: 'The Church became converted for the time being into a vast political agency, a great moral machine moving with resistless influence, united action, and a single will. Every priest who was examined was a canvasser; the canvas was everywhere – on the altar, in the vestry, on the roads, in the houses.'[26] And while an election was in progress in County Tyrone in 1911 a parish priest announced that any Catholic who should vote for the Unionist candidate 'would be held responsible at the Day of Judgment'.[27] A still more notorious example of clericalism in secular affairs, within the recollection of Englishmen, was the veto on the Military Service Act proclaimed from the altars of the Catholic Churches, which, during the Great War, defeated the application to Ireland of the compulsory service which England, Scotland, and Wales accepted as the only alternative to national defeat and humiliation.[28]

But these were only conspicuous examples of what the Irish Protestant sees around him every day of his life. The promulgation in 1908 of the Vatican decree, *Ne Temere*, a papal reassertion of the canonical invalidity of mixed marriages, followed as it was by notorious cases of the victimisation of Protestant women by the application of its principles, did not encourage the Protestants to welcome the prospect of a Catholic Parliament that would have control of the marriage law; nor did they any more readily welcome the prospect of national education on purely ecclesiastical lines.[29] Another Vatican decree that was equally alarming to Protestants was that entitled *Motu Proprio*, by which any Catholic layman was *ipso facto* excommunicated who should have the temerity to bring a priest into a civil court either as defendant or witness.[30] Medievalism like this was felt by Ulster Protestants to be irreconcilable with modern ideas of democratic freedom, and to indicate a temper that boded ill for any regime which would be subject to its inspiration. These were matters, it is true, – and there were perhaps some others of a similar nature – on which it is possible to conceive

[26] The statement has been quoted in Parliament by Hugh Arnold Forster (1855–1909) in a debate on clerical influence at elections. See Hansard, House of Commons Debates, 10 February 1893, vol. 8, col. 1095.

[27] A by-election took place in North Tyrone on 6 October 1911.

[28] The Military Service Act introduced conscription into the United Kingdom excluding Ireland in January 1916.

[29] The decree of *Ne Temere* (1907) required that all children of a mixed marriage be brought up as Catholics. Before that date tradition dictated that the boys in such a marriage would be brought up in the father's faith while the girls followed that of their mother.

[30] An act under Canon Law decreed by the Pope on his own initiative.

more or less satisfactory legislative safeguards being provided; but as regards the indefinable but innumerable minutiae in which the prevailing ecclesiastical standpoint creates an atmosphere in which daily life has to be carried on, no safeguards could be devised, and it was the realisation of this truth in the light of their own experience that made the Ulstermen continually close their ears to allurements of that sort.

The Roman Church is quite consistent, and from its own point of view praiseworthy, in its assertion of its right, and its duty, to control the lives and thoughts of men; but this assertion has produced a clash with the non-ecclesiastical mind in almost every country where Catholicism is the dominant religious faith. But in Ireland, unlike Continental countries, there is no Catholic lay opinion – or almost none – able to make its voice heard against clerical dictation, and consequently the Protestants felt convinced, with good reason, that any legislature in Ireland must take its tone from this pervading mental and moral atmosphere, and that all its proceedings would necessarily be tainted by it.

Prior to 1885 the political complexion of Ulster was in the main Liberal. The Presbyterians, who formed the majority of the Protestant population, collateral descendants of the men who emigrated in the eighteenth century and formed the backbone of Washington's army, and direct descendants of those who joined the United Irishmen in 1798, were of a pronounced Liberal type, and their frequently strong disapproval of Orangeism made any united political action an improbable occurrence.[31] But the crisis brought about by Gladstone's declaration in favour of Home Rule instantly swept all sections of Loyalists into a single camp. There was practically not a Liberal left who did not become Unionist, and, although a separate organisation of Liberal Unionists was maintained, the co-operation with Conservatives was so whole-hearted and complete as almost to amount to fusion from the outset.

The immediate cessation of class friction was still more remarkable. For more than a decade the perennial quarrel between landlord and tenant had been increasing in intensity, and the recent land legislation had disposed the latter to look upon Gladstone as a deliverer.[32] Their gratitude was wiped out the moment he hoisted the green flag, while the labourers enfranchised by the Act of 1884 eagerly enrolled themselves

[31] The United Irishmen were a secret society, inspired by the French Revolution, which engaged in a republican insurrection against the Crown in 1798.

[32] The Land Acts passed by the Westminster legislature between 1870 and 1909 were designed to reform tenancy rights and proprietorship in Ireland.

as the bitterest enemies of his new Irish policy.[33] The unanimity of the country-side was matched in the towns, and especially in Belfast, where, with the single exception of a definitely Catholic quarter, employer and artisan were as whole-heartedly united as were landlord and tenant in passionate resentment at what they regarded as the betrayal by England's foremost statesman of England's only friends in Ireland.

The defeat of the Home Rule Bill of 1886 brought relief from the immediate strain of anxiety.[34] But it was at once realised that the encouragement and support given to Irish disloyalty for the first time by one of the great political parties in Great Britain was a step that could never be recalled. Henceforth the vigilance required to prevent being taken unawares, and the untiring organisation necessary for making effective defence against an attack which, although it had signally failed at the first onslaught, was certain to be renewed, welded all the previously diverse social and political elements in Ulster into a single compact mass, tempered to the maximum power of resistance. There was room for no other thought in the minds of men who felt as if living in a beleaguered citadel, whose flag they were bound in honour to keep flying to the last. The 'loyalist' tradition acquired fresh meaning and strength, and its historical setting took a more conscious hold on the public mind of Ulster, as men studied afresh the story of the Relief of Derry or the horrors of 1641.[35] Visits of encouragement from the leaders of Unionism across the Channel, men like Lord Salisbury, Mr. Balfour, Mr. Chamberlain, Lord Randolph Churchill, fortified the resolution of a populace that came more and more to regard themselves as a bulwark of the Empire, on whom destiny, while conferring on them the honour of upholding the flag, had imposed the duty of putting into actual practice the familiar motto of the Orange Lodges – 'No surrender'.[36]

From a psychology so bred and nourished sprang a political temper which, as it hardened with the passing years, appeared to English Home

[33] The Third Reform Act, or Representation of the People Act, of 1884 extended the suffrage among male voters in the United Kingdom.

[34] The first Home Rule Bill was defeated in the House of Commons on 8 June 1886 by 341 votes to 311.

[35] The Siege of Derry was a major episode forming part of the Williamite Wars in Ireland. The Siege was relieved on 1 August 1689. The Irish Rebellion of 1641 led to wholesale violence against Protestants in due course described as a massacre.

[36] Robert Arthur Talbot Gascoyne-Cecil (1830–1903), 3rd Marquess of Salisbury, was Prime Minister from 1895 to 1902; Arthur Balfour (1848–1930) was Prime Minister from 1902 to 1905; Joseph Chamberlain (1836–1914) was Leader of the Opposition in 1906. Randolph Churchill (1849–95) became Chancellor of the Exchequer and Leader of the House of Commons. 'No Surrender' was a popular slogan of resistance.

Rulers to be 'stiff-necked', 'bigoted', and 'intractable'. It certainly was a state of mind very different from those shifting gusts of transient impression which in England go by the name of public opinion; and, if these epithets in the mouths of opponents be taken as no more than synonyms for 'uncompromising', they were not undeserved. At a memorable meeting at the Albert Hall in London on the 22nd of April, 1893, Dr. Alexander, Bishop of Derry, poet, orator, and divine, declared in an eloquent passage that was felt to be the exact expression of Ulster conviction, that the people of Ulster, when exhorted to show confidence in their southern fellow-countrymen, 'could no more be confiding about its liberty than a pure woman can be confiding about her honour'.[37]

Here was the irreconcilable division. The Nationalist talked of centuries of 'oppression', and demanded the dissolution of the Union in the name of liberty. The Ulsterman, while far from denying the misgovernment of former times, knew that it was the fruit of false ideas which had passed away, and that the Ireland in which he lived enjoyed as much liberty as any land on earth; and he feared the loss of the true liberty he had gained if put back under a regime of Nationalist and Utramontane domination. And so for more than thirty years the people of Ulster for whom Bishop Alexander spoke made good his words. If in the end compromise was forced upon them it was not because their standpoint had changed, and it was only in circumstances which involved no dishonour, and which preserved them from what they chiefly dreaded, subjection to a Dublin Parliament inspired by clericalism and disloyalty to the Empire.

The development which brought about the change from Ulster's resolute stand for unimpaired union with Great Britain to her reluctant acceptance of a separate local constitution for the predominantly Protestant portion of the Province, presents a deeply interesting illustration of the truth of a pregnant dictum of Maine's on the working of democratic institutions.

'Democracies', he says, 'are quite paralysed by the plea of nationality. There is no more effective way of attacking them than by admitting the right of the majority to govern, but denying that the majority so entitled is the particular majority which claims the right.'[*]

[37] William Alexander (1824–1911) was a Church of Ireland cleric.

[*] Sir S. H. Maine, *Popular Government*, p. 28. *Editorial note:* Henry Sumner Maine (1822–88) published a series of articles in response to the Third Reform Act and collected them in *Popular Government* in 1885.

This is precisely what occurred in regard to Ulster's relation to Great Britain and to the rest of Ireland respectively. The will of the majority must prevail, certainly. But what majority? Unionists maintained that only the majority in the United Kingdom could decide, and that it had never in fact decided in favour of repealing the Act of Union; Lord Rosebery at one time held that a majority in Great Britain alone, as the 'Predominant Partner', must first give its consent; Irish Nationalists argued that the majority in Ireland, as a distinct unit, was the only one that should count, Ulster, whilst agreeing with the general Unionist position, contended ultimately that her own majority was as well entitled to be heard in regard to her own fate as the majority in Ireland as a whole.[38] To the Nationalist claim that Ireland was a nation she replied that it was either two nations or none, and that if one of the two had a right to 'self-determination', the other had it equally.[39] Thus the axiom of democracy that government is by the majority was, as Maine said, 'paralysed by the plea of nationality', since the contending parties appealed to the same principle without having any common ground as to how it should be applied to the case in dispute.

If the Union with Great Britain was to be abrogated, which Pitt had only established when 'a full measure of Home Rule' had produced a bloody insurrection and Irish collusion with England's external enemies,[40] Ulster could at all events in the last resort take her stand on Abraham Lincoln's famous proposition which created West Virginia: 'A minority of a large community who make certain claims for self-government cannot, in logic or in substance, refuse the same claims to a much larger proportionate minority among themselves.'[41]

The Loyalists of Ulster were successful in holding this second line, when the first was no longer tenable; but they only retired from the first line – the maintenance of the legislative union – after a long and obstinate defence which it is the purpose of the following pages to relate.

[38] Archibald Philip Primrose (1847–1929), 5th Earl of Rosebery, served as Liberal Prime Minister of the United Kingdom from March 1894 to June 1895.

[39] The phrase self-determination had become widespread in the context of the nationalities debates sparked by the First World War and its aftermath.

[40] The Act of Union (1801) was introduced by William Pitt the Younger (1758–1806) as a response to the 1798 Rebellion in Ireland.

[41] West Virginia was formed in the context of the US civil war. On 31 December 1862 an enabling act was approved by Abraham Lincoln (1809–65) admitting the state to the Union on condition that a provision for the gradual abolition of slavery be inserted in the Constitution.

Index

Index

CAMBRIDGE TEXTS IN THE
HISTORY OF POLITICAL THOUGHT

Titles published in the series thus far

Aquinas *Political Writings* (edited and translated by R.W. Dyson)
Aristotle *The Politics and The Constitution of Athens* (edited and translated by Stephen Everson)
Arnold *Culture and Anarchy and Other Writings* (edited by Stefan Collini)
Astell *Political Writings* (edited by Patricia Springborg)
Augustine *The City of God against the Pagans* (edited and translated by R. W. Dyson)
Augustine *Political Writings* (edited by E. M. Atkins and R. J. Dodaro)
Austin *The Province of Jurisprudence Determined* (edited by Wilfrid E. Rumble)
Bacon *The History of the Reign of King Henry VII* (edited by Brian Vickers)
Bagehot *The English Constitution* (edited by Paul Smith)
Bakunin *Statism and Anarchy* (edited and translated by Marshall Shatz)
Baxter *Holy Commonwealth* (edited by William Lamont)
Bayle *Political Writings* (edited by Sally L. Jenkinson)
Beccaria *On Crimes and Punishments and Other Writings* (edited by Richard Bellamy; translated by Richard Davies)
Bentham *A Fragment on Government* (edited by Ross Harrison)
Bernstein *The Preconditions of Socialism* (edited and translated by Henry Tudor)
Bodin *On Sovereignty* (edited and translated by Julian H. Franklin)
Bolingbroke *Political Writings* (edited by David Armitage)
Bossuet *Politics Drawn from the Very Words of Holy Scripture* (edited and translated by Patrick Riley)
Botero *The Reason of State* (edited and translated by Robert Bireley)
The British Idealists (edited by David Boucher)
Burke *Pre-Revolutionary Writings* (edited by Ian Harris)
Burke *Revolutionary Writings* (edited by Iain Hampsher-Monk)
Cavendish *Political Writings* (edited by Susan James)
Christine de Pizan *The Book of the Body Politic* (edited by Kate Langdon Forhan)
Cicero *On Duties* (edited by E. M. Atkins; edited and translated by M. T. Griffin)
Cicero *On the Commonwealth and On the Laws* (edited and translated by James E. G. Zetzel)
Comte *Early Political Writings* (edited and translated by H. S. Jones)
Comte *Conciliarism and Papalism* (edited by J. H. Burns and Thomas M. Izbicki)
Condorcet *Political Writings* (edited by Steven Lukes and Nadia Urbinati)
Constant *Political Writings* (edited and translated by Biancamaria Fontana)
Dante *Monarchy* (edited and translated by Prue Shaw)
Diderot *Political Writings* (edited and translated by John Hope Mason and Robert Wokler)
Diderot *The Dutch Revolt* (edited and translated by Martin van Gelderen)

Diderot *Early Greek Political Thought from Homer to the Sophists* (edited and translated by Michael Gagarin and Paul Woodruff)
Diderot *The Early Political Writings of the German Romantics* (edited and translated by Frederick C. Beiser)
Emerson *Political Writings* (edited by Kenneth S. Sacks)
Emerson *The English Levellers* (edited by Andrew Sharp)
Erasmus *The Education of a Christian Prince with the Panegyric for Archduke Philip of Austria* (edited and translated by Lisa Jardine; translated by Neil M. Cheshire and Michael J. Heath)
Fénelon *Telemachus* (edited and translated by Patrick Riley)
Ferguson *An Essay on the History of Civil Society* (edited by Fania Oz-Salzberger)
Fichte *Addresses to the German Nation* (edited by Gregory Moore)
Filmer *Patriarcha and Other Writings* (edited by Johann P. Sommerville)
Fletcher *Political Works* (edited by John Robertson)
Sir John Fortescue *On the Laws and Governance of England* (edited by Shelley Lockwood)
Fourier *The Theory of the Four Movements* (edited by Gareth Stedman Jones; edited and translated by Ian Patterson)
Franklin *The Autobiography and Other Writings on Politics, Economics, and Virtue* (edited by Alan Houston)
Gramsci *Pre-Prison Writings* (edited by Richard Bellamy; translated by Virginia Cox)
Guicciardini *Dialogue on the Government of Florence* (edited and translated by Alison Brown)
Hamilton, Madison, and Jay (writing as 'Publius') *The Federalist with Letters* of *'Brutus'* (edited by Terence Ball)
Harrington *The Commonwealth of Oceana and A System of Politics* (edited by J. G. A. Pocock)
Hegel *Elements of the Philosophy of Right* (edited by Allen W. Wood; translated by H. B. Nisbet)
Hegel *Political Writings* (edited by Laurence Dickey and H. B. Nisbet)
Hess *The Holy History of Mankind and Other Writings* (edited and translated by Shlomo Avineri)
Hobbes *On the Citizen* (edited and translated by Michael Silverthorne and Richard Tuck)
Hobbes *Leviathan* (edited by Richard Tuck)
Hobhouse *Liberalism and Other Writings* (edited by James Meadowcroft)
Hooker *Of the Laws of Ecclesiastical Polity* (edited by A. S. McGrade)
Hume *Political Essays* (edited by Knud Haakonssen)
Jefferson *Political Writings* (edited by Joyce Appleby and Terence Ball)
John of Salisbury *Policraticus* (edited by Cary J. Nederman)
Kant *Political Writings* (edited by H. S. Reiss; translated by H. B. Nisbet)
King James VI and I *Political Writings* (edited by Johann P. Sommerville)
Knox *On Rebellion* (edited by Roger A. Mason)

Kropotkin *The Conquest of Bread and Other Writings* (edited by Marshall Shatz)
Kumazawa Banzan *Governing the Realm and bringing Peace to All below Heaven* (edited and translated by John A. Tucker)
Lawson *Politica Sacra et Civilis* (edited by Conal Condren)
Leibniz *Political Writings* (edited and translated by Patrick Riley)
Lincoln *Political Writings and Speeches* (edited by Terence Ball)
Locke *Political Essays* (edited by Mark Goldie)
Locke *Two Treatises of Government* (edited by Peter Laslett)
Loyseau *A Treatise of Orders and Plain Dignities* (edited and translated by Howell A. Lloyd)
Loyseau *Luther and Calvin on Secular Authority* (edited and translated by Harro Höpfl)
Machiavelli *The Prince, Second Edition* (edited by Quentin Skinner and Russell Price)
Joseph de Maistre *Considerations on France* (edited and translated by Richard A. Lebrun)
Maitland *State, Trust and Corporation* (edited by David Runciman and Magnus Ryan)
Malthus *An Essay on the Principle of Population* (edited by Donald Winch)
Marsiglio of Padua *Defensor minor and De translatione Imperii* (edited by Cary J. Nederman)
Marsilius of Padua *The Defender of the Peace* (edited and translated by Annabel Brett)
Marx *Early Political Writings* (edited and translated by Joseph O'Malley)
James Mill *Political Writings* (edited by Terence Ball)
J. S. Mill *On Liberty and Other Writings* (edited by Stefan Collini)
Milton *Political Writings* (edited by Martin Dzelzainis; translated by Claire Gruzelier)
Montesquieu *The Spirit of the Laws* (edited and translated by Anne M. Cohler, Basia Carolyn Miller and Harold Samuel Stone)
More *Utopia* (edited by George M. Logan and Robert M. Adams)
Morris *News from Nowhere* (edited by Krishan Kumar)
Nicholas of Cusa *The Catholic Concordance* (edited and translated by Paul E. Sigmund)
Nietzsche *On the Genealogy of Morality* (edited by Keith Ansell-Pearson; translated by Carol Diethe)
Paine *Political Writings* (edited by Bruce Kuklick)
William Penn *Political Writings* (edited by Andrew R. Murphy)
Plato *Gorgias, Menexenus, Protagoras* (edited by Malcolm Schofield; translated by Tom Griffith)
Plato *Laws* (edited by Malcolm Schofield; translated by Tom Griffith)
Plato *The Republic* (edited by G. R. F. Ferrari; translated by Tom Griffith)
Plato *Statesman* (edited by Julia Annas; edited and translated by Robin Waterfield)

Political Thought in Portugal and its Empire, c.1500–1800 (edited by Pedro Cardim and Nuno Gonçalo Monteiro)
Price *Political Writings* (edited by D. O. Thomas)
Priestley *Political Writings* (edited by Peter Miller)
Proudhon *What is Property?* (edited and translated by Donald R. Kelley and Bonnie G. Smith)
Pufendorf *On the Duty of Man and Citizen according to Natural Law* (edited by James Tully; translated by Michael Silverthorne)
Pufendorf *The Radical Reformation* (edited and translated by Michael G. Baylor)
Rousseau *The Discourses and Other Early Political Writings* (edited and translated by Victor Gourevitch)
Rousseau *The Social Contract and Other Later Political Writings* (edited and translated by Victor Gourevitch)
Seneca *Moral and Political Essays* (edited and translated by John M. Cooper; edited by J. F. Procopé)
Sidney *Court Maxims* (edited by Hans W. Blom, Eco Haitsma Mulier and Ronald Janse)
Sorel *Reflections on Violence* (edited by Jeremy Jennings)
Spencer *Political Writings* (edited by John Offer)
Stirner *The Ego and Its Own* (edited by David Leopold)
Emperor Taizong and ministers *The Essentials of Governance* (compiled by Wu Jing; edited and translated by Hilde De Weerdt, Glen Dudbridge and Gabe van Beijeren)
Thoreau *Political Writings* (edited by Nancy L. Rosenblum)
Tönnies *Community and Civil Society* (edited and translated by Jose Harris; translated by Margaret Hollis)
Tönnies *Utopias of the British Enlightenment* (edited by Gregory Claeys)
Vico *The First New Science* (edited and translated by Leon Pompa)
Vitoria *Political Writings* (edited by Anthony Pagden and Jeremy Lawrance)
Voltaire *Political Writings* (edited and translated by David Williams)
Weber *Political Writings* (edited by Peter Lassman; edited and translated by Ronald Speirs)
William of Ockham *A Short Discourse on Tyrannical Government* (edited by Arthur Stephen McGrade; translated by John Kilcullen)
William of Ockham *A Letter to the Friars Minor and Other Writings* (edited by Arthur Stephen McGrade; edited and translated by John Kilcullen)
Wollstonecraft *A Vindication of the Rights of Men and A Vindication of the Rights of Woman* (edited by Sylvana Tomaselli)

Lightning Source UK Ltd.
Milton Keynes UK
UKHW022154200522
403328UK00008B/116

9 781108 799133